New Life

A History of the New Life Churches of New Zealand, 1942–1979

Brett Knowles

Third Edition

EMETH PRESS
www.emethpress.com

New Life:
A History of the New Life Churches of New Zealand,
1942–1979

Copyright © 2015 Brett Knowles
Printed in the United States of America on acidfree paper

All rights reserved. No part of this book may be reproduced, or stored in a retrieval system or transmitted in any form or by any means, electronic, mechanical, photocopying, recording, scanning or otherwise, except as permitted by the 1976 United States Copyright Act, or with the prior written permission of Emeth Press. Requests for permission should be addressed to: Emeth Press, P. O. Box 23961, Lexington, KY 405233961. http://www.emethpress.com.

ISBN 978-1-60947-093-7

Library of Congress Control Number: 2015937689

For Adrienne:

Wind beneath my wings

Table of Contents

List of Figures vii
List of Tables ix
List of Abbreviations xi
Foreword to the First Edition xv
Preface to the Reprint Edition xvii
Acknowledgments xix
What's in a Name? A note on Nomenclature xxi
Chapter 1: Evacuation! 1
Chapter 2: For the Sake of 'The Name' 7
Chapter 3: The Bethel Temple Legacy 13
Chapter 4: Latter Rain! 21
Chapter 5: The Latter Rain Legacy 27
Chapter 6: Australian Developments 33
Chapter 7: Catalyst for change: The New Evangelicalism 39
Chapter 8: Day of small beginnings 49
Chapter 9: Breakthrough! 57
Chapter 10: Ron Coady and expansion in the South 65
Chapter 11: Filling the Pastoral Gap 71
Chapter 12: Parting of the Ways 77
Chapter 13: The Glory Years: 1960 to 1965 85
Chapter 14: The Nature of the Movement I: The Sectarian Impulse 93
Chapter 15: The Nature of the Movement II: The Antiecumenical
  Impulse 99

Chapter 16: The Nature of the Movement III: The Missionary Impulse 105
Chapter 17: The Indigenous Churches and the rise of the Charismatic Movement 113
Chapter 18: A tale of two churches I: The Palmerston North Christian Fellowship 119
Chapter 19: A tale of two churches II: Peter Morrow and the Christchurch New Life Centre 125
Chapter 20: Charismatic growth and its effect on the Indigenous Churches 133
Chapter 21: 'The times they are a-changing' 141
Chapter 22: The 1972 Jesus Marches 147
Chapter 23: The Moralist Movement and the Indigenous Churches 155
Chapter 24: Moralist Initiatives I: Accelerated Christian Education 163
Chapter 25: Moralist Initiatives II: The Save Our Homes Campaign 173
Chapter 26: Growth, Accountability and the Discipleship Controversy 183
Chapter 27: Moves towards Pentecostal unity: Ern Baxter and Jack Hayford 193
Chapter 28: The significance of the 1975 Snell's Beach Convention 199
Chapter 29: Towards Pentecostal Church Union? 207
Chapter 30: The Indigenous Churches in the 1970s: Growth and Dynamism 215
Chapter 31: Epilogue 223
Appendix I: The Pentecostals: See how they grow 227
Appendix II: Biographies 231
Appendix III: Maps: Growth of the Movement 241
Bibliography 249
Indexes (People and Places) 275
About the author 283

List of Figures

Figure 1: The *Tjinegara*, which brought the evacuating Bethel Temple Missionaries to New Zealand 3

Figure 2: Ray and Ruth Jackson, whose ministry laid the foundations upon which the New Life Churches were later to build 24

Figure 3: The congregation at Queen Street Assembly of God, Auckland, photographed during Rob Wheeler Campaign, May 1959 35

Figure 4: Rob and Beryl Wheeler and Ian and Mavis Hunt and their families on campaign, 1958–59 44

Figure 5: Map showing the locations of early Rob Wheeler campaigns and of early Full Gospel churches (1958–60) 50

Figure 6: The National Revival Crusade 1960 Easter Convention in Tauranga, with Rob Wheeler addressing the meeting 53

Figure 7: A.S. Worley, at the time of his Timaru campaign in 1960 59

Figure 8: Rob Wheeler's seventh Winter Bible School held in Auckland, 1966 74

Figure 9: Summer Training Camp, Nelson, *circa* 1968 75

Figure 10: Ron Coady praying for the sick during his Cotton Mill Crusade in Nelson, 1963 86

Figure 11: Rob Wheeler's tent campaign in Auckland, January 1962 88

Figure 12: Sandwich-board advertising for Rob Wheeler's August 1966 Wellington campaign 89

Figure 13: Some of the pastors of the movement at the Gunn's Bush Convention, Waimate, January 1964 109

Figure 14: Indecent Publications Tribunal: Total Submissions and
    Decisions 1964–74 144
Figure 15: Growth of the Movement in the North Island 246
Figure 16: Growth of the Movement in the South Island 247

List of Tables

Table 1: Total Pentecostal Adherents 1961–96, according to Religious Professions Responses in successive five-yearly New Zealand censuses 227

Table 2: *APCNZ*-affiliated Pentecostal pastors, listed by church affiliation, 1983–84 and 1986 228

Table 3: Pentecostal attendance, 1986 and 1990 229

List of Abbreviations

&	and
A.C.T.	Australian Capital Territory
ACE	Accelerated Christian Education
AOG	Assemblies of God
APC	Associated Pentecostal Churches [of New Zealand]
APCNZ	Associated Pentecostal Churches of New Zealand
B. Phil.	Bachelor of Philosophy
B. Theol.	Bachelor of Theology
B.A.	Bachelor of Arts
B.C.E.	Before the Common Era [equivalent to B.C. or Before Christ]
B.D.	Bachelor of Divinity
BE	Board of Elders of the Pentecostal Church of N.Z. (Inc.) Minute Book 1934–51
Bro.	Brother
CFTN	Canterbury Family Television Network
co.	company
comp.	compiler
Cor.	Corinthians
CPA	Concerned Parents Association
D. Phil.	Doctor of Philosophy
DAWN	Discipling a Whole Nation [name of parachurch group]
Dip. S.Th.	Diploma Scholar in Theology
Dr	Doctor
e.g.	*exempli gratia* [for example]
EC	Executive Council, Representing the Board of Elders of the Pentecostal Church of N.Z. (Inc.), Minute Book 1934–51
ed.	edition, edited
Eph.	Ephesians
et al.	*et alia* [and other things or persons]
etc.	*et cetera* [and the rest, and so on]

f.	folio [leaf of manuscript text]
ff.	following
Hon.	Honourable
i.e.	*id est* [that is]
ibid.	*ibidem* [in the same place]
ICNZ	Indigenous Churches of New Zealand
idem	in the same author
Inc.	Incorporated
Jnr.	Junior
Jr.	Junior
KJV	King James Version (of the Bible)
Ltd.	Limited
M.A.	Master of Arts
M.P.	Member of Parliament
M.Th.	Master of Theology
Matt.	Matthew
MHCF	Majestic House Correspondence Files
n.d.	no date [of publication]
n.p.	no place [of publication]
N.Z.	New Zealand
N.Z.L.R.	New Zealand Law Reports
Neh.	Nehemiah
No.	Number
NZBC	New Zealand Broadcasting Corporation
NZPD	*New Zealand Parliamentary Debates*
NZPF	New Zealand Pentecostal Fellowship
NZQA	New Zealand Qualifications Authority
p.	page
P.M.	Prime Minister
Ph.D.	Doctor of Philosophy
pp.	pages
Ps.	Psalm
Rev.	[Book of] Revelation, Reverend
rev. ed.	revised edition
RNZAF	Royal New Zealand Air Force
S.A.	Salvation Army
s.v.	*sub voce* [i.e. at place of word cited]
Sam.	Samuel
Sis.	Sister
Snr.	Senior
SPUC	Society for the Protection of the Unborn Child
St.	Street, Saint
trans.	translated
USA	United States of America
UWC	United Women's Convention
v.	verse, versus

vol.	volume
vols.	volumes
Wm.	William
WPEM	Wellington Pentecostal Evangelical Mission, Minute Book 8 July 1942–3 December 1951
YMCA	Young Men's Christian Association
YWAM	Youth with a Mission

Foreword to the First Edition

Brett Knowles has written a book which is both fascinating and significant. Fascinating, because few interested in religion can have failed to have heard of some of the events he refers to. Here are events central to the Charismatic movement in New Zealand and not insignificant to the Charismatic movement throughout the world. They are told here, with an eye to some of the fascinating detail which only someone who has been both a participant and a creative explorer could uncover in their detail. Significant, because Brett Knowles has shaped this story into a significant analysis incorporating both thoughtful history and analytical theology. He has quizzed the stories and gone behind them. He has unpacked the theology, and indicated its appeal and its strengths and weaknesses. I think this is the important mark of a movement which has made a turning point in its development when it can be open to this level of analysis. It does not come easily to a movement. It sees its miracles, its sagas of divine providence analysed, and the act of analysis can feel like an act of sacrilege. This is not the tone of Brett Knowles' book. This critical reader for one, came away with questions answered, ideas corrected, more respectful of a movement because I understood it better.

    I warmly recommend this book. New Zealand has played an important part in the Charismatic movement throughout the world, and Brett Knowles has given us the clear light of understanding of a very important part of the story.

Dr Peter J. Lineham
School of History, Philosophy and Politics,
Massey University,
Albany,
Auckland,
New Zealand, 1999.

Preface to the Reprint Edition

This book is a reprint edition of a work originally published in 1999 and 2000. The Third Millennium version (*New Life: A History of the New Life Churches of New Zealand, 1942-1979*),[1] published in September 1999, included photographs, but no footnotes. By contrast, the Edwin Mellen Press version (*The History of a New Zealand Pentecostal Movement: The New Life Churches of New Zealand from 1946 to 1979*),[2] published the following year, was directed at the academic community and thus included footnotes, but no photographs. Nevertheless, the text in each version was identical. The opportunity has now been taken to produce an edition that combines the features of both earlier versions.

Permissions have been obtained, where applicable, for this reprint edition. Third Millennium Publishing went out of business in 2005 and that version is thus out of print, although Edwin Mellen Press is still publishing the 2000 academic edition. The author is extremely grateful to the latter publishers for consent to produce this reprint under the banner of Emeth Press. This was the first time that such permission had ever been granted by Edwin Mellen Press[3] and the author records here his sincere appreciation for their generosity.

In this reprint edition, the text has been edited to conform to Emeth Press guidelines. The opportunity has been taken to make slight corrections of typography; where minor corrections of fact are made, these are usually indicated by means of an endnote. While the people and places indexes have been retained, the detailed miscellaneous index in the Edwin Mellen Press version has been omitted in this edition.

Thanks are also due to Kuda Zimba and Sandi Jull at the University of Otago Helpdesk, who facilitated the conversion of the map files in Figures 5, 15 and 16 into a format that could be incorporated in the text of the book.

Brett Knowles,

Dunedin, New Zealand 2014
http://brettknowlesnz.weebly.com/

Notes

1. Brett Knowles, *New Life: A History of the New Life Churches of New Zealand, 1942–1979* (Dunedin: Third Millennium Publishing, 1999).
2. Brett Knowles, *The History of a New Zealand Pentecostal Movement: The New Life Churches of New Zealand from 1946 to 1979* (Lewiston, NY: Edwin Mellen Press, 2000).
3. Professor Herbert Richardson, Editor-in-Chief, Edwin Mellen Press, e-mail correspondence with the author, 14 August 2014.

Acknowledgements

This book is the oral history of a significant group of New Zealand Pentecostal churches, the New Life Churches of New Zealand (originally called the 'Indigenous Churches'). It is based upon the author's honours dissertation[1] and doctoral thesis[2] at the University of Otago, and upon additional research into the early years of the movement. Primary data has come from oral interviews with pastors and congregational members of the New Life Churches and with others from outside the movement, corroborated by such documentary materials as were available. The author's policy has been to make use of extended quotations—with a minimum of editing—to allow the interviewees to tell their story as much as possible. The citation of these materials and of other sources, as well as the format and punctuation of the book, conforms to what is known as the Chicago style,[3] except where adapted to New Zealand conventions.[4]

The author was fortunate to have had the support of a stimulating and vigorous academic community. Dr Peter Matheson—now of Ormond College, Melbourne—was the author's mentor, and his historical and literary insights saved me from many a pitfall. The resources of the Hewitson Library at Knox Theological Hall and the Central and Hocken Libraries at the University of Otago were invaluable, as was the unstinting assistance of their librarians and staff. The University of Otago was generous in its bestowal of a three-year Postgraduate Scholarship to undertake doctoral research, and later of a Bridging Grant to enable the writing of this book. Professor Gerald Pillay acted as adviser and matchmaker, introducing the author to his publishers, Edwin Mellen Press. Bishop Ron Coady and Pastor Rasik Ranchord checked the initial drafts for accuracy, and Drs Peter Lineham and John Stenhouse and the Rev. Dr Allan Davidson read the manuscript and recommended it for publication. Dr Lineham also kindly contributed a preface. The Rev. Janet Marsh undertook a meticulous proofreading of the final text and any remaining errors are therefore the author's sole responsibility, as also are the interpretations placed on the historical data.

The author is particularly indebted to those who shared their experiences in the interests of history, and who granted permission for extracts from these interviews to be published in this book. This provided a valuable reservoir of material that would have been otherwise unobtainable. Thanks are also due to Ruth Henderson, Adrienne Knowles and—especially—the late Tina Lustenhouwer for their many hours of work transcribing the interview tapes. Others have also contributed to this work. Mr R.B. Wettering de Rooy of Nedlloyd Shipping Lines in London, and Dr C. Touwen-Bousma of the *Rijksinstituut voor Oolorgsdocumentatie* and the staff of the *Rijksmuseum Nederlands Scheepvaart Museum* in Amsterdam, supplied otherwise inaccessible material. This added greatly to the story of the evacuation from Indonesia that led to the arrival of the Bethel Temple missionaries in 1942. Mrs Cecily Worsfold graciously granted me the use of her late husband's research papers in Wellington, and Pastors Max Palmer and Alex Webster gave me access to the Majestic House Correspondence files in Christchurch. Earl Hurst of Timaru provided the photograph for the cover of the book and Allan Kynaston of Dunedin drew the maps at pages 50, 246 and 247.

Finally, the author wishes to pay tribute to the early participants in the movement, who first led him to Christ and under whose ministry he was nurtured in the life of the Spirit. This book is very much *our* story. And especially, to my wife Adrienne, to whom this book is dedicated, my grateful love and thanks.

Notes

1. Brett Knowles, 'For the Sake of the Name: A History of the "New Life Churches" from 1942 to 1965' (B.Theol. (Honours) Dissertation in Christian Thought and History, University of Otago, 1988).
2. *idem*, 'Some Aspects of the History of the New Life Churches of New Zealand 1960-1990' (Ph.D. Thesis in Church History, University of Otago, 1994).
3. As exemplified in Kate L. Turabian, *A Manual for Writers of Term Papers, Theses and Dissertations*, 4th ed. (Chicago: University of Chicago Press, 1973).
4. Following the model of Peter Devereux, ed., *The New Zealand Style Book*, rev. ed. (Wellington: GP Publications Ltd., 1993).

What's in a Name? A note on Nomenclature

The group now known as the New Life Churches of New Zealand forms one of the larger associations of Pentecostal churches in New Zealand. During its collective history it has had a number of name changes which have tended to reflect changes in the group's self-perception and corporate polity. The movement began in 1946 as a result of a secession from the Pentecostal Church of New Zealand. The unifying factor of these separatist Pentecostal churches was then the Bethel Temple doctrine of water baptism in 'the Name.' This was augmented by a strongly independent emphasis on the autonomy and sovereignty of the local church, inherited from the Latter Rain movement in 1948. Although these new churches did not adopt a collective title, the terms 'Bethel Temple' or 'Latter Rain' would be equally applicable to them at this stage.

A new evangelistic impulse began in late 1957, when Tommy Hicks' visit inspired Rob Wheeler and others to begin Full Gospel tent campaigns. Since Wheeler had moved away from an exclusive association with the Bethel Temple movement by 1954, this new movement was diffuse in corporate identity, although broadly focused on evangelism. Indeed, it was not until 1961 that the activity of Wheeler and his Full Gospel colleagues could be identified as being in any way distinct from other Pentecostal groups. This growing sense of identity owed much to the opposition that they received from other Pentecostal churches. Although Bethel Temple teaching and Latter Rain polity both remained characteristics of this Full Gospel movement, it was essentially a network of independent Pentecostal evangelists and pastors, rather than an association of churches.

It was not until 1965 that a corporate identity began to emerge. Up to this time, the individual churches in the movement were sometimes described as 'Free churches', 'Full Gospel' assemblies, or as 'assemblies based upon the New Testament pattern.' By 1965, a new term was coming into use. *Bible Deliverance*—a magazine published by Rob Wheeler—now began to refer to 'indigenous Full Gospel Assemblies'[1] and the movement's first combined project in August 1965—Operation Gideon—included follow-up booklets 'published by the Indigenous Full Gospel Churches of New Zealand.'[2] The title 'Indigenous Full Gospel Churches' had originated in a South Island Pastor's Conference in Timaru in November 1964,[3] and soon became the designation by which the incipient movement was usually known. It was used by Rob Wheeler in an address on the *NZBC* programme 'I Believe' in 1968[4] and was intended to convey the sovereign, autonomous nature of the local churches, which

> while keeping their sovereignty and local control, have come into fellowship with other ministers and congregations, sharing their convictions and experiences at conventions and crusades arranged for this purpose. Not all the Independent Pentecostal Churches in New Zealand work together in this way, but those who have been doing this in the last few years have been given a general, collective name—"The Indigenous Full Gospel Churches."[5]

The term 'indigenous' was used rather than 'independent', which was felt to have adverse connotations: 'The word "indigenous" simply means "native," "local," "belonging to the district," and we prefer this word to "independent," for who can really be independent in the strictest sense and still follow the teachings of Paul on Church life?'[6]

However, the term 'Indigenous Churches' was not a universally popular one. Most local churches called themselves 'New Life Centres' in the South Island, and 'Christian Fellowships' in the North. Consequently the name did not come into general use—it has facetiously been said that this was because no one knew how to spell 'indigenous'! Although census statistics show an increasing use of the name, most of the movement tended to use shorthand titles of 'our stream' or 'our move' in private references to the group as a whole.

As well as this, there was also an increasing, although unofficial, use of the terms 'New Life Centres' or 'New Life Churches' to describe the movement. This was a natural development, since many of the South Island churches used the title for their own local fellowships, and it was a logical step to extend this to the movement as a whole. A vote on the subject of a name change was taken at the 1988 Annual Pastors' Conference and the delegates unanimously rejected the title of 'Indigenous Churches of New Zealand.' The name 'New Life Churches of New Zealand' was chosen as the official title of the movement as a whole, and the local churches were to use this corporate name along with their local title.[7]

In this book, the following titles are used to describe the movement at different stages of its history. The terms 'Bethel Temple' or 'Latter Rain' are used during the period up to 1957. From 1957 to 1965, churches in the movement are referred to as 'Full Gospel' Assemblies or 'Full Gospel' Churches. After 1965, the terms 'Indigenous Full Gospel Churches' or 'Indigenous Churches' are used to denominate the movement. Finally, the title of the 'New Life Churches of New Zealand' is employed for the movement after 1988. The exception to this historical differentiation is when an earlier feature—for example, the practice of Singing in the Spirit—is continued through to the present-day movement. In such cases, the title 'New Life Churches' is used for the movement, even though this may appear anachronistic in the immediate context of the reference.

Notes

1. 'Outreach in Three Dimensions', *Bible Deliverance*, April 1965, 3; 'Ministers' Conference', *Bible Deliverance*, July 1965, 16.
2. *The Miracle of New Life* (n.p.: Indigenous Full Gospel Churches of New Zealand, [1965]), back cover.
3. A.R. Coady, Davis, California. Fax correspondence with the author, 12 March 1998.
4. The text of this address is to found in R.B. Wheeler, 'Indigenous Full Gospel Assemblies', *Church Bells*, July 1968, 32-33, and in Wheeler, 'I Believe', *Church Bells*, September 1968, 33-34. This was published as New Zealand Broadcasting Corporation, *I Believe: A series of talks broadcast over NZBC stations in 1967* (n.p. [Wellington]: New Zealand Broadcasting Corporation, n.d. [1968]).
5. R.B. Wheeler, 'Indigenous Full Gospel Assemblies', *Church Bells*, July 1968, 32.
6. ibid.
7. The Dunedin assembly, for example, advertises itself as 'Word of Life Pentecostal Church (a New Life Church).' 'Church Notices', *Otago Daily Times*, 12 December 1998, 45.

Chapter 1

Evacuation!

Surabaya, East Java: Wednesday, 4 February 1942...

It was midmorning when the first bombs began to fall. Although the sky was clear and a convoy of Allied warships in the Makassar straits had earlier sighted the formation of more than thirty Japanese bombers,[1] no warning of the impending attack had reached Surabaya. The element of surprise was complete as the planes swept over the city. In the streets below, those not fortunate enough to reach the comparative safety of the air raid shelters took cover where they could and huddled in fear as the impact of the bombs shook the ground. Not everybody ran for shelter, however. From the porch of his parents' home, five-year-old[2] David Jackson watched the bombing raid with unperturbed curiosity, not at first realising that these were enemy planes. By the time that the Jackson family became aware of the danger, it was too late to reach the safety of the shelters, which by now were full. There was nothing that they could do except to pray; and pray they did, standing unprotected in their home as the bombs fell. This first raid caused much damage, but when the bombers had flown back to their base in Southern Celebes, the Jacksons' house was the only one in their street that remained undamaged.[3]

The Jackson family were members of Bethel Temple, a large independent Pentecostal church in Seattle, Washington, led by Pastor W.H. Offiler. David Jackson's father Ray Jackson was a gifted Bible teacher and the church had sent the family to assist with its work in Indonesia in 1939.[4] Their arrival formed part of a strong missionary program run by Bethel Temple. This had resulted in a number of Pentecostal missionaries being sent out to various parts of the world in the 1920s and 1930s. Indonesia (then called the Dutch East Indies) soon became one of Bethel Temple's major fields of endeavour. Their missionaries Groesbeck and van Claver were the first Pentecostal missionaries to arrive in the country and their work, from 1921 to 1926, laid the foundations of Indonesian Pentecostalism. A second wave of Bethel Temple missionaries followed fourteen years later, with the arrival of Pastor W.W. Paterson and others in 1935. This led to the establishment of a Bible School at Surabaya,[5] which strongly influenced the Pentecostal movement in Indonesia. One specific legacy was an emphasis, particularly in the group of churches known as *Gereja Tabernakel* [Tabernacle Church], on the Tabernacle of Moses as a basis for the interpretation of the Old and New Testaments. This doctrinal emphasis and typological method were later to influence the New Zealand New Life Churches' teachings.

Ray Jackson initially worked with the Surabaya Bible School. His stay in Indonesia was short-lived, for the war in the Pacific broke out with the bombing of Pearl Harbour in December 1941, and the Japanese began their drive southwards towards Indonesia. Their rate of advance was prodigious and by the end of January 1942 the Japanese Navy was mounting a three-pronged attack on Java, by way of Sumatra, Borneo and Celebes. On 24 January 1942, the airfield at Kendari in Southwest Celebes fell, giving the Japanese control over the shortest sea routes to Australia, threatening Australia itself and bringing Surabaya within range of their bombers. These bombing raids began on 4 February and continued until the Japanese landings in Java twenty-four days later.[6] Since Surabaya was, after Singapore, the most important naval base in the Southwest Pacific, the bombing raids rapidly became more extensive, with a particularly heavy air attack on 19 February.[7] By 26 February, Surabaya was virtually a city under siege.

After the fall of Singapore on 15 February and the Japanese landings in Bali four days later, the military situation became increasingly desperate. As the threat of invasion came closer, the Dutch authorities decided to evacuate. They recommended that the Bethel Temple missionaries—some eighteen in all[8]—should split up and embark on three separate ships. The hope was that at least some of them would get through to safety. However, the missionaries insisted that they all be together and eventually left Surabaya on 20 February, aboard the *Tjinegara*, a 9,227 ton passenger liner of the Java-China-Japan line.[9] The *Tjinegara*, along with her sister ship *Tjitjalenka*, formed part of a large evacuation convoy of ships. This evacuation order came almost too late, since the Japanese had already landed on Bali and Dutch and American destroyers had battled Japanese troop carriers off the coasts of Bali the previous day.[10] Two Dutch minesweepers, the *Abraham Crijnssen* and the *Eland Dubois*, therefore escorted the convoy for the first two days out of Surabaya on its dangerous passage through the narrow Bali Straits.[11] By now, the remnants of the Dutch Navy had taken over the defence of Java. Furthermore, the Japanese invasion force had already set out from its assembly points at Cam Ranh Bay in French Indochina and at Jolo in the Sulu Archipelago. The first landings on Java came on 28 February and by 8 March the Dutch authorities had surrendered the island to the Japanese.[12]

After the convoy had cleared the Bali Straits, the two minesweepers—all that could be spared from the desperate defence of Java—returned to Surabaya and from that time the convoy was on its own. The Japanese capture of Timor on 20 February had reinforced their stranglehold over the eastern sea routes to Australia and their planes had bombed Darwin itself the previous day. Only the southward route remained open, although a carrier group of Japanese warships had already entered the Indian Ocean to intercept any attempt at evacuation by this route to Australia. On the fourth day out from Surabaya, a Japanese destroyer sighted the convoy and gave chase. David Jackson recalls that the missionaries all prayed and a fog came down and covered the ship for three days, forcing the Japanese destroyer to give up its pursuit.[13] Ultimately, out of the entire convoy, only two ships of the Java-China-Japan line were successful in getting through to safety. These were the *Tjitjalenka*, the largest and most modern ship of the line, and the *Tjinegara* itself.[14]

Figure 1: The *Tjinegara*, which brought the evacuating Bethel Temple Missionaries to New Zealand
(L.L. von Münching, Wassenaar, Netherlands)

After escaping around the south coast of Australia, the *Tjinegara* eventually reached Adelaide on 4 March. The ship made a further stop in Sydney before departing on 12 March for Wellington, en route to Balboa, Cristobal and New Orleans.[15] When the ship arrived in Wellington on Tuesday 17 March,[16] members of the Wellington Pentecostal Church of New Zealand hosted the Bethel Temple missionaries. During the four days that they were in Wellington, the missionaries conducted several meetings for their hosts and the newness of the Bethel Temple teachings generated considerable excitement. This led to an invitation to return to New Zealand after the war and to work with the Pentecostal Church of New Zealand.[17] During his stay in Wellington, his hosts took Ray Jackson sight-seeing up to Mount Victoria. There he noted the striking resemblance of the city and harbour to a dream or vision that he had experienced some time previously. He took this as an indication that he should return to New Zealand.

After four days in port, the *Tjinegara* resumed its voyage back to the United States on 21 March, eventually arriving in New Orleans on 19 April.[18] David Jackson alleged that the *Tjinegara* was sunk in the Gulf of Mexico shortly after landing the missionaries safely and that all hands were lost.[19] This is a persistent and long-standing legend in the New Life Churches, but is not the case. The *Tjinegara* made a return voyage from New Orleans to New Caledonia and Australia several months later. On 23 July, the ship weighed anchor at Brisbane en route to Noumea and on to the United States. Two days later, the Japanese submarine *I169* torpedoed the ship in the Capricorn Channel eighty miles east of Rockhampton. There were 117 people on board the *Tjinegara*: 72 crew members, 33 people taking care of the 470 horses being transported to Noumea, and 12 members of an American gun crew. All those on board were rescued, but the animals went down with the ship. The Dutch Nautical Inspectorate later held an investigation in San Francisco into the sinking and found that a junior officer had shut down the ship's engines, acting without an order being given. If this officer had not done so, the *Tjinegara* could have outrun the submarine. The abandonment of the ship was therefore premature and the loss of the ship and its cargo was avoidable.[20]

Following their safe arrival in the United States, most of the Bethel Temple missionaries returned to their home church in Seattle. Throughout the remainder of the war, the Pentecostal Church of New Zealand maintained contact by letter with several of them. In 1943, its Annual Convention acted on correspondence from Al Edmondson, one of the Bethel Temple missionaries,[21] and extended a call to him to the pastorate of the Wellington assembly.[22] Eventually, two of the missionaries returned to New Zealand in late July 1945[23] and were welcomed into their pastorates. Ray Jackson was placed into Auckland (despite the identification of his vision with Wellington) and Al Edmondson into Wellington. A third Bethel Temple missionary, John Banks, returned at the end of 1945 and was placed into Blenheim.[24] No one could have foreseen that the doctrines brought by these three pastors would ignite a controversy that would eventually destroy the Pentecostal Church of New Zealand.

Notes

1. David Thomas, *Battle of the Java Sea* (London: André Deutsch, 1968), 22.
2. The previous edition of this book incorrectly gave his age as seven years old at the time.
3. David Jackson, Interview, Timaru, 19 November 1987.

4. Hanny Mandie, General Secretary of the Indonesian *Gereja Pantekosta* (Pentecostal Church) movement, recalls their arrival that year. Hanny Mandie, Interview, Waikanae, 22 September 1987.
5. John Thomas Nichol, *The Pentecostals* (formerly *Pentecostalism*), rev. ed. (Plainfield, New Jersey: Logos International, 1971), 176–77.
6. Thomas, *Battle of the Java Sea*, 120–22.
7. 'Heavy Plane Losses: Japanese Over Java', *[Wellington] Evening Post*, 19 February 1942, 7.
8. David Jackson recalls twenty-eight missionaries. Jackson, Interview. However, the *Pentecostal Messenger* (the official publication of the Pentecostal Church of New Zealand) notes that the evacuation party that passed through Wellington in 1942 consisted of '18 East Indies missionaries.' 'Editorial Notes', *Pentecostal Messenger*, December 1943, 2.
9. K.W.L. Bezemer, *Geschiedenis van de Nederlandse Koopvaardij in de Tweede Wereldoorlog: Deel Twee [History of the Dutch Merchant Marine in the Second World War: Volume 2]* (Amsterdam: Elsevier, 1986), 708. Relevant sections translated for the author by Miss Nel van't Wout, Dunedin.
10. John Keegan, *The Second World War* (London: Hutchinson, 1989), 262.
11. L.L. von Münching, *De Nederlandse Koopvaardijvloot in de Tweede Wereldoorlog [The Dutch Merchant Fleet in the Second World War]* (Bussum: De Boer Maritiem, 1978), 88, cited by Dr C. Touwen-Bouwsma of the *Rijksinstituut voor Oolorgsdocumentatie* [Netherlands State Institute for War Documentation], Correspondence with the author, Amsterdam, Netherlands, 2 February 1990.
12. Thomas, *Battle of the Java Sea*, 149.
13. Jackson, Interview. Although this story was well known among the participants in the early New Life Churches, the author has been unable to obtain independent corroboration of the incident. Nevertheless, this story, and other similar stories of the miraculous, served to demonstrate that God had brought the Bethel Temple missionaries to New Zealand, thus legitimating their ministry there.
14. Bezemer, *Geschiedenis*, 708.
15. *Tjinegara* Report Sheet, from records held by the Historical Branch, *Ministerie van Verkeer en Waterstraat, Directoraat-General Scheepvaart en Maritieme Zaken* [Ministry of Transport (Land and Buildings), Director-General Shipping and Maritime Affairs], Rijswijk, Netherlands.
16. Wellington Harbour Board Records, Maritime Museum, Queen's Wharf, Wellington. The *Tjitjalenka* had arrived in Wellington the previous day.
17. Later to be renamed the Elim Church of New Zealand, Inc.
18. *Tjinegara* Report Sheet.
19. Jackson, Interview.
20. Bezemer, *Geschiedenis*, 1043ff., and von Münching, *De Nederlandse Koopvaardijvloot*, 267. Relevant sections translated for the author by the staff of the *Rijksmuseum Nederlands Scheepvaart Museum* [State Museum, Netherlands Shipping Museum] Amsterdam, and by Mr R.B. Wettering de Rooy of Nedlloyd Lines, London.
21. Board of Elders of the Pentecostal Church of N.Z. (Inc.), Minute Book 1934–51, Wellington [hereafter cited as *BE*], 10 December 1943, f.73.
22. *BE*, 20 December 1943, f.75. The Wellington assembly had 'tried by all the means in our power to induce [Edmondson] to stay' following the Bethel Temple

missionaries' visit in 1942. H.V. Roberts to Al Edmondson, 11 February 1944, James E. Worsfold Research Papers, Wellington [hereafter cited as Worsfold Papers]. The author is grateful to Mrs Cecily Worsfold for granting access to her late husband's files.
23. The Wellington Pentecostal Evangelical Mission, Minute Book 8 July 1942–3 December 1951, Wellington [hereafter cited as *WPEM*] records that a welcome tea would be held for Pastor and Mrs Edmondson on 8 August 1945. *WPEM* 30 July 1945, f.61. It appears that the Jackson family had arrived in New Zealand at the same time as the Edmondsons, since David Jackson recalls hearing sirens sounding in Auckland to mark the end of World War II in August 1945. Jackson, Interview.
24. *BE*, 11 December 1945, f.87d. A typed copy of the minutes for 11 December 1945, comprising six pages, were attached to f.87 of the Minute Book. The lower case letter 'd' refers to the fourth page of these minutes.

Chapter 2

For the Sake of 'The Name'

The ministries of the three Americans were highly successful and their Bethel Temple teachings attracted a following throughout late 1945 and early 1946, particularly in Auckland. The Pentecostal Church of New Zealand quickly seconded Ray Jackson and Al Edmondson to its Executive Council, with Jackson also being appointed the first Principal of its newly established Pentecostal Bible Institute.[1] These decisions received formal approval at the movement's Annual Convention in December 1945,[2] as did the appointments of Jackson, Edmondson and Banks as pastors of the Auckland, Wellington and Blenheim assemblies, respectively.[3] Jackson was the featured speaker at the Convention, addressing seven out of its fifteen meetings.

This enthusiastic acceptance by the Pentecostal Church of New Zealand makes Jackson's sudden letter of resignation to its Executive on 18 December 1945, just two days after the Convention, all the more surprising. Jackson's letter gave two reasons for his precipitate withdrawal. The first of these was the financial strain caused by his appointments which, in his view, had become 'a burden and problem' to the local church. Jackson 'deeply regret[ted] that we are a party to the cause of such concern' and insisted that he would 'be much happier...to labour without remuneration,...simply trusting the Lord to make provision.' The second reason appeared to be the more significant one. This was his desire to 'avoid any possibility of an unintentional transgression of the Manual of the Pentecostal Church of NZ Inc. or of the Board of Elders in representing them in an official capacity.' He therefore tendered his resignation as Principal of the Pentecostal Bible Institute and as Pastor of the Auckland Assembly. This, he believed, would 'enable me to proceed with my labours without the fear of the possibility of invoking your displeasure by transgressing any regulation of the Manual.'[4]

While financial considerations were no doubt a factor, Jackson's withdrawal may have been a reflection of his distaste for organisation and administration. This would have been entirely in keeping with his charismatic and somewhat autocratic personality. In his letter of resignation, Jackson reminded the Executive that 'it was not my desire to assume such titles' as 'Principal' or 'Pastor.'[5] He appears to have viewed the institutional structure of the Pentecostal Church of New Zealand as a hindrance to his charismatic freedom to minister. It is nevertheless important to note that he was happy to continue to work with the movement in an unofficial capacity. There was no evidence of discord, as the Executive was unanimous in urging him to reconsider his resignation.[6] Jackson appears to have remained in good standing, continuing (despite his resignation) to pastor the Auckland assembly and to head the Pentecostal Bible Institute. The Executive also readily granted approval to his proposed evangelistic campaign in Blenheim two months later, agreeing to pay his return travelling expenses.[7]

This delicate harmony was not to last. During the Convention, Jackson had introduced a characteristic Bethel Temple teaching known as 'the Name.'[8] Its proponents insisted on baptism in the name of the Lord Jesus Christ rather than that of the Father, Son and Holy Spirit. They held that the invocation of 'the Name' symbolised and actualised the presence of the Godhead and thus was the validating factor in baptism. It was therefore essential to administer baptism in the name of the Lord Jesus Christ, since only in this way could it be a true baptism.[9]

The new teaching seems initially to have caused little controversy, other than to stimulate a surge of rebaptisms. Indeed, the Annual Convention had made a point of sending greetings to Pastor Offiler of Seattle, the originator of the doctrine.[10] Contention eventually began to emerge in 1946, especially in Auckland, where Ray Jackson had taken over the pastorate of the assembly from Pastor H.V. Roberts, the Superintendent of the Pentecostal Church of New Zealand. During one of Pastor Roberts' absences in early 1946, Jackson had taught the new doctrine, apparently causing some dissension. By the time that Pastor Roberts returned to Auckland, open discord had developed in the congregation.[11]

At the local level, Pastor Roberts opposed the new doctrine because of its divisive effect on the congregation. As Superintendent of the Pentecostal Church of New Zealand, however, he exercised a wider influence. In part, this was because of his long service to the movement since its founding following the campaigns of Smith Wigglesworth in 1922 and 1923-24.[12] Because of Roberts' influence, and of the strong loyalty that he inspired in the other pastors in the movement,[13] the issue of 'the Name' quickly became a national one. The progress of the controversy is discernible in the minute books of the Wellington assembly, the movement's national Board of Elders and Executive Council,[14] and in some of the later correspondence relating to the issue.[15] Although these reveal no signs of incipient dissension until mid-April 1946, 'the Name' appears to have become a national issue by then. As a result, a special meeting of the Executive Council convened on 16 April to deal with the question.

The Executive Council noted that some members of the Wellington assembly had left because of the teaching of the doctrine by Pastor Al Edmondson and that this had also caused discord in the Auckland assembly. The Council members 'were perturbed that... [the doctrine of "the Name"] should be made an issue in any Assembly [and was] likely to cause a division.' Some of them voiced strong opposition, notably E.E. Pennington, a former pastor of the Wellington assembly, who labelled the doctrine 'entirely and absolutely unscriptural.'[16] Pastor Pennington was a longtime associate of Superintendent Roberts and had a reputation for the forthright way in which he spoke his mind.[17] Most of the other pastors and elders who were present appeared to share his view, with the sole exception of Dal Walker, editor of the movement's official magazine, the *Pentecostal Messenger*.

The response of the Wellington assembly may have been typical of the way in which the decision of the Executive Council was effected in the local churches. A series of meetings between its elders and Pastor Edmondson, held throughout late April and early May, attempted to resolve the controversy there. The elders made it clear that they were 'not in accord with this new teaching' and they therefore asked Pastor Edmondson to refrain from teaching it to prevent discord in the assembly. His reply was that he would preach on the doctrine whenever God told him. (Edmondson's response was not as defiant as it might appear, since the freedom to preach the truth as he saw it was an issue of principle for him. The minutes also record some hesitation in his responses, which may reflect his perception that he had been backed into a corner on the issue.) As a result of his refusal to comply with the elders' request, the eldership suspended him until the next committee meeting on 6 May.[18] At this final meeting, the elders asked him to submit a doctrinal explanation to a combined meeting of all the Pentecostal churches in Wellington.[19] On his declining to do so, he was immediately dismissed from the pastorate.[20] Pastors E.E. Pennington and Chas. Bilby replaced him as joint pastors until the eventual appointment of a new full-time pastor.[21]

Ray Jackson and John Banks both appear to have resigned the movement several weeks earlier than Al Edmondson.[22] Their departure does not initially appear to have been an acrimonious one, the Board of Elders noting that 'despite it all there had been no bitterness manifested between the dissenting brethren.'[23] Nevertheless, controversy over the issue continued with the publication of an article promoting 'the Name' in the April–May issue of the *Pentecostal Messenger*. This resulted in the magazine being hurriedly withdrawn from circulation and reissued with a replacement article. Its editor Dal Walker may have written the offending article, since the Board of Elders regretfully accepted his resignation from this post at the same time that they withdrew the magazine from circulation.[24] Walker had been a staunch supporter of the new doctrine, and eventually resigned his eldership role in the movement in September 1946.[25]

These resignations failed to halt the growing split within the ranks of the Pentecostal Church of New Zealand, and some of its members left with Jackson and his colleagues. Although the numbers involved do not appear to have been large, they represented an appreciable portion of its membership, since most Pentecostal churches at the time had small congregations.[26] This loss was traumatic for the movement, which never recovered from the divisions caused by the controversy. After struggling to survive for several years, its remnants eventually merged with the Elim Church of Great Britain to form the Elim Church of New Zealand (Incorporated) at the end of 1952.[27]

This exodus also led to the creation of a new group of independent Pentecostal churches. The initiative for this appears to have begun in Auckland, where many members of the congregation had been converted under Ray Jackson's ministry. These people prevailed upon him to stay and to pastor them rather than to return to the United States as he had intended. Jackson consequently set up a house church to cater for his followers, and this had grown into the largest Pentecostal church in Auckland by 1947.[28] Rob Wheeler, a participant in this church, recalls that 'we used to fast every Sunday morning [and then] have a Communion Service and fellowship. We had Bible Study on Tuesdays, Prayer Meetings on Thursdays, and Young Peoples' [meetings] on Saturdays. It grew until the houses weren't big enough.'[29] As a result of this growth, the church was compelled to move to larger premises in the Orange Hall in Newton Road, Auckland City.[30]

Similarly Al Edmondson's group in Wellington developed from house meetings into a good-sized church, meeting in a public hall. John Banks was less successful in Blenheim, the group there not developing beyond the house meeting stage. These three small Bethel Temple churches laid the foundations of a movement that was later to evolve into the New Life Churches of New Zealand. By the 1970s these churches would rank 'among the most dynamic forces in the religious life in New Zealand'[31] and comprise the second largest Pentecostal grouping in this country. Partly because of the legacy of their Bethel Temple forebears, they would also make a significant contribution to the emergence of the Charismatic Movement in New Zealand.

Notes

1. Executive Council, Representing the Board of Elders of the Pentecostal Church of N.Z. (Inc.), Minute Book 1934–51, Wellington (hereafter cited as *EC*), 2 October 1945, ff.29–30. The Executive was the governing body of the Pentecostal Church of New Zealand and was ultimately responsible to the Board of Elders at the Annual Convention.
2. *BE*, 8 December 1945, f.87a.
3. *BE*, 11 December 1945, f.87d.

4. Ray Jackson to General Secretary of Pentecostal Church of New Zealand [Chas. Bilby], 18 December 1945, Worsfold Papers.
5. ibid.
6. *EC*, 17 January 1946, f.34.
7. *EC*, 7 February 1946, f.35.
8. *EC*, 16 April 1946, f.37.
9. A mimeographed summary of 'the Name' doctrine as taught by the Indigenous Churches of New Zealand (i.e. the designation by which the New Life Churches were formerly known) was produced in the early 1960s. This was eventually published in 1975 as Kevin J. Conner, *The Name of God* (Portland, Oregon: Bible Temple—Conner Publications, 1975). Ron Coady recalls the baptismal formula derived from Bethel Temple and used by Ray Jackson and his disciples. This was: 'I baptise you in the Name of the Father, and of the Son, and of the Holy Ghost— THE LORD JESUS CHRIST, and into the likeness of His death that, like as Christ was raised from the dead from the glory of the Father, even so you also shall rise to walk in... newness of life.' Coady, Fax correspondence with the author, 12 March 1998.
10. *BE*, 17 December 1945, f.87f. Offiler's teaching on 'the Name' was set out in W.H. Offiler, *God, and His Name* (Seattle, Washington: Temple Publishing House, [1932?]).
11. Dorothy Walker, Interview, Wellington, 27 June 1996. Dorothy Walker was Superintendent Roberts' daughter. Her husband Dal was editor of the *Pentecostal Messenger*, the official magazine of the Pentecostal Church of New Zealand.
12. Roberts' ministry can be summarised from the references to him in James E. Worsfold, *A History of the Charismatic Movements in New Zealand* (Bradford: Julian Literature Trust, 1974), *passim*. He was the author of an account of an eyewitness account of Wigglesworth's campaigns. H.V. Roberts, *New Zealand's Greatest Revival* (Auckland: New Zealand Pelorus Press, 1951).
13. Dorothy Walker, Interview.
14. These are the only extant minute books. The author is grateful to Pastor Mike Knott of Wellington City Elim Church for granting access to these.
15. These include letters from Pastor H.V. Roberts and other leaders of the Pentecostal Church. Worsfold Papers.
16. *EC*, 16 April 1946, f.37.
17. Dorothy Walker, Interview.
18. *WPEM*, 1 May 1946, f.82.
19. *WPEM*, 6 May 1946, ff.84–85.
20. *WPEM*, 9 May 1946, f.85.
21. *EC*, 11 June 1946, f.38.
22. Superintendent Roberts notes that he had written to Jackson on 26 April, requesting him to return the equipment and account books of the Pentecostal Bible Institute. Harry Roberts to General Secretary, Pentecostal Church of New Zealand, 8 July 1946, Worsfold Papers. This indicates that Jackson had left the movement by that date. John Banks had resigned his pastorate in Blenheim by mid-April. *EC*, 16 April 1946, f.37.
23. *BE*, 31 May 1946, f.88a.
24. *BE*, 31 May 1946, f.88b. Dal Walker's enthusiastic support of 'the Name' created some difficulties for Superintendent Roberts, his father-in-law. Roberts ex-

pressed his exasperation with this situation and reviewed the removal of the offending article in a letter to Chas. Bilby, the General Secretary of the Pentecostal Church of New Zealand. Harry Roberts to Chas. Bilby, 23 May 1946, Worsfold Papers.
25. *BE*, 9 September 1946, f.90.
26. Superintendent Roberts notes that 'about twenty of [the] members' of the Auckland assembly had left with Jackson. H.V. Roberts to Ray Jackson, 3 July 1946, Worsfold Papers.
27. Worsfold, *History*, 191.
28. Rob Wheeler, Interview, Waikanae, 22 September 1987. Given that this was a house church, numbers would not have been large, despite Wheeler's claim that this was the 'largest Pentecostal church in Auckland.' This reflects the small size and sectarian status of Pentecostalism up to the 1960s.
29. ibid.
30. Rob Wheeler, Correspondence with the author, Whangaparoa, 2 March 1998.
31. Peter J. Lineham, 'Tongues must cease: The Brethren and the Charismatic Movement in New Zealand', *Christian Brethren Research Journal* 34 (November 1983): 16.

Chapter 3

The Bethel Temple Legacy

The Bethel Temple origins of these breakaway churches gave them a characteristic doctrinal framework and hermeneutical methodology. Their Pentecostal belief systems were based on a strongly fundamentalist attitude to the Bible[1] and a distinctive mode of Bible interpretation. The controversy that accompanied the birth of these churches also did much to shape their early character. It is therefore important to analyse what the main features of Bethel Temple doctrine were and why there should have been such vigorous opposition to it.

The doctrine of 'the Name' was not a teaching unique to New Zealand. Pentecostal historian Walter Hollenweger observes that almost the entire Indonesian Pentecostal movement uses this formula of baptism.[2] This may have been due to the influence of the Bethel Temple Bible School in Surabaya. Those who received the new revelation were enthusiastic in their communication of it and this led to its rapid spread. Dal Walker commented to the author in 1971 that he himself had converted T.L. Osborn, one of the major figures in American Pentecostalism, to this teaching.[3] The issue was therefore a widespread one, and resulted in a surge of rebaptisms into 'the Name.'

Although the controversy might, at first sight, seem to be an exercise in semantic hairsplitting, there were some important implications. At one level, the reaction of the Pentecostal Church of New Zealand was pastoral, stimulated by concern for the unity of the movement's congregations. As they correctly recognised, the teaching of 'the Name' had a potential to be highly divisive. Nevertheless, the vigorous opposition to the doctrine indicates that there were also interpretative issues at stake. These centred on three questions, which the Wellington Pentecostal Evangelical Mission minute book summarises as follows:

1. Is the Name of the Holy Ghost Christ[?]
2. That only those who are baptised into the Name of [the] Lord Jesus Christ have been correctly baptised, [and that]

3. Only those who are baptised into the Name of [the] Lord Jesus Christ are in the Bride of Christ.[4]

These questions illustrate the hermeneutical dimensions of the issue. Was 'Christ' the name of the Holy Spirit, and what legitimated this interpretation? Both sides in the controversy based their arguments on a fundamentalist approach to the Bible, in which the Scriptures were both the source and the final authority. It was clear from the New Testament that the name of the Son was 'Jesus', and it was also possible to argue from the Old Testament that the name of the Father was 'Lord.'[5] The Bethel Temple teachers went one step further, however, insisting that the term 'Christ' must be the name of the Holy Spirit:

> The Spirit is the Anointing. That is what He IS. His nature, Himself, His Name are one—CHRIST.[6]
>
> The name CHRIST means the ANOINTED, and it has pleased God that the Holy Spirit should be comprehended under this name. The Holy Ghost is and may only be expressed as the CHRIST, or the Anointed.[7]

In their view, the appellation 'Lord-Jesus-Christ' was indeed the triune name of the Father, Son and Holy Spirit. In response, the Pentecostal Church of New Zealand insisted that the words 'Father', 'Son', and 'Holy Spirit' were names of the Godhead rather than simply titles. To baptise in these names thus fulfilled the Scriptural requirements for the invocation of the Divine Name in baptism.[8]

To some extent, the controversy over 'the Name' was a product of the hermeneutical method of the Bethel Temple teachers, who legitimated their doctrines by an illuminist approach to the Bible. Offiler emphasised the need for direct spiritual revelation of the hidden truths of the Bible. This is demonstrated by his book *God and His Bible*, widely circulated among the forerunners of the New Life Churches in the early 1960s. He claimed that his doctrines did 'not follow any of the usual lines of modern Bible teaching, for much of the subject matter has come to the author by the direct revelation of the Holy Spirit of God.'[9] Bethel Temple adherents tended to accept these revelation truths uncritically, with the implications of these seldom being carefully examined. The weakness of their argument was that the term 'Christ' referred preeminently to the Messiah—the 'anointed one', namely Jesus the Messiah—and did not properly apply to the Holy Spirit, the 'anointer.' Their dependence on spiritual revelation rather than logical argument tended to obscure this distinction.

Offiler's emphasis on revelation was paralleled by his use of Bible typology. In his view, Old Testament incidents and events were types or shadows of heavenly things.[10] Thus, 'the Old Testament is filled with typical things, and every type, has its anti-typical revelation, and fulfilment. The typological studies, are filled with great blessing for all who will search.'[11] A striking example of his allegorical typology was that of 'the Sun, the Moon, and the Stars, [which] are a magnificent revelation of the Godhead Bodily,[12] as The Father, The Son, and The Holy Spirit.'[13] Other types include those of Abraham,

Isaac and Jacob as a threefold allegory of the Trinity; likewise, 'the Rod, the Rock and the Living Waters' (based on Numbers 20:8) and other Biblical analogies. Much of Offiler's typology follows a similar threefold pattern, reflecting his emphasis on the trinitarian being of God. This could apply to any part of the Old Testament and the Tabernacle of Moses was, in particular, an abundant source of allegorical types. The outer court of the Tabernacle symbolised the Mosaic dispensation of law; the holy place, the church age of grace; while the holy of holies, where God's presence dwelt, foreshadowed the millennial age of glory. This typological method of interpretation formed the basis of the hermeneutical methodology employed by the New Life Churches.

Offiler's teachings were also strongly millennial and dispensational, having marked similarities with those of J.N. Darby and the Brethren movement. He shared their view that human history was divided into dispensations of time, and held that there were three such dispensations. The first of these extended from 4000 B.C.E.[14] to 2000 B.C.E., and was the dispensation of the Father, i.e. from Adam, the 'father' of the human race, to Abraham, the 'father of those that believe.'[15] Likewise, the two thousand years from 2000 B.C.E. to the Christian era were the dispensation of the Son. This extended from Isaac, the only begotten son of the father (Abraham), to Jesus, the only begotten Son of the Father (God). The two thousand years of the Christian era comprised the dispensation of the Spirit. This began with the 'former rain' outpouring of the Spirit at Pentecost, and would come to a climax with the 'latter rain' outpouring at the end of the age. These made up six one-thousand-year 'days'[16] of the 'Redemptive Week', corresponding to the six 'days' of the 'Creative Week' of Genesis 1. The seventh day of rest foreshadowed the thousand-year reign of Christ during the millennium.

The effect of this legacy on the new movement was twofold. It generated a characteristic style of Pentecostal Bible teaching, and provided an hermeneutical methodology that gave full rein to the imaginative use of allegory and typology. Consequently, many of the New Life Churches' characteristic doctrines, such as their emphasis on the Tabernacle of Moses, came directly from their Bethel Temple antecedents. Of greater importance, however, was the ethos that these churches inherited. From their earliest beginnings, they were a Bible teaching movement, and emphasised the role of residential Bible Schools. Early examples include Rob Wheeler's Bible School in Tauranga from 1959 to 1966 and Ron Coady's Bible School in Nelson in 1963 and 1964. Peter Morrow's church later ran the New Life Family Bible College—eventually renamed the 'International School of Ministry'—in Christchurch from 1971 to 1993. There were also numerous small *ad hoc* nonresidential Bible Schools conducted in local churches by the pastors of the movement. As will be seen, this Bible teaching ethos made a major contribution to the beginnings of the New Zealand Charismatic Movement in the later 1960s.

Later opponents of 'the Name' teaching made much of its similarity to that of the 'Jesus Only' movement, which had emerged in American Pentecostalism in 1913.[17] This movement emphasised the authority of the name of Jesus, maintaining that while God is a threefold Being, Father, Son and Holy Spirit, there is but one Person, and that is Jesus. It therefore denied traditional trinitarian doctrine and baptismal practice, replacing these with a modalist view of God and with baptism in the name of Jesus, and as such, was considered heretical by other Pentecostal churches.

While there were some similarities between 'Jesus Only' doctrines and practices and those of the Bethel Temple teachers, the doctrinal assumptions of the two movements were quite different. Offiler's theology was emphatically trinitarian. His book *God and His Bible* categorically states, under the heading of 'the Godhead Bodily', that:

> The God whom we worship is always revealed in His Word as Three-fold in His Nature and Being. Never!—from the first word in the Book of Genesis to the last word in the Book of Revelation is the God of the Bible manifested as the singular, solitary numeral, or number, ONE. The Oneness of God is NOT numerical! He is a Oneness of thought and purpose. A Oneness of Ministry and Love. It is a Oneness of holy accord and harmony, and we repeat that the Oneness of God is NEVER numerical. He never means the number ONE.[18]

By using the title of the 'Lord Jesus Christ' to denominate the triune Being of Father, Son and Holy Spirit, Offiler and his followers sought to be faithful to a trinitarian understanding of God. However, their reliance on revelation, together with their lack of theological sophistication, led them into statements that were capable of misinterpretation. One example was their use of the phrase 'Fullness of the Godhead Bodily' (or sometimes simply 'Godhead Bodily') to describe the full revelation of God (Father, Son and Holy Spirit) through the life of Jesus. Because the 'Jesus Only' movement had used this phrase in precisely this sense, Offiler and his followers were accused of holding a similar unitarian theology. Nevertheless, they did not mean to suggest that the beings or identities of the Father, Son and Holy Spirit were in any way confused or overlapped. Their trinitarian understanding of God was quite different from the unitarian emphasis of the 'Jesus Only' groups.

Notwithstanding these differences, 'the Name' teaching in New Zealand was equated with 'Jesus Only' doctrine (as for example, by James Worsfold).[19] Rob Wheeler insists that this equation was made by Pastor Roberts and other Pentecostal leaders from the earliest stages of the controversy.[20] It is therefore surprising that nowhere in the primary records of the dissension is any reference made to this imputed unitarianism. No condemnation of Bethel Temple views on the Trinity appears in the various minute books of the Pentecostal Church of New Zealand, nor in the correspondence between the protagonists in the controversy. Furthermore, neither the extracts from Pastor H.V. Roberts' pamphlet *Beware of the New Revelation on Water Baptism*, cited by Worsfold,[21] nor Pastor E.E. Pennington's mimeographed pamphlet on 'the Name',[22] make any reference to unitarian tendencies. This silence is significant, for if the doctrine had indeed been perceived as unitarian, this would have been sufficient to totally damn its teachers in the eyes of their Pentecostal colleagues.[23]

Despite Wheeler's claim, the earliest opponents of the doctrine may not have initially seen 'the Name' teaching as 'Jesus Only.' The claim that it was unitarian appears to have been a somewhat later categorisation, which apparently became the standard perception in the 1950s and early 1960s. Rob Wheeler complains that

> No matter how hard [Ray Jackson] tried to convince [the other Pentecostal churches] he was not "Jesus Only," they just would not believe [him].... It was only the second generation of myself, Peter Morrow, Ron Coady and so on that finally put that bogey to rest.... It wasn't just our theology that did it; it was the fact that the true "Jesus Only" church had started in New Zealand [in 1969],[24] and the Pentecostal groups could see that we were totally different, and then they believed us.[25]

The most vigorous animosity appears to have come in the early 1960s, culminating in the formation of the New Zealand Pentecostal Fellowship [hereafter cited as *NZPF*] in 1966.[26] This opposition is evident from the Doctrinal Statement that forms part of the Constitution adopted by the *NZPF*, which inserts a qualifying word 'only' into the clause on Baptism. This reads: '[we believe]... in the ordinance for Believers of Baptism by immersion in the Name of the Father, Son and Holy Ghost (only).'[27] The clause therefore specifically excluded the formula of baptism 'in the Name of the Lord Jesus Christ', and so barred those groups that promoted this formula from participation in the *NZPF*.[28] One of the first actions of the *NZPF* was to publish a booklet by Ralph Read, then General Superintendent of the Assemblies of God. This strongly attacked 'the formula of "oneness" teachers' (i.e. the imputed teaching of 'the Name').[29] Read claimed, in response to a question 'does the issue of "the Name Baptism" go deeper than the question of the formula?', that

> Many [of these teachers] deny the fundamental teaching of the Godhead by which we mean that the Godhead exists in three distinct eternal Persons, Father, Son and Holy Ghost and that these three are one. The fundamental understanding of the Trinity involves this and this is denied by many "Oneness" teachers who give new meanings to old terms. Others say unless you are baptised in "the Name" you may be in the body of Christ but not in the Bride of Christ.[30]

Some of Read's statements do refer to Bethel Temple teachings, such as the need to be baptised in 'the Name' to be in the Bride of Christ. Nevertheless, the booklet appears to fall into the trap of assuming the identity of this teaching with that of the 'Jesus Only' movement. In so doing, it misrepresents the trinitarian theology of the Bethel Temple teaching on 'the Name' and imputes an unfair charge of unitarianism to the forerunners of the New Life Churches.

The teaching of 'the Name', and the vigorous opposition that it later attracted, created boundaries of identification for these churches. Although this emphasis had become rather less prominent by the mid-1950s, it did provide an initial rallying point. By the 1960s, the Bethel Temple ethos of Bible teaching had become a more important characteristic than the single doctrinal issue of 'the Name.' Nevertheless, the unyielding opposition from other Pentecostal groups reinforced a sense of 'us and them' and helped to create a legacy of sectarian identity for the forerunners of the New Life Churches. This legacy was augmented by the arrival of the Latter Rain movement in New Zealand.

Notes

1. Robert Mapes Anderson, *Vision of the Disinherited: The Making of American Pentecostalism* (New York: Oxford University Press, 1979), 5: 'the Pentecostals have always prided themselves on their commitment to what they believe to be the "Fundamentals" of historic Christianity.'
2. Walter J. Hollenweger, *The Pentecostals*, trans. by R.A. Wilson (London: SCM Press Ltd., 1972), 71.
3. Dal Walker, Comment to author, Tawangmangu, Indonesia, 1971.
4. *WPEM*, 1 May 1946, f.81.
5. This is because the English translators of the King James Version had rendered the divine name of *YHWH* (for which the Jews substituted *adonai* or 'lord' in reading the text) as LORD. The capitalisation of the whole word in the English indicates that this is a substitution, rather than an exact translation, of the Hebrew text.
6. This followed from the Bethel Temple belief that the name given to a person in Scripture reflected that person's essential being or nature. For example, Abraham, i.e. 'Father of a multitude' (Gen.17:5); Jesus, i.e. 'Saviour' (Matt.1:23). To understand the significance of the person's name was to know the real person.
7. Cited by H.V. Roberts, *Beware of the New Revelation on Water Baptism* (Auckland: Church Army Press, 1946), and thence by Worsfold, *History*, 188. Capitalisation as cited. Roberts' book represented the official response of the Pentecostal Church of New Zealand. A large extract is reproduced in Worsfold, *History*, 184–90.
8. *EC*, 11 June 1946, f.38.
9. W.H. Offiler, *God and His Bible, or The Harmonies of Divine Revelation* (Seattle, Washington: Bethel Temple, 1946), 11. This book contained the essence of Offiler's teaching on the Bible, divided into 120 specific topics.
10. Offiler based this methodology on Hebrews 8:5, which describes the Old Testament priesthood as being 'the example and shadow of heavenly things' (King James Version, hereafter cited as *KJV*).
11. Offiler, *God and His Bible*, 172. The somewhat idiosyncratic punctuation is as cited.
12. Offiler uses the phrase 'Godhead Bodily' (Colossians 2:9 *KJV*) to denote the Trinity.
13. Offiler, *God and His Bible*, 172. He discusses this particular type, which forms the basis of his Trinitarian understanding, at greater length in *idem*, *The Majesty of the Symbol, or Bible Astronomy* (Seattle, Washington: By the Author, 1933).
14. Offiler believed, as did Archbishop Ussher in the seventeenth century, that the world was created in 4004 B.C.E.
15. Romans 4:11.

16. Based upon a literalist interpretation of 2 Peter 3:8, 'one day is with the Lord as a thousand years, and a thousand years as one day' (*KJV*).
17. An excellent account of the issues involved in the rise of the 'Jesus Only' movement is given in Vinson Synan, *The Holiness-Pentecostal Movement in the United States* (Grand Rapids, Michigan: William B. Eerdmans Publishing Co., 1971), 153-63 and 220-22.
18. Offiler, *God and His Bible*, 34. Emphasis and punctuation as cited.
19. Worsfold, *History*, 182, note 7. Worsfold continued to maintain this identification as late as 1989. James Worsfold, Correspondence with the author, 14 January 1989, Brett Knowles Research Papers, Dunedin.
20. Wheeler, Correspondence with the author, 2 March 1998.
21. Roberts, *Beware of the New Revelation on Water Baptism*, 24-31, cited by Worsfold, *History*, 184-90.
22. E.E. Pennington, Pamphlet on 'the Name' controversy, 1946, Worsfold Papers.
23. Worsfold does cite a paragraph from Donald Gee, *The Pentecostal Movement, Including the Story of the War Years (1940-1947)* rev. ed. (London: Elim Publishing Company, 1949), 124-25, to justify the condemnation of the Bethel Temple teaching as unitarian. Worsfold, *History*, 183, note 7. However, Gee's passage refers to the New Issue controversy in the Canadian and American Pentecostal movements during the late 1910s and early 1920s. Worsfold's assumption, that the Bethel Temple teaching on 'the Name' is identical with that of the New Issue (or 'Jesus Only') teachers of a generation earlier, begs the question. In any case, Gee's statement cannot be applied to the later movement, since he specifically limits it to the period between 1920 and 1924. Gee, *The Pentecostal Movement*, 125.
24. According to David Barrett, the United Pentecostal Church, a unitarian (i.e. 'Jesus Only') Pentecostal group, arrived in New Zealand in 1969, and by 1982 had established forty churches with approximately 4,000 affiliated members. It also conducted a Bible School with twenty-five students attending. David B. Barrett, ed., *World Christian Encyclopaedia: A Comparative Study of Churches and Religions in the Modern World, AD 1900-2000* (Nairobi: Oxford University Press, 1982), s.v. 'New Zealand', Table 2, 'Organized Churches and Denominations in New Zealand.' However, Wheeler considers Barrett's statistics for the New Zealand wing of this unitarian Pentecostalism to be 'gross exaggeration.' Wheeler, Correspondence with the author, 2 March 1998.
25. Wheeler, Interview.
26. The membership of this Pentecostal umbrella group comprised the Apostolic Church, the Assemblies of God, the Elim Church, and the National Revival Crusade. Worsfold, *History*, 312-13.
27. Cited in Worsfold, *History*, 314.
28. Ian Clark, Interview, Auckland, 28 February 1990. See below, chapter 27, page 194.
29. Ralph R. Read, *Water Baptism: The Formula and its meaning. A Study of the Trinitarian Formula of Matthew 28 v.19 and the Formula of 'Oneness' Teachers: A Guide and a Refutation* (Christchurch: New Zealand Pentecostal Fellowship, 1966). I am grateful to James Worsfold for a copy of this booklet.
30. ibid., 9-10.

Chapter 4

Latter Rain!

After more than a year of ministry in the new Bethel Temple churches, Ray Jackson and his family returned to the United States in 1947, and John Banks took over his pastorate in Auckland. Rob Wheeler recalls that the Jackson and Edmondson families had returned home because they were homesick and discouraged because of the fierce Pentecostal opposition directed against their work.[1] Another factor was the news of a third generation of healing evangelists[2] that was then emerging in America, spearheaded by William Branham.[3] Wheeler believes that Jackson had heard reports of Branham's ministry and consequently felt that he needed to return to the United States to see at first hand what was taking place.[4] Jackson's time in America was to be significant, both for himself and for the development of the churches he had left behind in New Zealand.

While in America, Ray and Ruth Jackson attended some meetings in North Battleford, Saskatewan, Canada, where a revival had broken out in February 1948 at the Sharon Orphanage and Schools, attracting worldwide attention. The accounts of this revival reveal marked similarities between it and the revival at Charles F. Parham's Bible School in Topeka, Kansas, which had launched the Pentecostal movement some forty-seven years earlier. Parham wrote of the Topeka outpouring that, following a student's request for prayer and the laying on of hands for the Baptism of the Spirit,

> I had scarcely repeated three dozen sentences when a glory fell upon her, a halo seemed to surround her head and face, and she began speaking in the Chinese language, and was unable to speak English for three days.
>
> Seeing this marvellous manifestation of the restoration of Pentecostal power,... we decided as a school to wait upon God. We felt that God was no respecter of persons and what He had so graciously poured out upon one, He would upon all.[5]

This revival marked the beginning of the Pentecostal movement, which later spread worldwide from Azusa Street in Los Angeles from 1906 onwards.

The North Battleford awakening began, as did that in Topeka, in a Bible School where the students had gathered to study the Word of God with fasting and praying. As also had happened in Topeka, there were similar divine irruptions. According to Ern Hawtin, a participant in the North Battleford awakening, God suddenly moved into their midst in a 'strange new manner.' Hawtin reported that

> Some students were under the power of God on the floor, others were kneeling in adoration and worship before the Lord. The anointing deepened until the awe of God was upon everyone. The Lord spoke to one of the brethren. "Go and lay hands upon a certain student and pray for him." While he was in doubt and contemplation, one of the sisters who had been under the power of God, went to the brother saying the same words, and naming the identical student he was to pray for. He went in obedience and a revelation was given concerning the student's life and future ministry. After this a long prophecy was given with minute details concerning the great thing God was about to do. The pattern for the revival and many details concerning it were given.[6]

From these beginnings, gifts of healing and prophecy began to operate, with the result that people began to come from every part of North America and of the world to participate in this revival. These camp meeting-conventions conducted by the teachers at the Sharon Bible School marked the beginning of what later became known as the Latter Rain movement.[7]

The emphases of this new radically independent Pentecostal movement brought it into conflict with other Pentecostal groups.[8] John Nichol characterises it as 'a counteraction to the growing denominationalism of the Pentecostal movement', but observes that this soon became 'an organisation of come-outers, replete with tenets of faith and a charismatic leadership.'[9] However, Nichol's reference to organisation may not be entirely accurate. Richard Riss concurs that the movement did represent a 'reaction against the denominationalism that had developed within Pentecostalism', but denies that there was a progression towards organisation. He observes that 'no denomination... arose out of the Latter Rain movement.... There remain countless independent churches throughout North America that became established during this time.'[10] The Latter Rain emphasis on the autonomy of the local church prevented these independent churches from coalescing into an organised denominational movement.

Pentecostalists generally understood the term 'Latter Rain' as referring to an outpouring of the Holy Spirit 'upon all flesh... in the latter days.' They based this belief upon Scripture references such as Joel 2:23ff., Zech.10:1, and Hos.6:3. Consequently, there was an ongoing expectation in Pentecostalism for a latter-day outpouring of the Spirit and each new revival (such as the 1948 movement) tended to be seen as a fulfilment of this expectation. Despite this, the North Battleford brethren were cautious, maintaining that 'in spite of all the talk about Latter Rain... the Latter Rain has not yet come and if so, only in very, very limited measures.'[11] Nevertheless, others quickly identified the movement with the promised Latter Rain, and the name stuck. It was this movement, rather than that of Offiler and Bethel Temple, that produced the characteristic Latter Rain teaching in New Zealand.[12]

Ray Jackson was the channel through which the new movement arrived in this country and was able to integrate the Latter Rain teachings successfully with his earlier Bethel Temple doctrines. This combination laid the foundation of the New Life Churches' characteristic distrust of structural organisation, their strong emphasis on the autonomy of the local church, and many of their distinctive doctrines and practices. Jackson had received the laying on of hands with prophecy at the North Battleford meetings and been ordained as an Apostle to New Zealand for the Latter Rain. This caused him to meet considerable opposition from Bethel Temple in Seattle (to whom he was still affiliated), and this opposition followed his return to New Zealand in 1949. John Banks, Jackson's successor in the Auckland pastorate, received a telephone call from Bethel Temple warning him not to have anything further to do with Jackson, as he had 'fallen into heresy.' This placed Banks in a very difficult position, as he had already arranged a public meeting to welcome the Jacksons back to the church that they had founded. Banks told Ray Jackson at the door of the church that he was not welcome on the platform, nor would he be able to discuss or talk about his involvement in the North American revival. Jackson wrote:

> I was too stunned to fully realise what he said and just followed him up to the platform like a puppy dog, and sat down. The song service became one of the longest ever—no one knew what to do with me on the platform and it had been announced that I would not be permitted there. Finally, to break the embarrassment of the whole situation, the Pastor said to the congregation very curtly, "you know him!" I stood up, and for minesterial [sic: ministerial] courtesy simply said "hello," which sounded so ridiculous. Then I jumped at a straw, calling my wife to testify to give me further time to get my bearings.
>
> My wife had not heard what he had told me at the entrance, so she just went ahead and did the very thing he had not wanted. I looked away, telling the Lord I had nothing to do with this. So I said, "now, I'm taking my liberty, Lord," and plunged in to tell the folks what I had witnessed in America. I didn't talk too long, but when I stopped, it seemed as though the people literally ran to the altar, and God came down. I made my exit.[13]

For several days after this, John Banks questioned Jackson concerning the Latter Rain and finally opened the door for further meetings, and, as Jackson wrote, 'that's how things started in New Zealand. People came from everywhere, and we saw the same things we had witnessed in America. It was the first time for singing in the Spirit in the South Pacific, and many other things.'[14]

Banks' acceptance of Jackson's message had the effect of combining the Bethel Temple churches in New Zealand with the new movement. The arrival of the Latter Rain marked a new stage in the prehistory of the New Life Churches in New Zealand. However, it also met with widespread opposition. There were several early converts, such as Pastor Allan Thrift, who accepted the Latter Rain message and amalgamated his small independent Pentecostal church in Takapuna with the movement. Ray Jackson and Allan Thrift later toured the country and visited every Pentecostal church they could, asking if they could share the Latter Rain message. Without exception, the door was shut in their faces. The reaction of other Pentecostal churches therefore forced the new movement into separatism at its inception. This opposition was not only to the Latter Rain message, but also to Jackson's Bethel Temple origins; memories of the split from the Pentecostal Church of New Zealand were still fresh. Against such opposition, the movement spread very slowly.

Figure 2: Ray and Ruth Jackson, whose ministry laid the foundations upon which the New Life Churches were later to build
(David Jackson, Nambour, Queensland, Australia)

Another early group of converts to the Latter Rain teaching was a house church pastored by Mrs Edna Robb in Tauranga. Mrs Robb was a convert of the Revival Fire Mission campaigns of A.H. Dallimore in Auckland in the early 1930s. During a family visit to Tauranga in late 1939, she had shared her Pentecostal testimony with a number of people. As a result of her enthusiastic witness, Pastor Alf Gracie of the Devonport Revival Fire Mission received an invitation to come to Tauranga to begin meetings at the Otumoetai school. After shifting permanently to Tauranga in early 1940, Mrs Robb took over the pastorship of these meetings 'as the only Spirit-filled person here at the time.' She continued to lead this house church until 1950, when it amalgamated with Ray Jackson's Latter Rain movement. This group formed the nucleus of the church that later developed into the Tauranga Christian Fellowship after 1954.

This church recently celebrated its fiftieth anniversary, which makes it effectively the oldest of the New Life Churches of New Zealand.[15]

Other results were meagre. A Latter Rain church was established in Lower Hutt and an attempt made to start a similar church in Whangarei. Elsewhere a few house meetings and individuals in Timaru, Blenheim and Christchurch accepted the new message. By 1950, there were only three churches in the North Island, namely, Auckland, Lower Hutt and Tauranga, and three house meetings in the South at Blenheim, Christchurch and Timaru. These churches and house groups constituted a network of believers linked by personal association with Jackson and his Latter Rain message, rather than a formal association of churches. The house meetings tended to be short-lived, and of the churches, only Tauranga was to have any major influence on the future development of the movement, the focus of which now began to shift to Australia.

Notes

1. Wheeler, Correspondence with the author, 2 March 1998.
2. After the earlier ministries of John Alexander Dowie in the 1880s, and the Jeffreys brothers and Smith Wigglesworth in the 1920s.
3. Accounts of William Branham's life and ministry are given in Hollenweger, *The Pentecostals*, 354–56, and (in more detail) in David Edwin Harrell, Jnr., *All Things are Possible: The Healing and Charismatic Revivals in Modern America* (Bloomington, Indiana: Indiana University Press, 1975), 27–41, 159–65.
4. Wheeler, Interview.
5. Charles Fox Parham, 'The Latter Rain', *The Apostolic Faith* XXVIII (April 1951): 4, cited in Nichol, *The Pentecostals*, 28.
6. E. Hawtin, 'How This Revival Began', *The Sharon Star*, 1 August 1949, 3, cited in R.M. Riss, 'Latter Rain Movement', in *Dictionary of Pentecostal and Charismatic Movements*, ed. Stanley M. Burgess, Gary B. McGee, and Patrick H. Alexander (Grand Rapids, Michigan: Zondervan, 1988), 532–34.
7. The fullest accounts of the Latter Rain movement (or the 'New Order of the Latter Rain', as it was sometimes called) are to be found in Richard M. Riss, *Latter Rain: The Latter Rain movement of 1948 and the Mid-Twentieth Century Evangelical Awakening* (Etobicoke, Ontario: Honeycomb Visual Productions, 1987), and *idem*, 'Latter Rain Movement', in Burgess *et al.*, *Dictionary*, 532–34. Edith L. Blumhofer, *The Assemblies of God: A Chapter in the Story of American Pentecostalism*, 2 vols. (Springfield, Missouri: Gospel Publishing House, 1989), 2: 53–67, offers a critical perspective on the movement. Other treatments are somewhat meagre. Nichol, *The Pentecostals*, 237–38, makes only a brief reference to the Latter Rain, and although Hollenweger, *The Pentecostals*, 72ff., refers to the Latter Rain Assemblies of South Africa, this group appears to be a different movement (although using a similar name), since it was based in South Africa, and was active in the 1920s.
8. Blumhofer, *The Assemblies of God*, 2: *passim*. Blumhofer's account, although written from an Assemblies of God perspective, is critical of the Assemblies of God for rejecting the Latter Rain movement.
9. Nichol, *The Pentecostals*, 238.

10. Riss, *Latter Rain*, 77.
11. George Hawtin, 'Apostolic Work in Europe', *The Sharon Star* (1 May 1950), 1, quoted in ibid., 75.
12. Peter Lineham mistakenly calls Offiler's movement the Latter Rain (Lineham, 'Tongues must cease', 15). The error is understandable, since the movement in New Zealand became, as a result of Ray Jackson's influence, a combined Bethel Temple-Latter Rain movement. The two groups were not initially connected, for while Offiler shared the general Pentecostal expectation of a coming outpouring of the Spirit, he would not necessarily have identified this with the North Battleford movement.
13. Ray Jackson to Richard Riss, 16 March 1977, quoted in Riss, *Latter Rain*, 134–35. Since the author was unable to gain information from Ray Jackson due to his ill health, Riss' account of the arrival of the Latter Rain movement in New Zealand was invaluable. The author is grateful to his publishers for permission to reproduce this and other material. Ray Jackson underwent open heart surgery in 1988, and died in February 1990.
14. ibid.
15. 'Tauranga Christian Fellowship: Jubilee Reunion 1939–1989', Tauranga, 1989. (Mimeographed.) 2–3.

Chapter 5

The Latter Rain Legacy

Several sources have combined to shape the beliefs and practices of the New Life Churches. The Bethel Temple movement laid their hermeneutical and doctrinal foundations, and the controversy over the issue of 'the Name' created a boundary between them and other Pentecostal groups. The Latter Rain movement reinforced these boundaries and contributed a radically independent format and charismatic models of leadership. While the doctrines and beliefs of these churches eventually moved beyond those of their Bethel Temple antecedents in the 1960s, their collective organisation remained modelled on Latter Rain patterns until the 1980s. The influence of this movement was therefore the more important one for the future development of the New Life Churches.

In sociological terms, the Latter Rain movement was charismatic in ethos, restorationist and perfectionist in doctrine, and strongly antiorganisational in church polity. These attributes were reflected in six specific emphases. The first of these was the impartation of the gifts of the Spirit through the laying on of hands.[1] This contrasted with the traditional Pentecostal method of tarrying, or waiting in prayer, until God sovereignly baptised the seeker in the Holy Spirit. Although examples of the laying on of hands for the Baptism of the Spirit appear in the early history of Pentecostalism, the custom later appears to have become less common. The Latter Rain movement therefore restored, rather than created, this practice. Although Rob Wheeler comments that it was considered at the time to be 'bizarre',[2] the laying on of hands has now become a standard feature of Pentecostal and Charismatic groups.

The laying on of hands was also a means, together with prophecy, of recognising and setting apart charismatically gifted individuals as ministries to the Body of Christ. The Latter Rain movement saw this process as a restoration of the fivefold ministry of apostles, prophets, evangelists, pastors and teachers (Ephesians 4:11) which would bring the Church to perfection. The roles of the apostles and prophets received particular stress, as also did the recognition and ordination of anointed individuals to these offices.

These two doctrinal emphases reflected the charismatic ethos of the movement, as well as its strongly restorationist belief system. Latter Rain adherents believed that God was bringing back to His last-days Church the experiential appropriation, lost since the time of the Book of Acts, of the foundation truths of Hebrews 6:1–2. (This loss did not imply a lack of knowledge or of belief, but rather of an experiential living out of these truths.) Thus repentance from dead works and faith towards God were viewed as having been restored through Martin Luther, and baptisms through the Anabaptist and early Pentecostal movements. The laying on of hands emphasis of the Latter Rain movement was the fourth step in this process of restoration to the Church. The final two truths of resurrection from the dead and eternal judgement awaited experiential restoration in the future.

The expectation that the Church would be restored to the measure of the stature of the fullness of Christ[3] led to a third, strongly perfectionist, emphasis known as 'the manifestation of the sons of God.'[4] Early Latter Rain publications make reference to this triumphalist 'vision of the Manifestation of the Sons of God in the last days of this dispensation. This mighty army was seen conquering all before it. Sickness and disease were vanishing, and all evil spirits were seen scattered before the triumphant power of God's people.'[5] The North Battleford wing of the movement saw these manifest sons of God as being an army of victorious saints who would enter into all that God had promised the Church in the last days. Not all sections of the movement espoused this extreme perfectionism, although Bill Britton of Springfield, Missouri[6] later became a prominent exponent of the Sons of God doctrine.

A fourth Latter Rain teaching, the Three Feasts of Israel, restated this belief in a less stridently triumphalist form. This interpreted the three Old Testament feasts of Passover, Pentecost and Tabernacles as prophetic symbols of God's purpose for His Church. The Feast of Passover, in which the Passover Lamb was killed in commemoration of Israel's deliverance from Egypt, was fulfilled in 'Christ our Passover [being] sacrificed for us.'[7] Likewise, the Feast of Pentecost foreshadowed the descent of the Holy Spirit in the second chapter of Acts. The Feast of Tabernacles presaged the future perfection of the Church in the end of the age. In New Zealand, this particular teaching was unique to the early New Life Churches.[8]

The charismatic ethos and antiorganisational temper of the Latter Rain movement were exemplified in its emphasis on praise and worship. This incorporated several characteristic practices such as spontaneous singing in the Spirit, raising of hands and other physical expressions of worship, which have now become standard features in the Pentecostal and Charismatic movements. However, the claim that these practices had their origins in the Latter Rain movement is not entirely correct, since this movement represented their revival rather than their introduction *de novo*. Singing in the Spirit, for example, had been a feature of Pentecostalism in the early years of this century,[9] when 'the "heavenly choir" joined by various people in spontaneous harmony, attracted considerable interest. Those who heard it or participated in it claimed they could never adequately describe its beauty or sacredness.'[10] An early participant recalled his experience of it:

> There was a low murmur of sound from several directions over the congregation. This grew in volume until six persons were on their feet singing in rich harmony a song in the Spirit. Their eyes were closed, but without any confusion these persons moved from their various locations to the front of the hall, where they stood together singing in tongues in beautiful unison, then in harmonizing parts. To me was granted the glorious privilege of being one of [the participants in] this first such sensation of the Spirit's power. The sensation was like being a pipe from which poured forth the wonderful melody from deep within my being.[11]

The phenomenon of singing in the Spirit was especially prominent in the campaigns of Maria Woodworth-Etter in the early 1900s.[12] It also occurred in the 1904 Welsh Revival, possibly stimulated by the characteristic Welsh phenomenon of *hwyl*,[13] and in the early Pentecostal movement in New Zealand.[14] However, it appears to have fallen into desuetude in later Pentecostalism. This may have been the consequence, at least in part, of a progression towards Pentecostal organisation. Singing in the Spirit appears to have reflected not only a desire for charismatic freedom in worship, but also a response to the routinisation of the Pentecostal movement and a vigorous aversion towards structural organisation.[15]

This antipathy was the most distinctive emphasis of the Latter Rain movement, which claimed (with some justification) that the Pentecostal movement had lost its charismatic fervour, becoming more organised and hence more denominational. Since the Latter Rain movement considered all organisation to be 'Babylonian' and antithetical to the freedom of the Spirit, the denominational Pentecostal churches were therefore apostate, backslidden and deserving of rebuke.[16]

This antiorganisational polity had considerable resonance with the views of the early Pentecostal movement itself, which, from its very beginnings, tended to regard organization with suspicion. Just four months after the start of the Azusa Street revival, Frank Bartleman records, with a mixture of dismay and righteous indignation, that

> "Azusa" began to fail the Lord also, early in her history. God showed me one day that they were going to organize, though not a word had been said in my hearing about it. The Spirit revealed it to me. He had me get up and warn them against making a "party" spirit of the Pentecostal work. The "baptized" saints were to remain "one body," even as they had been called, and to remain free even as His Spirit was free, not "entangled again in a yoke of (ecclesiastical) bondage." ... That spirit has been the curse of every revival body sooner or later. ...
>
> Sure enough the very next day after I dropped this warning in the meeting, I found a sign outside "Azusa" reading "Apostolic Faith Mission."[17] The Lord said: "That is what I told you." They had done it.[18]

Bartleman's views on the evils of organisation reflected the mainstream of early Pentecostal thinking. The Latter Rain movement revived this emphasis at a time when many Pentecostal groups had become more organised,[19] and was therefore able to exploit a potent residual core of belief.[20] It laid major stress on the independence and sovereignty of the local church, insisting that the principle of local autonomy was not to be vitiated by any system of external authority. Any church polity that vested governmental jurisdiction in a central body was denominational and hence 'Babylonian.'

In essence, the Latter Rain movement was a fellowship of churches rather than a denomination. It modelled its method of dealing with relationships between the various local churches on the practice of the Swedish Independent Assemblies of God, which, as Everett Moore observed,

> believe in a very close organization of the church on the local level but fear the ill effects of an organization on the national scale. Their national conventions are much the same as those of the groups which admit their classification as a denomination with one clear-cut exception: no minutes are kept of the deliberations of such meetings. The resolutions are not binding on the local churches but merely serve for their guidance.[21]

The New Life Churches have always held to a vigorously undenominational polity and their antipathy towards structural organisation reflects the importance that they placed on the autonomy of the local church. This has been the most significant and enduring of the features that they inherited from the Latter Rain movement.[22] They were scrupulous in their avoidance of any form of organisational structure, and each indigenous local church tended to follow its own independent course. (They saw this as the New Testament pattern of church government, which, to some extent, parallels the views of the Brethren movement. However, given the strong opposition of the Brethren to all things Pentecostal and the attitude of the forerunners of the New Life Churches towards other groups, neither side would have cared to acknowledge the similarity.)

To summarise: the New Life Churches have inherited a number of features from the Latter Rain movement, among which were the practices of the laying on of hands and singing in the Spirit. However, the most important legacy was the emphasis on the autonomy of the local church, which provided them with their distinctive polity of independence. Although this emphasis still has its advocates, it has now become dysfunctional to some extent because of the movement's growth. Nevertheless, their antipathy to any organisational linkage between the autonomous local assemblies generated much of the early movement's energy and reflected its desire to be free to follow the charismatic leadings of the Holy Spirit.

Notes

1. Although all of the nine charismatic gifts could be thus imparted, those of tongues, prophecy and the word of knowledge appear to have been the most emphasised in practice.
2. Wheeler, Interview.
3. Ephesians 4:13 (*KJV*).
4. The phrase is taken from Romans 8:18-23 (*KJV*).
5. George R. Hawtin, 'Editorial', *The Sharon Star*, 1 April 1949, 2, cited in Riss, *Latter Rain*, 96. Capitalisation as cited.
6. For a biographical note on Britton's life, see R.M. Riss, 'Britton, Bill', in Burgess *et al., Dictionary*, 98-99.
7. 1 Corinthians 5:7 (*KJV*).
8. Bruce Wást, Comment to author, Dunedin, 1 October 1989. Wást is pastor of the Word of Life Pentecostal Church, Dunedin. For an example of this Latter Rain teaching on the Three Feasts of Israel, see Ron Coady's seven-part series on 'The Feasts of the Lord' in *Bible Deliverance*, April-October 1959.
9. Occurrences of the heavenly chorus during the 1906 Revival at Azusa Street are recorded in Frank Bartleman, *What really happened at Azusa Street?* ed. John Walker (Northridge, California: Voice Christian Publications, 1962), 31-32.
10. Blumhofer, *The Assemblies of God* 1:145. Blumhofer cites an example of the phenomenon which occurred during a service at Elim House in Rochester, New York, in 1908.
11. Gordon P. Gardiner, 'Out of Zion...Into the World', *Bread of Life* 31 (February 1982): 6, cited in ibid., 1:142.
12. Riss, *Latter Rain*, 83ff. According to Riss, Mrs Woodworth-Etter's account of the phenomenon in her book *Signs and Wonders God Wrought in the Ministry for Forty Years* (Indianapolis, Indiana: By the Author, 1916) provided a catalyst for its resurgence some thirty years later in the Latter Rain movement. For a biographical note on her life, see W.E. Warner, 'Woodworth-Etter, Maria Beulah', in Burgess *et al., Dictionary*, 900-901.
13. *Hwyl* is defined by the *Oxford English Dictionary*, 2nd ed., s.v. '*Hwyl*', as 'an emotional quality which inspires and sustains impassioned eloquence; also, the fervour of emotion characteristic of gatherings of Welsh people.' Audrey Way, formerly secretary of Knox Theological Hall, and herself of Welsh origins, describes it as arising from a state of *hiraeth*, a 'deep, deep, longing.' Audrey Way, Comment to author, Dunedin, 1990. The phenomenon therefore includes excitement, emotion and yearning, often expressed in spontaneous, heartfelt singing. Perhaps the best example of *hwyl* is that of a Welsh crowd at a Rugby test match at Cardiff Arms Park!
14. James Worsfold, for example, recalls singing in the Spirit as a child in the early days of New Zealand Pentecostalism. James Worsfold, Comment to author, Wellington, September 1990.
15. These characteristics were later incorporated into the doctrine of The Tabernacle of David. For examples of the movement's exposition of this, see Kevin J. Conner, *The Tabernacle of David* (Portland, Oregon: Conner Publications, 1976); Rob Wheeler, 'David's Tabernacle', *Bible Deliverance*, December 1965, 9-10,12; and Bro. [Ron] Coady, 'I will build again the Tabernacle of David', *Restoration*, January-June 1967, 8-10.
16. Nichol, *The Pentecostals*, 238.

17. This title represented an association with the Apostolic Faith Movement of Charles Fox Parham. William J. Seymour, the leader of the Azusa Street mission, had links with Parham. Blumhofer, *The Assemblies of God*, 1:104–5.
18. Bartleman, *What really happened at Azusa Street?* 41–42. Bartleman's response was to leave this group and to start up another Pentecostal Mission.
19. For an incisive study on the ways in which Pentecostal movements are organised, see Luther P. Gerlach and Virginia H. Hine, *People, Power, Change: Movements of Social Transformation* (Indianapolis: Bobbs-Merrill Company, 1970), 34ff.
20. Blumhofer observes that the 'continuity of their message with the rhetoric of early Pentecostals assured them ... a hearing.' Blumhofer, *The Assemblies of God*, 2:56.
21. Everett LeRoy Moore, 'Handbook of Pentecostal Denominations in the United States' (M.A. Thesis, Pasadena College, June 1954), 117–18, cited in Riss, *Latter Rain*, 59.
22. Australian Latter Rain proponents Victor Hall and Murray Wylie disagree that this emphasis on autonomy came from Ray Jackson's teaching of the Latter Rain movement. Instead, they insist that the focus of the original movement (in both Canada and Australasia) was the 'coming together of the body [of Christ]', i.e. 'the unity and maturity of the church in the lead-up to Christ's return' and contend that Ray Jackson's concentration was on the 'bringing of the body of Christ *together*, and ... leading it on to maturity.' They therefore argue that the emphasis on autonomy was a particularly New Zealand one. Victor Hall and Murray Wylie, *Journey to Ephesus: In Search of a Lampstand. A Biography of Restoration.* 2nd edition (Forest Glen, Vic.: Seedlife Publications, 2004), 109–10. Emphasis as cited.

Chapter 6

Australian Developments

After his return from America in 1949, Ray Jackson remained in New Zealand for about a year. He later moved to Sydney at the invitation of Dr Len Jones,[1] who had accepted the Latter Rain message and thought that it would sweep Australia. However, the movement attracted even greater opposition there than had been the case in New Zealand, particularly from the Apostolic Church.[2] Its leaders charged that Jackson 'had spoilt [the Apostolic Church] work and was divisive and was ruining their vision' in Australia.[3] There was some justification in these charges, although Jackson appears to have shrugged off the opposition, claiming that 'the [Latter Rain] work... continued to spread.'[4] In reality, only three churches resulted from the Australian venture: Sydney, Melbourne and Bendigo.

A more important consequence for later developments in New Zealand was that Jackson was able to recruit a number of Australian followers who later became leaders in the movement in the 1960s. These were graduates of Jackson's Bible Schools, particularly of that held at the home of Mrs Margaret Wonders, 6 Stratford Avenue, West Ryde, Sydney, for four months in early 1952.[5] (This was the only Bible School that Ray Jackson was to conduct in Sydney, his base of operations later shifting to Melbourne.) Conditions were primitive in the extreme. Of the 21 students, 18 lived on the premises, enduring cramped living conditions. The female students had the use of the house, while the 10 or 11 male students slept in a garage-*cum*-bunkroom. Rob Wheeler recalls that this was 'an incredible place—redback spiders and all.'[6] The ruggedness of the conditions had an unintended benefit in that they produced a close-knit relationship between the students that later had its effect on the movement. These students included future leaders such as Rob and Beryl Wheeler, Peter Morrow, David Jackson, Ron and Muriel Coady, Kevin and Joyce Conner, Mike Bensley and others.

The major emphasis of the school was on relationships, prayer, and worship and praise, reflecting Jackson's Latter Rain emphasis on the charismatic operation of the Spirit. Although there were set lectures, these were secondary to what the Spirit of God was doing and saying, rather than the backbone of the course. Mike Bensley remembers that 'the whole emphasis was waiting on God'; the students met together

> to wait on God and imbibe of restoration and revival truths taught by Ray Jackson and other ministries such as David Schoch and Omar Johnson who visited during our time there.... Our days commenced early with prayer and waiting on God, and we were taught to be sensitive to the Holy Spirit and to flow with the anointing in what the Lord wanted to bring forth.[7]

This emphasis on responding to the prompting of the Holy Spirit meant that the school timetable was highly flexible. Rob Wheeler recalls that 'we would meet together for prayer at nine [o'clock]; we might still be singing in the Spirit at one o'clock in the afternoon.'[8]

This developed consciousness of the presence of God had its outworking in public meetings held in a local hall, and in meetings of other Pentecostal churches that the students would visit. Ron Coady says that 'we would begin to sing together and the Spirit of God would fall upon the congregations (and that is not an exaggeration) until, in the end, when we would come into a church, people would say "whatever you do, don't let them sing—because if you do, the service will be taken out of your hands!"'[9] The students' singing in the Spirit became a vehicle for the Holy Spirit in bringing the consciousness of the presence of God upon the congregation. This Latter Rain practice caused consternation among those who were in charge of these meetings, since they were unable to continue with their set programmes. Naturally, the invasion of other churches did not endear Jackson or his students to existing Pentecostal groups. Rob Wheeler observes that

> Ray Jackson was very evasive as far as the Pentecostal pastors were all concerned.... Kevin [Conner], David [Jackson] and I were present when Ray was talking among [Pentecostal] leaders.... They were quite abusive to Brother Jackson, and one of them said "Well, we don't like you; you're the scorpion, [but] what we're afraid of is the scorpion's eggs." And that was Kevin, and David and myself.[10]

The other Pentecostal churches saw the rising generation of students in Ray Jackson's school as a greater threat than Jackson himself. Wheeler observes that the charge of evasiveness was, to some extent, justified. He recalls that '[Jackson] became extremely evasive over his wording for water-baptism, whereas Kevin [Conner] and I delighted to explain in detail the misconceptions of "Jesus Only" in relation to water baptism.'[11]

Pentecostal reaction to this provocative situation produced something of a martyr complex in the ethos of Jackson's Australian churches that was still evident more than twenty years later.[12] While praise and worship remained a constitutive factor in the self-identity of these churches, now called the 'Associated Mission Churches of Australia', there was also a sectarian antipathy to other churches. Members of this group appeared to delight in invading other churches to spread their message. Chant records a conversation with one of Jackson's members who 'had recently been to another Pentecostal assembly and started a "spirit of praise" that had spread through the whole assembly. To him, he had done what God wanted. Little consideration was given to the ethics of invading another work and introducing a form of worship without the approval of the leadership there.'[13] This antipathy to other Pentecostal churches appears to have remained as strong in the 1970s as it had been in the 1950s.

After the completion of the Sydney Bible School, some of the students travelled back to New Zealand. Peter Morrow, David Jackson and Rob Wheeler hitchhiked throughout New Zealand endeavouring to arrange Latter Rain meetings, but with very little success. Morrow and David Jackson also worked for some time with Youth for Christ, while Ron Coady returned to secular employment, eventually moving to New Zealand in May 1957. Throughout the mid-1950s, there was little growth in the Latter Rain churches (despite the general boom in mainstream New Zealand church life). By 1957, there were still only four churches (Auckland, Wellington, Tauranga and Whangarei) and a handful of cottage meetings.

Figure 3: The congregation at Queen Street Assembly of God, Auckland, photographed during Rob Wheeler Campaign, May 1959
(Rob Wheeler, Auckland)

The opposition to the Latter Rain churches from other Pentecostal groups compounded their exclusion from the mainstream of New Zealand Christianity. Throughout the 1950s, both the Australian and New Zealand wings of this movement were small sectarian groups with limited horizons beyond their own religious vision. This was also true of the New Zealand Pentecostal movement as a whole, as was their small size and sectarian ethos. Hazel Houston, for example, describes the Assemblies of God at the time as being, with the sole exception of the Auckland Queen Street Assembly of God, 'small and hardly recognisable as Pentecostal.'[14] Ian Clark comments that in the 1950s Pentecostalism was

> a very small and a very ingrown movement. They were making all sorts of efforts to break out of a very constricted kind of a mode, but I think, in modern terms, they were *totally* irrelevant. That would be a good way of describing it. Nice people, who met in little upstairs halls above a butcher shop (things like that).... [They] met at Oddfellows' Halls and that sort of thing, and it really was pretty "grotty."... It was like David: all those who had a grudge, or owed money, or [were in] trouble with the law; they would join themselves to him.[15] But [now] there's been a transformation: you get people from many different professions in [the Pentecostal movement] today.[16]

This 'very constricted...mode' was not entirely due to the sectarian ethos and social composition of the Pentecostal movement. Of equal importance was the sometimes strenuous opposition that it received from other churches, including the evangelical groups with which it had much in common. Bryan Gilling quotes Rev. J.A. Clifford, principal of the Baptist Bible College from 1961 to 1973, as saying that in the 1959 Billy Graham Crusade, the Pentecostals 'were carefully excluded.... If anybody had Pentecostal leanings they weren't allowed to be in on counselling or anything like that.'[17] Other examples of this policy include the exclusion of Pentecostal young people in Timaru from membership of the local Youth for Christ, despite their support for its activities. This was largely due to Baptist and Brethren domination of Youth for Christ; the sectarian separation was not, in this case, a product of Pentecostal exclusiveness.

The Latter Rain churches suffered from a double isolation. Not only did they share the exclusion of their fellow Pentecostals from the mainstream of New Zealand religious life by the major churches, but these Pentecostal groups themselves also opposed them. Their Latter Rain attitude of undenominational separatism reinforced the effects of this exclusion. As a result, these churches represented a narrowly focused sectarian group of independent Pentecostal churches both in Australia and New Zealand. The New Zealand churches were, however, developing in different ways from Jackson's works in Australia, and although the contacts with Jackson continued, his influence in New Zealand began to decline. Indeed, the Australian churches felt that their New Zealand colleagues had compromised their position by going beyond the original Bethel Temple teaching on 'the Name' as the basis of fellowship. There was something of a conscious decision by the New Zealand churches to go their separate way from their Australian counterparts. This decision was an individual one for each local church, rather than the result of a collective consensus. Rob Wheeler remembers having to make this break as early as 1954.[18] This was not a turning away from their previously held principles, so much as a broadening of the basis for fellowship. The Australian churches were, and have remained, more separatist than those in New Zealand.[19]

A Conference in Melbourne attempted to bring the two groups of churches together in 1973. However, this proved abortive, since the New Zealand churches had, by then, developed in markedly different ways from their Australian counterparts. Pastor Shaun Kearney made a comment at the conference that summed up the differences when he said 'you Australians have all one "father"; the churches in New Zealand have many "fathers."'[20] Kearney meant by this that the Australian churches owed their existence to the ministry and teachings of Ray Jackson (their 'one father'). Conversely, the New Zealand churches had arisen through the ministry of a number of 'fathers', not all of whom had been associated with Jackson. The Australian and New Zealand churches had developed in different ways, and there was no basis for a merger.

This breaking of links with Jackson may have been significant for the later expansion of the New Zealand churches. Chant records that there were only about 15 Mission Churches in Jackson's movement in Australia in 1973.[21] This compares markedly with the rapid growth of the Indigenous Churches in the 1960s and 1970s. Jackson's charismatic and somewhat autocratic leadership style may ultimately have proved restrictive for the Australian churches. By breaking with Jackson, while still retaining his hermeneutical methodology and Latter Rain ethos, the New Zealand churches laid the foundations for their expansion over the next twenty years. However, the single most important catalyst of this expansion was to emerge in 1957.

Notes

1. Len Jones was the founder of a Wellington-based Pentecostal missionary agency, the Slavic and Oriental Mission, later renamed 'World Outreach.'
2. Riss, *Latter Rain*, 135–37.
3. Reported by Cecil Cousen, cited in ibid., 137. Cousen was a long-standing pastor of the British Apostolic Church, who had participated in the Latter Rain movement while in Canada in 1949. ibid., 94–95, 105–7.
4. Ray Jackson, cited in ibid., 136.
5. Mike Bensley, a student in Jackson's Sydney Bible School, recalls the visit of Latter Rain apostle Omar Johnson to the Bible School. His wife Mary confirms that this took place in 1952. Mike Bensley, Interview, Waikanae, 24 September 1987; Mary Bensley, correspondence with the author, February 1998.
6. Wheeler, Interview.
7. Bensley, Interview.
8. Wheeler, Interview.
9. Ron Coady, Taped Interview in response to Questionnaire, Davis, California, 24 March 1988.
10. Wheeler, Interview. Corrections to text of Wheeler's interview made from Wheeler, Correspondence with the author, 2 March 1998.
11. Wheeler, Correspondence with the author, 2 March 1998.
12. Barry Chant, *Heart of Fire* (Adelaide: Luke Publications, 1973), 178.
13. ibid.

14. Hazel Houston, *Being Frank: The Frank Houston Story* (London: Marshall Pickering, 1989), 100. Mrs Houston's book is a biography of her husband Frank Houston, who was Superintendent of the Assemblies of God from 1966 to 1977.
15. The reference is to 1 Sam.22:2: 'And every one that was in distress, and every one that was in debt, and every one that was discontented, gathered themselves unto [David]; and he became a captain over them' (*KJV*).
16. Clark, Interview. Clark was specifically referring to the Assemblies of God (of which he was for some years General Secretary). His observation is, however, valid for the whole Pentecostal movement.
17. Rev. J.A. Clifford, cited in Bryan D. Gilling, 'Retelling the Old, Old Story: A Study of Six Mass Evangelistic Missions in Twentieth Century New Zealand' (D. Phil. Thesis in History, University of Waikato, 1990), 253.
18. Wheeler, Interview.
19. Its character in the 1970s is well described by Chant, *Heart of Fire*. Chant mentions Kevin Conner, Peter Morrow and Rob Wheeler, and comments that 'none of these men is now associated with the Mission Church movement in Australia.' ibid., 179, note 4.
20. Shaun Kearney, Comment at Asian-Pacific Ministers' Conference, Melbourne, June 1973. Kearney was then pastor of the North Shore Christian Fellowship.
21. Chant, *Heart of Fire*, 175.

Chapter 7

Catalyst for change: The New Evangelicalism

Towards the end of the Second World War, a major resurgence of religion began to occur in many parts of the world. It is not accurate to describe this as an American evangelical awakening, since it took no single form, and was not limited to any particular theological perspective or geographical area. Nevertheless it was most prominent in the United States,[1] where it built upon a pervasive sense of public anxiety reflecting the altered realities of the Cold War era. This insecurity enhanced the perceived desirability of traditional American religion, which now functioned as a patriotic bulwark against the menace of the dreaded Reds, particularly in the McCarthy era of the 1950s. Traditional forms of religion therefore provided a source of reassurance in the face of a frightening new world.

In America, this religious revival manifested itself in a number of different ways.[2] At one level, it reflected new and generalised forms of American civil religion, in which religious tradition became a constituent part of the American Way and patriotism and religious commitment merged into congruent terms. This convergence was exemplified by President Eisenhower's statement in 1954 that 'our government... makes no sense unless it is founded on a deeply felt religious faith—and I don't care what it is.'[3] Other strands of this religious resurgence included theological and liturgical renewals that affected many American churches, and, in particular, the rise of what became known as the New Evangelicalism. This New Evangelicalism was not a monolithic fundamentalism, but rather a multifaceted subculture, manifestations of which included the Billy Graham Crusades, the healing evangelism of Oral Roberts and others, and the Latter Rain movement.[4] The revival of American religion was as much a cultural, civil and social resurgence as a purely religious one.

This revitalisation of religious life extended beyond the American Continent. Churches in New Zealand also enjoyed vigorous growth from the end of the Second World War up to the end of the 1950s. Their growth reflected the social changes caused by burgeoning economic development, and the population growth and urbanisation associated with the postwar baby boom.⁵ In response to these challenges, and to the increasing suburbanisation of New Zealand society, most churches undertook building and extension programmes, and placed a conscious emphasis on evangelism. In so doing, they were making use of the almost unprecedented opportunities made available to them. A notable example of this vigorous activity was the New Life Movement in the Presbyterian Church,⁶ which reflected that church's mood of optimism and renewed sense of mission. Another was the Baptist Church Extension Programme, which had its period of maximum effectiveness in the late 1950s, with some 24 Baptist churches being established in the five years from 1955 to 1960.⁷

Although the growth of New Zealand churches throughout the 1950s was clearly part of a worldwide phenomenon, the emphasis here was on reconstruction rather than the rehabilitation of traditional cultural and religious values. However, this dissimilarity of emphasis did not necessarily mean that there was no public anxiety in this country, or that New Zealanders were isolated and insulated from developments in other parts of the world. Participation in the expanding international communications network, especially following the introduction of television in the early 1960s, and the increasing popularity of overseas travel helped to extend New Zealanders' awareness of global issues. This raised consciousness paralleled a gradual loosening of ties with Britain, and a corresponding reorientation towards the United States. Because of this shift of focus, American influence in New Zealand became considerable, both in the secular and religious fields. The 1959 Billy Graham Crusade provides the clearest example of the way in which this changed orientation affected New Zealand religion.

The Billy Graham Crusade was, on the face of it, highly successful. Graham himself claimed that he had 'preached to more people in six days in New Zealand than in any other week of my ministry.'⁸ Some of the Crusade's supporters hailed it as 'the time when New Zealand has been closest to a general spiritual revival.'⁹ The statistics of the Crusade give some indication of its impact, at least in the short term, on the religious consciousness of the country. These show that 574,300 people had attended during the twelve days of the Crusade, 185,000 of them at the landline meetings in other centres, and that 17,493 people had made decisions for Christ.¹⁰

However, these impressive figures do not tell the whole story. More than a third of these respondents had come to make a 'reaffirmation of faith', or to gain 'assurance of salvation' or 'restoration.'¹¹ Since these categories presuppose some degree of previous Christian involvement, this indicates that many of these converts (and, by implication, much of the Crusade attendance) comprised those already within the ambit of the churches. Furthermore, less than a quarter of the converts were incorporated into the life of the Church.¹² John Pollock, Billy Graham's biographer, claimed that this loss was due, at least in part, to a lack of follow-up by the churches, and cites several such instances of neglect.¹³ However, not all the churches were unsympathetic to the converts of the Crusades. A contrary opinion was that of Janus (a Methodist commentator on current events), who referred to the 'thorough and worthy' quality of this follow-up.[14] Nevertheless, the author has interviewed a number of people (now members of the New Life Churches) who were converts of the Billy Graham Crusade, and their experience tends to confirm Pollock's claim.

There appears also to have been a failure to sustain the momentum generated by the Crusade. Pollock further lamented that 'many individual churches failed to learn in time that a Crusade should not be a single burst of activity but part of a continuing programme of evangelism.'[15] It is perhaps unreasonable to expect that the excitement of the Crusade could be maintained for an extended period, particularly after Graham and his colleagues had left New Zealand. The fact remains, however, that the Crusade does not appear to have been as successful in its goal of reaching unchurched New Zealanders as its supporters claimed it to be.

The Crusade did have some long-term effects on New Zealand Christianity, the most significant of which was the importation of a largely self-sufficient American evangelical subculture. Some sections of the New Zealand Church welcomed this American style of Evangelicalism, and its innate dynamism helped to modify and to reorient New Zealand Evangelicalism towards a less institutional style. The identity of evangelical Christians became more firmly centred in their personal relationship with Christ, in which denominational labels became comparatively unimportant. Since the Pentecostal movement tended to pride itself on its nondenominationalism, this less denominational evangelical identity contributed towards Pentecostal expansion in the 1960s and 1970s. In particular, the emphasis of the Full Gospel healing evangelists on personal commitment to Christ was a significant factor in their gaining a hearing in post-Billy Graham New Zealand.

Although Billy Graham was the most prominent of the postwar evangelists, he was not the only exemplar of the Evangelical expansion. In the United States, the emergence of a new generation of healing evangelists, initially spearheaded by William Branham, and later by Oral Roberts, created a new reservoir of support for the Pentecostal movement after 1947.[16] Later, as the healing revival subsided in the United States, this spread around the world. Oral Roberts was one of the most successful healing campaigners and his success both reflected, and helped to foster, the rapidly expanding constituency of these healing evangelists.[17] His effectiveness was multiplied by his numerous publications, which found a wide acceptance and helped to spread the message of the healing movement beyond its traditional sphere of influence. Because this healing revival was recognisably a Pentecostal phenomenon, its success helped to lay the foundations for the worldwide expansion of Pentecostalism over the next twenty years.

In the United States, the healing revival reached its peak in 1952, and continued unabated until the mid-1950s. However, it had begun to lose its momentum by 1956 and was changing its focus to become an international movement. This change of direction built upon the extensive communications networks established by the healing evangelists through their books, magazines and mailing lists. In New Zealand, Pentecostal groups were well-informed of what was happening in the United States. The Slavic and Oriental Mission in Wellington ran a well-stocked bookshop known as the 'Evidence Book Depot', which engaged in the importing and distributing of Pentecostal books and publications. It also published a monthly magazine called *The Evidence*, which gave extensive publicity to the healing revival in America. This helped to spread the ideas and theology behind the healing movement long before the arrival of a number of American Pentecostal evangelists in the later 1950s.[18] Nevertheless, the arrival of these evangelists was to provide a catalyst for the revival of the healing movement in New Zealand.

A forerunner of the postwar resurgence of healing in New Zealand emerged in September 1957,[19] when Assemblies of God evangelists Ray Bloomfield and Frank Houston began meetings among rural Maori at Waiomio, near Kawakawa in Northland.[20] Although this revival was highly successful and continued until Houston relocated to Lower Hutt in 1959, it nevertheless remained an isolated incident, and had little effect beyond one or two local areas. The real beginnings of the postwar healing movement in this country came in late 1957, with the arrival of the American evangelist Tommy Hicks, best known for a spectacularly successful campaign in Argentina in 1954. In that campaign 'the attendance [had] never dropped below 60,000 a night, and on at least one night was reported by the Buenos Aires newspapers to have passed 200,000.'[21] Even President Péron himself was reported to have been healed of eczema in response to Hicks' prayers.[22]

Hicks therefore arrived in New Zealand with a considerable reputation, and all the Pentecostal churches strongly supported his two healing campaigns in Wellington and Christchurch. He appears to have had some success, with numbers of decisions for Christ being recorded and people testifying of having received healing during the campaign.[23] However, his campaigns had a more significant indirect effect, in that they stimulated others to adopt this style of evangelism. Rob Wheeler recalled that Hicks represented 'our first exposure to an evangelist, really.... Ron Coady and myself got fired up on evangelism.'[24] Others were similarly inspired, including Norman and Gilbert White of the Apostolic Church, independent Pentecostal pastor Ian Hunt, and Wheeler's colleague Mike Bensley.

Stirred by Hicks' campaigns, Wheeler returned to his Latter Rain church in Tauranga, bought a 36-foot by 18-foot ex-army tent, and resigned his pastorate to begin evangelistic campaigns using the tent as a transportable church. Wheeler regarded Oral Roberts as 'my hero'[25] and consciously modelled his method of Pentecostal evangelism on Roberts' tent crusades in the United States. He began by forming a nonprofit society—the Word of Faith Ministry— to facilitate 'the propagation of the Full Gospel.'[26] The term 'Full Gospel', originally a description of the characteristic teachings of early Pentecostalism,[27] reflected his new understanding of evangelism. It referred to the full power of the Gospel, namely, salvation, divine healing and the Baptism of the Spirit, as God's complete provision for the whole person. Wheeler also later published a magazine, *Bible Deliverance*, to maintain communication with his associates and converts.[28]

The Full Gospel healing revivalism of Wheeler and his colleagues was significant for several reasons. Firstly, it built upon a tradition of alternative medicine, derived in part from Maori forms of healing,[29] and periodically revived by the activities of healers from within New Zealand and overseas. The visit of John Alexander Dowie in the late 1880s represented the first wave of the healing movement in New Zealand. This constituency was reinforced and expanded in the 1920s by a second generation of healing campaigners, including Smith Wigglesworth,[30] J.M. Hickson[31] and T.W. Ratana.[32] News of the postwar healing movement in the United States also stimulated this interest, which was further quickened by the visit of Hicks and other healers.[33] The campaigns of Wheeler and other Full Gospel evangelists therefore represented a third wave of healing revivalism, and tapped into a renewed public awareness of the practice of divine healing.

Secondly, the Full Gospel evangelists' emphasis on salvation through personal faith in Christ also enabled them to make use of the momentum generated by the Billy Graham Crusade. Although Wheeler and his colleagues had already been campaigning for more than a year before the arrival of Billy Graham in 1959, the effects of this Crusade reinforced their effectiveness and enlarged their audience. The less institutional style of Evangelicalism resulting from the Crusade also facilitated the formation of nondenominational Pentecostal churches following Wheeler's campaigns.

Thirdly, the unconventional evangelistic methods of the Full Gospel campaigners had some appeal. Wheeler's tent campaigns, while patterned upon American models, represented a departure from the normal forms of New Zealand church life. The unconventionality of his methods enabled him to benefit from a reaction to social conformity that was beginning to emerge in the late 1950s. The rapid expansion of State Housing suburbs, where families were supplied with standardised low-cost Government-subsidised housing, exemplified both the conformity and the cult of domesticity that characterised the 1950s. This suburban growth and conformity was paralleled by a rapid proliferation of the mainstream churches, particularly between 1955 and 1959.

Something of a social breakout began later in the decade. This was initially located in the 'bodgie and widgie' generation, where it found expression in new styles of dress and music, which served to demonstrate a rejection of traditional patterns of social behaviour.[34] In a different form, it was also reflected in the declining constituencies of the mainstream churches after 1960, particularly amongst young people. This was not necessarily a rejection of religion *per se*—since the 1960s were notable for the appearance of new patterns of religion—but rather of the forms in which it was practised. Unconventional forms of religion, such as Pentecostalism and the tent campaigns of Rob Wheeler and his colleagues, therefore appealed to those disenchanted with the traditional churches at the end of the 1950s.

Fourthly, and most importantly, the revivalism of Wheeler and his colleagues created a network of Full Gospel evangelists and independent Full Gospel churches. While Wheeler was one of the first in New Zealand to launch into this type of Pentecostal healing campaign, other Pentecostal workers and groups also began to adopt the same patterns and methods of evangelism. The White brothers (Norman and Gilbert) of the Apostolic Church began tent crusade evangelism at the same time as Wheeler, followed later by Ian Hunt and Graeme Jacks,[35] as well as by Mike Bensley and others. There was extensive cooperation between these evangelists. Ian Hunt, for example, assisted Wheeler in many of his earlier campaigns, and contributed articles to *Bible Deliverance*. In this way, an informal network of independent Full Gospel evangelists was created, sharing a common desire to 'extend our Saviour's kingdom.'[36]

Figure 4: Rob and Beryl Wheeler (left) and Ian and Mavis Hunt (right) and their families on campaign, 1958–59. Picture taken from cover of *Bible Deliverance*, May 1959.

(Rob Wheeler, Auckland)

This network laid the foundations for what later would become the New Life Churches of New Zealand. At this stage, however, its boundaries were very ill-defined. The links of fellowship were personal, rather than institutional or denominational. Wheeler later described it as 'just . . . a bunch of ministers who are all buddies and . . . friends just sharing together. There was no sense of a "stream" [i.e. movement] of our own.'[37] This was not an association of Pentecostal churches, nor was it a movement in any organisational sense. The basis for fellowship was not the acceptance of Bethel Temple doctrine or Latter Rain polity, but a shared concern for healing evangelism. Nevertheless, the informality of this network fitted well with Latter Rain ideals of independence and enabled the Full Gospel evangelists to reach across Pentecostal denominational barriers. As will be seen, it contributed to the emergence of the New Life Churches of New Zealand.

Notes

1. Sydney E. Ahlstrom, *A Religious History of the American People* (New Haven: Yale University Press, 1973), 949-63, offers the best short treatment of this resurgence in America. Winthrop S. Hudson, *Religion in America* (New York: Charles Scribner's Sons, 1965) 382-91, also gives a useful account.
2. Hudson describes this return to religion as 'formless and unstructured, manifesting itself in many different ways and reinforcing all religious faiths quite indiscriminately.' Hudson, *Religion*, 383. Ahlstrom, however, is able to distinguish five overlapping types of revival that made up the postwar religious resurgence in America. Ahlstrom, *Religious History*, 954-63.
3. *Christian Century* 71 (1954), cited in *Christianity Today*, 8 May 1961, and thence in Ahlstrom, *Religious History*, 954.
4. Randall Balmer, *Mine Eyes have seen the Glory: A Journey into the Evangelical Subculture in America* (New York: Oxford University Press, 1989). Balmer's account is a superbly articulate analysis of the various types of American Evangelicalism in the 1980s. He writes from the perspective of a former evangelical, and is able to combine objective analysis and critical detachment with an insider's understanding of, and empathy with, the complex subculture that he describes.
5. Keith Sinclair, A *History of New Zealand*, rev. ed. (Harmondsworth, Middlesex: Penguin Books, 1984), 298-99.
6. The best intensive study of this movement is I.G. Marquand, 'The New Zealand Presbyterian New Life Movement: A Case Study in Church Growth' (M.Th. Thesis in Church History, University of Otago, 1977). This is supplemented at several important points by Owen Rogers, 'The New Zealand Presbyterian New Life Movement' (B.D. Dissertation in Church History, University of Otago, 1990). It should be noted that the title of the 'New Life Churches of New Zealand' has no apparent connection with the Presbyterian New Life Movement.
7. S.L. Edgar, *A Handful of Grain*, The Centenary History of the Baptist Union of New Zealand, vol.4, 1945-1982 (Wellington: New Zealand Baptist Historical Society, 1982).
8. Billy Graham, cited in *Christchurch Star*, 9 April 1959, and thence in Warner Hutchinson and Cliff Wilson, *Let the People Rejoice* (Wellington: Crusader Bookroom Society, 1959), 130.
9. Cited in Bryan Gilling, 'Mass Evangelism', in Douglas Pratt, ed., *'Rescue the Perishing': Comparative Perspectives on Evangelicalism and Revivalism*. Waikato Studies in Religion, Vol. 1 (Auckland: College Communications Ltd., 1989), 49. Gilling does not record the source of this claim.
10. Hutchinson and Wilson, *Let the People Rejoice*, 142-46. However, Gilling cautions against uncritical acceptance of these figures. Gilling, 'Mass Evangelism', in Pratt, *'Rescue the Perishing'*, 49-52; and *idem*, 'Retelling the Old, Old Story.' These give important surveys of the Billy Graham Crusades in the wider context of New Zealand Evangelicalism.

11. Some 6,606 (or 37.76% of the total) of the converts fell into these three categories. Hutchinson and Wilson, *Let the People Rejoice*, 144.
12. Only 4,167 (or 23.82%) of the converts were referred to the churches. Gilling, 'Retelling the Old, Old Story', 289, argues that this indicates the comparative ineffectiveness of this form of mass evangelism.
13. John Pollock, *Billy Graham: The Authorised Biography* (London: Hodder and Stoughton, 1966), 263.
14. *New Zealand Methodist Times*, 25 April 1959, 697, cited in Gilling, 'Retelling the Old, Old Story', 288.
15. Pollock, *Billy Graham*, 257.
16. The best critical coverage of this healing revivalism in America is Harrell, *All Things are Possible*.
17. While a résumé of Oral Roberts' career is given in ibid., 41-52, the major critical biography is *idem*, *Oral Roberts: An American Life* (Bloomington, Indiana: Indiana University Press, 1975).
18. The most important figures in the transmission of the ideas and theology of the healing revival to New Zealand were Oral Roberts and T.L. Osborn. Harrell, *All Things are Possible*, 63-66 and 169-72. Osborn was less well known in America than Roberts, since he focused his efforts on missionary campaigns outside the United States and produced tons of free literature for distribution in foreign countries. This literature consisted exclusively of his sermons and books, translated into the languages of the various mission fields. The effect of this massive literary productivity was to spread the message of the healing revival, of which Osborn's writings provide a typical example, worldwide.
19. An account of this is given in Hazel Houston, *Being Frank*, 94ff. Houston incorrectly dates this revival as c. 1955-56, a mistake repeated in the earlier editions of this book. However, Ian Clark correctly dates it as September 1957 (Clark, *Pentecost at the Ends of the Earth: The History of the Assemblies of God in New Zealand (1927-2003)* (Blenheim: Christian Road Ministries, 2007), 89) and this is confirmed by Ray Bloomfield's report in *New Zealand Evangel* (Ray Bloomfield, 'Thus hath God wrought...,' *New Zealand Evangel*, May 1958, 15-16.
20. Frank Houston later became General Superintendent of the Assemblies of God in New Zealand.
21. 'But what about Tommy Hicks?' *Christian Century* LXXI (7 July 1954), 814, cited in Nichol, *The Pentecostals*, 224. For an extended account of this revival, see Edward Miller, *Thy God Reigneth: The Story of the Revival in Argentina* (Burbank, California: World Missionary Assistance Plan, 1968).
22. Miller, *Thy God Reigneth*, 35.
23. Worsfold, *History*, 194.
24. Wheeler, Interview.
25. ibid.
26. *Bible Deliverance*, April 1959, 2.
27. Nichol, *The Pentecostals*, 7-8.
28. *Bible Deliverance* is a valuable source for the development of the Full Gospel movement in the early 1960s, and of the churches that resulted from these campaigns.
29. For examples of these, see Edward Shortland, *Maori Religion and Mythology* (London: Longmans, Green and Co., 1882), 31-32; Elsdon Best, *Maori Religion and My-*

thology: Being an Account of the Cosmogony, Anthropogony, Religious Beliefs and Rites, Magic and Folk Lore of the Maori Folk of New Zealand, Dominion Museum Bulletin No.10, Section 1 (Wellington: Government Printer, 1924), 233ff.; and Bronwyn Elsmore, *Like Them That Dream: The Maori and the Old Testament* (Tauranga: Tauranga Moana Press, 1985), *passim*. Elsmore deals with the topic in greater detail in *idem, Mana from Heaven: A Century of Maori Prophets in New Zealand* (Tauranga: Moana Press, 1989).

30. The best survey of Wigglesworth's ministry as part of the 1920s Revivalist movement is Douglas Ireton, 'A time to heal: the appeal of Smith Wigglesworth in New Zealand 1922-1924' (B.A. (Honours) Dissertation in History, Massey University, 1984).
31. For a critical account of Hickson's healing ministry, see Stuart Mews, 'The revival of spiritual healing in the Church of England 1920-26', in W.J. Sheils, ed. *The Church and Healing: Papers read at the twentieth summer meeting and the twenty-first winter meeting of the Ecclesiastical History Society* (Oxford: Basil Blackwell for the Ecclesiastical History Society, 1982), 299-331.
32. A brief summary of Ratana and his ministry is given in Elsmore, *Like Them That Dream*, 167-71.
33. The visit of British faith healer Dr Christopher Woodard in 1958 created vigorous public debate on the subject of healing. For an example of this, see 'Letters to the Editor', *Otago Daily Times*, 18 June-14 July 1958. Woodard was a Harley Street physician and author of several books on healing. Christopher Woodard, *A Doctor Heals by Faith* (London: Max Parrish, 1953); *idem, A Doctor's Faith holds fast* (London: Max Parrish, 1955). He believed that 'all disease originates in the spirit and can be cured by a right attitude to things.' Woodard, *A Doctor Heals by Faith*, 55-56. His approach to healing was therefore rather different from that of the Full Gospel evangelists. The latter, for their part, saw divine healing by the power of God as being a component part of, and witness to, the Full Gospel. Nevertheless, the publicity surrounding Woodard's visit helped to further the Full Gospel cause.
34. For a survey of these social trends, and of the controversy that surrounded them in the 1950s, see Redmer Yska, *All Shook Up: The Flash Bodgie and the Rise of the New Zealand Teenager in the Fifties* (Auckland: Penguin, 1993). Bodgies were distinguished by their dress style of long drape-cut coat, stovepipe trousers, crepe-soled shoes, fluorescent socks and string ties. Widgies, the female counterpart of bodgies, wore sweaters, black tight toreador pants, large belts, straight gaberdine skirts with a split at the back, and low-heeled slip-on pump shoes.
35. 'New Zealand: Evangelism', *Bible Deliverance*, November 1960, 12.
36. I.A.S. and R.N., 'Easter Conventions: Devonport Report', *Bible Deliverance*, May 1959, 14.
37. Wheeler, Interview.

Chapter 8

Day of small beginnings

Wheeler was quick to imitate the example set by Hicks' campaigns in late 1957. Within a month, he had launched into Full Gospel evangelism, conducting his first tent campaign at Mount Maunganui, across the harbour from his home base in Tauranga. This first attempt produced 'practically nothing' in the way of results.[1] However, Wheeler was to have greater success on the East Coast, where he had been invited by Mike Bensley to conduct a campaign among Ngati Porou in the remote Hicks Bay-Rangitukia area in early 1958. A Maori woman was sovereignly healed of blindness while sitting in the meeting and, as a result, this campaign became, in Wheeler's words, an 'absolute landslide.'[2] As a result, he and his colleague Ian Hunt concentrated their efforts on the East Coast and Bay of Plenty areas throughout the summers of 1957–58 and 1958–59.[3] Their campaigns contributed to the opening of four new Maori Full Gospel churches by 1959. These were at Rangitukia, Waihau Bay and Te Araroa (where a church building programme was under way by mid-1959) on the East Coast, as well as at Te Teko in the Bay of Plenty.[4] Another church started the following year at Tokomaru Bay. *Bible Deliverance* reported that by November 1960,

> the Maori Full Gospel work on the East Coast... has developed and expanded from one assembly with a full-time resident Missionary, [i.e. Rangitukia] to five assemblies under the care of four missionaries. One assembly now has its own Deacons and apart from an occasional visit from the missionaries, they are progressing as a sovereign assembly running their own affairs.[5]

The term 'missionary' is significant, since *Bible Deliverance* consistently uses it for those who worked among Maori,[6] and the linkage between Full Gospel evangelism and missionary work was a strong one. Tommy Hicks had his greatest successes in Argentina in what was regarded as a missionary campaign, and the worldwide missionary-evangelism of T.L. Osborn was also well-known in New Zealand Pentecostalism. The East Coast Maori work was therefore seen as a mission field and quickly became an important base for Wheeler's early successes.

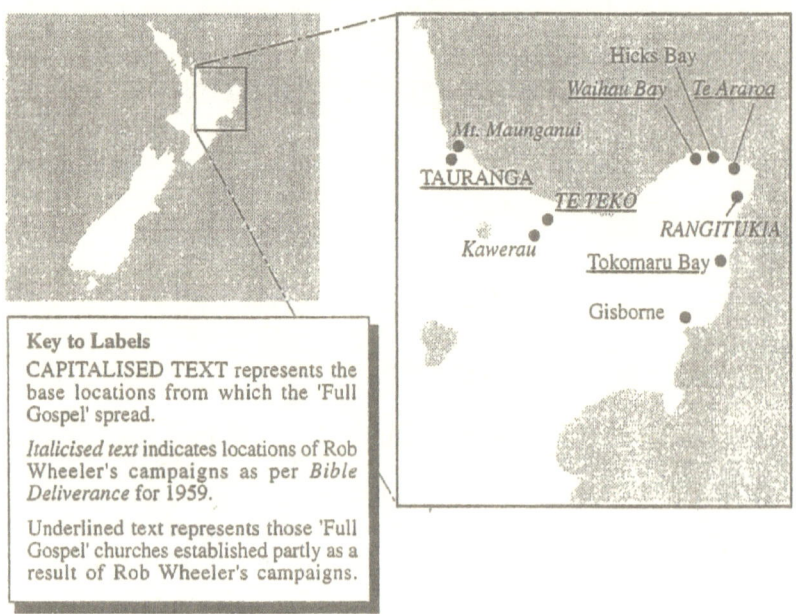

Figure 5: Map showing the locations of early Rob Wheeler campaigns and of early Full Gospel churches (1958–60)

Wheeler's campaigns on the East Coast built upon the work of others, particularly Bruce and Fay McGregor, who had moved to Hicks Bay in 1955 to begin Full Gospel missionary work among Maori. The McGregors later shifted to Rangitukia, where they were able make greater inroads into the community and to set up an assembly there that became the base for the East Coast work. Nevertheless, there were difficulties: 'opposition from established, lifeless [churches], together with practically no support, was all part of the programme.'[7] However, the East Coast work had progressed sufficiently to conduct its first Convention at Easter 1959. This took place on a *marae*[8] at Rangitukia, and attracted Full Gospel believers from Tauranga, Waihau Bay, Te Araroa and other areas of the East Coast, as well as many of the local people.[9] Wheeler's tent campaigns both contributed to and reinforced this growth and, as will be seen, affected the development and expansion of his evangelistic ministry.

Similarly, Wheeler's campaigns in the Bay of Plenty built upon and consolidated the foundations that had been laid by two small house groups in Whakatane[10] and Te Teko.[11] The way in which the Te Teko house group developed into a fully fledged assembly provides a good example of the catalytic effect of these campaigns. A commemorative booklet put out by the Te Teko church states that although a small house group had been meeting in homes in Te Teko since 1957,

> TeTeko Fellowship really came about by Bro.Rob Wheeler & Ian Hunt having a combined Tent Campaign on the vacant section next to the TeTeko Police Station. The result was that Bro.Rob wrote to Bro & Sis Thrift in Australia who were preparing to return to N.Z. and suggested to them that they might like to estab[l]ish a work in TeTeko that would take care of the results of the Tent Campaign.... Thus it was that on the 19th.July 1969 [*sic*: 1959] that the work was commenced in the TeTeko Memorial Hall, Sis.Puti Waikato's Fish shop, and Bro.& Sis. Campbell's farm at Otakeri [*sic*: Otakiri]....
>
> These meetings continued over 1959–60 with little impact being made on the Maori Community as a whole, in fact there were quite a number of incidents that revealed the hostility of many of the locals to this unwelcome "new Church" that had come amongst them.... [T]he turning point... of what eventually became the Move of God in TeTeko and the surrounding districts [came] in 1961.
>
> It began with Sis.Wiha McCauley coming to the TeTeko Memorial Hall and was healed-delivered-and saved, she told and testified to her family, who came and received Christ, and they in turn told their families and the whole thing began to snowball in TeTeko, Te Mahoe, Waiohou & Kawerau. It was wonderful to sit back, as it were, and see the Lord Sovereignly working without the aid or assistance of man.[12]

The Te Teko assembly provides a typical example of the way in which Wheeler's campaigns contributed to the establishment of a local Full Gospel church. It also demonstrates the way in which a significant healing sometimes provided the catalyst for a breakthrough into the wider community and of the sense of divine sovereignty that accompanied this breakthrough. The Te Teko assembly capitalised on this opening, and, under Thrift's leadership, became a strong centre of expansion in the Bay of Plenty area and among Maori further afield.

Wheeler's evangelistic successes on the East Coast opened further doors of opportunity to him, and other Pentecostal groups began to invite him to conduct campaigns. These were usually held in churches and public halls during the winter months when tent campaigns were no longer possible. One early example was the combined Pentecostal citywide Auckland crusade under the auspices of the Full Gospel Businessmen's Fellowship International in May 1959.[13] By this time, a dual pattern was emerging in the ministries of Wheeler and his associates. On the one hand, these Full Gospel evangelists used tent-churches and local halls as venues and campaigned, when invited, on behalf of other churches where these existed and were cooperative. However, in other areas with no Pentecostal churches, the campaigns were pioneer ventures, undertaken with the aim of establishing a local Full Gospel assembly. Wheeler describes their purpose as follows:

> New Zealand was sceptical to Full Gospel work, as most towns have no Assemblies that preach this message and what they have heard was twisted or only half true. A sane, sound, balanced ministry and pattern had to be presented to capture the land for the Deliverance ministry, and leave good assemblies behind in every town.... We are not out to build our own denomination, or set up churches with our name over the door. We are not working against our

fellow brethren, preaching this same message, but rather we are working with them, to the utmost of our ability, to strengthen their Assemblies and send new converts to them.... Already we have been thrilled to conduct campaigns in eight established Full Gospel [i.e. Pentecostal] Assemblies from five different groups of Churches as well as various other groups throughout the land.... [As well as this] we have successfully used marquees in areas where there are no Full Gospel Assemblies, and this season, working with Ian Hunt, we have seen four new assemblies opened and "growing up" in the liberty of the Spirit. These works are independent and self-governed with a "Shepherd" in charge of them.[14]

The pattern of Wheeler's ministry was threefold. He worked with, and at the invitation of, existing (usually Pentecostal) churches and channelled back his converts to them. He also worked in cooperation with other evangelists. However, where there was no Pentecostal church in the area, Wheeler and his colleagues would endeavour to set up an independent local Full Gospel assembly from the results of the campaign. At this stage, Peter Morrow was following up the converts of Wheeler's campaigns and gathering them into house meetings that would lay the foundation for later development into a fully fledged local assembly.

The emerging network of independent Full Gospel evangelists (including Wheeler and his colleagues) was not a homogenous group, nor was the basis of its fellowship acceptance of Bethel Temple doctrine or of Latter Rain polity. The links were personal, rather than organisational or doctrinal, with a focus on evangelism. Consequently the independent Full Gospel churches that developed from their campaigns were simply gravitational accretions of like-minded believers. These independent congregations had little corporate identity beyond their relationship with Christ and their fellowship with those who shared their faith.

Nevertheless, some significant links of fellowship with other Pentecostal groups did develop from Wheeler's campaigns. One such resulted from his June 1959 campaigns for Pastor Vin Brown of the Wellington National Revival Crusade. While on holiday on the East Coast, Pastor Brown had come across one of Wheeler's tent campaigns, and was impressed by what he heard. As a result, he invited Wheeler to minister in the churches of the National Revival Crusade,[15] and Wheeler became a frequent visitor to this group of churches. Although Wheeler did not share this movement's British Israel doctrinal emphasis, there were similarities in a common distrust of organisational structures, and a shared concern for evangelism. Wheeler and Pastor Edna Robb of Tauranga were invited to speak at the 1959 National Revival Crusade Easter Conference[16] and Wheeler conducted at least four campaigns in National Revival Crusade churches in 1959 and 1960. These informal links of fellowship took a more institutional form during this movement's Easter Conference in Tauranga the following year. An impromptu and informal meeting of the pastors of some 18 assemblies (apparently comprising the 12 National Revival Crusade churches, and six churches linked with Rob Wheeler and his associates) was held during the Conference. This gathering took the opportunity of meeting together to discuss vital matters pertaining to the future of the movement.... It was decided, among other things, to change the name of the movement from "National Revival Crusade" to "United Full Gospel Fellowship" thus opening the door to any independent Full Gospel Groups of like precious faith who would like to enjoy the benefits of fellowship. Although the name was changed, the principles remain the same, the New Testament pattern of locally governed assemblies continuing to operate without interference, yet each sharing fellowship and mutual ministry for the building up of the Kingdom of God.[17]

Figure 6: The National Revival Crusade 1960 Easter Convention in Tauranga, with Rob Wheeler addressing the meeting
(Rob Wheeler, Auckland)

The United Full Gospel Fellowship represented a convergence, rather than an association, of independent Full Gospel churches with the National Revival Crusade churches. It attempted to provide a common basis of fellowship for Full Gospel believers from varied backgrounds. This fellowship was not based on Wheeler's Bethel Temple teaching, nor on the British Israel emphasis of the National Revival Crusade churches, although a mutual abhorrence of extralocal organisation did provide a common denominator. Nevertheless, the Fellowship was ineffective during its short lifetime, and most converts of Wheeler's campaigns were unaware of its existence, having little sense of identity apart from their own local assembly. As will be seen, these links dissolved in acrimony at the disastrous United Full Gospel Fellowship 1961 Annual Convention.

A more substantive basis of identity for Wheeler's converts was provided by his teaching materials, and later, by his Bible School in Tauranga. By mid-1959, *Bible Deliverance* was announcing the availability of free cyclostyled sets of Wheeler's teaching notes. These comprised his studies on the subjects of Salvation and Healing, Sanctification, Water Baptism, Holy Spirit Baptism, Gifts of the Spirit, Church Order for the Gifts and Bible Ministries.[18] These titles indicate that this was an elementary set of studies intended for new converts. The following year saw the launch of a Winter Bible School in Tauranga, with evening classes three nights a week for four months and offering a considerably extended curriculum.[19] Much of this comprised Bethel Temple material such as 'Bible Numbers', 'Studies on Daniel and Revelation', 'The Great Revival', 'Bible Chronology' and, especially, 'The Name of God.' Wheeler and Ron Coady did the bulk of the teaching, and this Bible School did much to establish a doctrinal core of identity for the Full Gospel churches established as a result of Wheeler's campaigns. The availability of the Bible School notes in cyclostyled form helped to disseminate a typical Bethel Temple hermeneutic approach to Scripture. Other Full Gospel pastors used them in their own local church Bible Schools and this reproduced an ethos of Bible teaching, inherited from Ray Jackson Snr. and passed on by Wheeler and his associates. Given that these churches held a strongly independent Latter Rain polity of autonomy, Wheeler's Bible School helped to give the emerging Full Gospel movement an associative centre that it otherwise would not have had.

To summarise: the campaigns of Wheeler and his associates were often followed by the setting up of local Full Gospel churches to consolidate the results of the campaign and to care for the converts. Many of these local, autonomous, self-governing assemblies, sometimes collectively known as the 'Indigenous [Full Gospel] churches', formed the nucleus of what were later to become the New Life Churches of New Zealand. At this early stage, however, this emerging group of independent Pentecostal churches cannot yet be characterised as a movement. Its links were personal, rather than institutional, and the identifying characteristics were its Bethel Temple style of Bible teaching promoted by Wheeler's Bible School, its Latter Rain polity of autonomy, and its passion for evangelism. Furthermore, not all the independent assemblies established by the Full Gospel evangelists associated themselves with this emerging group of churches. Norman White, for example, was associated with the Apostolic Church. Ian Hunt's Open Door Mission in Palmerston North remained an independent church for some years, but later became part of the Elim Churches of New Zealand. Nevertheless, the Indigenous Churches—later renamed the New Life Churches—were the main beneficiaries of this Full Gospel evangelism, and from this day of small beginnings would expand exponentially over the next five years.

Notes

1. Wheeler, Interview. Similarly, Ron Coady recalls that one of his first campaigns on his own account, in Te Araroa in June 1960, was 'quite a flop.' Coady, Interview.
2. Wheeler, Interview.
3. 'Regions Beyond—the Missionary Page: The East Coast Maori Work', *Bible Deliverance*, April 1959, 8-9. *Bible Deliverance* refers to tent campaigns at Te Araroa, Rangitukia, Waihau Bay, Kawerau and Te Teko during this period.
4. R. Wheeler, 'Without a Vision—The People Perish', *Bible Deliverance*, May 1959, 21-22.
5. 'New Zealand: The Maori Work', *Bible Deliverance*, November 1960, 12.
6. This paternalism towards Maori was not confined solely to the Full Gospel evangelists. Allan Davidson comments, in the context of a discussion of Anglican, Methodist, Roman Catholic and Presbyterian Maori work, that 'a mission mentality, seen in Pakeha paternalism, has dominated a great deal of the churches' in-

volvement with Maori for much this century.' Allan Davidson, *Christianity in Aotearoa: A History of Church and Society in New Zealand* (Wellington: Education for Ministry, 1991), 133a.
7. 'Regions Beyond—The Missionary Page: The East Coast Maori Work: Rangitukia', *Bible Deliverance*, April 1959, 9.
8. A *marae* is defined as 'the courtyard (usually grassed) of a Maori meeting-house, the centre of tribal life; often now used of the whole complex of courtyard, meeting-house, and ancillary buildings and grounds.' H.W. Orsman, ed., *The Dictionary of New Zealand English: A Dictionary of New Zealandisms on Historical Principles* (Auckland: Oxford University Press, 1997), s.v. 'Marae.' For a detailed account of the Maori customs and protocol relating to the *marae*, see Hiwi and Pat Tauroa, *Te Marae: A Guide to Customs and Protocol* (Auckland: Heinemann Reed, 1988).
9. 'Easter Conventions—Rangitukia Report', *Bible Deliverance*, May 1959, 15.
10. Tera Woelders, 'A Dutch couple find Christ', *Bible Deliverance*, August 1959, 18, refers to the start of regular Saturday night meetings in Whakatane 'two and a half years ago' (i.e. circa February 1957).
11. 'Te Teko Report', *Bible Deliverance*, May 1959, 8.
12. 'Te Teko Fellowship—25th Anniversary Celebrations, 1961-1986', [1986]. (Mimeographed.) 5. Punctuation, capitalisation and spacing as cited. I am grateful to Pastor Allan Thrift for a copy of this booklet.
13. This was held at the Auckland Queen St Assembly of God, then the flagship of New Zealand Pentecostalism. W.E. Scott, 'The Auckland Revival Crusade', *Bible Deliverance*, June 1959, 9.
14. R. Wheeler, 'Without a Vision—The People Perish', *Bible Deliverance*, May 1959, 21-22.
15. Later renamed the Christian Revival Crusade. See Worsfold, *History*, 292-96, for an account of this movement.
16. I.A.S. and R.N., 'Easter Convention: Devonport Report', *Bible Deliverance*, May 1959, 14.
17. V. Brown, 'The Tauranga Easter Convention Story (Part 1): United Full Gospel Fellowship', *Bible Deliverance*, May 1960, 7.
18. *Bible Deliverance*, June 1959, 13.
19. *Bible Deliverance*, March 1960, 15.

Chapter 9

Breakthrough!

As the Full Gospel healing campaigns of Wheeler and his associates gained momentum, the arrival of evangelists from overseas compounded their effect. A return visit by Tommy Hicks was scheduled for September and October 1959, but he was unable to come. His place was taken by an independent American evangelist, A.S. Worley from Greenville, South Carolina, who had come to New Zealand in mid-October 1959 at the invitation of Dr Len Jones.[1] Brother Worley (as he was known) was to have great influence on the development of the Full Gospel movement in New Zealand. In personality, he was quietly spoken, gentle and humble, and preached simply and positively. An observer noted that 'the promises of God, and the rights and privileges of God's people were so simply explained, that people felt ashamed of their unbelief.'[2] Worley's positive faith was contagious, and it is noticeable that the reported sermons of Rob Wheeler, and, more particularly, Ron Coady, show this emphasis from this time on.[3]

Brother Worley was one of the featured speakers at the National Revival Crusade 1960 Easter Convention in Tauranga, where his challenging and faith-building messages had a powerful motivating effect.[4] Ron Coady recalled that God challenged him at this Convention to give up his secure secular job in the Army and his part-time teaching role in Wheeler's Bible School, and to begin healing campaigns.[5] Worley also achieved some measure of success in his healing campaigns as he ministered independently around the country, wherever a door was opened to him. However, he was to have his greatest effectiveness in the South Island, and his campaign in Timaru during June and July 1960 would acquire legendary status in the history of the New Life Churches.

Timaru was a religiously conservative city, and seemingly not at all open to Pentecostalism, being referred to in Pentecostal circles as 'preacher's graveyard.'[6] Although there had been attempts by various Pentecostal groups over the years to start a church in Timaru, there was only one minuscule independent Pentecostal group, meeting regularly in the Orange Hall in Bank

Street. Although this group did not always use a corporate title, it sometimes advertised itself by titles such as 'Pentecostal Fellowship' or 'Full Gospel Mission.'[7] This small independent assembly was pastored for some months in 1959 and 1960 by an itinerant Assemblies of God worker, Laurie Murray. During his tenure as pastor, its weekly newspaper advertisement appeared under the heading of 'Assemblies of God.' However, Murray was quite unflattering in his description of his congregation, describing them as 'about half-a-dozen old-timers who had either just managed to hold on in the face of general despising and rejection; or maybe their forthright and ever-exuberant witness had frightened people for miles around.'[8] It probably is not surprising that Murray's tenure was comparatively short-lived, as was this group's affiliation with the Assemblies of God. Following A.S. Worley's first Timaru campaign in April 1960, the group's weekly advertisement reverted to the heading of 'Full Gospel Mission.' It therefore appears that links with the Assemblies of God were not strong, and may have been due to Murray's influence.

The Full Gospel Mission included among its members Ada Pollock (neé Saunders) and her husband, Jimmy. Ada Pollock and her sisters were well-known in Pentecostal circles, having been founding members of the Pentecostal Church of New Zealand, established in 1924 as a result of Smith Wigglesworth's healing campaigns.[9] Zona Knowles, who became a member of this group in April 1960, emphasises that the Saunders sisters were Pentecostal (i.e. Pentecostal Church of New Zealand) rather than Assemblies of God adherents. Furthermore, it was Ada Pollock herself, rather than the Timaru group who had invited Worley to Timaru for his first campaign in April 1960.[10]

The invitation to Worley arose out of his Dunedin campaign in February 1960, when an elderly Timaru couple attended and received healing from numerous ailments, including a painful eye condition that caused almost total blindness.[11] (Worley recalls that 'the old man who had been prayed for in Dunedin had been healed of his blindness. He had been showing his friends that he had been healed by taking his rifle and striking matches by shooting the head off the match.'[12]) Ada and Jimmy Pollock, who had been praying for many months for a revival in Timaru, had also attended the Dunedin meeting and invited Worley to come to Timaru for a campaign.

Worley began his first campaign in Timaru on 6 April 1960, and continued for six days. Although there were some results, the Worleys then left Timaru with no intention of ever returning. Worley was later to say that 'Timaru was the only place he had ever come back to twice.'[13] However, Ada Pollock was not the sort of person to take 'no' for an answer, and she prevailed upon the Worleys to return for a second campaign. This began in the New Century Hall, Barnard Street, Timaru on 17 June 1960, and attracted an audience of about 60 people in the first meeting. The campaign was intensive, with two meetings each day, six days a week. By the end of the second week, attendances had risen to approximately 200 in the afternoon teaching meeting.[14] Ron Coady had come down from Tauranga to assist Worley in the teaching meetings in the afternoon, while Peter Morrow was one of the songleaders for the evening meetings.

Figure 7: A.S. Worley, at the time of his Timaru campaign in 1960
(Zona Knowles, Timaru)

Healings were the most prominent feature of the Timaru campaign. After the first week, full-page advertisements appeared in the local paper claiming healings of 'heart trouble, asthma, complete deafness, stroke, arthritis and other complaints.'[15] The advertisement that appeared on 4 July added that 'well over 100 people [had] accepted Christ' and a 'boy with [a] club foot, had it restored to normal.'[16] This particular healing created much interest; so much so that the *Timaru Herald* wrote up a three-column article on it two days later.[17] This article proved to be the turning point of the campaign and from then on attendances at the meetings grew dramatically. By its third week, the Worley Mission had become one of the major topics of conversation in the town.

The author attended the Worley mission and was one of the more than 600 people converted to Christ during the five-week campaign. A personal recollection[18] will serve to capture the atmosphere of these meetings:

> I was present at the evening meeting of Wednesday 6th July in the New Century Hall. The hall was packed out: approximately 250–300 people being seated, and others standing several rows deep all around the walls of the building. I managed to obtain a seat on top of the bookstall at the rear of the hall; others were seated on the floor beneath my feet. (These particular people were taking

notes of the sermon—I had never seen anyone do this before!) The atmosphere was electric with expectancy—the "healings" had drawn people from all over the South Island to these meetings. The fervent singing was one of the hall marks of the campaign: in particular, the hymn that was to become the "trademark" of the Timaru campaign being sung with "all stops out":

> "He lives, He lives, Christ Jesus lives today!
> He walks with me, and talks with me, along life's narrow way.
> He lives! He lives! Salvation to impart!
> You ask me how I know he lives?
> He lives! within my heart."[19]

The preaching was simple, straightforward and positive: it was characterized by a positive faith and an emphasis on the person and ministry of Jesus. At the conclusion of the sermon, an "altar call" was made for people to "make a decision for Christ": people were asked to bow their heads, and those who wanted to "receive Christ" were invited to raise their hands as a sign of their commitment to Christ. The "converts" were then invited to come forward to the front of the hall, where they were led through the "sinner's prayer" by the evangelist, in which they "asked Jesus to come into my heart and be my personal Saviour." They then signed a "Decision Card," which served both as a record of the occasion, and also provided the convert's name and address for follow-up. Forty-three people responded to this "altar-call" that particular night. The reaction of the congregation was extraordinary: it was quite common for complete strangers to get up from their seats and to come up and warmly shake the hands of the "converts" returning to their seats. One of the early converts (Lilian Wright) remembers this as being one of the particular features of the campaign: "you could *feel* the love of God in the meetings: the air was full of it."[20]

After the "altar call," a "prayer line" was called for the sick, and these people came forward, and were individually prayed for by Brother Worley. The atmosphere was expectant and reverent: there was no sense of "hype." Often the speaker would operate the gift of the "Word of Knowledge," by which he would describe the condition (usually physical) of people in the audience, and invite them to come forward for prayer for this need. This "gift" was seen as a stimulus to faith: the revelation of the physical need was understood as an indication that the condition would be healed after prayer. Many people were healed: Lilian Wright, for example, told me that her husband had been healed of an arthritic back, and never had any trouble with it again.[21]

However, there were also those who were not healed, or who only obtained temporary relief. Thus the Worley campaign inevitably led to controversy, which was exacerbated by opposition from ministers of the established churches. These ministers preached against the mission from their pulpits, often without having attended the meetings for themselves, and wrote letters to the editor of the newspaper. An examination of the 'Church Notices' column in the *Timaru Herald* during the period of the Worley campaign will give some indication of the extent of this opposition. Most church advertisements simply recorded the time of their services, with no details of the sermon topic being given. The clubfoot healing on 26 June marked the turning point of the campaign. The following Saturday's 'Church Notices' in the *Timaru Herald* show that a number of churches preached that weekend on topics relating to the healing campaign. The sermon titles indicate that the campaign was seen as a danger[22]; church newsletters from the period confirm that this perception was widely held. Certainly, many of these ministers acted from a genuine sense of pastoral concern, but some, unfortunately, descended to attacking or ridiculing the person of the evangelists. An example of this ridicule—although possibly not specifically related to the Worley campaign—is an unattributed newspaper clipping of a letter to the editor from a local Presbyterian minister. This pointed out that if miracles were wrought as a sign of God's power, then why hadn't anyone been healed of baldness?[23] (This was a personal slight at the expense of Ron Coady, who was noticeably bald and who was assisting in the campaigns.)

One of the most controversial issues was that of 'teeth filling.' Claims were made that people had received fillings of gold, silver and other materials in their teeth as a sign of the power of God. Controversy over these claims helped to focus further attention on the campaign, and it received widespread publicity as a result. This controversy eventually reached the debating chamber in Parliament. The Rev. Clyde Carr, M.P. for Timaru, referred to the claims of teeth filling and asked 'could the Minister [of Health] or the Director of Dental Hygiene look into the matter?'[24] He also requested the Minister of Health 'to take action to prevent the malpractices of quacks and unqualified people who assumed duties for which they were not equipped.'[25] The response of the Minister was not recorded.

A newspaper article in the *Timaru Herald* on 2 September summarised the controversy to date over the campaigns and noted that the teeth filling claims were 'too vague for reasonable analysis.'[26] The article reported that the South Canterbury Dentists' Association had offered the evangelist the use of their facilities to prove his claims. Fifteen days later, the *Timaru Herald*, in an editorial headed 'Faith-Healing Mission', again commented on the events of the past three months. While generally *laissez-faire* in tone, it claimed that the clubfoot healing had not yet been documented,[27] and printed a statement from the South Canterbury Dentists' Association on the issue of teeth filling. This stated that 'from records held by the respective dentists it has been made clear that in no cases can the claims be substantiated, each new filling now present having been placed in the mouth at an earlier date by the dentist concerned, as proved by reference to the dentist's records.'[28]

(However, against this must be set the claims of, for example, Marion Winnington, who insists that 'both Peter and Janet [her two oldest children] as children each received several fillings. Subsequently, Janet's dentist denied having put these fillings in. At the time, dentists generally were strongly opposed to the miracle tooth fillings, and in an effort to support his Dental Association, he attempted to remove the fillings and replace them with his own.'[29] A 'Testimony of an Auckland Dental Surgeon' is cited by Mary Henderson in favour of the phenomenon.[30] However, this testimony relates to a later occurrence of teeth filling in Auckland rather than to the current occurrence of the phenomenon in Timaru. As the dentist concerned had recently been secretary of the Auckland Full Gospel Businessmen's Fellowship International,[31] his testimony was not an impartial one.)

The *Timaru Herald* editorial went on to state that doubts on the authenticity of the cures did not necessarily reflect on the sincerity or integrity of the evangelists. Their convictions, and those of the claimants to divine healing, were genuine ones, honestly believed. Worley himself had been cooperative with their reporter's intentions, and had encouraged testimonies from those healed. In doing so, he cautioned against extravagant claims, and offered no objection to independent verification of specific cases of healing.[32]

Although the campaign officially ended on 24 July, Worley stayed on in Timaru for several weeks after this. This campaign marked the emergence of Full Gospel evangelism as an identifiable movement in the South Island. Over 600 people had made decisions for Christ in the five and a half weeks of the campaign, and a sizeable portion of these remained to form the nucleus of a church. Ron Coady commented that these converts were 'all kinds [of people]... from every [part of the] spectrum. The wealthy, the poor, the middle class, the upper class, teenagers....'[33] Some of these converts had been attracted from other churches; others had no church connections at all; and still others had been converted in the campaigns and had returned to their churches. However, as Bert Schoneveld has pointed out, 'Pentecostal fellowships have, in terms of commitment to the Church, benefited by gaining from the non-Pentecostal churches some of their keenest members.'[34] Schoneveld found that, for Pentecostal converts, the most appealing feature of Pentecostal churches was 'the centrality of Christ.'[35] He further observes that the 'the overwhelming reason why... [the converts] came to the Pentecostal Churches was that it offered them *life*.'[36] These perceptions are reflected in Worley's comments during an address to a gathering of about 60 people on Tuesday 2 August 1960, on the subject of forming a church in Timaru. Worley said, in part, that:

> Now you have tasted the good Word of God and have come in contact with the living Christ... you will never be satisfied with anything less than this you have tasted.... There has to be a place where people can come and receive the spiritual benefits for which their faith is reaching out.... You can never be satisfied again with mere forms and ceremonies and Social Gospel. Only the living Christ with His miracles of healing and the fellowship of born-again believers will ever bring true joy and satisfaction to your hearts.... The purpose of the meeting this morning is to talk with you about organizing a... faith mission.[37]

Ron Coady commented on the need to form a local assembly after the campaign:

> The reason why a church was formed—what was going to happen to these converts? There were those who were fighting the teaching of divine healing. The traditional churches didn't want it. We were heretics, and so forth. The baptism of the Spirit, speaking in tongues, was fought stupendously.... [These were] pre-Vatican II days, and before the renewal

had hit the major denominations. This is what happened—and we had to do something with the people.[38]

Consequently an assembly was formed in Timaru to care for the new converts. The majority of Laurie Murray's small Full Gospel Mission congregation appear to have transferred their allegiance, becoming members of this new church. The Full Gospel Mission itself ceased to exist, and Murray himself moved on to Westport. The short life-span of this group, and the ease with which its members could shift their denominational allegiance and transfer to another church, appears to be a typical feature of New Zealand Pentecostal groups. The primary identity of the new assembly, known as the 'Christian Fellowship Mission', lay in its emphasis on evangelism. As will be seen, it became a launch pad for the growth of the Full Gospel movement in the South Island.

Notes

1. A somewhat uncritical authorized biography of Worley is Robert E. Grice, *Apostle to the Nations: An Authorized Biography of A.S. Worley, a Man of Faith and Miracles* (Walhalla, South Carolina: Faith Training Center, n.d. [1990]). This biography appears to be based on Worley's recollections, but is quite confused on the sequence of his ministry in New Zealand.
2. 'Evangelist and Mrs. Worley visit Tauranga', *Bible Deliverance*, November–December 1959, 10.
3. For example, Ron Coady's article in *Bible Deliverance*, April 1960, 13–15, entitled 'YOU', states: 'This article is about YOU! It is about what you *are*, what you *have*, and what you can *do*. . . .' Emphasis as cited.
4. V. Brown, 'The Tauranga Easter Convention Story (Part 1): United Full Gospel Fellowship', *Bible Deliverance*, May 1960, 6–9.
5. Coady, Interview.
6. Mary Henderson, *From Glory to Glory: A History of the Timaru New Life Centre 1960–1980* (Timaru: Dove Print, 1980), 4.
7. 'Religious Notices', *Timaru Herald*, July 1959–December 1960. The use of this latter title did not imply a connection with the Full Gospel campaigns of Rob Wheeler and others.
8. Laurie Murray, *Where to, World 1977?* (Palmerston North: By the Author, n.d. [1977]), 25. Murray's portrayal of the somewhat eccentric character of this group appears to be an accurate one. They were quite typical of many smaller Pentecostal groups in New Zealand then.
9. Worsfold, *History*, 167, 172 and 175.
10. Zona Knowles, Comment to author, Timaru, 26 November 1989.
11. The testimony of this couple is given in 'Blind, Arthritis, Thyroid, Duodenal Ulcer: Healed through Prayer!' *Bible Deliverance*, August 1961, 11 and 13.
12. Worley, cited in Grice, *Apostle to the Nations*, 24.
13. Worley, cited by Lilian Wright, Interview, Timaru, 18 November 1987.
14. Ron Coady, 'It happened in Timaru', *Bible Deliverance*, August 1960, 8.
15. *Timaru Herald*, 28 June 1960, 13.

16. *Timaru Herald*, 4 July 1960, 6.
17. 'Parents say Prayer Transformed Boy's Twisted Foot: Now Walks Unaided', *Timaru Herald*, 6 July 1960, 12.
18. Extended quotation from Knowles, 'For the Sake of the Name', 31-33.
19. A.H. Ackley, 'He lives, He lives, Christ Jesus lives today!' No.631, *Redemption Hymnal* (Revised Edition Eastbourne, Sussex: Elim Publishing House, 1955). Copyright 1933 by Homer A. Rodeheaver. Copyright renewed 1961, The Rodeheaver Co. (A Div. of Word, Inc.). All rights reserved. International copyright secured. Permission requested 10 February 1999.
20. Lilian Wright, Interview. Emphasis as cited.
21. ibid.
22. E.g. in the Baptist church advertisement: 'What is the Baptism of the Holy Spirit?— An examination of Divine Healing, and Speaking in Tongues, its purposes and perils.' *Timaru Herald*, 2 July 1960, 4.
23. Although this unidentified clipping from the 'Letters to the Editor' column was found in the archives of the Timaru New Life Centre, it could not be located in the *Timaru Herald* files for the period (July–October 1960). Nevertheless, it does illustrate the personal ridicule that some of these healing campaigners attracted.
24. *New Zealand Parliamentary Debates* [hereafter cited as *NZPD*], vol.324, 2544 (23 September 1960).
25. 'Timaru Faith Healing Mission Discussed By Mr. Carr in House', *Timaru Herald*, 24 September 1960, 12.
26. 'South Canterbury Dentists Offer Evangelist Facilities To Prove Claims', *Timaru Herald*, 2 September 1960, 12.
27. The *Timaru Herald* reported 11 days later that this child had since undergone a second operation on his deformed foot. 'Second Operation on Infant's Deformed Foot', *Timaru Herald*, 28 September 1960, 10.
28. 'Editorial: Faith-Healing Mission', *Timaru Herald*, 17 September 1960, 12.
29. Marion Winnington, comment made at the 25th Jubilee celebrations of the Timaru New Life Centre, October 1985.
30. Wm. E. Scott, Principal, Auckland Dental Surgeries, Letter 15 February 1961, cited as 'Testimony of an Auckland Dental Surgeon', in Henderson, *From Glory to Glory*, 6-7.
31. W[m].E. Scott, Secretary, 'The Auckland Revival Crusade', *Bible Deliverance*, June 1959, 9.
32. 'Editorial: Faith-Healing Mission', *Timaru Herald*, 17 September 1960, 12.
33. Coady, Interview.
34. E.J. [Bert] Schoneveld, 'An exploration in Protest' (Research Essay, Knox Theological Hall, 1982. (Typescript.)), Appendix, 5.
35. ibid., Appendix, 7.
36. ibid., Appendix, 6. Emphasis Schoneveld.
37. A.S. Worley, 'Excerpts from an address by A.S. Worley', cited in Henderson, *From Glory to Glory*, 8.
38. Coady, Interview.

Chapter 10

Ron Coady and expansion in the South

After the end of the Timaru campaign, Ron Coady returned briefly to Tauranga to wind up his affairs there. He then came back to Timaru together with Paul Collins, who had just graduated from the Tauranga Bible School, and took over the responsibility of the new assembly. Until this time, Coady had copastored with Rob Wheeler and taught in Wheeler's Bible School in Tauranga, and supported himself by secular employment in the Army. He had been stirred by Worley's messages at the National Revival Crusade 1960 Easter Convention and had resigned his secular job to go into full-time ministry. He had, up to this time, regarded himself as a Bible teacher rather than as an evangelist, and his experience in Timaru was something of a new beginning for him. His teaching meetings in the afternoon during the Worley campaign complemented the evangelistic work of Worley, but Coady soon began to adopt Worley's methods, and to develop his own style of evangelism.

Australian-born Coady is one of the most interesting figures in the history of the movement. He was formerly a Roman Catholic, and according to his booklet *I Shall Not Want*[1] had had to leave home when he became a Christian. He had been given an ultimatum by his Catholic mother to return to the Catholic Church or to leave home. He chose to do the latter. It appears that he had once been in a monastery, since the final meeting of his evangelistic campaigns was often given over to his life story, entitled 'Why I left the monastery.'[2] It is therefore ironic that Coady adopted a semi-Catholic orientation after his departure from New Zealand in 1970, and came to place emphasis on the Apostolic Succession. He saw this succession as a logical extension of the Latter Rain doctrine of laying on of hands. This led him to accept ordination in the Syro-Chaldean church of South India in 1972. He has been based in Davis, California for some years and was, until the end of 1989, Bishop of a church with Syro-Chaldean connections, the Catholic Apostolic Church: Glastonbury Rite. Coady has now resigned his episcopal See, and returned to his first love, healing evangelism.[3]

Rob Wheeler accurately describes Coady as 'dynamic—a dynamo.'[4] From the time that he began his evangelistic work, a new aggressiveness is discernible in the method as well as the message of the Full Gospel movement in the South Island. Coady's campaigns helped to create an identity for the movement; some of his early converts in Southland were (and in some cases, still are) known by the perjorative title of 'Coadyites.' Coady made Timaru his base, and, together with Paul Collins, from there launched out into evangelistic campaigns. The dramatic expansion of the movement over the next few years in the South Island is directly attributable to these campaigns.

The South Island was largely virgin territory as far as the Full Gospel message was concerned. Consequently, Coady seldom met with the restrictions that Wheeler would sometimes find in cooperating with existing Pentecostal churches in his North Island campaigns. It must be admitted, however, that Coady (as befitted his dynamic and aggressive approach) would not have been inclined towards cooperation, particularly in view of the opposition that the movement encountered. Indeed, he *gloried* in opposition. After a campaign in Dunedin in which he was threatened that he would never leave alive if he returned for further meetings, he not only returned, but was labelled as 'the man they couldn't hang'![5] Although more flamboyant and aggressive than most of his Full Gospel colleagues, Coady did reflect the general feeling of the movement in the South Island, particularly after 1961.

From Timaru, outreaches were held to Geraldine and Waimate, and, in December 1960, Coady and Paul Collins conducted a ten-day campaign in Invercargill. The Timaru assembly's newsletter 'Signposts of Faith' reported, possibly with a degree of hyperbole, that over 200 decisions for Christ were recorded during this campaign and that 'multitudes received deliverance from sin, sickness and disease. The blind received their sight, the deaf heard, the dumb spoke, cripples walked and ran, teeth were miraculously filled and skin diseases were cleansed.'[6] Coady recalled that 'one man had a metal elbow, and God miraculously healed him.'[7]

In December 1960, 'Signposts of Faith' jubilantly noted that 'over the past six months we have seen over 1,200 people in Timaru, Waimate, Geraldine and Invercargill record decisions for the Lord Jesus Christ.' The newsletter then sets out an ambitious seven-point 'Harvest Plan for 1961', which included evangelistic and pastoral goals both within Timaru and beyond. These included the achieving of 2,000 decisions for Christ, the raising of £1,000 for overseas missions, and the establishment of three new permanent Full Gospel Missions in the South Island during 1961. Each of these new Missions was to be both a local church and an evangelistic centre: 'these Missions are to be completely autonomous and self-supporting, with their own deliverance ministries.' Local goals in Timaru included the formation of a Soul Clinic for counselling, follow-up and prayer ministry, and the setting up of a Gospel Training Centre and a Gospel Publishing Division.

Finally, the Timaru congregation aimed to erect a church building within the next twelve months.[8]

The proposed polity of these autonomous and self-supporting Missions reflected a Latter Rain emphasis on the independent local church, as well as a response to opposition. Coady later commented that

> it was not the intention to establish churches. The intention was to meet the needs of the people... to make Christ known to all men [sic], to preach the message of salvation, to reach the unchurched. We would loved to have turned the people over to the churches, but how can you turn people over to those who oppose you and fight you and preach against you? So churches were formed out of the meetings as of a necessity to care for those who were born into the Kingdom of God.[9]

A second breakthrough in the South occurred in Gore, where Paul Collins began an evangelistic campaign on 1 March 1961. About 40 people attended the first meetings. After a few days, Paul Collins was joined by Coady and the campaign began to gain momentum, numbers increasing throughout the 26 days of the campaign. On the final night, the hall was 'crammed to capacity; sliding doors were opened—people stood or sat anywhere they could; the platform had little space left for the preachers to move about. God had visited this spiritually starved town.'[10] The *Otago Daily Times* gave the campaign four-column front-page treatment, reporting that the audience had 'increased to nearly 400, and nightly more than 100 people stand in the healing line.'[11] More than 450 decisions for Christ were recorded during the campaign, many of these being teenagers,[12] and 'miracles of healings took place too numerous to mention',[13] including, as in the Timaru campaign, teeth filling. Although the *Otago Daily Times* reported some scepticism about the healings,[14] this particular sign created great interest, crowds coming from surrounding districts to witness it for themselves. The crowds were so great that 'during the prayer time for the sick on one occasion, Brother Coady called for assistance in prayer as the line was so long, and a Presbyterian minister came forward to lay hands on the sick for the first time in his experience.'[15]

The Gore campaign may have benefited from a local tradition of revivalism, since the nearby Waikaka valley (from which a number of the converts had come) had experienced a number of revivals since the 1880s.[16] It also continued the momentum generated by Worley's success in Timaru eight months earlier. These two healing campaigns, together with those of Rob Wheeler in the North Island, were among the most spectacular outcomes of the two-year healing revival that took place from 1960 to 1962.[17] The main focus of this revival was on salvation and healing, although the baptism of the Spirit became a more prominent feature after mid-1961. These campaigns represented a major breakthrough for the Full Gospel movement and laid the foundations for its expansion throughout the country. Over the five years from 1960 to 1965, most localities in New Zealand were the target of some form of Full Gospel evangelism.

Following the campaigns, local Full Gospel churches were often set up to consolidate the results and to care for the converts. These local, autonomous, self-governing assemblies, sometimes collectively known as the 'Indigenous [Full Gospel] churches', formed the nucleus of what were later to become the New Life Churches of New Zealand. However, although many of the converts of the Full Gospel campaigns eventually gravitated towards the Indigenous Churches, not all the independent groups established by these revivalists associated themselves with this embryonic movement. Norman White, for example, remained associated with the Apostolic Church. Ian Hunt's Open Door Mission in Palmerston North remained an independent church for some years, later becoming part of the Elim Churches of New Zealand. Nevertheless, the Indigenous Churches (later renamed the 'New Life Churches') were the main beneficiaries of this Full Gospel healing movement.

Following the Gore campaign, arrangements were made for 'regular weekly meetings to be continued in Gore as the people want[ed] to know more of this New Testament Christianity.'[18] This placed an enormous workload on Coady, who still had the responsibility of the Timaru assembly: 'With no one to follow up and establish a Full Gospel assembly on the Bible pattern, Brother Coady made the long journey by train from Timaru to hold one meeting weekly on Friday nights, travelling down Thursday and returning Saturday. This he did consistently for many months.'[19] Ray Necklen eventually moved from Pukekohe to Gore in September 1961 to assume the pastorate there. Evidently the transition did not go smoothly, and Necklen recalled that there had been 'plenty of trials and disappointments' during his first twelve months in Gore. Nevertheless, 'the original Mission that was commenced with that campaign is standing true and strong today ... [and] there is a solid core of believers at Gore.' The congregation had bought a section for building, and were able to erect a meeting hall on this site during 1962 and were also able to host a combined South Island Convention that Easter.[20]

Full Gospel expansion was also taking place in the North Island. The same sense of optimism and achievement is reflected in Wheeler's editorial in the January 1961 issue of *Bible Deliverance*: '1960 was a wonderful year! More souls, healings, miracles, baptisms, exploits of faith, than any previous year, But 1960 is behind us, and now it is history. By God's grace, we shall make 1961 one hundred per cent greater.'[21] Wheeler's evangelistic ministry was growing both in extent and effectiveness. By the beginning of 1961 he had added another section to his tent to give a seating capacity of 400 to 500 people.[22] He now began to campaign in the South Island as well as in the North. During 1961, he conducted tent campaigns in Blenheim, Timaru, Invercargill, Dunedin, Oamaru and Christchurch in the South, besides Tauranga and Hastings in the North. An editorial in *Bible Deliverance* captured the increasing sense of opportunity and urgency that pervaded this period:

> Greetings from the South Island! It is harvest time. There is much work to be done in a short time. We are working from daylight until 1 and 2 in the

morning with calls, meetings, writing and future plans.... Now we are in Dunedin ready to commence ten nights of meetings here before going on to Invercargill. Brother Coady and Brother Collins are campaigning in Gore. Brother Johnson is in Timaru. Brother White at Invercargill. Brother Hunt at Foxton and others are hard at the ingathering throughout the land in tents, halls, churches and missions.... It is harvest time![23]

This extract also demonstrates the cooperative nature of Full Gospel evangelism.

Wheeler was also branching out into other forms of ministry. His plans for 1961 included overseas evangelism, literature, tape recordings, child evangelism, Bible School, missionary outreach, and correspondence ministries as adjuncts to his campaigns.[24] He also sought to gain access to radio broadcasting facilities later that year and, to this end, *Bible Deliverance* petitioned for time on the National radio stations to be made available.[25] This project was not immediately successful, although Wheeler's Word of Faith Ministry was on the air in Australia by March 1962.[26]

The momentum generated by the Full Gospel campaigns of Wheeler, Coady and their associates would continue to increase until the mid-1960s. Although this expansion represented the emergence of a new movement, the boundaries of its identity were not yet well-defined.[27] Events in 1961 would provide the stimulus for a consolidation of identity and thus facilitate the formation of the Indigenous [Full Gospel] Churches. This rapid growth also brought problems in its wake, as is highlighted by the experience of the Timaru and Gore assemblies. How were converts of the campaigns to be cared for, particularly in towns where no churches had cooperated, or where there was no Full Gospel work? If a Full Gospel assembly was set up after the campaigns, where would its leaders come from? As will be seen, several different measures were employed in response to these problems, each of them contributing to the future development of the New Life Churches.

Notes

1. Bro. [A.R.] Coady, *I Shall Not Want* (Nelson: Faith Enterprises, n.d.).
2. 'The Message of Deliverance comes to Mosgiel', *Revival News*, May 1962, 6.
3. A.R. Coady, Correspondence with the author, Davis, California, 1988–91.
4. Wheeler, Interview.
5. Reported in 'The Man they couldn't hang visits Timaru', *Gospel Truth* 6 (December 1964), 3.
6. Christian Fellowship Mission, Timaru, 'Signposts of Faith', n.d. [December 1960].
7. Coady, Interview. This individual was the brother-in-law of Pastor Reg Highstead of the Wanaka Christian Fellowship.
8. Christian Fellowship Mission, Timaru, 'Signposts of Faith', n.d. [December 1960].
9. Coady, Interview.
10. Ray Necklen, 'First Anniversary', *Revival News*, September 1962, 8.

11. 'Religious Upheaval caused in Gore by Claims of Divine Healing', *Otago Daily Times*, 24 March 1961, 1.
12. 'The Gore Campaign—Southland', *Bible Deliverance*, April 1961, 4.
13. Necklen, 'Anniversary', *Revival News*, September 1962, 8.
14. 'Religious Upheaval', *Otago Daily Times*, 24 March 1961, 1.
15. 'Gore Campaign', *Bible Deliverance*, April 1961, 4.
16. David Jull, a Ph.D. student at the University of Otago, refers to several waves of revival in the Waikaka area in 1886, 1903 and 1928, which created an ongoing residue of revivalist expectation. David Jull, Comment to author, University of Otago, Dunedin, 1998.
17. Peter Morrow offers this designation, and sharply differentiates the 1960–62 healing revival from the Charismatic renewal of the late 1960s. Peter Morrow, Interview, Dunedin, 30 July 1990.
18. 'Gore Campaign', *Bible Deliverance*, April 1961, 5.
19. Necklen, 'Anniversary', *Revival News*, September 1962, 9.
20. ibid.
21. Rob and Beryl Wheeler, 'Editorial', *Bible Deliverance*, January 1961, 2.
22. 'New Zealand: Evangelism', *Bible Deliverance*, November 1960, 12; Rob and Beryl Wheeler, 'Editorial', *Bible Deliverance*, January 1961, 2.
23. Rob and Beryl Wheeler, 'Editorial: A Call to Action!!!' *Bible Deliverance*, Easter 1961, 2.
24. Rob and Beryl Wheeler, 'Editorial', *Bible Deliverance*, January 1961, 2.
25. 'Operation "Sound Barrier,"' *Bible Deliverance*, April 1961, 15.
26. 'Stop Press! "Sound Barrier" Bro/ken' [sic], *Bible Deliverance*, April 1962, 10.
27. Note Wheeler's reference to Coady and Collins, American campaigner Everett Johnson, Apostolic evangelist Norman White and independent Pentecostal evangelist Ian Hunt as working together at the 'ingathering throughout the land.' Rob and Beryl Wheeler, 'Editorial', *Bible Deliverance*, January 1961, 2.

Chapter 11

Filling the Pastoral Gap

The spectacular success of the Timaru and Gore campaigns in the South Island and, to a lesser extent, of Wheeler's campaigns in the North, sparked further expansion of the Full Gospel movement. This expansion created problems for the young movement, and the issue of how to take care of the converts of the campaigns became increasingly urgent as success followed success in 1961 and 1962. Although there was a shared concern for pastoral follow-up of the converts, this was a secondary rather than a primary focus, since the movement's first priority was for evangelism. Consequently the accelerating growth in the number of churches quickly outstripped the limited availability of pastors.

Three stopgap measures were employed to meet this pastoral shortfall. Firstly, evangelists visiting an assembly with no resident pastor might stay on for some weeks as a short-term pastor. This was augmented by the appointment of a team of deacons to supervise the affairs of the assembly, which both supplemented the role of these temporary pastors and provided a measure of continuity. The third, and in the long term the most effective, measure was the rapid development of Bible Schools to train workers to meet the pastoral need in the movement. These Bible Schools were to play an important role in the creation of doctrinal boundaries for the emergent Full Gospel Churches.

By 1961, a regular succession of Pentecostal ministers from overseas was visiting New Zealand. These individuals frequently stood in as temporary pastors, both in assemblies that had no permanent pastor yet, or where, as in the case of Timaru, the pastor was absent on campaign work elsewhere. Thus, although Ron Coady held the overall responsibility for the Timaru assembly for 17 months up to December 1961, a number of visiting ministries acted as short-term pastors during his absences on campaign. These visitors included Pastor Allan Thrift from Te Teko, Pastor Roy Tregenza from the Canadian Assemblies of God, Dr Everett Johnson of Sacramento, California, and others.

However, this measure was a stopgap one, since few of these visiting ministers stayed longer than five or six weeks. Some dissatisfaction with this arrangement became apparent during the first Annual General Meeting of the Timaru Christian Fellowship Mission held on 9 December 1961. The minutes of the meeting include (*inter alia*), the following entries:

> Lengthly [sic] discussion followed re the matter of the Pastor's... extensive absence in Gore and not visiting locally....
> Much discussion followed on... the problem of us having a perminant [sic] Pastor or relying on roving Ministry.[1]

In both cases, the remit was held over to a future meeting where Pastor Coady could be present. His absence from the Annual General Meeting provides a classic illustration of the problem.

A second solution was the appointment in many churches of a body of deacons to supervise its physical and financial affairs. This complemented, rather than replaced, the role of visiting ministry as temporary pastors, since the understanding was that 'the deacons had control of the temporal goods of the church. The elders had control of the spiritualities.'[2] This pattern was of long standing, since Ray Jackson's Auckland Bethel Temple church, established after the secession from the Pentecostal Church of New Zealand, had appointed elders and deacons as early as 1946. This format of church government was well-established in the North Island churches associated with Wheeler. This presbyterial and diaconal structure forms an interesting contrast to Wheeler's emphatic comment that Jackson was the '*sovereign pastor*' of the Auckland church.[3] Jackson's strong and capable style of ministry tended towards the autocratic, and may have provided something of a role model for the pastoral function in the New Life Churches.

Several factors combined to make the South Island experience of the deacon's role a somewhat difficult one, as is illustrated by the experience of the Timaru assembly. The first of these was simply lack of experience. Coady commented that the 'deacons were appointed by myself... with the approval of the people. They were chosen from the people.'[4] However, because almost all of the people were converts of the recent campaigns, these deacons were, in David Jackson's words, 'pretty fresh and new and novices.... [Coady] learned quite a few things out of that.'[5] Secondly, the absence, at this stage, of appointed eldership meant that control of the spiritualities devolved on the Pastor, rather than on any collective body of spiritually qualified people. In spite of the movement's theoretical patterns of spiritual oversight (i.e. Pastor-Elder-Deacon), the structural model was really a Pastor-Deacon one. A third factor, however, rendered this structural model impracticable in the circumstances. This was the sustained absence of the Pastor on campaign work and the consequent succession of temporary Pastors. The vacuum in ongoing spiritual leadership meant that the deacons gradually assumed a *de facto* eldership function. As Lilian Wright, whose husband

Jim had been the head deacon in the Timaru assembly, put it, 'the deacons had the oversight while the pastor was away.'[6]

It is therefore not surprising that when David Jackson arrived in Timaru to become the permanent pastor in December 1961, there was an immediate conflict of authority. While the diaconate had, through the necessity of the circumstances, assumed a role of spiritual leadership in the Timaru church, the movement understood the pastoral role in centralised, autocratic, terms. A split in the Timaru Christian Fellowship Mission became inevitable, coming to a head in April 1962, when Jackson and two-thirds of the congregation left to form a new church, the Timaru Missionary Revival Centre.[7] This sad episode had the effect of removing the offices of elders and deacons from the structure of the South Island Indigenous Churches for more than ten years. When the Timaru New Life Centre finally ordained its first elders in 1974, it did so despite the grave misgivings expressed by the pastors of the other South Island churches. The ministry functions of elders and deacons are today much more a part of the South Island churches than was the case thirty years ago.

The most effective long-term measure to meet the shortage of pastors was that of the Bible School. The role of Bible teaching had always been an important one in the movement. Wheeler had opened his Tauranga Bible School in the late 1950s, and his editorial in the first issue of *Bible Deliverance* contains as much of an emphasis on teaching as on preaching and healing.[8] The Bible School was usually held over the winter months from July to September when Wheeler was not conducting campaigns, and comprised evening classes three nights a week, with two lectures each night. By 1962, the student body of the Bible School had grown to more than 80 students. These came from all around New Zealand.[9]

The growth of the student body was paralleled by a change in the way in which the Bible School was perceived. Originally it was essentially a meeting for systematic Full Gospel Bible study, but it soon became a vehicle for training workers to fill the pastoral gaps arising from the rapid growth of the movement. A comparison of the notices placed in *Bible Deliverance* announcing the 1960 and 1961 schools will demonstrate the changing perception of its role. The 1960 Winter Bible School was advertised as 'an outstanding opportunity to study the Full Gospel Truths of the Bible', and the list of subjects follows a traditional Bethel Temple curriculum.[10] The 1961 notice is far more urgent in tone. 'The Harvest is Great! The workers are few! The Lord has need of you! Plan now to attend our Full Gospel "Faith Training School" for Christians of all churches.' An explanatory note is added: '*This is not starting a new denomination!* It is an honest attempt to meet the tremendous need for trained workers to help bring in the harvest in all churches and cities, everywhere.' The course was extended to four nights weekly and topics included 'Living by Faith, Full Gospel Basic Principles, Evangelism and Demonology, Prophecy [and] Bible Exegesis' as well as the usual Bethel Temple subjects.[11]

Figure 8: Rob Wheeler's seventh Winter Bible School held in Auckland, 1966. Front row (from left): Mary Bensley, Mike Bensley, Rob Wheeler, Kevin Conner.

(Rob Wheeler, Auckland)

Rob Wheeler later claimed that as a result of this Bible School, 'Tauranga became a "seed basket" to provide the pastors for churches all over New Zealand.... We had taken two-thirds of that church [Tauranga] out and put them in the field.'[12] Not all the Bible School students, however, went into full-time ministry, nor did all the pastors come through this particular school. Allan Thrift began a short-term evening Bible School in Te Teko in July 1962, which attracted more than 50 students in its first year of operation, including a number of future pastors and missionaries.[13] Ron Coady opened a more intensive full-time three-month Bible School in Nelson in 1963, which ran for two years, and from which a number of students went out into full-time pastoral work. Later, Peter Morrow opened his New Life Family Bible College in 1971, which offered a full-time one-year course and which attracted students from overseas as well as from various churches in New Zealand.

While these Bible Schools aimed at the training and equipping of workers to fill the pastoral gaps in the rapidly growing movement, they also had three important side effects. Firstly, all of these schools were conducted by pastors who had either studied in Ray Jackson's Bible School in Australia, or who, like Pastor Allan Thrift, had worked closely with Jackson. Although Jackson had not had any direct influence on the New Zealand movement since the early 1950s, his Bethel Temple doctrines and hermeneutical methodology had been absorbed by his students. These students—by now the leaders of the New Zealand movement—in turn passed these on through their Bible Schools to the next generation of students. Thus, although there were no direct connections with Jackson, his legacy of Bible teaching continued to influence the emerging Indigenous Churches.

Figure 9: Summer Training Camp, Nelson, *circa* 1968. Ron Coady at extreme right in front row; Keith Holt (Coady's co-pastor in Nelson in the late 1960s) second from left in back row.
(Bernie McNabb, Richmond, Nelson)

A second important side effect was that the notes from the Tauranga Bible School became the standard texts for Bible teaching in the Indigenous Churches. Ron Coady observes that, for his part,

> We still have all the Bible notes that were prepared for the night [Bible] School in Tauranga, which became the basis of teaching for later on for the Bible School in Nelson. The various students who attended the Bible School have used that teaching that was imparted to them then, which later became the foundational teaching of many of the congregations in the indigenous Full Gospel works in New Zealand.[14]

The teaching materials of the Tauranga Bible School were reproduced and replicated in other Full Gospel Bible Schools. As a result they provided a doctrinal model for the emerging movement, and consequently also acted as a source of identity. They also became a focus for opposition, and the hostility that the movement was to face from some Pentecostal churches after 1961 was directly stimulated by issues of doctrine. Indeed, the reemergence of controversy over 'the Name' in 1961 (paradoxically at a time when this doctrine was less emphasised in the movement) may owe something to the perceived effectiveness of Wheeler's Tauranga Bible School. The opposition that he encountered after 1961 was specifically directed at his teaching, rather than at his evangelism.

A third, although unintended, benefit of the Bible Schools was the creation of a network of fellowship among the students, which continued after these students had moved to other centres to pastor churches. The links between the graduating students strengthened the informal pastoral bonds that comprised the cohesive factor in the early movement. Thus the original links of fellowship between Wheeler and his Full Gospel colleagues were extended and reinforced by the students of the movement's Bible Schools, and formed connections upon which the movement was to build. As will be seen, the opposition that it faced from other Pentecostal groups also helped to strengthen these doctrinal boundaries of identity.

Notes

1. Christian Fellowship Mission, Timaru, Minutes of Annual General Meeting, 9 December 1961. (Handwritten.)
2. Coady, Interview.
3. Wheeler, Interview. Emphasis as cited.
4. Coady, Interview.
5. Jackson, Interview.
6. Lilian Wright, Interview.
7. Later to be renamed the Timaru New Life Centre.
8. 'Editorial', *Bible Deliverance*, April 1959, 2.
9. 'Editorial', *Bible Deliverance*, June 1962, 2.
10. 'Notice: Winter Bible School', *Bible Deliverance*, March 1960, 15.
11. 'Notice: Winter Bible School', *Bible Deliverance*, April 1961, 16. Emphasis as cited.
12. Wheeler, Interview.
13. 'Te Teko Fellowship', 6 and 13. A summary of the results of the 1962 School is given at 22: 'Out in Full-time Ministry in N.Z., 6 couples and families. Part-time Ministry in N.Z., 1 couple. In Mission Work overseas, 1 couple and family (in Cook Island [sic]).... As Elders in Various Assemblies, 4 men and 2 of their wives. Deacons in Various Assemblies, 10 men and 2 of their wives. Youth Leader, 1 man. So of these 53 students, 35 are holding places of responsibility that they have been trained for, both at home and abroad.'
14. Coady, Interview.

Chapter 12

Parting of the Ways

Although the new movement was expanding rapidly by 1961, its collective boundaries were still diffuse, since it saw itself as being a stream of revival, rather than an association of churches. Two events took place in April of that year that did much to modify and relocate the collective boundaries of the movement and to give it an associative identity.[1] The first of these was the disastrous Wellington United Full Gospel Convention, which led to the alienation of participants in the United Full Gospel Fellowship. The second was the confrontation between Wheeler and several Christchurch Pentecostal pastors following his combined Christchurch campaign in mid-April. The two events represented a turning point for the movement. Indeed, it is only from this point on that it can be differentiated as a separate group, distinct from other Pentecostal bodies, and eventually becoming identified by the title of the 'Indigenous Churches.'

In early April 1961, the United Full Gospel Fellowship held an Easter Convention at Pastor Vin Brown's National Revival Crusade church in Vivian Street, Wellington. More than 500 people attended the Convention from both the North and the South Islands.[2] The main speaker was Dr Everett Johnson from Sacramento, California, who had begun his New Zealand campaign in Pastor Ray Necklen's church in Pukekohe on 15 January 1961. Johnson was described as 'different entirely from what we have been used to' and as a 'prophet of joy and liberty.'[3] His methods and preaching style were radical, with his main concern being to get people liberated in the praises of God, whereby they lost their inhibitions in the worship of God. To this end, he employed loud, enthusiastic, jazzy music and singing and banged his enormous tambourine 'in an effort to get a response from the congregation.'[4] Johnson was known as 'the Rock and Roll preacher'—a title he took some pride in—and was totally uncompromising in his methods. Two of his favourite sayings were 'Get in, get out, or get run over!' and 'Something is going to change around here, and it won't be me!'[5] This loud demonstrative praise was presented as Scriptural,[6] and as being the means by which the ministry of the Holy Spirit was released in the members of the congregation.

Johnson proved to be too much for some sections of the audience at the Easter Convention, and, according to an article in the *New Zealand Truth*, 'caused no little embarrassment with his methods.'[7] The article quotes Pastor Vin Brown, the convenor of the Convention, as saying that 'it was all very distressing. We engaged him on the recommendation of one of our ministers. We want to forget the whole thing as soon as possible. Some things that were said, we couldn't agree with at all.'[8] However, a letter from 'One of the Ministers' to the Editor took issue with the Convenor's statement.[9] This letter said that 'these statements were not the feelings of the United Full Gospel Fellowship, but only of about half of the ministers and of only about 20 per cent of the people.'[10]

It is therefore evident that a difference of opinion had arisen. In particular, conflict had developed between the desire of many in the congregation to continue in free worship in the Spirit and the convenor's insistence on adherence to the Convention programme. Johnson and his followers castigated this as an 'attempt to control the people and restore them to the programme order.' As they saw it, 'it was God, not the people, who deliberately ignored and over-ruled the programme of men to institute this new visitation and experience in the hearts of His children.'[11] A parting of the ways between the flesh and the Spirit was therefore inevitable.

Although no reports of the Convention appear in *Bible Deliverance*,[12] names of some of Wheeler's associates that had been prominent in earlier periodicals and articles are, from this time on, noticeably absent. It would appear that the divergence of opinion had generally followed time lines. The younger, more recently established Full Gospel churches appear to have accepted this message and the older, longer-established and more staid National Revival Crusade churches had rejected it. Johnson's ministry appears to have had something of the same effect at congregational level also. Mary Henderson, in describing the reactions to his activities, commented that 'for some, this latest move was unacceptable and a number of people left the church.'[13]

This teaching of uninhibited praise and liberty had some indirect effects on the development of the Indigenous Churches. Coady's campaigns, in particular, reflected the lack of concern for public opinion that had characterised Johnson's ministry. Some aspects of the music and songs of the later movement, such as the exuberant type of worship known as 'warfare praise', may also have had their origins here. A negative indirect effect was that the Full Gospel Churches became less concerned with what people outside the movement thought of them, with the result that tact in dealing with others was equated with compromise. This could, and did, lead to derogatory comments concerning other churches, although it must be remembered that the traffic in this was two-way. Worley became alarmed at what was happening, and published a disclaimer in the May 1961 issue of *Bible Deliverance* that said, in part, that

> Brother Worley is most anxious to work in harmony with established Full Gospel assemblies throughout the country and, in a note received from him as the magazine goes to press, he wished to make it known through *Bible Deliverance* pages, that he and his party were not in agreement with the methods and ministry of those who consistently condemn the established Denominations and their Pastors.... The result [is] ... a lost influence for the Full Gospel testimony.[14]

Nevertheless, this attitude also had some positive effects. The new 'liberty' helped to reinforce an increased aggressiveness in evangelism that, in turn, led to further expansion of the movement. Moreover, the lack of concern for public opinion was perhaps not a bad thing, given the opposition that the Full Gospel Churches faced.

The opposition faced by the movement was not simply a product of Full Gospel aggressiveness. Wheeler had also faced restriction and opposition from the very beginning of his evangelistic ministry, sometimes from the selfsame cooperating churches for whom he conducted campaigns. After his early successes on the East Coast, invitations had slowly begun to come from other Pentecostal churches, one of the first being from Pastor Vin Brown of the Wellington National Revival Crusade. As Wheeler put it, then 'the *AOG* [Assemblies of God] opened a few doors—very carefully. Then the Apostolic—very carefully.... The [Apostolic and *AOG*] pastors had us under observation.'[15] This hesitancy appears to be a result of the continuing identification, at least in the minds of these pastors, of Bethel Temple teaching with that of the 'Jesus Only' groups. The Latter Rain practice of laying on of hands for the Baptism of the Spirit was also a point of disagreement. Wheeler consequently felt it necessary to be cautious in his preaching and presentation. He commented that these doors were opening to him 'purely from an evangelistic point of view.... I wasn't touching Water Baptism.... I wasn't even touching the Baptism in the Spirit, because it was such a "dicey" subject. Salvation and Divine Healing were *it*! ... I was working with the existing [Pentecostal] churches, with the line getting more narrow all the time.'[16]

For Wheeler, the breaking point came with a tent crusade in Christchurch in April 1961, sponsored by the Apostolic, Assemblies of God and Elim churches. Wheeler recalls that this was an 'incredible crusade' in which approximately 100 conversions were recorded and about 50 people baptised in the Holy Spirit. Nevertheless, he was confronted after the last meeting by the pastor chairing the campaign, who, while acknowledging that it had been a great crusade, charged that Wheeler's Bible School appeared to teach 'Jesus only' doctrine. According to Wheeler, the pastor's words were that 'I have vowed to stamp these people out if it takes the last breath in my body!'[17] Furthermore, if this was what Wheeler taught, then he would be stamped out in the same way. Thus, despite the success of the campaign and the benefits to the cooperating churches, the result was that, in Wheeler's words, 'we left on that kind of disinterested [*sic*] note.'[18]

The results of this divergence of the ways were to prove traumatic for Wheeler. Because of this Pentecostal opposition, he was unable to attend the Universal Evangelists' Seminar sponsored by Oral Roberts in Tulsa, Oklahoma in 1961. Although Wheeler had been nominated as one of the New Zealand delegates, the Assemblies of God in both Australia and New Zealand threatened to withdraw support from the Oral Roberts organisation if he went. Invitations from Pentecostal churches to conduct campaigns became more infrequent, and Wheeler was later to adopt the more aggressive approach of Coady.

At this point, it should be noted that, despite the official rejection of the Full Gospel movement by the Pentecostal churches, some pastors kept a good attitude and maintained links with it. Frank Houston, later to become General Superintendent of the Assemblies of God, was one such pastor. He was a frequent visitor in the 1960s to the Timaru Missionary Revival Centre, where he had family connections with some of its congregation. Houston had a gentleman's agreement with its Pastor David Jackson that as long as the Missionary Revival Centre remained in Timaru, then the Assemblies of God would not attempt to open a work there.[19] Houston's openness eventually fostered revival in the Assemblies of God, and this followed him on his emigration to Australia.

The collapse of links of fellowship after the disastrous 1961 Easter Convention, and Wheeler's rejection by the Christchurch Pentecostal ministers in April 1961,[20] forced the Full Gospel Churches to adopt a separatist identity. Chas. Bilby[21] made the observation to Wheeler that 'you have one of two options: you will drop right out, or, [the Pentecostal churches] have forced you to establish your own "stream."' Wheeler recalls that his response to this was '"Right!"... So from then on... there [were] no holds barred.'[22] He began to adopt some of the more aggressive evangelistic methods of Coady, and to campaign in opposition to the existing Pentecostal churches. Up to this time, the growth of the movement had been stronger in the South Island, but this more combative approach now sparked an increased momentum in the North Island also.

Opposition from Pentecostal and mainstream churches therefore had some significant effects on the development of the Full Gospel Churches in the early 1960s. It fostered their sectarian ethos and reinforced a sense of alienation from other churches and from the world. In so doing, it helped to create and to define the movement's boundaries, and contributed to its growth.[23] The catalytic role of persecution in this process of change is acknowledged by participants in the movement. Wheeler, for example, links the spontaneous combustion that characterised this period of growth with the movement's rejection by other Pentecostal churches.[24] A comparison of the Full Gospel Churches in the North and the South Islands will demonstrate the nexus between a trenchant response to opposition and a clear-cut sectarian identity. Opposition appears to have been stronger in the South, and the churches established there as a result of Coady's campaigns were sometimes labelled 'Coadyites.' There do not appear to be any corresponding allusions to 'Wheelerites' in the North Island.

In part, this is because the origins of these churches were more diversified than was the case in the South. However, it also appears to reflect the vigorous response of the South Island wing of the movement to the opposition that it faced.

The effect of this response was to create sectarian boundaries in what was originally a somewhat ill-defined undenominational movement. The opposition which many local assemblies faced seems to have produced a strong sectarian identity, combined with an antipathy towards other churches. A good example of this process was the Western Districts Christian Mission in Tuatapere (now relocated at Orepuki and renamed 'Orepuki Christian Centre'). This assembly was founded as a result of Coady's campaign there in May 1962 and met with strenuous opposition from its inception. While some of this opposition may be due to the conservatism of rural Southland, Coady's report emphasises its religious basis: 'Opposition was flowing.... Clergy began visiting homes, where they had never been known to go before, warning the people. Tape recordings were taken into homes, and still are, denouncing the Baptism of the Holy Ghost as demonism. People were warned not to come as this was of the devil.'[25] The Tuatapere church continued to experience considerable persecution and harassment throughout its early history.[26] As a result, it became notable in the movement for being the wildest and most inflammatory of the Full Gospel Churches, with a high level of polemic against other churches and against the wider society. The Tuatapere church therefore epitomised the link between persecution (whether actual or perceived), and sectarian attitudes to the wider society.

The events of April 1961 led to a parting of the ways between the Full Gospel evangelists and their congregations on the one hand, and older, more denominational Pentecostal groups on the other. This created a sense of 'us and them', and in so doing, strengthened the identity of the emerging Indigenous Churches. The perception of opposition, whether justified or not, created new boundaries for the movement and reinforced the aggressive attitudes generated by Everett Johnson's ministry. Thus, although few in the New Life Churches today would care to acknowledge the connections, the 1961 United Full Gospel Fellowship Convention was a crucial one for the development of the movement's identity. It also accelerated its aggressive expansion over the next three years.

Notes

1. An interesting article, examining the way in which collective boundaries are modified and relocated, is Adam Seligman, 'Collective Boundaries and Social Reconstruction in Seventeenth-Century New England', *Journal of Religious History* 16 (1991): 260–79. I am grateful to Rev. Dr Peter Matheson for this reference.
2. 'Communities represented were Devonport, Tauranga, Pukekohe, Hamilton, Wanganui, Timaru, Thames, Te Awamutu, Wellington, Christchurch, Masterton,

Ruatoria, Howick, New Plymouth, Palmerston North and possibly others.' 'Hundreds from 15 Communities to Wellington', *'Harvestime' [sic]*, May 1961, 3. The majority of these communities represented National Revival Crusade churches, but there was also a significant representation of the new churches established as a result of the recent Full Gospel campaigns.
3. United Full Gospel Fellowships, 'Newsletter', Wellington, February 1961, 2. (Mimeographed.)
4. Henderson, *From Glory to Glory*, 13.
5. Personal knowledge.
6. Johnson's teaching was anchored by references such as Ps.47:1 'O clap your hands, all you people, shout unto God with the voice of triumph'; Ps.98:4 'Make a joyful noise, all the earth; make a loud noise, and rejoice, and sing praise'; and Ps.33:3 'Sing unto Him a new song; play skilfully with a loud noise.'
7. 'Dental president's challenge to hot gospeller', *New Zealand Truth*, 11 April 1961, 18.
8. ibid.
9. Although not identified in *New Zealand Truth*, this letter was from Pastor Necklen, since an apology from him later appeared in *Bible Deliverance*. 'Apology', *Bible Deliverance*, October 1961, 5.
10. 'Truth Readers Have Their Say: Hot Gospeller', *New Zealand Truth*, 2 May 1961, 29.
11. Brother Everett Johnson, 'LATTER RAIN FALLS! During Wellington Convention God Moved! Man Moved! God Won!' *'Harvestime'*, May 1961, 6.
12. The only extant report on the Convention is in the strongly partisan publication *'Harvestime.'* This was published as a single-issue magazine so 'that all may know the full truth and the facts behind the visit and ministry in New Zealand of Evangelist Everett Johnson.' Ray Necklen, 'Editorial', *idem*, 2. The report itself forms part of a highly biased and polemic lead article.
13. Henderson, *From Glory to Glory*, 13.
14. 'Newsflashes', *Bible Deliverance*, May 1961, 7. It is ironic, however, that Worley's disclaimer should appear on the same page as the preliminary reports of the Christchurch campaign that led to the confrontation between Wheeler and the pastors of the cooperating churches.
15. Wheeler, Interview.
16. ibid. Emphasis as cited.
17. Although Wheeler does not identify this pastor, this was evidently Pastor Ralph Read of the Sydenham Assemblies of God, who later published a booklet vigorously refuting the use of 'the Name' in water baptism. Read, *Water Baptism: The Formula and its meaning*.
18. Wheeler, Interview.
19. Personal knowledge.
20. Wheeler also met with a similar rejection two years later from the Australian churches for whom he conducted campaigns. This is demonstrated by a cyclostyled circular letter from the Windsor Full Gospel Church in Brisbane, Australia, over the signature of its pastor Ian Munro, and headed 'Dis-association from "Word of Faith" Bible School.' The letter takes issue with what it describes as 'controversial and unacceptable doctrines *definitely identifiable as "Latter Rain" teachings*' and asserts that these had caused '*untold havoc*' in Australian Pentecostal churches. It goes on

to identify these *'divisionary doctrines'* as Wheeler's teachings on 'Water Baptism' and the 'Definition of the Godhead' and links these with those of Ray Jackson. Evidently these doctrines refer to the invocation of 'The Name' in water baptism. The letter announced that consequently the Windsor Full Gospel Church *'now completely dissociates itself from the "Word of Faith" organisation (of which Bro. Wheeler is the principal)....'* Windsor Full Gospel Church, Circular letter, Windsor, Brisbane, Australia, 2 June 1963. (Cyclostyled.) Emphasis as cited.

21. Bilby was Secretary of the Slavic and Oriental Mission in Wellington, and a widely respected figure in the New Zealand Pentecostal movement.
22. Wheeler, Interview. Emphasis as cited.
23. Gerlach and Hine have pointed out that persecution (either real or imagined) is one of five key factors that are crucial for the lift-off of a movement. Gerlach and Hine, *People, Power, Change*, xvii.
24. Wheeler, Interview.
25. 'Revival fires continue to burn in Tuatapere', *Revival News*, October 1962, 3.
26. For example, a group of young people from Timaru (including the author) visited the Tuatapere church in January 1963 for a weekend of meetings. These young people had the interesting experience of rocks being thrown on to the roof of the pastor's house at four o'clock in the morning, accompanied by derisory shouts of 'Hallelujah.' The meeting that Sunday night was conducted by the Timaru young people, largely without the presence of the pastor, who was outside the hall dealing with four men who had come to beat him up. Since the pastor (Alister Lowe) was strongly built, had recently been in the Territorials, and was skilled in unarmed combat, these four men did not get things all their own way!

Chapter 13

The Glory Years: 1960 to 1965

The Timaru and Gore campaigns were only the beginnings of the movement's rapid growth, which was to continue until at least 1965. At the beginning of 1962, Coady moved from Timaru to Invercargill, and from there conducted a number of campaigns, mostly in the lower half of the South Island. These were not the product of a planned strategy. As he put it, 'we [simply] went where we felt the Spirit would have us go, as we waited upon the Lord and we felt God speak to us to go to a place.'[1] Often there were invitations from people who had come across the campaigns in other towns. The campaign in Tuatapere, for example, came about 'because one family had attended the meetings in Invercargill and Gore... [and had asked] "will you come to our town?"'[2] The result was that over 70 people came to Christ in these meetings out of a total population of 110 people in the town. Alister Lowe, who was the songleader for the campaign, remained behind to pastor the work, which, in spite of considerable opposition—or possibly because of it[3]—grew into an enthusiastic and vibrant church.

Other campaigns were held in Dunedin and Mosgiel—these for the Assemblies of God—and in Stewart Island, Ashburton, Christchurch, Nelson and other centres. Coady later summarised the results of the first two years of campaigns in the South Island:

> It is now a little more than two years since we came to labour for the Lord here in the South Island [in June 1960] and so much has happened in that time. We have seen indigenous full gospel works established in Timaru, Waimate, Gore, Invercargill and now Tuatapere.... Since February of this year [1962] fifteen campaigns have been held as far north as Nelson to as far south as Stewart Island. All five cities [i.e. Invercargill, Dunedin, Timaru, Christchurch and Nelson] have seen campaigns and just on six hundred decisions for Christ have been recorded. Signs and wonders and miracles have attended the preaching of the Word of God. Lives have been transformed, broken bodies healed and many filled with the Spirit....
>
> Since March of this year [1962] we have made Invercargill our working base, but now we are moving on and making Nelson our centre to work

from, this being a strategic point between the two islands. There is much land to be possessed for the Lord.[4]

The momentum of Coady's campaigns continued from Nelson. A large One Thousand Souls For Christ Crusade was held in the Nelson Cotton Mill at the end of 1962, and 170 decisions for Christ were recorded.[5] This was followed by campaigns in Motueka, Takaka, Blenheim and Kaikoura, and return visits to Tuatapere, Stewart Island, Invercargill, Gore, Dunedin, Timaru and Christchurch. Besides this itinerant evangelism, Coady also pastored the Nelson assembly, by now numbering several hundred people, produced a monthly magazine (*Revival News*) and conducted two three-month full-time Bible Schools! Coady's energy reflected a sense of optimism and opportunity, and was perhaps typical of the movement as a whole, especially in the South Island. As a result, there were 13 Indigenous churches in the South Island—as well as on Stewart Island and the Chatham Islands—by September 1964, all of them founded within the previous four years.[6]

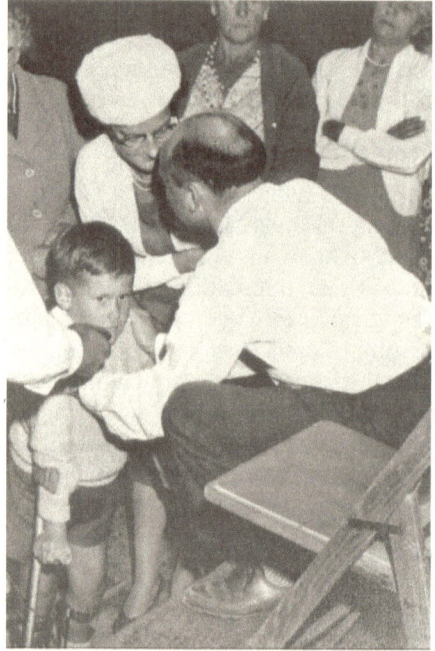

Figure 10: Ron Coady praying for the sick during his Cotton Mill Crusade in Nelson, 1963. Picture taken from cover of *Revival News*, March 1963.
(A.R. Coady, Davis, California., U.S.A.)

As new assemblies were established, many of them also became involved in the ongoing work of evangelism. An example of this was Coady's Ashburton campaign, held in mid-1962. *Revival News* reported that

> The people of the Missionary Revival Centre, Timaru, which is pastored by Brother David Jackson, sponsored the Ashburton campaign and long before the campaign was due to commence spent much time in visiting every home [in Ashburton] with literature, shops with posters and covered the campaign with prayer and fasting.
>
> The opening night saw a bus load of folk from Timaru in the meeting. Young people came each night to assist with the musical side of the services.... [After the campaign] Brother Jackson has commenced follow-up meetings and we ask the readers to remember Ashburton in prayer.[7]

A personal anecdote will convey something of the ethos of this congregational involvement. The author was part of the team from Timaru who worked to prepare the way for Coady's campaign in Ashburton. Permission was obtained from the town Council to hold open-air meetings on the grass median strip running through the centre of town. The first of these attracted some 600–700 listeners on the opposite side footpath, and members of the open-air team crossed the road to engage in face-to-face witnessing with the audience. The author was confronted by one of the local policemen, who promptly ordered him back to the other side of the road, and threatened with arrest if he ventured across the road again. An intellectually handicapped local man—unconnected with the open-air team—made matters worse for this policeman by standing in the middle of the main road traffic songleading as the open-air group sang. The policeman then hit him over the head with his flashlight, dragged him off the road and arrested him.

Teams of people from Timaru also visited Ashburton every Saturday to go from door to door offering an invitation to the forthcoming campaign. However, this bore little immediate fruit since, as *Revival News* acknowledged,

> there was much opposition in the town to the full gospel message, from both churches and business houses. Many expressed their desire to attend the meetings but were afraid to do so because of repercussions. [Consequently] crowds were not great (one night we were down to three people), but... the last night saw well over 120 people in the hall.[8]

Although no assembly resulted at the time from Coady's campaign and from the intensive work that had preceded it, the effort was not wasted. Eventually members of Peter Morrow's church in Christchurch were able to start house meetings in Ashburton, and from these small beginnings the Ashburton New Life Centre was formed.

The Kaikoura New Life Centre had a similar history. An Elim pastor, Murray Jenkins, arranged for a Holiday and Healing Festival in Kaikoura over the 1963–64 New Year holiday period. A number of young people from Timaru, including a singing group known as 'The Firebrands', assisted Coady in the campaign, which resulted in 33 decisions for Christ.[9] Jenkins continued to hold meetings in Kaikoura until he and his wife went to India as missionaries at the end of 1964 after attending Coady's Nelson Bible School.

After a short and largely unproductive pastorate by one of Jenkins' fellow students from the Bible School, the assembly went into recess for several years. It was revived later in the 1960s by workers from the Christchurch New Life Centre, and by the 1970s had grown to a congregation of more than 150 people. Two observations came be made from the experience of the Ashburton and Kaikoura churches. Firstly, an assembly was not always formed immediately after a campaign, and a number of attempts were sometimes necessary before the foundations of a permanent Indigenous Church were successfully laid. Secondly, the success of a campaign often depended on having local contacts to provide a focal point for converts of the campaign and to facilitate the founding of a local assembly.

Figure 11: Rob Wheeler's tent campaign in Auckland, January 1962. Picture taken from cover of *Bible Deliverance*, February 1962.
(Rob Wheeler, Auckland)

These observations are also applicable to the North Island, although the growth of the movement there was more complex than in the South.[10] Despite his perceived rejection by the Pentecostal churches in Christchurch, Wheeler had continued to conduct crusades wherever invitations were extended. While some of his campaigns were conducted with the cooperation of the existing Pentecostal churches, others were held in the face of opposition. Nevertheless, the movement continued to grow despite this opposition and Wheeler became more somewhat aggressive in his approach. As he was later to put it, 'we were very uncooperative when opposed.... There were no holds barred!'[11] The pace of the summer tent campaigns became more intensive: 'From town after town...we would go all summer....We would go for two or three weeks; we would finish on a Sunday night. Beryl and I would pull the tent down on Sunday night, pack the truck... and start Monday night in the next town.'[12]

In some cases, these campaigns were held in direct opposition to the existing Pentecostal churches in the town: 'I had to get my motivations right.... I used to take extreme delight in going to a town to put the tent right on [the doorstep of] the Assemblies of God, and getting them to come out. I marvel at the grace of God in our crusades... with that kind of an attitude!'[13] Yet, despite 'that kind of an attitude' (now deplored by Wheeler), this aggressive evangelism resulted in a considerable number of churches being established in the North Island. *Bible Deliverance* claimed at the end of 1964 that 'new Assemblies, based upon New Testament lines, are coming into existence at the rate of one or two a month, all over New Zealand.'[14] Wheeler calls this period of growth 'spontaneous combustion!' and likewise asserts that 'at one stage, between Ron Coady and myself, we were opening a new church every two weeks.'[15]

Figure 12: Sandwich-board advertising for Rob Wheeler's August 1966 Wellington campaign

(Rob Wheeler, Auckland)

In many ways, 1964 marked the peak of this period of increase. By the end of that year, Wheeler had conducted campaigns in most parts of the North Island. A change in the pattern of evangelism was, however, beginning to emerge, and the emphasis began to shift from short-term evangelistic campaigns to a longer-term church planting approach. In making this transition, the evangelistic purpose still remained the same, Wheeler insisting that

> We do not intend to lessen the pace of evangelism, or slacken down on our outreaches [but] rather to intensify, consolidate, and then multiply them, but in a definite detailed way that the work will not scatter and disappear in years to come. We are not starting another denomination, but endeavouring to build again the pattern of Christian life and indigenous assembly order, according to the Book of Acts, and the Epistles.... Crusades will no longer be into a city—ten days—and out of the city on to the next. Now they will be longer, touching all aspects of the Full Gospel.... Converts will be taken care of, and where there is no existing assembly doing an aggressive job for the Gospel, we will establish one, and take care of it, until it is able to stand on its own.[16]

The Auckland campaign, held at Western Springs in late November and early December 1964 was an example of this changed pattern. 'This crusade had been quite different from others we have held in the last seven years. Different, because we have set our hand to a different task than [sic] before, that is, to actually establish a New Testament pattern Church, from the Crusade.'[17] This four-week crusade was only the first step, and weekly services continued with further suburban tent crusades throughout Auckland over the next few months.[18] The direct result of this intensive and continuing campaign was the establishing of two new assemblies in Auckland.

The five-year period from 1960 to 1965 was a period of primary growth for the emerging Indigenous Churches. These were glory years for the movement, which, despite some strong opposition, had grown tenfold—from six to more than sixty churches—in the five years to 1965. The movement had already formed its distinguishing characteristics, and was beginning to develop an independent Pentecostal identity. The nature of the movement and of its relationship to the wider society will be examined next.

Notes

1. Coady, Interview.
2. ibid.
3. Indeed, a comment to this effect was made to Coady by an elderly Tuatapere couple. 'Young man, we have been believers for 45 years, preachers have come and gone in this town, but you are the first one that has received such persecution. So we have come along as these meetings must be of God.' Reported in 'Revival fires continue to burn in Tuatapere', *Revival News*, October 1962, 3.
4. Brother and Sister Coady, '*Eben-Ezer*: The Stone of Help', *Revival News*, October 1962, 2.
5. 'Closing Scenes of the Cotton Mill Crusade: Closing Service', *Revival News*, March 1963, 5.

6. 'Churches throughout New Zealand and Australia', *Gospel Truth* 5 (September 1964), 8. This list is, however, incomplete for the North Island.
7. 'We take the Word of Life to Ashburton and Christchurch', *Revival News*, September 1962, 3.
8. ibid.
9. 'Spread the Tidings Round: Kaikoura Holiday and Healing Festival', *Revival News*, January/February 1964, 8.
10. Wheeler refers to 'multiple fathers' of the movement in the North Island. He meant by this that there were a number of people who pioneered the growth of the movement. He names Allan Thrift, Norman White and Ross Davies as examples of these. Wheeler, Interview. Wheeler himself should also be included in this list.
11. ibid.
12. ibid.
13. ibid.
14. 'Editorial: Christmas Greetings', *Bible Deliverance*, November–December 1964, 2.
15. Wheeler, Interview.
16. 'Editorial: Make the Pattern Right', *Bible Deliverance*, February 1964, 2.
17. R.B.W., 'Auckland Crusade at Western Springs', *Bible Deliverance*, November–December 1964, 6.
18. ibid., 7.

Chapter 14

The Nature of the Movement I: The Sectarian Impulse

From their earliest beginnings the Indigenous Churches—later to be renamed the 'New Life Churches'—represented a diffuse grouping of independent or nondenominational Pentecostal assemblies. They were characterised by an autonomous Latter Rain polity, and by a hermeneutic methodology inherited from their Bethel Temple predecessors. The adherents of the movement located the core of their identity, both individual and corporate, in their relationship with Christ. Their tendency to describe themselves simply as 'Christian' or 'undenominational Christian' was not, in itself, unusual. It appears to reflect a wider trend, possibly stimulated by the 1959 Billy Graham Crusade, towards noninstitutional forms of Evangelicalism. This shift of emphasis is demonstrated by the increase in the census figures for 'Christian' in the 1960s and 1970s.[1] As Bill Hotter—an adherent of the Christchurch New Life Centre from its inception—put it: 'it was difficult to say exactly *what* we were back then. We were simply "Christians"—not "Pentecostals" or "New Life Centre" people—we did not have any identifying "tag."'[2]

This lack of corporate focus had some negative effects for the movement. The loyalty of its members was directed towards a style of belief, rather than towards a denomination or group of churches. Consequently, there was initially little sense of corporate belonging beyond that of the local assemblies, which were in effect simply gravitational accretions of like-minded believers. An example of this diffuse sense of identity is the way in which an association developed between the early Full Gospel campaigners and the National Revival Crusade. Although Wheeler later stated quite emphatically that this latter group was '*not* our move',[3] this appears to be a judgement in retrospect. Nothing in *Bible Deliverance* suggests that any differentiation was made *at the time* between the National Revival Crusade and Wheeler and his Full Gospel colleagues. Rather, both groups were viewed as simply fellowships of people who loved the Lord, and the niceties of where a person belonged were relatively unimportant.

This lack of focus also had some advantages for the movement. It enabled it to capitalise on the informal ecumenism that had resulted from the Billy Graham Crusade and facilitated an appeal to those disenchanted with traditional institutional Christianity. The ease with which a person could join the movement and the comparative absence of formal membership qualifications made it attractive to those seeking a simpler, less institutional form of Christianity. (This is not to say that the movement did not have criteria for membership. Participation depended upon persons being born-again Christians—that is, having received Christ as their personal Saviour, and on their experience of the Baptism of the Holy Spirit. These factors did not function as formal criteria, the fulfilling of which admitted a person to membership in a local church, but as informal, but essential, qualifications that linked a person to Christ.) Because membership of an Indigenous Church tended to include only those currently attending its services and actively involved in its ongoing life, formal regulators of membership such as church rolls were unnecessary. The intrinsic weakness of the movement's diffuse and informal corporate linkages was counterbalanced by a strong sectarian sense of difference from the world, which created a collective boundary and hence a sense of identity.

This informality of belonging also was characteristic, although possibly to a lesser extent, of Pentecostalism as a whole. This facilitated the movement of people between Pentecostal churches, and across the boundary between Pentecostal and mainstream churches. Despite the diffuseness of its identity, the Pentecostal movement was nevertheless strongly sectarian, and a pronounced sense of difference from the world provided a significant boundary for groups within its sphere of influence. To categorise the movement as sectarian is not necessarily to make a value judgement, but simply to recognise its sociological character and its relationship to its social context. Nevertheless, it generally has been acutely conscious of its sectarian status, and has tended to view the designation as a pejorative epithet. Colin Brown gives an example of this: 'At an Extension Studies' seminar at Victoria University in July 1976 a spokesman for classical Pentecostalism took strong exception to the designation "sect" as applied to Pentecostalist churches and it was quite clear that it was the pejorative associations of the term which troubled him.'[4] Brown interprets this reaction as due to the increasing respectability of the Pentecostal movement. However, it may also be a product of their reluctance to be included in the same category as, for example, Mormons and Jehovah's Witnesses, who would generally be regarded by Pentecostal churches as nonChristian.

What does it mean to be sectarian? Sociologist Michael Hill refers to Max Weber's classic analysis of sectarianism, which included 'the twin features of exclusiveness and elitism...,[as well as] the sectarian emphasis on the recruitment of committed adults... and the tendency... to separate from their surrounding society.'[5] Other analyses include those of Ernst Troeltsch, who built upon Weber's observation that all movements emerge as sects, and with the passage of time and the process of growth, become more denominational and churchlike. Another is that of Bryan Wilson, who categorises Pentecostalism as a conversionist sect, in which evangelism is central and which bases its beliefs on a literal interpretation of the Bible.[6] Wilson observes that while this type of sect is the one most likely to evolve into a denomination, it is nevertheless 'distrustful of, or indifferent towards, the denominations and churches which at best have diluted, and at worst betrayed, Christianity; it is hostile to clerical learning and especially to modernism; it is opposed to modern science, particularly to geology and to evolutionary theories; [and] it disdains the artistic values accepted in the wider society.'[7]

Although movements cannot always be pigeonholed tidily into convenient well-defined categories, it is nevertheless true that the Indigenous Churches had a strongly conversionist sectarian ethos. Evangelism was, largely, their *raison d'être*, and this enabled them to appeal to a broad religious constituency. However, in defining themselves as born-again Christians, in contrast to denominational Christians, adherents of the movement tended to denigrate other forms of religious belief and experience that did not coincide with their own. The corollary of their individualistic emphasis on a personal commitment to Christ was often nonacceptance of other ways of approach to God.[8]

What were the sectarian characteristics of these churches? Two elements of Wilson's analysis are particularly relevant to a study of the early movement and its sectarian ethos. These are its attitudes to the values of the wider society, and its attitudes to other churches.[9] Adherents of the Indigenous Churches rejected the values of the world, believing that the Christian life offered greater fulfilment. Several examples of this attitude can be found in the *Gospel Truth*, a short-lived periodical published by the Timaru Missionary Revival Centre from July 1964 to April 1965. The first issue is devoted to teenagers, and the front-page article, headed 'Teenagers find answers', includes statements such as:

> Being a Christian is the most satisfying life anyone can imagine. The worldly life looks so exciting, but is like biting into a luscious-looking apple, only to find it has no flavour and is rotten at the core.
>
> The Christian life is the reverse; to some it looks stodgy and uninteresting on the outside, but when you enter in, you never want another thing, except more of the Christian life. It is the answer to the quest for adventure, which is in every young person. Being a Christian is thrilling; there is no end to the newness.[10]

The magazine includes a number of testimonies from some of the young people of the church. These are headed by titles such as 'I Was a Teddy Girl', 'Former Jockey Now Bible Student', 'Dancing Was My Life', and 'I wanted a Kick out of Life.' The common motif of these articles is that each of these young people was 'trying to satisfy a longing in my soul', and only found real happiness when they became a born-again Christian. One teenage girl who had 'trained [as a Highland dancer] for eight years and during that time won nearly 100 prizes, including medals and cups' now said that

> As a young person I can testify that the Lord takes all worldly desires away because he puts something more lasting in its place. I kept up my dancing for some time but I knew I had lost all interest in it. When I went to dances I just didn't enjoy them any more, and when the excitement was over I was left with nothing. I am only interested now in serving the Lord.[11]

This rejection of worldly activities was a corollary of one's experience with Christ, which, in theory, satisfied a person so completely that there was neither need nor desire for the things of the world. Instead, the person's desire was now set on serving the Lord. The satisfaction of finding and fulfilling God's purpose for their lives provided a powerful, and genuine, motivation for these young people to reject the enticements of the world. The Timaru Missionary Revival Centre was typical of other churches in the movement in that this motivation was reinforced by a strong emphasis on, and preparation and training for, going to the mission field. (It should be noted that since not all these young people were able to go to the mission field, the result of this narrow, highly idealistic emphasis was eventually frustration and disillusionment in many cases. The establishment of Youth with a Mission [*YWAM*] later provided an outlet for some of this youthful idealism. This international, interdenominational, organisation encouraged young people into short-term service on mission fields around the world. Since it did not require lengthy periods of preparation, nor insist on long-term mission service, *YWAM* became popular as an easily accessible avenue for Christian young people to serve overseas.)

A further example of the way in which the Indigenous Churches rejected societal values may be seen in their hostile attitude towards higher education. To some extent, this antipathy was a legacy of the anti-intellectualism that characterised most Pentecostal groups, reflecting the comparatively meagre educational level of many of their adherents.[12] However, there was also an element of fear that Pentecostal young people who went to university would lose their faith, and possibly also their moral integrity, through their exposure to the university milieu. The opposition to education was therefore based on a pastoral concern, and functioned as a mechanism of sectarian social control. Accordingly, university study was discouraged, usually by means of unspoken attitude, but occasionally by direct dissuasion.

However, there was also an issue of principle behind this rejection of education. The Bible was the only source of authority; what more did the Christian need? Since Christ was the answer to all one's longings, it was impossible to admit that any source of fulfilment existed outside one's own Christian faith. While the Indigenous Churches were not the only Pentecostal group to hold this view, they were, however, less restrictive than, for example, Ray Jackson's Associated Mission Churches of Australia.[13] This strong antipathy towards education was rather more pronounced in these Australian churches than was the case in their New Zealand counterparts. Nevertheless, it did reflect a traditional Pentecostal anti-intellectualism that had some parallels in the Indigenous Churches.

A personal anecdote will illustrate the attitude of this Australian group towards education. During a visit to Singapore in April 1972, the author unexpectedly met up with a friend who was a former fellow member of the Timaru Missionary Revival Centre. This young man had been involved with Ray Jackson's Melbourne Bible School since 1965, and consequently was well-imbued with its distinctive Bethel Temple teachings. He had been sent out as a missionary to Indonesia in early 1971, and happened to be visiting Singapore at the same time as the author. He was scheduled to preach that Sunday morning in the Chinese Assembly of God church where we had met. A number of young people in this church had won scholarships for university study in America, and were preparing to travel overseas to further their education. In conversation before the service, my friend expressed alarm at this emphasis on university education. He saw this as representing a danger to these young people, and declared vehemently 'I'm going to put a stop to this!' His sermon that morning was based on Daniel 1:8-14, and drew a parallel with the four Hebrews who refused the food from the Babylonian king's table—which he likened to worldly university education. He insisted that 'God has meat [i.e. "revelation"] for you that the world never dreams of!' His point was that these young people should likewise refuse the meat from the king's table of university education and be fed by the revelation knowledge of God's Word. He was, however, unsuccessful in his attempt to dissuade these young people from pursuing their university education.

This example, although somewhat extreme, does demonstrate the thinking behind the opposition to university study from Pentecostalism generally and the Indigenous Churches in particular. It represented a sectarian rejection of worldly values and a belief that all that the Christian needed was to be found in the revelation knowledge of God's Word. University study and participation in worldly pursuits were therefore discouraged. These sectarian attitudes began to change in the later 1960s, partly as a result of the changing sociological mix of the movement, and partly through the influence of the Charismatic Renewal. These changing attitudes also moderated the strong antipathy of the Indigenous Churches towards other churches.

Notes

1. The census figures for 'Christian (No Other Designation)' from 1956 to 1981 are: 1956: 7,662; 1961: 12,130; 1966: 21,548; 1971: 33,187; 1976: 52,478; and 1981: 101,901. Cited in Michael Hill, 'The Decline of Church-Based Religiosity and the Rise of Sectarianism', in *Religion in New Zealand Society*, 2nd ed., edited by Brian Colless and Peter Donovan (Palmerston North: Dunmore Press, 1985), 142.
2. Bill Hotter, Comment to author, Christchurch, December 1989. Emphasis as cited. The title 'New Life Centre' in any case would be an anachronism, as the name was not used by the Christchurch assembly until the 1970s.
3. Rob Wheeler, Comment to author re Dissertation, Auckland, 1989. Emphasis as cited. This comment was a response to the author's mistaken identification of the

Full Gospel churches with the National Revival Crusade. Knowles, 'For the Sake of the Name', 25ff. Wheeler disagreed strongly with this analysis.
4. Colin Brown, 'How Significant is the Charismatic Movement?' in *Religion in New Zealand Society*, 2nd ed., edited by Brian Colless and Peter Donovan (Palmerston North: Dunmore Press, 1985), 104.
5. Michael Hill, 'The Decline of Church-Based Religiosity', 120. Hill's article gives a useful summary of the historical development of various sociological theories of sectarianism. ibid., 119–24. See also *idem*, 'Religion', in *New Zealand: Sociological Perspectives*, ed. Paul Spoonley, David Pearson and Ian Shirley (Palmerston North: Dunmore Press, 1982), 185.
6. Bryan Wilson, ed., *Patterns of Sectarianism: Organization and Ideology in Social and Religious Movements* (London: Heinemann, 1967), 26. Wilson analyses the patterns of sectarianism and distinguishes four separate classes of sect. His analysis is summarised in Hill, 'The Decline of Church-Based Religiosity', 121ff.
7. Wilson, *Patterns of Sectarianism*, 27.
8. A favourite text for preaching was 1 John 5:12 (*KJV*): 'He that hath the Son hath life; and he that hath not the Son of God hath not life.' No other form of religious experience was valid except that of 'asking Jesus into your heart to be your personal saviour.' It was in this sense that one received Christ, and so received 'power to become... sons of God' (John 1:12 *KJV*).
9. Attitudes to other churches will be discussed in the next chapter.
10. 'Teenagers find answers', *Gospel Truth*, July 1964, 1.
11. 'Dancing was My Life', ibid., 3.
12. An extreme example of anti-intellectualism in the early American Pentecostal movement is cited in Nichol, *The Pentecostals*, 77. Nichol cautions that this 'represents the thinking of a radical group within Pentecostalism; however, the sentiment expressed does reflect the anti-intellectualism of many of the early Pentecostals.' Although some remnants of this attitude still exist in Pentecostalism today, the antipathy towards education is now much less pronounced, and Pentecostals may be found doing graduate and postgraduate courses in most educational institutions.
13. There were some personal and doctrinal, although not organisational, connections between these Australian churches and the Indigenous Churches. However, these churches were much more separatist and isolationist in ethos and emphasis than were their New Zealand counterparts. See Chant, *Heart of Fire*, chapter 14, for an account of this group.

Chapter 15

The Nature of the Movement II: The Antiecumenical Impulse

One of the most conspicuous features of the early movement's sectarian ethos was its strongly antiecumenical stance. Bryan Wilson's analysis of conversionist sectarianism is clearly applicable to the Indigenous Churches. They could accurately be described as 'distrustful of, or indifferent towards, the denominations and churches which at best have diluted, and at worst betrayed, Christianity; [and]...hostile to clerical learning and especially to modernism.'[1] This distrust was a product both of their exclusivist Bethel Temple and Latter Rain roots and of the opposition they had received from other churches.

Although this mood of antipathy was quite widespread throughout the Indigenous Churches, it was not uniform in its intensity. While some sections of the movement were quite hostile in their opposition to the denominational churches, others were more conciliatory. Worley, for example, was concerned to make it known that 'he and his party were not in agreement with the methods and ministry of those who consistently condemn the established Denominations and their Pastors.'[2] The difference in attitude between Worley and his successors is aptly summed up in a comment, overheard by the author, from a refined, elderly lady, one of Worley's converts, in Timaru. This lady sadly remarked after hearing a sermon that included a number of derogatory allusions to the denominational churches that 'Mr Worley never used to talk like that!'[3] Wheeler also sought to be as unobjectionable as possible for the sake of his evangelistic campaigns, and Peter Morrow had a more open attitude to the mainstream churches than did many of his colleagues. Other sections of the movement, however, were much less restrained, and appeared to take delight in criticism of the established churches.

There were two main foci of this antipathy towards the denominations. The first of these centred on the perceived dead formalism of the churches. Worley told his converts in Timaru that, as a result of their encounter with the living Christ, 'you can never be satisfied again with mere forms and ceremonies and social Gospel.'[4] His comments reflected the commonly held Pentecostal view that the mainstream churches were dead and formal, and lacked the power of the Holy Spirit. While he was comparatively mild in his criticisms, others were far more scathing in their attack. This appeared to be particularly the case in those churches associated with Coady. Yet it would be unfair to place the blame for this on Coady, since he was merely the most articulate proponent of this general antipathy, rather than the creator of it. Others in the movement were equally critical of dead formalism and several examples may be cited of this. One appears in the *Gospel Truth*, the first issue of which sets out the purpose of the paper. The *Gospel Truth* sought to 'proclaim the good news of the Truth that will liberate men and women from sin, formality, dead religion, sickness and poverty, and bring them into contact with a living Christ.'[5] Another was Wheeler, who, in spite of his earlier endeavours to be conciliatory, reported in 1965 that 'In the last two years we have seen and preached a new phase of deliverance, and that is to the Christian, bound and tied in tradition, Religious formality and denominationalism.... The message is... Bible deliverance from sin, sickness, demons, fear and sectarianism.'[6] The antagonism towards dead religion was therefore a widespread one, and was reinforced by the opposition that the movement faced.

While a number of examples may be cited of this antagonism, it must be pointed out that the traffic was two-way. One such example was the visit of a young Presbyterian representative to the Timaru assembly in 1961, who observed the meeting and wrote a very derogatory and rather inaccurate report on it.[7] The response of the Timaru congregation was interesting. Coady, then its pastor, obtained a copy of the report and read it out during a meeting, and each derogatory statement about the meeting was greeted with hoots of laughter. The exception was the final statement of the report, which said, in effect, that 'by the end of the meeting, some of the young people were so "worked up" that they were speaking in tongues.' This parting shot was greeted by growls of anger from the congregation. They appeared to feel that although they could live with the derogatory comments of others, to malign the Baptism of the Spirit was to cheapen an experience that was precious to them.

The second focus of antipathy was to the Roman Catholic church and the World Council of Churches. This antiecumenical emphasis was shared by other groups such as the Westminster Fellowship of the Presbyterian Church of New Zealand and the Bible Truth Society, whose articles were sometimes reprinted in the movement's periodicals.[8] G.L. Hart, the founder of the Bible Truth Society, appears to have been a Fundamentalist rather than a Pentecostalist, and was a prolific producer of antiecumenical articles and pamphlets in the early 1960s. However, it is significant that one of his most vehement articles appeared in *Bible Deliverance* alongside a report on the August 1964 Massey Conference. This Conference helped to lay the foundations of the Charismatic movement in New Zealand and produced a degree of informal ecumenism among the participants, including Pentecostalists. The report stated that 'For the first time in the History of New

Zealand, we saw Christians and ministers from the BAPTIST-ANGLICAN-PRESBYTERIAN-BRETHREN-S.A. [Salvation Army], of whom many had received the baptism of the Holy Ghost, also many from the PENTECOSTAL churches all gathered together to worship the Lord under one roof.'[9] The antidenominationalism of the Indigenous Churches became less pronounced as the Charismatic movement gathered momentum, and as links of fellowship began to be forged between Pentecostalists and mainstream church participants in the Charismatic Renewal.

This antiecumenical attitude is demonstrated in a number of articles in the movement's publications, of which Kevin Conner's series entitled 'Who is the Harlot Church?'[10] provides a good example. Conner began by asking a rhetorical question: 'Who is the Harlot Church, is it Protestantism, Modernism, Roman Catholicism or is it the World Council of Churches?'[11] He then went on to insist that 'if you know the truth about the Church of the Lord Jesus Christ, it should set you free from denominationalism, if you know the truth about the Body of Jesus Christ, it should set you free from sectarianism.'[12] His articles presented a sustained call to come out from the false church that was being gathered, by means of the World Council of Churches, to the 'Babylonian' system of the Roman Catholic church. Since Conner was widely respected in the movement as a Bible teacher, his views carried much weight.

Coady's attitude to Roman Catholicism and to the World Council of Churches was more hostile. Although little anti-Catholic or antiecumenical polemic appears in the first few issues of his magazine *Revival News*, the November 1962 issue launches into a full-scale attack on the Second Vatican Council. His editorial in that issue states that

> History is in the making....
>
> As I write this, the infamous Vatican Council is sitting, scheming to make a grand compromise in order to sweep within its folds, in one great swoop, the present day modernistic Protestant denominations.
>
> Rome, the mother of harlots [Rev.17] is opening her doors to welcome back her Protestant daughters....
>
> The doctrines of justification by faith only in Christ, the free forgiveness [sic] of sins, the efficacy of the Blood of Christ as the only purging agent of sin, the Bible alone as the rule of faith in doctrines and morals have been undermined and discarded in Protestant churches by traitorous clergy who call themselves the ministers of the Lord....
>
> The call is going forth again to the people of God "COME OUT OF HER MY PEOPLE." Union with Rome will force the true people of God to COME OUT.[13]

Almost all the articles in this particular issue are polemic, directed against the Roman Catholic church and the World Council of Churches, and later issues of *Revival News* continued the attack. Evidently the Second Vatican Council, then just beginning, was viewed with extreme suspicion, and perhaps not a little fear. The Council was seen as setting the stage for the return to Rome of the Protestant churches and the emergence of the scarlet woman of Revelation 17. This was interpreted as the rise of the false church [i.e. 'Babylon'] from which the true believers must come out. In the eyes of the Indigenous

Churches, the modernism of the Protestant denominations, and their willingness to enter into dialogue with the Catholic church was proof of their identification with this 'Babylonian' system.

This strong antipathy towards the denominational churches, and towards the Roman Catholic church in particular, was especially vigorous during the early years of the movement. Gordon Copeland, for example, was a member of Coady's Gospel Lighthouse church in Nelson in the early 1960s. He recalls that he and the other young people of the church would often engage in face-to-face witness with Catholics to convince them of the error of their Roman Catholic ways. Not surprisingly, these aggressive attempts at conversion proved to be unsuccessful.[14] This antagonism was returned with interest, as is demonstrated by a report on one of Coady's Nelson campaigns. *Revival News* reported that 'the local Catholic Youth Organisation had stated that Roman Catholic Youth would be present each night to disrupt the services and true to their word this they did, night after night.'[15] It was not until the later 1960s that this attitude of hostility towards the denominational churches began to change.

The sectarian ethos of the Indigenous Churches was inherited from their Bethel Temple, Latter Rain and Pentecostalist antecedents. The movement's nondenominational polity was based on a belief that denominationalism was 'Babylon', from which they had come out. (Denominationalism was defined as any system of centralised church government or church structure whereby the affairs of a local assembly could be directed or controlled from Headquarters.) An example of this nondenominational polity was the Tauranga Christian Fellowship—effectively the movement's oldest church, since it was founded in 1939, and amalgamated with the Bethel Temple movement of Ray Jackson in 1949. This is described as 'a non-denominational church' in a clipping from a local newspaper in 1984.[16] Another example is the reference in a national magazine three years later to the Auckland Christian Fellowship, 'a non-denominational evangelical group.'[17]

The movement likewise distrusted organization as the enemy of the charismatic freedom of the Spirit. This reflected the views of the early Pentecostalists, who generally saw charismatic freedom and organisational structure as not only mutually incompatible, but also as antithetical. Frank Bartleman, the diarist of the Azusa Street revival, was one of the more vigorous proponents of this point of view. Charles Fox Parham, the originator of The Apostolic Faith movement in 1901, had a somewhat different perspective on the subject of organization, and his views should be set off against those of Bartleman.[18] However, Pentecostalism has tended to disregard Parham and his views, and Bartleman therefore is a more accurate representative of the predominant ethos of the movement.

This aversion to denominationalism was reinforced by the millennial eschatology of the Indigenous Churches. They viewed the ecumenical movement as leading to a false world superchurch, which they identified with the scarlet woman of Revelation 17, and consequently were strongly opposed to formal links with other churches. As they saw it, genuine ecumenism was a thing of the spirit, based on the fellowship in the Spirit between individual Christians, rather than on organisational alliances between denominations. Only those who were born again and filled with the Spirit could share this spiritual fellowship, and these constituted the true Church, the Bride of Christ.

As will be seen, the antiecumenical attitudes of the Indigenous Churches would be moderated by the influence of the Charismatic Renewal in the late 1960s, and by changes in the Pentecostal movement in the 1970s. However, the Latter Rain principle of autonomy remained a potent force in the movement, as is indicated by continuing references to nondenominational local churches at the end of the 1980s.[19] Nevertheless, the application of this principle was modified and a more centralised style of polity began to develop during the 1980s. There had already been some moves in this direction with the movement's first nationwide collective venture in 1965. This was Operation Gideon, which was to significantly affect the future development of the movement.

Notes

1. Wilson, *Patterns of Sectarianism*, 27.
2. 'Newsflashes', *Bible Deliverance*, May 1961, 7.
3. Ron Coady comments that this lady's remark was not entirely accurate. He observes that 'on many occasions, at the close of a service, Brother Worley would advise the people to attend churches where Christ was preached in His saving and healing power. He was fond of quoting the Scripture "Why seek ye the living among the dead" [and] ... would follow this up by commenting "you will not find the living Christ in dead churches,", referring to the traditional denominations.' Coady, Fax correspondence with the author, 12 March 1998. Nevertheless, Worley was milder in his criticisms than were other sections of the movement.
4. A.S. Worley, cited in Henderson, *From Glory to Glory*, 8.
5. 'The Gospel Truth?' *Gospel Truth*, June 1964, 1.
6. 'Outreach in Three Dimensions', *Bible Deliverance*, April 1965, 2. By Wheeler's account, he would have begun to preach this 'new phase of deliverance' in early 1963. The hardening of his attitude appears to be in response to the increasing opposition that he faced in his campaigns. See Knowles, 'For the Sake of the Name', 47–48.
7. Attempts to locate a copy of this report proved unsuccessful, despite searches in the archives of the Hewitson Library and in this church's parish records, as well as contact by letter with its former minister.
8. An example of this is G.L. Hart, 'All roads lead to Rome: Church Unity or Religious Unity', *Bible Deliverance*, October 1964, 12–13.
9. 'What happened at Massey? Most unique convention in History of N.Z.', *Bible Deliverance*, October 1964, 15. Reprinted from *Gospel Truth*, August 1964, 6. Capitalisation and punctuation as cited.
10. Kevin Conner, 'Who is the Harlot Church?' *Gospel Truth*, February–April 1965, *passim*. This series was not completed, as the periodical ceased publication with the April 1965 issue.
11. ibid., February 1965, 4.

12. ibid. This is a classic example of Latter Rain come-outism.
13. 'Coming Events Cast Their Shadows', *Revival News*, November 1962, 2. Capitalisation and emphasis as cited.
14. Gordon F. Copeland, *Faith that works* (Lower Hutt: Barnabas Christian Trust, 1988), 19–20; 'Healing and Happiness Festival', *Revival News*, September 1963, 6–7.
15. 'Healing and Happiness Festival', *Revival News*, September 1963, 6–7.
16. Reproduced in 'Tauranga Christian Fellowship: Jubilee Reunion 1939–1989', 29.
17. Jeff Hayward, 'Back to Fundamentals', *More*, December 1987, 211.
18. For a discussion of this issue, see James R. Goff, Jnr., *Fields White Unto Harvest: Charles F. Parham and the Missionary Origins of Pentecostalism*. Fayetteville: University of Arkansas Press, 1988, *passim*.
19. See above at footnotes 16 and 17.

Chapter 16

The Nature of the Movement III: The Missionary Impulse

One of the features that has characterised the movement from its inception has been a strong emphasis on missionary work. This is probably not surprising, given that its foundations had been laid by three Bethel Temple former missionaries to Indonesia. Two of the earliest missionary couples supported by these churches were Dal and Dorothy Walker, who went to Indonesia in 1949,[1] and Graham and Pam Truscott, who arrived in India at the end of 1959.[2] The early movement also strongly supported missionaries through the Slavic and Oriental Mission in Wellington, a Pentecostal missionary agency founded in 1932 by Dr Len Jones. A missionary page was a regular feature in *Bible Deliverance*, and although initially the reports in this were limited to missionary work among Maori, the scope of this expanded as the movement itself grew. By the end of 1961, *Bible Deliverance* was reporting news of missionaries currently serving in India, Indonesia and Japan, and of others about to go to Southeast Asia, the Pacific Islands and Dutch New Guinea.[3]

Missionary work was emphasised at congregational level also. David Jackson, for example, placed great importance on preparing the members of his Timaru congregation to serve God on the mission field. The name adopted for the Timaru church during his pastorate demonstrates his vision:

Some wonder why we call ourselves "Missionary Revival Centre." . . .

- *Firstly* we believe God wants us to be missionary minded, to lift up our eyes and behold the fields ripe unto harvest, to uphold the missionaries already on the front lines in prayer and with our financial support. We like to keep our platform open to any recommended, sincere and genuine missionaries.
- *Secondly*, because we believe in revival. . . .
- *Thirdly*, we pray that this will be a centre where missionaries will hear the call, prepare and go to answer the call of God.[4]

David Jackson's strong emphasis on missions permeated every aspect of the Timaru church's life. It was a matter of principle for this church that whenever it was in financial need, it would take up a missionary offering. This was an application of the Biblical promise of 'give, and it shall be given to you'—as the church gave to missionaries, its own financial needs would be met.5 Jackson's missionary vision went further than mere financial support, however. Henderson comments that

> After the walls of Jerusalem had been restored (Neh.11:1) the people voluntarily tithed 10% of themselves to dwell in the city of God. Our Pastor felt that he could not be content until we, as a church, tithed 10% of ourselves to the Mission Fields. At one stage with only 80–90 of a congregation, we were financially supporting nine workers [from the Timaru congregation] on the harvest fields.6

This strong missionary emphasis was typical of most of the Indigenous Churches. While this was a natural extension of their evangelistic ethos, some of these missionary ventures had important indirect effects for the development of the movement.

The most significant of these missionary ventures was that of Paul and Bunty Collins, who went to Thailand in July 1962 to begin missionary work there. After working in Bangkok and Chiangmai for some months, they came to the conclusion that the missionary activity of the Christian Church was not even counteracting the population growth, let alone reaching the unevangelised world. In reality, the church was losing ground, rather than increasing the proportion of Christians in the population. They became convinced that literature distribution was the key to reaching Thailand,7 and consequently set up an office in Bangkok, in conjunction with the Slavic and Oriental Mission, to produce, print and distribute Gospel literature.

Collins' strategy for literature evangelism was to conduct Newspaper and Magazine Crusades, as well as to print and supply Gospel literature for distribution. He describes these as follows: 'A newspaper crusade is an illustrated Gospel message in cartoon form. It is presented as a full-page advertisement in leading newspapers. It contains a complete message of Salvation with an inquirer's coupon at the bottom of the page so that everyone may reply.'8 One of Collins' converts in Chiangmai was Adirek, a gifted and nationally known Thai cartoonist, and he prepared the Gospel cartoons using some of the characters that he had created in secular cartoon work. The results of these ad-vangelism crusades were dramatic: 'so far, over 22,000 replies have come in altogether. One newspaper crusade alone brought in over 1,800 replies.'9 A six-lesson Bible Correspondence Course was sent to each inquirer, and follow-up was carried out in conjunction with the local Thai churches, where these existed.

Collins' work in Thailand had several important indirect effects for the movement in New Zealand. Firstly, his literature office was called the New Life Centre and the succinctness of this title appealed to many of the New Zealand churches, who adopted it as their own local assembly name. Thus the Timaru Missionary Revival Centre changed its name to 'Timaru New Life Centre', the Christchurch Revival Centre became the 'Christchurch New Life Centre', and other churches adopted similar titles. The adoption of this name was more prevalent in the South Island than in the North, which tended to use titles such as 'Auckland Christian Fellowship', 'Tauranga Christian Fellowship' rather than variations of New Life. Eventually, the Indigenous Churches of New Zealand as a movement changed their collective title to the 'New Life Churches of New Zealand' in 1988.

A second, more important, effect was that many of the movement's churches had provided financial backing for several newspaper crusades, and their success raised the idea of doing the same thing in New Zealand. The initiative for this began in the South Island, and appears to have originated with Coady, who was a particularly strong supporter of the Collins' work in Thailand.[10] Consequently a pastoral conference was convened in Timaru in late November 1964, when fourteen pastors, representing ten of the '14 free indiginous [sic] assemblies in the South Island' gathered to discuss the idea.[11] The South Island pastors agreed to undertake the project, which was, however, to be on a larger scale in that the full-page advertisement was to appear simultaneously in every newspaper in the South Island. The idea caught on in the North Island also. In early April 1965, a meeting at Johnsonville of 'some 26 pastors representing 44 of the indigenous full Gospel Assemblies in the North Island' met together to discuss the proposed evangelistic outreach.[12] Eventually a 'National meeting of the Ministers of the Indigenous Full Gospel Churches of New Zealand' was arranged for early July at Akatawara to complete arrangements for the project, by now called Operation Gideon.[13]

The first full-page cartoon advertisement in the Operation Gideon outreach appeared in the national press on 5 August 1965.[14] Over 1,000 replies were received to this advertisement, and there was considerable activity in the Letters to the Editor column of many daily newspapers.[15] Although these replies represented direct results from Operation Gideon, the indirect results were to be more significant, in the long term, for the Indigenous Churches. The pastoral gatherings convened to discuss and arrange the outreach stimulated a process of convergence and had the effect of cementing fellowship between the pastors in the movement. The Timaru Conference seems to have been particularly influential in this regard. The report on this refers to 'the desire for greater unity' and to a drawing together and uniting of the South Island pastors in love by the Holy Spirit.[16] This Conference was later held up as an exemplar of unity at the unsuccessful Melbourne Conference between the New Zealand Indigenous Churches and Ray Jackson's Mission Churches of Australia in 1973. Similarly, *Revival News* comments that at the Akatawara conference, 'History was made. Never before had Ministers from Free Indigenous Churches throughout New Zealand met on such common ground.... This Full Gospel Conference at Akatawera [sic] [was] the first of its kind ever, but not the last.'[17]

Although published reports of these and other conferences are uniformly positive, there appear to have been some difficulties in maintaining the unity of the movement up to this point. Coady mentions the resolving of 'any thought of division between the North and the South Islands in going two different directions when Rob Wheeler and other brethren from the North Island were in conference together.'[18] The inference of his passing comment is that up to this time there had been differences in approach between the North and South Island churches, and that these conferences had achieved a resolution of these. Coady later explained in correspondence with the author that

> the mounting division [between the North Island and South Island churches] was over expressions in worship. Since 1961 the churches in the South Island had adopted a more high-spirited model, i.e. joyous shouting, marching, hand-clapping, dancing[,] exuberant singing, the use of tambourines, guitars, etc.[19]
>
> The North Island churches were more low key in their forms of worship, i.e. more devotional. This was a legacy from the Latter Rain. The high-spirited forms of worship in the South Island were considered "manifestations of the flesh." So it appeared that the two groups, while continuing to love and respect each other, would go their separate ways.
>
> The division was averted after I shared with the ministerial brethren what God had revealed to me after the Annual Convention in Nelson Easter 1965, concerning "The Restoration of the Tabernacle of David."[20] (This teaching would later become a world-wide proclamation.) The ministers concluded that exuberant expressions of worship were part of God's plan in restoring the fullness of worship in spirit and in truth.[21]

Given the rapid expansion of the movement over the previous five years, it is perhaps not surprising that stresses should have arisen. Although churches in the movement had often held conventions where the local churches could meet together for fellowship, these were usually regional rather than national. Examples include the 1962 Easter Conventions at Gore[22] and Waiohau,[23] the 1963 Easter Convention at Nelson,[24] the 1964 New Year Convention at Gunns' Bush,[25] and the 1964 Easter Conventions at Murupara, Whakatane and Gore.[26] Consequently the movement tended to become regionalised, and this divide was particularly evident between the North Island and South Island churches. The Timaru and Johnsonville Pastors' Conferences, and especially the Akatawara National Conference, were significant in that they marked the first time when all the pastors of the movement had come together in a single gathering.[27] These conferences were also important in that they represented the first occasion on which all the Indigenous Churches had joined to implement a common purpose. The movement's first nationwide Combined Convocation held in Nelson at Easter 1965 also helped to cement the unity of the movement's pastors and congregations.

Operation Gideon therefore represented a step away from the movement's strong emphasis on local autonomy towards a recognition that to minister effectively, the churches had to work together and on a national basis. Some sort of teamwork was evidently necessary between the churches. With Operation Gideon the loosely linked movement of approximately 60 individual local churches began to develop into a group with a national identity. It therefore represents the first steps towards a corporate national unity and identity.

Figure 13: Some of the pastors of the movement at the Gunn's Bush Convention, Waimate, January 1964. Back row (from left): Peter Morrow (Christchurch), Kevin Conner (Australia), David Jackson (Timaru), Ron Coady (Nelson), Shaun Kearney (Wellington), Bill Salisbury (Whangarei), Alister Lowe (Tuatapere), Ray Necklen (Gore). Front row (from left): Bill Brannen, Ron Jackson, Ray Jackson (evangelists-at-large), Welburn Findlay (Invercargill).

(Timaru New Life Centre, Timaru)

To summarise: the missionary impulse of the movement had important, although indirect, effects on its future development. The conferences convened to discuss and implement Operation Gideon also helped to cement a new unity and a sense of corporate identity among the Indigenous Churches. Although the ethos of the movement remained strongly sectarian—particularly in its attitude towards other churches, a major change in orientation was under way. In part, this represented a transition from evangelical campaigns to evangelical churches. The amalgamation of Wheeler's *Bible Deliverance* magazine with Ray Necklen's *Church Bells* in June 1966 and the demise of Ron Coady's *Revival News* six months later reflected this transition. *Church Bells* continued until September 1968, and was essentially an in house news magazine for the movement, rather than a periodical produced by an evangelistic ministry as its predecessors had been. This change of focus, together with the cooperative effort of Operation Gideon, marked the beginning of the movement's evolution into an identifiable association of churches. With the appearance of the Charismatic movement in the later 1960s, the separatist sectarianism of the Indigenous Churches also began to be modified.

Notes

1. Dorothy Walker, 'Indonesia have I loved: Dal N. Walker 25 Years of Missionary Service 1949–1974' (Solo-Jateng, Java, Indonesia: Dorothy Walker, [1974]), 4. Worsfold incorrectly dates their departure as 1946. Worsfold, *History*, 299.
2. As befitted a movement with diffuse boundaries of identity, the church affiliation of these missionaries is not entirely clear. The Walkers had been involved in the 1946 secession from the Pentecostal Church of New Zealand. However, they appear to have returned to this church—now named the Elim Church—despite continuing to maintain strong links of fellowship with the early Indigenous Churches. Worsfold is ambiguous on the affiliation of the Walkers and the Truscotts, since he includes them among those missionaries sent out by the Elim Church (ibid., 195) and among the Indigenous Churches' missionaries (ibid., 299).
3. 'Missionary Newsflashes', *Bible Deliverance*, November 1961, 12.
4. 'What's in a Name?', Timaru Missionary Revival Centre, 'Newsletter', no date, 3. (Mimeographed.) Knowles Papers.
5. Henderson, *From Glory to Glory*, 16–17.
6. ibid., 24.
7. 'It seems to us that only the mass media, such as literature, ... will be able to stem the tide.' Paul and Bunty Collins, 'Thailand races to a lost eternity', *Bible Deliverance*, August 1963, 6.
8. Paul Collins to Ron Coady, 'Let's Finish the Job', *Revival News*, March 1966, 6–7.
9. ibid.
10. 'Gospel Bombardment: Attack on New Zealand', *Revival News*, August 1965, 7.
11. 'Great Pastoral Conference Held in Timaru', *Gospel Truth*, February 1965, 1.
12. 'Ministers' Conference', *Bible Deliverance*, July 1965, 16.
13. 'Gospel Bombardment', *Revival News*, August 1965, 6–7,11.
14. ibid., 11.
15. 'Exciting results from "Operation Gideon,"' *Revival News*, October 1965, 4.
16. 'Great Pastoral Conference', *Gospel Truth*, February 1965, 1.
17. 'Gospel Bombardment', *Revival News*, August 1965, 11.
18. Coady, Interview.
19. This exuberant worship appears to have been a product of Everett Johnson's ministry. See above, chapter 12.
20. See above at chapter 5, footnote 15.
21. Coady, Fax correspondence with the author, 12 March 1998.
22. 'Days of Heaven on Earth!' *Revival News*, May 1962, 12–14.
23. 'Newsflashes', *Bible Deliverance*, June 1962, 9.

24. 'Some see VISIONS, Some PROPHESY, Others FILLED with the HOLY GHOST at the Easter Gatherings in Nelson', *Revival News*, May 1963, 3–5. Capitalisation as cited.
25. 'Gunns Bush Camp Meetings', *Revival News*, January/February 1964, 8.
26. 'Easter Conventions...', *Bible Deliverance*, March 1964, 16.
27. The only previous National Conferences (in 1960 and 1961) had been those of the National Revival Crusade, rather than of the Indigenous Churches.

Chapter 17

The Indigenous Churches and the rise of the Charismatic Movement

The year 1965 was a significant one for the development of the Indigenous Churches. The various pastoral conferences and conventions held in preparation for Operation Gideon strengthened the corporate identity of the movement. This coincided with a focal change from evangelistic campaigns to church planting and consolidation, and with the emergence of the Charismatic renewal within the New Zealand denominational churches.[1] This movement, which shared the emphasis on the infilling of the Holy Spirit so characteristic of classical Pentecostalism, owed much, at least in its early stages, to the support of its Pentecostal cousins. Although there were no direct organisational connections between the Pentecostal and Charismatic movements, a number of Pentecostal leaders had some influence on the early development of the renewal. However, this influence was two-way, as the Charismatic movement also exercised a moderating effect on the sectarian ethos of many Pentecostal churches, including the Indigenous Churches.

The Anglican Church was one of the earliest groups affected by the Charismatic movement. The beginnings of the renewal date from 1965, when Charismatic activity began in Palmerston North at All Saints' parish and at Massey University, principally as a result of the ministry of Father Ray Muller.[2] Neil observes that 'over half of the [Massey University] students baptised in the Spirit at this time [1966] were Anglicans, more than the total number of classical Pentecostals in Palmerston North, and this situation reflects the considerable personal influence of Father Muller in shaping the charismatic movement.'[3] Other, more disruptive, effects of the Charismatic movement were also felt in other churches. An example of this was the withdrawal of the Awapuni Baptist church from the Baptist Union about 1969, largely as a result of a division over the Charismatic issue.[4] (This church later became the Palmerston North Christian Fellowship, and is now affiliated with the New Life Churches.) The increasing momentum of the renewal was reinforced by the visit of Father Dennis Bennett in September and October 1966, which stimulated public awareness of the Charismatic movement in the mainstream churches.

The years 1965 and 1966 were therefore significant for the emergence of the Charismatic movement in New Zealand. Nevertheless, this was not a unified movement, springing up from a single source, and following a single course. Rather, as Ken Wright, an early participant, comments, 'God broke through from quite a number of different angles and different "streams" almost simultaneously during the early [and] mid-1960s.... It's very difficult to attribute the overall development of the [Charismatic] movement ... to any one particular thing or church.'[5] Commentators have not always recognised the diversity of the Charismatic movement in New Zealand, and its prehistory has often been overlooked. Both Colin Brown in particular, and Allan Neil to a lesser extent, tend to gloss over the period before 1965. Peter Lineham, however, traces the early progress of the movement from 1959 to 1965,[6] and Eric Hodgkinson emphasises the diversity of those groups that participated in the Pentecostal and Charismatic movements from the 1960s onwards.[7]

In this chapter, an attempt will be made to sketch some of the early developments that led to the emergence of the New Zealand Charismatic movement in the 1960s. This owed more to individual influence at a personal level than to any organisational or institutional efforts. There were a number of examples of this, chief among them two Brethren visitors from overseas, Campbell McAlpine and Arthur Wallis, who helped to lay the foundations of the movement in this country.[8] McAlpine had arrived in New Zealand in 1959, and was widely accepted as a preacher and convention speaker in Brethren and Baptist circles, and in interdenominational groups such as Youth for Christ. Although his dynamic sermons were memorable, it was his 'winning personality and ... aura of saintliness'[9] that enabled him to make a deep impact on those with whom he came in contact. However, he had experienced an infilling of the Spirit in South Africa in the late 1950s, and his acceptability in the Brethren assemblies began to wane when this became known. From then on his ministry was largely confined to cottage meetings in private homes, where he was able to share his Charismatic testimony in greater detail. After conducting the Tell New Zealand Crusade in 1963, in which he sought to place a copy of John's Gospel in every home in the country, McAlpine left New Zealand in September that year. He returned briefly to address the conference at Massey University in August 1964.

Arthur Wallis built upon the foundation that McAlpine had laid. Like him, he also had great acceptability among the Brethren assemblies, as well as in wider Evangelical circles. He had been invited to New Zealand to speak at a Brethren camp in April 1963, and remained in this country until the end of the following year. His influence on the emerging Charismatic movement was crucial. While in New Zealand, he 'helped to bring Charismatics who were not in Pentecostal churches into contact with each other, and to assist them to retain their own identity separate from other Pentecostals.'[10]

Wallis was one of the organisers of the Massey University Conference in August 1964, together with Frank Carlisle of Wellington, a Charismatic member of the Brethren Church. Wallis and McAlpine were the main speakers at this Conference, as well as Tom Marshall, a Charismatic Baptist, also from Wellington. A number of other speakers, including several Pentecostal ministers—for example, Trevor Chandler, Frank Houston and Rob Wheeler—shared their testimonies of how they had been baptised in the Holy Spirit. This Conference was a landmark for the Charismatic movement in New Zealand. An article in *Gospel Truth* reported that over 300 people had attended the conference, including a number of the Full Gospel ministers. The article names these as 'Rob Wheeler, of Tauranga; Ralf Reid [*sic*: Ralph Read], of Christchurch [Assemblies of God]; Norman and Gilbert White, of Feilding [Apostolic]; Alister Lowe of Tuataperi [*sic*]; Ian Hunt, of Palmerston N[orth]; David Jackson, of Timaru; Allen Thrieft [*sic*], of Whakatane; Frank Houston, of Lower Hutt [Assemblies of God]; Duncan Ferguson, of India; Chas. Bilby, of Wellington [Elim]; Milton Greenslade, of Timaru; Dr. Greenway, of Hamilton [Apostolic], and others.'[11] It is evident from the number of different Pentecostal groups included under this rubric that the term 'Full Gospel' was equivalent to 'Pentecostal', so far as the author of the article was concerned. The article also commented on the

> gracious spirit of love and fellowship one towards the other as each one dropped their denominational tags....
> Believe it or not—as these ministers were all thrown in together, a spirit of love flowed between them and between other denominational ministers.... Truly God was knitting hearts in a bond and fellowship between all His ministers.[12]

This conference therefore helped to forge links between the participants in the Charismatic movement, as well as between them and the classical Pentecostal groups. It also laid the foundations for the outbreak of the movement in Palmerston North and elsewhere in 1965. Annual transdenominational Conferences, featuring overseas and local participants in the Charismatic renewal, became something of an established model for the movement in the following years. Ken Wright observes that

> There was no doubt at all that the nature of the ministries that we brought into the country at that time, plus the ministries that Des Short was having... with his major Conventions [in Tauranga],[13] had a tremendous influence overall upon the whole move of the Spirit in the country, as well as, of course, the ongoing influence of the likes of Peter Morrow, Frank Houston, Rob Wheeler and [others] had a great, great, impact in these areas, to name just a few.[14]

Wright's latter comment shows that there was also considerable early influence on the movement from New Zealand Pentecostals. Neil observes that almost all those experiencing Charismatic renewal up to 1965 had done so through the Pentecostal churches.[15] In the case of the Assemblies of God, this influence can be traced back to Ray Bloomfield, who was an effective evangelist, especially among the Maori people in Northland and elsewhere, in the late 1950s. Ian Clark comments that 'Ray [Bloomfield], although he held *AOG* [Assemblies of God] credentials, was always a very free spirit, and he... wasn't typical of many *AOG* people at the time.'[16] Bloomfield moved to the United States and Canada in early 1960, and consequently had little direct influence on the course of events in New Zealand. However, his unsectarian attitudes were inherited by his assistant Frank Houston, who had worked with him for three years, and who became pastor of the Lower Hutt Assembly of God in December 1959.[17] Houston played a decisive role in the development of the Assemblies of God, spearheading its growth in the 1960s, and becoming its General Superintendent in 1966.[18]

However, Houston's openness to the independent Pentecostal churches, including the Indigenous Churches,[19] and to the denominational churches was of even greater significance than were his activities in the Assemblies of God. Houston's ministry, as well as that of his assistant Trevor Chandler,[20] also helped to create links with mainstream church members that greatly assisted the growth of the Charismatic movement. Ken Wright observes that 'The major effect... upon [the Charismatic movement in] our region at that time... really was the influence of Frank Houston's church in Lower Hutt, and Trevor Chandler, who came up here [to Palmerston North] on a number of occasions and took house meetings and other meetings.'[21] The influence of Houston and Chandler, together with that of McAlpine and Wallis and the momentum generated by the 1964 Massey Conference, helped to lay the foundation for the Charismatic movement in Palmerston North.

However, Houston and Chandler were not the only examples of the personal, rather than organisational, influence of the Pentecostal movement on the Charismatic renewal. Similar examples included the ministry of Peter Morrow and other Pentecostal pastors in Christchurch. The campaigns of Rob Wheeler and Ron Coady,[22] as well as those of the White brothers from the Apostolic church, and of other Pentecostal evangelists, were also significant. At a congregational level, the face-to-face witnessing of individual Pentecostal believers had considerable impact. A corporate influence on the Charismatic movement was that of the Apostolic Church, who throughout the country

> had quietly... for a number of years felt led of God to belong to the local ministers' fraternals. That... gave them an open door to be able to... proclaim and share the truth of Pentecost, in a low key role, which had considerable impact because of their faithfulness and their obvious love and fellowship with... vastly different ministers from totally contradictory theological backgrounds.[23]

Wright contrasts this openness with the attitude of 'a lot of other Pentecostal churches... [who] were closed and suspicious' of other churches. This suspicion was also evident in the Pentecostal movement in the United States, where Edith Blumhofer refers to 'initial Assemblies of God hesitations about the charismatic movement.'[24] She links these hesitations with the inherent antiecumenicalism and anti-Catholicism of the Assemblies of God in the 1960s.[25] She further argues that the Latter Rain movement and the healing evangelists of the 1950s laid the foundation for the emergence of the Charismatic movement in the 1960s.[26]

Another important catalyst in the expansion of the Charismatic movement was that of publications from overseas. David Wilkerson's book *The Cross and the Switchblade*, published in 1963,[27] was by far the most influential of these, and was widely read in New Zealand.[28] An example of its influence is given in David Balfour's testimony in *Logos* magazine.[29] (*Logos* was published in Christchurch from August 1966 on, and was effectively the voice of the New Zealand Charismatic movement until August 1970, when it shifted to Australia.) Balfour's story is quite typical; an examination of the various testimonies published in *Logos* shows that the role of literature was very important indeed in the spread of the Charismatic movement. Later examples include John Sherrill's *They speak with other tongues*,[30] Michael Harper's *As at the Beginning*,[31] and Dennis Bennett's *Nine O'Clock in the Morning*.[32]

There was therefore neither a single source for the Charismatic renewal, nor a unified manifestation of it. The combination of stimuli that helped to produce the movement varied from place to place, and different churches experienced it in different ways and gave different responses to it. Two churches that demonstrate the diversity of the Charismatic movement are the Palmerston North Christian Fellowship and the Christchurch New Life Centre. These will be examined in the next two chapters.

Notes

1. The best overall coverage of the Charismatic renewal in New Zealand up to 1974 is that of Allan G. Neil, 'Institutional Churches and the Charismatic Renewal: A Study of the Charismatic Renewal in the Anglican Church and the Roman Catholic Church in New Zealand' (Diploma S.Th. Thesis in Church History, Joint Board of Theological Studies, 1974). Other useful surveys are those of Brown, 'How Significant is the Charismatic Movement?' [1985]; Nola Ker, 'Religion and Society in Interaction in New Zealand.' M.A. Thesis in Sociology, Victoria University of Wellington, 1984; and Lineham, 'Tongues must cease.' An analysis of specific aspects of the movement is offered by Michael David Myers, 'Organizational Change in the Auckland Catholic Charismatic Movement' (M.A. Thesis in Anthropology, Auckland University, 1978). Another is that of M.T. Vincent Reidy and James T. Richardson, 'Roman Catholic Neo-Pentecostalism: The New Zealand Experience', *Australia and New Zealand Journal of Sociology* 14 (1978): 222-30. Both of these analyses focus on the Catholic Charismatic movement. Eric Hodgkinson, 'The Independent Pentecostal Movement', Research Essay in New Zealand Religious History, Massey University, 1989 (Handwritten.), examines the beginnings of the Charismatic movement in the Manawatu area, and corrects Neil's thesis at several key points.
2. Brown, 'How Significant is the Charismatic movement?' [1985], 105.
3. Neil, 'Institutional Churches', 88.
4. The earlier edition of this book, following Colin Brown, stated that the Awapuni Baptist Church left the Baptist Union in 1965. (Brown, 'How significant is the Charismatic movement?' [1985], 108). However, its former pastor, Ian Drinkwater, dates this secession in 1969 or later (Ian Drinkwater, e-mail correspondence with

author, 30 September 2014). This date is confirmed by the Centenary History of the Baptist Union of New Zealand, which states that Awapuni Baptist was founded in 1960 and 'survived only ten years', which would place its withdrawal about 1969–70 (Edgar, *A Handful of Grain*, 27).
5. Ken Wright, Taped interview in response to Questionnaire, Palmerston North, April 1990. Wright was originally a Presbyterian elder, and later an elder in the Awapuni Baptist Church following its secession from the Baptist Union. He eventually became a pastor in the Palmerston North Christian Fellowship.
6. Lineham, 'Tongues must cease.'
7. Hodgkinson, 'Independent Pentecostal Movement.'
8. For the development of the Charismatic movement up to the 1964 Massey Conference, see Lineham, 'Tongues must cease', *passim*.
9. ibid., 23.
10. ibid., 40.
11. 'Most Unique Convention in History of New Zealand', *Gospel Truth*, August 1964, 6. The author is not named, but may have been David Jackson, the publisher of the *Gospel Truth*. Most of this article was reprinted in *Bible Deliverance*, October 1964, 15. Spelling as cited.
12. ibid.
13. See Worsfold, *History*, 219, for examples of these.
14. Ken Wright, Interview.
15. Neil, 'Institutional Churches', 88.
16. Clark, Interview.
17. Houston, *Being Frank*, 113.
18. Worsfold, *History*, 217.
19. See above at chapter 12, page 80.
20. Chandler was originally a Baptist lay missioner who had himself been baptised in the Spirit in Houston's meetings in the late 1950s. Lineham, 'Tongues must cease': 22.
21. Ken Wright, Interview.
22. ibid. Wright states that Ron Coady's campaign with the White brothers in Feilding in late 1964 was particularly influential on the emergence of the Charismatic movement in the region.
23. ibid.
24. Blumhofer, *The Assemblies of God*, 2:53.
25. ibid., 2:103–5.
26. ibid., 2:86.
27. A later edition was David Wilkerson, John and Elizabeth Sherrill, *The Cross and the Switchblade*, movie ed. (Old Tappan, New Jersey: Fleming H. Revell Company, 1975).
28. Lineham, 'Tongues must cease': 20.
29. *Logos*, August 1966, 7.
30. John L. Sherrill, *They speak with other tongues* (London: Hodder and Stoughton, 1967).
31. Michael Harper, *As at the Beginning* (London: Hodder and Stoughton, 1965).
32. Dennis J. Bennett, *Nine O'Clock in the Morning* (Watchung, New Jersey: Charisma Books, 1972).

Chapter 18

A tale of two churches I: The Palmerston North Christian Fellowship

Two of the Indigenous Churches—the Palmerston North Christian Fellowship and the Christchurch New Life Centre—illustrate the cross-pollination between Pentecostal churches and the emergent Charismatic movement. However, two cautionary comments must be made at the outset. Firstly, the reference to these two churches as specific examples is not intended to suggest that the Charismatic movement was confined to Palmerston North and Christchurch. Rather, the renewal was widespread and multifaceted, and was particularly strong in Auckland in its earlier stages.[1] However, since these two churches have now both become New Life Churches, they provide good examples of the ways in which this group of churches and the Charismatic movement have influenced and changed each other. Secondly, the emphasis on the Indigenous Churches does not necessarily imply that they had a greater influence on the renewal than the other Pentecostal churches such as the Apostolic Church or the Assemblies of God. Nevertheless, some scholars, for example Peter Lineham, have stressed the role of the Indigenous Churches. In his words, it was the Bethel Temple missionaries, 'chief among them Ray Jackson, who were to break the barriers which prevented the Pentecostal sects from making an impact in the mainstream churches.'[2] However, the influence of Frank Houston and Trevor Chandler of the Assemblies of God should be set off against Lineham's statement. The Indigenous Churches were an example of, rather than the *sine qua non* of, Pentecostal influence on the emerging movement.

One of the churches that was most strongly influenced by the Charismatic movement in its initial stages was the Awapuni Baptist church in Palmerston North. Ian Drinkwater, its pastor, had been baptised in the Spirit in the early 1960s. The result was that 'people who were getting renewed in the Spirit ... were drawn like magnets ... [and] quite a move of God broke out' in that church.[3] Awapuni Baptist Church thus became a focal point for an early fellowship of Charismatics in Palmerston North. Ken Wright—then a Charismatic Presbyterian elder—recalls that he used to 'go down and help the

[Baptist] pastor out with the evening services and [attend] my own church in the morning.'[4] The Charismatic activity of this group in Palmerston North appears to have preceded that of Ray Muller, and indeed to have been a factor in bringing Muller to his experience of the Holy Spirit. Hodgkinson observes that

> in Palmerston North there was strong input, especially into Ray Muller's ministry.... It has been generally accepted (Brown and Neil[5] state this) that the Rev. Ray Muller the curate at Anglican All Saints Church received the Baptism in the Spirit through a prayer meeting at St. Giles Presbyterian Church, Kilburnie [sic: Kilbirnie] in August 1965. Ken Wright... disputes this and said that he'd prayed for Muller prior to this and that Muller had received it with signs of glossolalia.[6]

Although Awapuni Baptist Church formed a focal point for the early Charismatics in Palmerston North, the boundaries of this group extended beyond the membership of that church. The group was quite influential on the emerging Charismatic movement, in that it laid the foundations for much of its later development. Hodgkinson notes that 'Neil[7] implies that Ray Muller had set up the Christian Advance Tape Library in 1965-66. Actually it was set up by a group consisting of Ian Drinkwater (Baptist minister at Awapuni Baptist Church), Ray Muller [Anglican], Ian Hunt [Independent Pentecostal] and Ken Wright [Presbyterian]. Ian Hunt physically ran the library.'[8] This tape library later evolved into the Christian Advance Ministries, which spearheaded the Charismatic movement in New Zealand after 1973. The group was also responsible for the invitation of overseas Charismatic speakers to this country. Hodgkinson says, again quoting Wright, that

> one day while praying as a group in Ken Wright's home, Ray Muller suggested that they contact Rev. David Du Plessis and invite him to New Zealand. This group helped Ray Muller to organize his visit in February 1966. The same group also invited Dennis Bennett in September/October 1966 and Rev. Michael Harper in August/September 1967.[9]

The visits of these overseas speakers considerably advanced the Charismatic movement in New Zealand, and provided the model for the later transdenominational Conferences that formed a prominent feature of Charismatic activity after 1972.

Despite the rapid expansion of the Charismatic movement, there were also some difficulties. The Awapuni Baptist Church seceded from the Baptist Union about 1969—in part over the Charismatic issue—and became 'an independent church with an eldership who were all formerly Baptist or Brethren.'[10] Wright explains that

> The church itself had come into quite a bit of disfavour, really, with the... Baptist movement generally, as it was the first... Charismatic Baptist church in the country.... There was quite a sort of inner conflict within the assembly with people who did not want to change with the renewal, and also pressure coming from outside the assembly from the Baptist Union.... Some people that remained in the church at that time... were actual [Baptist]

members, although... quite a good number of [the] people attending... would not take on Baptist Union membership.... So the remaining actual Baptist members voted themselves out of the Union, and decided to form a new Charismatic Fellowship.[11]

Wright was invited, along with the elders of the former Awapuni Baptist Church, to join the eldership of the new group, which was called the 'Palmerston North Christian Fellowship.' The new church grew steadily, renting an old picture theatre in the city centre in 1974 to accommodate the growing congregation, and later changing its name to 'Palmerston North Christian Centre.' The church was subdivided into two in December 1981—in part due to differences over leadership styles—with the Palmerston North New Life Centre being established in the northern part of the city. According to Wright, the combined congregations of the two churches at the end of the 1980s totalled about eleven hundred to twelve hundred people.[12]

The new Palmerston North Christian Fellowship was strongly evangelistic, as its predecessor, the Awapuni Baptist church had also been. It was heavily involved with groups such as Teen Challenge New Zealand, Youth for Christ, Christian Advance Ministries and other parachurch organisations. It was not, however, initially affiliated to any group of churches, although there were strong personal ties with others in the Charismatic and Pentecostal movements. Wright comments that

> In the mid-60s,... through the... respect for... the likes of Peter Morrow and Rob Wheeler,... when we became an open Christian fellowship ourselves, we felt the need to associate or identify with a particular group of churches, and basically... not on doctrine or theology but on the basis of friendship and relationship with these dear folk. We brought our church into an affiliation with them, and have remained in that state since, and continue to enjoy that relationship with the wider representation of the New Life Churches of New Zealand. In actual fact, our local fellowship has always been very much open and involved with the total Body of Christ, and we have gained favour and acceptance with a large range of different church fellowships and groups, but, nevertheless, still felt it necessary to have that broader identification and fellowship and relationship with these dear brethren.[13]

Not all Charismatic groups made this 'broader identification,' since

> At the same time there was also a developing group of people who were caught up in a "twilight zone," where they couldn't really go all the way with Pentecost and they couldn't go all the way with their "mainstreams," and so lots of independent indefinite little fellowships sprang up out of that. And I suppose initially that would also [have] been something [of] the nature of our fellowship in its early origins, but we recognise the wider Body of Christ so much that we didn't isolate; [in] fact we became more involved with it.[14]

The Palmerston North Christian Centre is therefore representative of a particular subset of the Charismatic movement. While there was some classical Pentecostal assistance of this group in the initial stages,[15] it had a largely Charismatic identity, rather than a Pentecostal one.[16] Once the momentum of the renewal had begun to accelerate, the Charismatic movement began to distance itself from classical Pentecostalism and to develop an independent, more mainstream, identity. Despite this process of detachment, however, some Charismatic groups found themselves in something of a limbo between the mainstream and the Pentecostal churches. These groups tended to add another stratum to the variety of independent Pentecostal churches already in existence.[17] As Hodgkinson puts it:

> From the mid-1960s to the 1970s there arose another grouping of churches whose leaders had their roots in fundamental evangelical churches like the Baptist and Open Brethren.... Arising out of the charismatic influence in the [Brethren] assemblies a new grouping of independent Pentecostal churches got established. In many respects they were similar to the Brethren Assemblies (emphasis on Eldership, Priesthood of All Believers, on open meeting where anybody could participate) yet with the charismatic emphasis on Baptism in the Spirit.... The influence of men with Brethren and Baptist backgrounds were [sic] considerable—McAlpine, Wallis, Milton Smith, Tom Marshall, Trevor Chandler, Frank Garrett, and Wyn Fountain.
>
> Over a period of 10–15 years from 1964 churches such as Awapuni Christian Fellowship (now Palmerston North Christian Fellowship), Kapiti Christian Fellowship, Upper Hutt Christian Fellowship, Fairlie New Life Centre [and] Western Suburbs Christian Fellowship [were founded]. Today there are over 50 churches that have plural leadership that are Pentecostal in nature.[18]

Some of these churches formed a distinct nucleus around the person of Hudson Salisbury, and are sometimes known as the plurality group—a reference to their plural leadership by a college of elders.[19] The Palmerston North Christian Centre, however, linked itself with those churches represented by Peter Morrow and Rob Wheeler, i.e. the Indigenous Churches. In so doing, they, and other churches that had their origins in this substratum of the Charismatic movement, brought several differences of emphasis into the Indigenous Churches.

Firstly, many of these churches stressed a Brethren polity of plural leadership, i.e. the corporate leadership of the autonomous local assembly by an eldership comprising several elders of equal rank and authority. This contrasted markedly with the polity of strongly individualistic leadership by the local pastor, inherited by the Indigenous Churches from their Bethel Temple antecedents and patterned on the rather autocratic pastoral style of Ray Jackson. Secondly, these churches brought with them a more open attitude to the wider church than had been the case in the Indigenous Churches to this point, although this antidenominational stance itself was also changing. Thirdly, these churches had considerably less antipathy towards the building up of organisational links with other local assemblies.

The influx of these Charismatic churches also gradually altered the composition of the Indigenous Churches as a movement. Pastor Rasik Ranchord clearly recognised this variety, when, during discussions that led to the adoption of the title 'New Life Churches' for the movement, he jocularly suggested that it be called the 'Liquorice Allsorts Churches'![20] The origins of the individual churches were extremely varied. The Tauranga Christian Fellowship, for example, was founded in 1939—seven years before the movement was to begin as a result of the secession from the Pentecostal Church of New Zealand. This local assembly owed its origins to converts of the 1932 Dallimore campaigns in Auckland.[21] The Timaru New Life Centre was the result of a specific Full Gospel campaign—the Worley Revival—held in Timaru in 1960.[22] By contrast, the Fairlie New Life Centre was effectively a charismatic ex-Brethren Assembly; likewise, the two Palmerston North New Life churches originated from the charismatic Awapuni Baptist Church.[23]

The influence of these adopted churches, reinforced by that of individual Charismatics who had transferred from denominational churches to Pentecostal groups, did much to broaden the sectarian outlook of the Indigenous Churches. Contact with other Charismatic groups also contributed to an erosion of the movement's traditional antidenominationalism. This broadening of outlook helped to lay a foundation for Pentecostal involvement in the nascent moralist movement in the 1970s, and was a factor in the structural evolution of the New Life Churches in the 1980s.[24]

Notes

1. This section of the movement has been well documented by Merritt and by Myers. N.F.H. Merritt, *To God be the glory: the first 10½ years of the Charismatic Renewal in St. Pauls* (Auckland: St. Paul's Outreach Trust, 1981); Myers, 'Organizational Change.'
2. Lineham, 'Tongues must cease': 15.
3. Ken Wright, Interview.
4. ibid.
5. Neil, 'Institutional Churches', 85.
6. Hodgkinson, 'Independent Pentecostal Movement', 12–13. Hodgkinson subsequently noted that the issue of the time of Muller's first encounter with the Holy Spirit is unclear. Eric Hodgkinson, e-mail correspondence with the author, 10 February 1998.
7. Neil, 'Institutional Churches', 95.
8. Hodgkinson, 'Independent Pentecostal Movement', 13.
9. ibid.
10. ibid, 9.
11. Ken Wright, Interview.
12. ibid.
13. ibid.
14. ibid.
15. Neil comments that, in the context of the Charismatic movement in Palmerston North, 'there was little direct classical Pentecostal influence.... This is in sharp contrast to events before 1965. Until then the charismatic experience was mediated almost exclusively through classical Pentecostals.' Neil, 'Institutional Churches', 88.

16. One major difference between the Charismatic movement and the classical Pentecostals is that Charismatics generally do not subscribe to the Pentecostal insistence on glossolalia as the only evidence for the infilling of the Spirit.
17. Nichol comments that there were fifty-four Pentecostal churches in New Zealand at the beginning of the 1960s, seventeen of which were 'unaffiliated with any national or international Pentecostal organisation.' Nichol, *The Pentecostals*, 179. Worsfold briefly refers to these in a chapter headed 'The Independent Churches and Groups.' Worsfold, *History*, 297-303. Included in these were a small number of churches that later evolved into the New Life Churches.
18. Hodgkinson, 'Independent Pentecostal Movement', 8-9. Of the five churches cited, two—the Palmerston North Christian Fellowship [Centre], and the Fairlie New Life Centre—are now New Life Churches. New Life Churches of New Zealand, '1990 Directory of Pastors and Churches', Christchurch, 1990. (Mimeographed.) Hodgkinson later noted that a number of these plural leadership churches have now moved to recognition of 'a leader among leaders' and the formal recognition of informal *de facto* leadership. Hodgkinson, Correspondence with author.
19. Hodgkinson quotes Hudson Salisbury's estimate that this group comprises about fifty such assemblies, with approximately 2,500 adult adherents. Salisbury, cited in Hodgkinson, 'Independent Pentecostal Movement', 1, note 1, and 8-9.
20. Rasik Ranchord, cited in Wheeler, Interview.
21. See 'Tauranga Christian Fellowship: Jubilee Reunion 1939-1989' for its history.
22. Henderson, *From Glory to Glory*, 4.
23. Hodgkinson, 'Independent Pentecostal Movement', 9. Awapuni Baptist was renamed 'Awapuni Christian Fellowship' in 1968, and 'Christian Centre' in 1974. Its name was later changed to the present 'Palmerston North Christian Fellowship' in 1984, three years after John Walton's 'Palmerston North New Life Centre' had become a separate church. Hodgkinson, Correspondence with author.
24. John Walton, who became one of the leaders of the New Life Churches following Rob Wheeler's retirement, due to ill health, in 1989, exemplifies this change of origin and outlook. Walton came originally from the Exclusive Brethren, and later was an adherent of Awapuni Baptist Church. John Walton, Interview, Pleasant Valley, Palmerston, Otago, 4 February 1989; Mark Toomer, 'National church leader "walks with his people,"' *Challenge Weekly*, 8 May 1996, 5. Walton became prominent in the New Life Churches in the 1980s. His elevation to joint leadership of the movement—alongside Peter Morrow, who had been associated with the movement since the early 1950s—demonstrates the changing character of the New Life Churches.

Chapter 19

A tale of two churches II: Peter Morrow and the Christchurch New Life Centre

Pentecostal links with the Charismatic movement appear to have been more pronounced in Christchurch than was the case in Palmerston North.[1] In particular, Peter Morrow and the Christchurch Revival Fellowship had considerable influence in the early stages of the movement. Morrow had visited Christchurch at the invitation of Terry Collins in October 1962 to conduct a weekend of meetings. Collins was then pastoring a small Full Gospel church of about 25 people, which he had established the previous year. He felt that it was time for him to move on into other areas of ministry, so Morrow stayed on in Christchurch and took over the pastorate of the church. Morrow recalls that conditions were not easy, although the congregation grew to about 70 to 80 people over a period of about three years. The meetings were held in the old *YMCA* Hall in Oxford Terrace, a feature of which was the rain coming in through the roof and running down the walls at the back. Some of the members of the congregation used to spend the whole of the evening services in the downstairs chapel praying while the service went on upstairs. One of these intercessors, Andreé Dornan, commented to Morrow in 1963 that she felt that God was going to 'give him a "move"'—i.e. that there was going be a revival in that church. Morrow's initial response to her was 'Great!' but he later commented that 'the "move" happened in a *totally* different way than I thought.'[2]

About 1965, the Christchurch Revival Fellowship opened an upstairs coffee bar on the corner of Tuam and Durham Streets.[3] This coffee bar, named 'Adullam's Cave',[4] was patterned on David Wilkerson's Teen Challenge outreach in *The Cross and the Switchblade*, and was intended to facilitate the reaching of young people from off the streets. (Christian coffee bars such as this became a feature of many church outreaches in the later 1960s. These provided a Christian counterpart to the secular coffee bars that formed a prominent part of the youth culture of the 1960s.[5]) Morrow recalls that Adullam's Cave was a dilapidated room... [that] became a coffee lounge just for kids off the street.... We didn't know that was the place God was going to use to baptise multiplied hundreds with the Baptism of the Holy Spirit... in the next three years.... We thought it was going to be used for... [reaching] some of the kids in the street, and we did [that] on Friday and Saturday [evenings]. But it was mainly... used for people on Thursday [evenings] to get the Baptism.[6]

As well as facilitating the outreach to young people, Adullam's Cave was the venue for teaching meetings every second Thursday evening, and here 'Some 50 to 60 non-Pentecostals, including Roman Catholics, Anglicans, Presbyterians, Methodists, and a few Baptists and Brethren came for teaching on the Baptism of the Holy Spirit.... There was a new turnover every two weeks.... They came for teaching and then went back to their own churches.'[7] The steady turnover of denominational people attending these teaching meetings continued for some three years, with the result that during this time hundreds of people from all denominations experienced the Baptism of the Spirit there.[8] The excitement of the period is captured by an article in *Church Bells* that stated:

> We praise God for the "moving of the Spirit" not only in our midst but also among different denominational circles. Especially prominent is the move of God in the *Presbyterian Church at Leiston* [sic: Leeston] where 18–20 have now been baptised in the Holy Ghost *including the* minister and his wife. Scarcely a week goes by without reports coming in of someone, maybe *Presbyterian, Methodist, Baptist or Anglican receiving the baptism in the Holy Spirit.*[9]

However, Adullam's Cave represented only the initial stage of the Charismatic movement in Christchurch. Gaynor Loryman, writing in 1973, reported that while the Charismatic movement in Christchurch started in 1965 among Protestants and in 1968 among Roman Catholics, it 'has really gained momentum only in the last 18 months.'[10] The figures given by Loryman's informants indicate that although the movement was strategically placed for future growth, it was still comparatively small at that stage in Christchurch. According to these informants, some 500 Roman Catholic Charismatic participants—including thirty priests—met weekly in eighteen groups of ten to fifty people each. There were about thirty to forty Anglican Charismatics who were meeting in ten groups, and the pastor of the influential Spreydon Baptist Church had estimated more than a quarter of his congregation to be Charismatic. However, Loryman does not mention the Presbyterian wing of the movement, which, as Colin Brown points out, was particularly strong in Christchurch and in nearby Leeston.[11]

There appears to be at least three distinct phases in the movement's development in Christchurch. The first of these, beginning about 1965 and focused to some extent on Adullam's Cave, had its greatest influence among Protestants. A second phase, starting in 1968, saw the start of the movement in the Catholic church. That year Peter Morrow had spent some time talking to the Catholic priests at the Redemptorist monastery. He had prayed for three priests—Fathers John McGill, Cecil Dennehy and Bruce McGill—who were later to be very influential in the Catholic Charismatic movement.[12]

Catholic layman Gordon Copeland emphasises the role of these three men in initiating Catholic prayer groups in Wainuiomata and elsewhere in 1969. These groups, in which Copeland himself was a participant, helped to foster an expansion of the Catholic Charismatic movement after 1973. His account corrects that of Reidy and Richardson, who locate the beginning of the New Zealand Catholic Charismatic movement in Auckland in early 1970 and attribute this to the seminal influence of overseas literature.[13] Reidy and Richardson also state that 'Later in the same year, a second group of Roman Catholics initiated Pentecostalism in their Church in Christchurch as a result of their contact with an independent Pentecostal Church—the New Life Revival Centre. Growth since 1970 has tended to be either outwards from these two cities or "spontaneous."'[14] However, as Copeland records, and Loryman confirms, Catholic Charismatic activity in Christchurch had begun in 1968, i.e. two years before the beginnings in Auckland. The difference in the two dates is explained by the reluctance of the early Catholic participants to identify themselves publicly with the movement. Loryman comments that Father Dennehy had kept quiet for two years about his Charismatic experience, waiting for a Roman Catholic bishop to be baptised in the Spirit. He saw this as providing the necessary episcopal legitimation for his experience. This happened in the United States in 1970, and Dennehy then felt free to acknowledge his involvement with the movement. The Catholic Charismatic movement did not therefore develop its own separate identity until 1970, although it had functioned as something of an underground movement up to this time.

The effect of this reticence was that in the early stages, Catholic participants in the Charismatic movement were instructed by Protestants in most cases.[15] However, there had already been some contribution from the Christchurch Revival Fellowship to the Catholic community before this. Rasik Ranchord, then Peter Morrow's co-pastor, recalls that the Fellowship had

> managed to get a tape of the "move" among the Catholic people in Notre Dame University in South Bend, Indiana [in 1967], and we began to circulate that among the Catholic community.... We were quite keen to see them being ministered to in this area [i.e. the Baptism of the Spirit], without necessarily trying to get them to come and "join" us.... At that stage [1967] ... we were probably the first Pentecostal church that was involved in the Charismatic move [in Christchurch].[16]

As a result of this, some Catholic people began to become involved with the Revival Fellowship's Bible studies, then conducted in Adullam's Cave, and later in the New Life Centre in Lichfield Street. There were no strings attached to these teaching meetings, and people were free to come without pressure being placed on them to join the Fellowship.[17] This lack of pressure was reinforced by the fact that the Christchurch assembly, at this stage known as the 'Christchurch Revival Fellowship', was a separate entity from the New Life

Centre. This latter title related to a teaching centre in Lichfield Street, run by Morrow and Ranchord, together with other Charismatic teachers. As with Adullam's Cave, the New Life Centre represented neutral territory, and people from nonPentecostal churches therefore felt free to attend the teaching meetings held there.

Ranchord sees this as being a unique factor in the early stages of the Charismatic movement in Christchurch. He observes that

> We did get some "flak" from people from the Pentecostal movement thinking that we were "compromising." At that stage, the main feel[ing] among these churches was "come out," and so, seeing we were teaching these people without making them necessarily come out to us, [it] was quite, quite, quite different.... We found [that] ... we did have quite an influence among them, and what it was, probably, that God blessed was ... an openness of spirit, to minister without getting them to "join" us. That was quite different; they didn't feel "trapped" or feel "threatened."[18]

The particular contributions of Peter Morrow and the Christchurch Revival Fellowship to the Charismatic movement were twofold. Firstly, they did much to foster the openness of spirit to other denominations and church groups that characterised the Charismatic movement in Christchurch. Ranchord comments that he had been educated in Catholic schools, and that Morrow had come from an Anglican background. He believes that this 'exposure ... had given us ... a good ... attitude ... towards these people from the denominational churches.'[19] However, in the case of the Christchurch Catholic Charismatic movement, this good attitude was due as much to the openness of Bishop Ashby to it as to the nonsectarian attitude of Morrow and Ranchord.[20] Consequently the Christchurch movement appears to have been the most successful of the Catholic Charismatic movements in New Zealand, and was much more ecumenical than its counterpart in Auckland.[21] The bonds of fellowship were warm and genuine. Morrow, for example, spent some time at the Redemptorist monastery, talking to the priests there until midnight. He recalled

> leaving Cecil [Dennehy] at twelve o'clock (and he certainly had a very, very, wonderful love for God), and I remember him asking me "what do you think of ecumenicalism, Peter?" ... I remember him lifting up his hand and saying "when the Protestants lift up Jesus, and *they* see only Jesus, and the Catholics lift up Jesus, and *they* see only Jesus, we're going to come together in Jesus." And I said, "Cecil, that's *my* language; I think we're going to get on well together!"[22]

The openness of this fellowship had the effect of producing an informal ecumenism among those who shared the experience of the Baptism of the Spirit. Indeed, to many of the participants in the Charismatic movement, this was the *true* ecumenical movement.

A second significant contribution of the Christchurch Revival Fellowship to the Charismatic movement was an emphasis on Bible teaching. This itself was a legacy of its Bethel Temple antecedents. Ranchord comments that

> We found that there were a lot of hungry people that didn't have anywhere to go for teaching, because Bible teaching was so little emphasised, or appeared to be, in their own churches. And, like one man said, ... [when] a Catholic became a Charismatic, the first thing he ... [did was to buy] a Bible. So there was a great need for teaching, and we found people just flocked in to receive teaching this way.[23]

By contrast, Myers refers to the lack of good teaching in the Auckland Catholic Charismatic movement: 'they were spiritually hungry but they weren't getting anything.'[24] This led to the diminution of the movement there after 1973–74.

This emphasis on Bible teaching appears to have had a strong appeal for many in the Charismatic movement. The uncritical, although clear and authoritative, emphasis on 'the Bible says' seems to have been as attractive to the new Charismatics in the late 1960s as it had earlier been to their Pentecostal counterparts. The result was an influx into the teaching meetings, both at Adullam's Cave and later at the New Life Centre in Lichfield Street. There was little direct pressure placed on Charismatics to join Pentecostal churches, although there was steady growth throughout the later 1960s in the Christchurch Revival Fellowship's meetings. This growth made necessary a shift from the *YMCA* to the larger Horticultural Hall in Cambridge Terrace. Ranchord recalls that 'After some of those early stages, [people] seemed to be ... mainly coming to the New Life Centre.... We did get quite a few people ... from among the churches. But, at no stage, was it because we *forced* them to join us: we left that decision to them.... It was a point of how the Lord led them.'[25]

However, the Christchurch Revival Centre was not the only Pentecostal group that benefited from this influx. Many of the younger Charismatics, known as 'the Jesus People', gravitated to the Sydenham Assembly of God in the early 1970s. As Neil comments, 'the years 1967 to 1971 were the "heyday" for independent Pentecostals and the Assemblies of God especially in Christchurch and Auckland. Both the Assemblies of God, Queen Street, Auckland, and the New Life Centre, Christchurch ... had a marked upsurge of growth in this period.'[26] Morrow believes that the Charismatic movement contributed to the numerical growth of the Christchurch New Life Centre only 'indirectly ... [since] most of the people went back to their own churches.'[27] Nevertheless, the hunger of the new Charismatics for Bible teaching appears to be a major factor in this expansion.

To summarise: the influence exerted by the Christchurch New Life Centre—then called the Christchurch Revival Fellowship—on the Charismatic movement was quite different from that of the Palmerston North Christian Centre. This reflected the dissimilar origins of the two churches. The bloodlines of the Christchurch New Life Centre ran through the Bethel Temple and Latter Rain movements. As an Indigenous Pentecostal assembly, it was typical of the first generation of the movement that later evolved into the New Life Churches of New Zealand. By contrast, the Palmerston North Christian Centre had its origins in the Baptist and Brethren movements, and became affiliated with the Indigenous Churches following its secession from the Baptist Union.

This diversity of origin was reflected in the polity and ethos of the two churches. Whereas the Christchurch New Life Centre emphasised the role of the individual pastor (or, in this particular case, pastors), the Palmerston North Christian Centre was governed by a plural eldership. Furthermore, the Christchurch New Life Centre was primarily a teaching church, although individual personal contacts were also an important component of its contribution to the Charismatic movement. By contrast, the Palmerston North Christian Centre directed its energies towards evangelism and the holding of transdenominational Conventions. Each of these churches influenced, and was influenced by, the emerging Charismatic movement in different ways.

Notes

1. Neil comments that in Christchurch, most participants in the Charismatic movement had come into the renewal through the Pentecostal churches. Neil, 'Institutional Churches', 93.
2. Peter Morrow, Interview, Christchurch, 13 May 1988. Emphasis as cited.
3. See P. Morrow, 'Coffee Bar', *Church Bells*, June 1966, 5 and 18, which includes a photograph of Adullam's Cave.
4. The reference is to David's place of refuge recorded in 1 Sam.22:1.
5. For an example, see 'Christian Keen-Teen Canteen', *Revival News*, June 1965, 9, which features the Nelson-Richmond church's coffee bar.
6. Morrow, Interview [1988].
7. Peter Morrow, cited in Gaynor Loryman, 'Growth of the Pentecostal Movement: A new relationship with Christ', *Christchurch Star*, 27 October 1973, 7.
8. Morrow, Interview [1988].
9. 'Church News: Christchurch', *Church Bells*, September 1966, 21. Emphasis as cited.
10. Loryman, 'Growth of the Pentecostal Movement.'
11. Brown, 'How Significant is the Charismatic Movement?' [1985], 106.
12. Copeland, *Faith that works*, 36.
13. Reidy and Richardson specifically refer to the influence of David Wilkerson's book *The Cross and the Switchblade* and of Kevin Ranaghan's book *Catholic Pentecostals*.
14. Reidy and Richardson, 'Roman Catholic Neo-Pentecostalism', 222.
15. Loryman, 'Growth of the Pentecostal Movement.'
16. Rasik Ranchord, Interview, Christchurch, 21 November 1989.
17. ibid.
18. ibid.
19. ibid.
20. Neil, 'Institutional Churches', 152.
21. ibid., 177.
22. Morrow, Interview [1988]. Emphasis as cited. Dennehy's openheartedness may also have been a product of the influence of the Second Vatican Council.
23. Ranchord, Interview.

24. Myers, 'Organizational Change', 109–10.
25. Ranchord, Interview. Emphasis as cited.
26. Neil, 'Institutional Churches', 109–10.
27. Morrow, Interview [1988].

Chapter 20

Charismatic growth and its effect on the Indigenous Churches

A third phase in the development of the Charismatic movement began in 1971. A major expansion of the renewal was then starting in many mainstream churches, and this gained momentum over the next two years.[1] Consequently, the period from 1971 to 1973 has been described as a boundary line between the period of the pioneers and the time of ingathering for the Charismatic movement.[2] To some extent, it also marked the start of a process of polarisation between the Pentecostal and Charismatic movements and the beginnings of an increasing sense of Charismatic identity.

Until 1971, the early Charismatics had tended to follow the lead of their Pentecostal mentors.[3] With the expansion of the renewal in the historic churches, however, and especially with the introduction of programmes such as the Life in the Spirit Seminars,[4] the Charismatic movement began to establish an independent identity. This process was reinforced by the launching of Christian Advance Ministries in 1972, and led to a distancing between the Charismatic movement and the classical Pentecostals. A corollary of this was a rejection of Pentecostal cultural baggage such as an insistence on glossolalia as the only evidence for the infilling of the Spirit and an uncritical emphasis on 'the Bible says.' Neil comments that the Charismatic movement had 'borrowed from the classical Pentecostals in the areas of their greatest weakness: exegesis and systematic theology' and uncritically accepted its 'speech patterns, prayer postures, mental processes and expectations.'[5] However, the 1973 Summer School, organised by the newly formed Christian Advance Ministries, reinforced a move away from the 'predominant [i.e. classical Pentecostal] theological interpretation of charismatic experience.'[6] The year 1973 therefore marked a coming of age of the Charismatic movement in New Zealand.[7]

Despite the growing divergence in ethos and emphasis between the two movements, the Charismatic renewal nevertheless owed much to classical Pentecostalism. Pentecostal individuals and groups had provided the stimulus, particularly at the personal and the organisational levels, by which many

Christians from the historic churches came into the experience of the Baptism of the Spirit.[8] However, Pentecostal patronage of the Charismatic movement was not limited to this initial process of catalysis. Charismatics often faced considerable opposition from their churches during the early stages of the renewal. As a result of this, 'many left the institutional church either because they were forced out, or because they could express their faith in a new setting without restraint or embarrassment.... Thus amid theological confusion and misunderstanding on both sides, people were forced to leave and join Pentecostal groups.'[9] (Neil gives the example of several Anglican Evangelical theological students from Christchurch, who were baptised in the Spirit through Rob Wheeler's ministry in 1961. He claims that these students were 'forced out and reluctantly left the Anglican church to join the Assemblies of God. Two of them are now Anglican priests—a situation which is now [i.e. in 1974] possible because of a more tolerant and accepting attitude towards charismatic expression in the Church.'[10])

Although Pentecostal churches often provided a haven for Charismatics disowned by their churches, the influence of Pentecostal teaching on the theological framework of the renewal was of greater significance. In part, this was a response to the perceived need in the movement for spiritual leadership and for clear Bible teaching. This need was identified by Michael Harper, following a visit to New Zealand in August and September 1967. He commented that 'there is a great need for wise and strong spiritual leadership in the present situation [i.e. the circumstances of the Charismatic movement in the face of heavy opposition]. There is a hunger for clear and authoritative [sic] Bible teaching.'[11] Until 1971, this was largely, although not exclusively, provided by Pentecostal churches, particularly in the case of Christchurch.

This emphasis on Bible teaching was the single most important overall contribution of classical Pentecostalism to the Charismatic movement in its early years. It helped to provide the initial categories and conceptual frameworks within which the Baptism of the Spirit was understood. In this respect, the contribution of the Indigenous Churches, with their strong Bible teaching ethos inherited from their Bethel Temple antecedents, was particularly significant. Rob Wheeler believes that the Indigenous Churches had a particularly important effect on the Charismatic movement. However, this was not 'as a stream, [but]... individually.'[12] He makes this comment in the context of Morrow's involvement with the renewal, and, as already been observed, teaching was a crucial factor in Morrow's and Ranchord's influence on the Charismatic movement in Christchurch. It was not until the Charismatic movement began to develop an independent identity after 1971 that this Biblically oriented Pentecostal conceptual framework began to be replaced by a more theologically nuanced Charismatic interpretation and ethos.

The Charismatic movement also had some reciprocal effects on the Pentecostal churches. In the case of the Indigenous Churches, the most important of these was that it served as a catalyst for the beginnings of a breakout from their sectarian mentality. However, this did not take place immediately and the Charismatic renewal at first appeared to catch the classical Pentecostal movement by surprise. Neil notes that 'for many independent Pentecostals, especially those who had "come out" from the historic denominations, a charismatic renewal *within* the traditional Church [was] anathema and an impossibility.'[13]

Consequently, attitudes within many of the Indigenous Churches to the Charismatic renewal were initially ambivalent. These were a product of the movement's traditional emphasis on nondenominationalism, and were epitomised in an article by Rob Wheeler in *Bible Deliverance*, entitled 'Will God revive the Historic Churches?'[14] While the article rejoiced in the outpouring of the Holy Spirit upon denominational people, which was 'thought impossible ten years ago', it also warned that

> you cannot place new wine in old bottles. That is, you cannot keep the outpouring of the Holy Spirit within the confines of Historic religion. It may last for a time, but eventually there comes a break. You may be able to stay there, and even be accepted for a time, but in the end you face a decision to either compromise on your experience and convictions and begin to "water down" your testimony (or else keep quiet altogether) or else graciously step out, and fellowship where freedom of worship and operation of the Gifts is allowed. You cannot successfully do both.[15]

Wheeler's views as expressed in the article were a fairly accurate articulation of the movement's Bethel Temple-Latter Rain heritage of come-outism, and were widely shared in many of the Indigenous Churches at the time. Nevertheless, this was not a universal conviction. These views would not have been fully endorsed, for example, by Peter Morrow and Rasik Ranchord in Christchurch, nor by the Palmerston North group of which Ken Wright was a part. Wheeler's article also adduces practical reasons why coming out from the mainstream churches should be necessary, arguing that 'it is impossible to maintain the "glow" of the Spirit . . . by staying in the orthodox churches.'[16] Even Pentecostal churches came under its blanket condemnation of denominationalism:

> Does this mean then, that orthodox christians receiving the Baptism of the Holy Spirit should join "Pentecostal" denominations who claim to have the liberty of worship and operations of the Gifts of the Spirit? Facts show that this is NOT happening, for thousands of Christians are receiving the Baptism of the Holy Spirit all over the land, but do not join up with recognised Pentecostal Churches. Is this because most Pentecostal groups in their turn, have become "old wineskins" set hard by their councils and boards? I am convinced that this is so, for hundreds of Full Gospel christians are leaving their Assemblies also, and stepping out of their "historic" church into house meetings, cottage groups and so-called "Independent" groups, where Denominationalism is not recognised or desired, and where the Spirit of the Lord can continue to restore His Truths and Gifts to His People. . . . God is reviving PEOPLE . . . but not denominations. God is pouring out His Spirit on all MEN everywhere . . . but not upon movements. God is restoring New Testament Christianity to individuals for one reason . . . to

bring them out of tradition and formality into a true Holy Spirit inspired unity that is God's answer to the Satanic inspired "World unity of Churches."[17]

Despite the considerable hyperbole (e.g. 'thousands of Christians are receiving the Baptism'), Wheeler's article is valuable as an explication of a commonly held perception in the movement at the time. Nevertheless it is significant that his article should have appeared in *Bible Deliverance* just six months after a report in the same magazine on the Massey Conference held in August 1964. This had described a 'gracious spirit of love and fellowship one towards the other [at the Conference] as each one dropped their denominational tags... [and] a spirit of love... between them and other denominational ministers.'[18] Wheeler's article demonstrates that although there was an acceptance, at least in theory, of Charismatic Christians in other denominations, there was still a strong antipathy towards denominationalism and particularly towards the World Council of Churches. The reported change of attitude at the Massey Conference does not appear, at this stage, to have penetrated very deeply into the thinking of the Indigenous Churches. Their come-outism remained largely intact, since they expected that Charismatics in the historic churches would eventually have to come out of the old wineskins of the denominational systems, including those of the organised Pentecostal churches.

An example of this attitude was the reaction of the congregation of the Timaru Missionary Revival Centre, when it was visited, about 1966, by Reverend David Edmonds, one of the first Charismatic Methodist ministers. Reverend Edmonds shared his testimony of how he had been baptised in the Spirit. The overall reaction of the congregation was one of *shock* that someone should have received the Spirit without having come out of their church. However, there could be no doubt of the reality and genuineness of his experience, and as a result of testimonies such as these, the exclusive and antiecumenical attitudes of the movement began to melt.

Two factors helped to stimulate a gradual change in the antipathy of the Indigenous Churches towards the denominational churches. The first of these was the example of Peter Morrow and Rasik Ranchord in Christchurch and of their more conciliatory attitude towards other churches. Wheeler, somewhat ruefully, acknowledges that

> Peter Morrow has been the "giant" of relationship with the Charismatic stream. I remember Peter rebuking the lot of us—we were becoming a cult of our own—and we always said "Peter, you're too 'wide'!" But a couple of years later, we appraised the situation, and he did the right thing. But he's the one who has championed the cross-relationship with churches.[19]

Morrow's influence helped to stimulate the beginnings of the Charismatic renewal in Christchurch, and to moderate the vigorous antidenominationalism of the Indigenous Churches. The expansion of his church in the 1960s and 1970s,[20] in part due to an influx of Charismatic Christians, provided him with a strong base from which to recruit and to train pastors and missionaries. Morrow established two Bible Schools in Christchurch—the New Life Family

Bible College, later renamed the International School of Ministry, in Thorrington Road, Cashmere and the Living Springs Bible School at Governor's Bay—to provide this training. Several Charismatic ministers from other churches—e.g. Reverend Owen Woodfield of the Opawa Methodist Church and Reverend David Balfour of the Anglican Church—also shared in the teaching at these schools. This interchurch cooperation did much to stimulate open attitudes in Morrow's students. The placing of many of these students into pastorates and other positions of leadership in the Indigenous Churches and elsewhere helped to spread these attitudes.

Another moderating influence on the sectarianism of the Indigenous Churches was the influx of Charismatics into the Pentecostal churches. This influx was both individual and corporate. On an individual level, it comprised those people who 'were from the historic churches and were baptised in the Spirit.... [These people] remained in the Pentecostal setting in order to continue to receive teaching and fellowship, while generally maintaining a fairly minimal allegiance within their own parishes.'[21] Many of these Charismatics eventually transferred their allegiance to Pentecostal churches. This influx was also corporate, in that Charismatic churches, such as the Awapuni Baptist Church, sometimes became linked, either formally or informally, with Pentecostal groups. The effect of this individual and corporate influx was a dilution of the antidenominational ethos of the Indigenous Churches.

To summarise: in their early stages, the Indigenous Churches, like most Pentecostal groups, were strongly sectarian, demonstrating a marked antipathy towards other churches and towards the World Council of Churches in particular. While this antipathy reflected a traditional Pentecostal distrust of denominationalism and organisation, it was to some extent also a response to the opposition of other churches towards Pentecostalism. Nevertheless, the Pentecostal movement did much to foster and to nurture the emerging Charismatic renewal. The emphasis of the Indigenous Churches on Bible teaching, and the conciliatory attitude of a number of people in the movement enabled them to have some influence upon the beginnings of the Charismatic movement.

Charismatic individuals and churches often linked informally with Pentecostal groups for fellowship and teaching; but in so doing, they helped to change the attitude and ethos of those Pentecostal groups with which they fellowshipped. A particularly influential example of this was the *Full Gospel Businessmen's Fellowship International*,[22] which created a broadly based independent forum for the sharing of Charismatic testimonies. This parachurch group did much to break down barriers, both between the Pentecostal and Charismatic movements, and between these two groups and mainstream Christianity.

Thus, as the renewal expanded, the sectarian suspicions of the Indigenous Churches were gradually eroded, and they benefitted greatly from an influx of Charismatic Christians and groups in the 1970s. The Indigenous Churches and the Charismatic movement therefore influenced and changed each other. On the one hand, the teaching ethos of the Indigenous Churches contributed to the thinking of the early Charismatic movement; conversely, the renewal helped to cause a gradual erosion of their isolationist ethos. This stimulated a broadening of the Indigenous Churches' sectarian horizons. This process was to accelerate in the 1970s.

Notes

1. Loryman, 'Growth of the Pentecostal Movement.'
2. Donald Battley, 'Charismatic Renewal: A View from Inside', *Ecumenical Review* 38 (January 1986): 49.
3. ibid. Neil also refers to 'the great influence exerted by classical Pentecostals on those charismatic Christians in the historic churches between 1967 to 1971.' Neil, 'Institutional Churches', 97.
4. These seminars were produced by the Word of God Community in Ann Arbor, Michigan, which had associations with the Notre Dame Charismatic movement. Neil, 'Institutional Churches', 139-40. Battley observes that these Seminars 'gave [the Charismatic Movement] tools that the Pentecostals had never developed.' Battley, 'Charismatic Renewal': 49.
5. Neil, 'Institutional Churches', 106-7.
6. ibid., 134. Neil discusses this classical Pentecostal theological interpretation in ibid., 11ff.
7. ibid., 131.
8. Hodgkinson, 'Independent Pentecostal Movement', 12.
9. Neil, 'Institutional Churches', 84.
10. ibid., 84, note 2.
11. Michael Harper, 'Report from New Zealand', *Renewal*, October-November 1967, 21, cited in ibid., 108.
12. Wheeler, Interview.
13. Neil, 'Institutional Churches', 59. Emphasis as cited.
14. Rob Wheeler, 'Will God Revive the Historic Churches?' *Bible Deliverance*, April 1965, 13-15.
15. ibid., 14. Capitalisation as cited.
16. ibid.
17. ibid., 14-15. Emphasis as cited.
18. 'Most Unique Convention in History of New Zealand', *Gospel Truth*, August 1964, 6, reprinted in *Bible Deliverance*, October 1964, 15.
19. Wheeler, Interview.
20. This had grown from approximately 115-20 people in 1964-1965, to a comfortably full large auditorium—seating 800-1000 people—at the Horticultural Hall in Cambridge Terrace, Christchurch, by 1980. Morrow, Interview [1988]. In the late 1970s, the Christchurch New Life Centre bought and renovated the old Majestic Theatre in Manchester Street, renaming it 'Majestic House.' Since 1980, this has been the central focus of many of the church's activities.
21. Neil, 'Institutional Churches', 93.
22. The story of this group is told in Demos Shakarian, John and Elizabeth Sherrill, *The Happiest People on Earth* (Old Tappan, New Jersey: Spire Books, 1975). The first

FGBMFI chapter in New Zealand was established in the mid-1960s, and by 1975, there were sixteen chapters. ibid., 161.

Chapter 21

'The times they are a-changing'

While the Charismatic movement significantly affected the isolationist ethos of the Indigenous Churches from the late 1960s on, a second factor was equally important for their future development. This was the rise of the permissive society, which questioned traditional institutions of authority[1] and challenged conventional codes of conduct. Nowhere was the process of social change during the Swinging Sixties more evident than in the sphere of sexual morality. The relaxation of ethical standards threatened traditional lifestyles and provoked a moral protest movement that was particularly important in altering the stance of the Pentecostal movement and of the Indigenous Churches in the 1970s.

The opening shots in what became known as the Sexual Revolution were fired when the unexpurgated version of D.H. Lawrence's *Lady Chatterley's Lover* was published in England in 1960.[2] Of even greater importance was the invention, and consequent mass availability, of the Birth Control Pill:

> More women—14 million in the United States and 60 million world-wide—use the pill than any other reversible method of contraception. The pill was the biggest break-through for giving women control over their reproductive lives of anything that came along until legalised abortion.... The sexual revolution [was] born on 9 May 1960 when the U.S. Food and Drug Administration approved the pill.[3]

The availability of the Pill had the effect of removing the threat of pregnancy for millions of women, thus giving them greater control over the consequences of their sexuality. This contributed to the loosening of traditional constraints on sexual relations.

The role of the media was also important. The worldwide liberalisation of media standards removed many of the restraints on what was considered fit to report. Furthermore, the visual impact of television enabled a more direct and personalised communication of information and ideas, since events were not just reported to happen, but in many cases were *seen* to happen. (A classic example of this was the summary execution, in full view of the television camera, of a Viet Cong suspect by a South Vietnamese police chief in the late 1960s. The cold-bloodedness of the execution came across clearly, and images such as these helped to fuel the growing protest movement against the Vietnam War.) The media, and particularly television, were therefore powerful catalysts for change, and affected the ethos of the era. Attitudes to sexuality and morality became more relaxed throughout the 1960s as a result of these and other factors.

A conservative reaction had begun to emerge by 1970 in New Zealand. A network of protest groups—including the Society for the Promotion of Community Standards, the Society for the Protection of the Unborn Child and the Concerned Parents' Association—appeared in the early 1970s. There were also other, less narrowly focused, protests such as the 1972 Jesus Marches. This reaction was anchored in conservative forms of Christianity and in the perception that traditional lifestyles, based on Judaeo-Christian standards of morality, were threatened.[4] Pentecostal churches were heavily involved in this network, and the development of the Pentecostal movement as a whole in the 1970s became characterised both by growth and by increasing moralist activism. This was particularly true of the Indigenous Churches.

The increasing permissiveness of the 1960s was exemplified by a number of specific issues that provoked vigorous debate and led to various forms of organised protest. These were the issues of homosexuality, contraception and abortion, and pornography and censorship. Several other issues, such as sex education in schools and second-wave feminism, also provoked specific responses from the Indigenous Churches and other conservative groups in the 1970s.

The moral issue that appeared to receive the least attention during the 1960s was that of homosexuality.[5] This may have been due to its comparatively low profile at this stage. Much of the public debate revolved around a recognition of the anomalous legislative situation whereby homosexuality was prohibited whereas lesbianism was not.[6] Controversy over the issue was renewed at intervals throughout the 1970s, although the legislation remained unchanged until the passing of the Homosexual Law Reform Bill in 1985. This Bill finally removed the legislative restrictions on homosexual activity between consenting adults, but not without massive moralist opposition that culminated in the Homosexual Law Reform Petition.

A second, more contentious, issue in the 1960s and 1970s was that of contraception and abortion.[7] The liberalisation of attitudes to contraception in the early 1960s, in part stimulated by the availability of the Pill, had its counterpart in attitudes to abortion later in the decade. The ambiguity of the abortion legislation, together with the liberalisation of abortion laws overseas, led to increasing pressure for revision of the law in New Zealand.[8] This sparked a conservative reaction, led by the Society for the Protection of the Unborn Child [*SPUC*], formed in Auckland in March 1970 specifically to fight the abortion issue. *SPUC* was strongly, although not exclusively, supported by Catholics, with additional support coming from members of the Fundamentalist churches and from the Mormons. The formation of liberal, pro-abortion, countermovements soon followed. These groups were largely nonsectarian and did not have the conservative religious motivation that dominated *SPUC* activities.[9]

Even at this early stage of the moralist debate, there was seen to be a clear demarcation between conservative religion on the one hand, and the emerging women's movement on the other. While this conservative opposition represented an attempt to maintain a traditional Judaeo-Christian ethic in the face of a rapidly changing social morality, it was also partly a response to the process of change itself.[10] The ongoing debate between these opposing political pressure groups ensured that considerable public controversy continued and intensified during the 1970s.[11] This led eventually to reform of the abortion laws in 1975, and to the passing, two years later, of the Contraception, Sterilisation and Abortion Bill legalising abortion, subject to certain conditions.

The debate between pro-life and pro-choice campaigners continued into the 1980s. The former stressed the right of the foetus to live; the latter, the right of the woman to choose either to continue or terminate her pregnancy. A more radical feature of antiabortion activity in the 1980s was the formation of rescue groups. Among other things, these groups engaged in the picketing of abortion clinics and in attempting to dissuade women seeking an abortion from going through with their purpose.[12] Other antiabortionists continued to test the legality of abortion clinics through the courts, and to exploit the loopholes in the current legislation to prevent the carrying out of abortions. The Indigenous Churches were strongly pro-life, and the Christchurch New Life Centre at one stage made use of the similarity in titles, issuing sets of bumper stickers that proudly proclaimed: 'New Life is pro-life.'

A third, more high-profile, issue in the later 1960s was that of pornography and censorship. In New Zealand, the law relating to this was contained in the Indecent Publications Act 1963, which set up an Indecent Publications Tribunal specifically to rule on issues of censorship and pornography. The Tribunal was both prompt and efficient, and in the first ten years there was only one appeal to the Courts against its decisions.[13] The extent of the spread of pornography in the late 1960s and early 1970s can be demonstrated by an analysis of the 832 publications classified by the Tribunal up to 1974.[14] These included books, magazines, periodicals and films; the performance of live stage shows such as *Oh! Calcutta!* also came under its jurisdiction.

Indecent publications of all kinds clearly became more widespread in the late 1960s. The workload of the Tribunal was initially relatively static at an annual rate of 20 submissions or less until 1967, but had jumped to 143 submissions by 1971. The number of submissions again rose by a further 54% to reach a peak of 221 for 1972. Thereafter, the level of submissions began to decline. The quantitative increase in submissions during this period appears to be matched by a qualitative change also. The proportion of publications that were determined indecent or restricted increased to a peak of 90.95% in 1972. The actual number of indecent or restricted

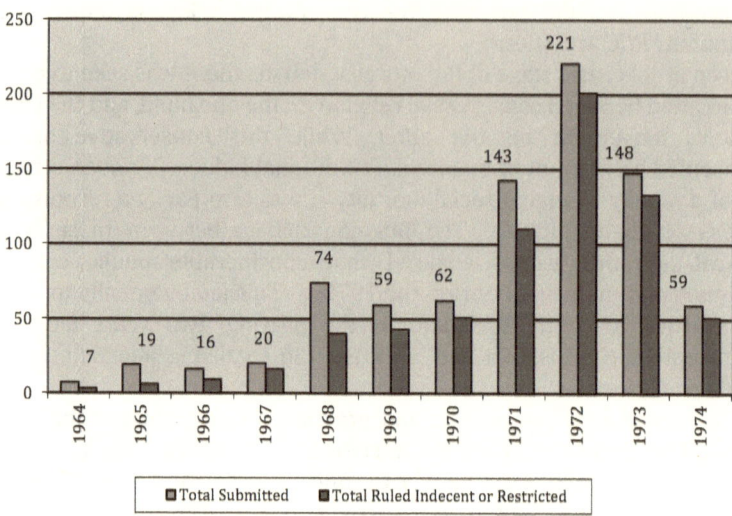

Figure **14**: Indecent Publications Tribunal: Total Submissions and Decisions 1964–74

publications in 1972 (i.e. 201) was five times that recorded in 1968 (i.e. 40). These statistics are presented graphically in Figure 14.[15]

The increasing number of publications ruled indecent or restricted helped to strengthen public perceptions of the accelerating growth rate in pornography. A controversial tour of New Zealand in October and November 1969 by the stage show *Oh! Calcutta!* proved to be the straw that broke the camel's back. In the eyes of some sections of the community, this stage show, which included scenes involving nudity, was symbolic of the decline in moral standards and of the spread of the permissive society. The following year a petition against the show was organised by Miss Patricia Bartlett, and gathered nearly 50,000 signatures. This petition was presented to Parliament, and asked for a definition of indecency so that no scenes showing nudity or sexual intercourse could be included in any public entertainment. Although the petition was rejected by Parliament, it resulted in considerable publicity for Miss Bartlett.[16]

The rejection of Miss Bartlett's petition, together with the blaze of publicity that followed, led to the formation of the Society for the Promotion of Community Standards in November 1970. This group, which to some extent was synonymous with Miss Bartlett herself, rapidly became the most prominent of the moral campaign groups in the 1970s. Together with *SPUC*, formed the same year to contest the abortion issue, it marked the beginnings in New Zealand of a conservative Christian reaction against the permissive society. As Allanah Ryan observes, this was also significant from a wider perspective, since their creation 'mark[ed] the beginning of a moralist movement in New Zealand. While in the early seventies these two groups hardly represented a *movement* (in the sense that we have one in the late eighties), they were definitely a *new* kind of conservatism.'[17] Although pressure groups such as these focused on narrowly defined single issues, they also represented and tapped into a general sense of unease among conservative Christians.

A wider ground swell expression of this concern over the changing moral values of society came with the Jesus Marches in 1972. These marches, initially intended as a conservative Christian protest over the perceived disintegration of morality in New Zealand, were catalytic for later developments in the 1970s. In particular, they would initiate trends that would modify the shape of Pentecostalism in this country. Thus the relaxation of moral standards that characterised the Swinging Sixties led to a conservative reaction that was to significantly affect the development of the Indigenous Churches in the 1970s.

Notes

1. Jürgen Habermas categorises this challenge to institutional authority as a legitimation crisis. Jürgen Habermas, *Legitimation Crisis*, trans. Thomas McCarthy (Boston: Beacon Press, 1975), *passim*.
2. John Capon, . . . *and there was light: The story of the Nationwide Festival of Light* (London: Lutterworth Press, 1972), 88.
3. 'Pill Remains Top Choice', *Timaru Herald*, 7 May 1990, 7.
4. 'Fundamentalist moral campaigners very often share the common world view of a threatened lifestyle.' Michael Hill, 'Religion and Society: Cement or Ferment?' in *Religion in New Zealand*, ed. Christopher Nichol and James Veitch (Wellington: Tertiary Christian Studies Programme of the Combined Chaplaincies and the Religious Studies Department, Victoria University, 1980), 224. See also Hill, 'Religion', in *New Zealand: Sociological Perspectives*, 187.
5. The best history of the homosexuality question in New Zealand up to 1983 is Richard Bowman, 'Beyond the Pink Triangle: the New Zealand public's attitudes towards homosexuality', in *Shades of Deviance: A New Zealand Collection*, ed. Michael Hill *et al*., (Palmerston North: Dunmore Press, 1983), 99–113.
6. New Zealand Homosexual Law Reform Society, *50/50: Fifty Questions and Answers about Homosexuality and the Law* (Wellington: New Zealand Homosexual Law Reform Society, 1968), 7.
7. For a succinct, but impartial, historical summary of the abortion controversy in New Zealand up to 1981, see Martin Vaughan and Angela Varelas, 'To be or not to be: the abortion controversy in New Zealand', in Hill *et al*., *Shades of Deviance*, 114–25. Another perspective on the abortion issue is presented in George Bryant, *The Church on Trial* (Whangarei: Whau Publications, 1986), chapter 9, 'Abortion.' A more liberal approach is that of M.W. Doyle, 'Recent Developments in the Abortion Law', in *Legal Abortion in New Zealand: A Review of Opinions and Politics 1970–1977*, ed. W.A.P. Facer (Auckland: New Zealand Rationalist Association, 1977), 5.
8. Jocelyn Brooks, *et al*., *Ill Conceived: Law and Abortion Practice in New Zealand* (Dunedin: Caveman Press, 1981), 31. This book, written from a pro-abortion

stance, gives a more detailed account of the abortion controversies than that of Vaughan and Varelas.
9. ibid., 46.
10. Colin Brown observes that 'so long as the pace of social change continues and security continues to elude us, ... the forces of conservatism will be strongly represented in the churches.... Religions have a special attraction to those made anxious by the pace of change and for whom security in other areas appears elusive.' Colin Brown, 'Religion in New Zealand: Past, Present and Future', in *Religion and New Zealand's Future*, ed. Kevin J. Sharpe (Palmerston North: Dunmore Press, 1982), 17.
11. One of the more vigorous critics of the antiabortion movement was Dr Erich Geiringer, whose book *SPUC 'em all! Abortion Politics 1978* (Waiura, Martinborough: Alister Taylor, 1978) paints an unflattering portrait of *SPUC*. However, his book does give some indication of the intensity of the abortion debate.
12. For an example of this activity (code-named Operation Rescue), see Lynne Loates, 'State of Siege', *More*, February 1990, 64–70.
13. Ed Dearn, *Pornography Degrades* (Sydney: Renda Publications, n.d.), 71. The appeal referred to is Robson v. Hicks Smith and Sons Ltd. [1965] *N.Z.L.R.* 1113. This was brought against the decision of the Indecent Publications Tribunal that the paperback version of D.H. Lawrence's *Lady Chatterley's Lover* could not be ruled indecent since an identical hard-cover version was already freely available. Indecent Publications Tribunal, Decision 18, delivered 7 April 1965, gazetted 14 April 1965. *New Zealand Gazette* (Wellington: Government Printer, 14 April 1965), 534–35.
14. Stuart Perry has compiled several indexes of the decisions of the Tribunal. Stuart Perry, *Indecent Publication Control in New Zealand* (Wellington: McCrae Publishers, 1975), 25–54.
15. For a detailed analysis of these statistics, see Knowles, 'Some Aspects of the History of the New Life Churches', 140–44.
16. Tony Reid, 'Patricia Bartlett versus Moral Rot', *New Zealand Listener*, 15 November 1980, 25. Reid's article is somewhat derogatory in tone. Alison Kirkman, 'Propriety Promoted: Patricia Bartlett and the Society for the Promotion of Community Standards', in Hill *et al.*, *Shades of Deviance*, 26–40, includes an interesting analysis of the ways in Miss Bartlett's media image was constructed.
17. Allanah Ryan, 'Remoralising Politics', in *Revival of the Right: New Zealand Politics in the 1980s*, ed. Bruce Jesson, Allanah Ryan and Paul Spoonley (Auckland: Heinemann Reed, 1988), 57. Emphasis as cited.

Chapter 22

The 1972 Jesus Marches

The Jesus Marches represented a grass roots conservative Christian response to the changes in society[1] and were catalytic for the future development of the Pentecostal movement in New Zealand. The impetus for the marches—and for similar marches, such as the Festival of Light in Britain[2]—came from apprehension over the deteriorating moral standards of society and the perceived need to protest this decline. Indeed, the scripture 'Righteousness Exalts a Nation' that appeared on placards carried by the marchers 'was virtually the theme and heart of the Jesus Marches—a genuine concern for the moral state of the nation.'[3] Initial reports characterised the event as a March for Righteousness[4] and as 'designed to encourage higher community standards, to promote recognition of Biblical authority, and to foster prayer.'[5] Rasik Ranchord, a participant in the Auckland march, observes that it was intended to bring about

> an awareness of a need for righteousness in the country, and ... [to raise] up the profile of Christians; they needed to be more visible, and [to] let their convictions be *known* more widely. And so there was a rally to show that whilst [there was] decadence on one hand, ... there were lots of people that stood for righteousness.... "Righteousness exalteth a nation"—that Scripture—became one of the rallying points.... We came to lift up righteousness, and this was one of the ways that we could demonstrate that.[6]

The motivation of the Jesus Marches was therefore grounded in the perceived need for the Christian community to make a stand for righteousness.

Although there were no direct connections with the British Festival of Light, the indebtedness of the New Zealand Jesus Marches becomes obvious when the Statements of the respective Executive Committees are compared.[7] In some sections, the statements are word-for-word identical. Nevertheless, the New Zealand marches appear to have been more fundamentalist and revivalistic in orientation than was the case in Britain. While prayer meetings for the marches were common to both countries, in New Zealand there was a strong emphasis placed on national repentance and revival.[8] Thus the Maori evangelist Muri Thompson, speaking at the rally held outside the Chief Post Office after the Auckland march, called for the Prime Minister to declare 'a day of prayer, fasting, repenting and self-humbling.'⁹ Furthermore, the Charter of Righteousness presented at that rally 'almost demanded that the civic authorities introduce a society based on New Testament principles.'[10] The aggressiveness of this demand naturally provoked a negative response from those to whom the Charter was addressed. By the time of the later marches, however, this somewhat hard-line attitude had mellowed.

The Jesus Marches attracted considerable public attention. The Auckland march on Friday 5 May 1972 received front-page treatment by the *New Zealand Herald* under the headline 'Jesus People Reign in Queen Street.'[11] Its success led to spontaneously generated Jesus Marches in other parts of the country. Ranchord recalls that

> Other people got inspired, and ... many other cities took it up. ... It almost seemed like a kind of "spontaneous combustion." People seemed to gravitate towards an idea like that and ... joined in. ... We felt that the Lord was definitely speaking [to many people]; that's why the idea spread. ... There was no kind of a central committee or anything like that[12]; each particular region did their own "Jesus March." ... It was left to the local committee to contact the local churches and to ... [share] the vision and [talk] about what they would do in that particular area, and [take] it off from there.[13]

This claim to spontaneity does not preclude the role of organisation in the spread of Jesus Marches. Muri Thompson had done much to publicise the idea throughout New Zealand in early 1972,[14] and the establishment of a Board of Reference provided a corporate focal point.[15] Nevertheless, participation in the marches was largely spontaneous. In local areas, 'organising committees sprang up spontaneously, [each] consisting mainly of laymen in the 20 to 30 age group, with ministers often acting in advisory capacities.'[16] Although these committee members represented many different churches, Pentecostal Christians were heavily involved. Rob Wheeler, for example, was Secretary of the Auckland Executive Committee[17] and the Christchurch Committee included a predominance of Evangelical, Pentecostal and Charismatic Christians.[18] The Jesus Marches were therefore essentially a lay movement as well as a young peoples' movement, and owed much to the impetus generated by the Pentecostal and Charismatic movements. Blyth Harper, Administrator and Prayer Convenor of the Auckland Jesus March, observed that 'the main thrust, in terms of planning and initial participation, came from charismatic Christians, especially the Maori Evangelist, Mr. Muri Thompson.'[19]

Although the nature of the Jesus Marches changed as the series progressed, this had always been somewhat ambiguous. Despite the strong emphasis on 'righteousness exalts a nation', the lines were blurred between an evangelistic witness of Jesus and a demonstration of moral protest. This is demonstrated by an advertisement for the march in *Challenge Weekly*. This is headed (in bold type and capitals) '**MARCH FOR JESUS**', while a second line, in smaller type, describes it as 'A March for Righteousness.'[20] Consequently, it is not surprising that on the night, 'What began as an idea of a formal protest march against the permissive society, ended with many of the 10,000 [participants] skipping and dancing their way down the street in the exuberance and joy of their love for Christ and oneness with one another.'[21] This was also a characteristic of the marches in other centres. 'The original call to national righteousness, protesting against the moral landslide, tended to be swallowed up as the marches progressed, by a positive celebration of the Name, power and presence of Jesus.'[22]

An example of the change in emphasis can be seen in the case of the Christchurch Jesus March, held on Friday 15 September 1972. This is evident both in the moderate nature of the Address to the Mayor[23] and in the slogans on the banners carried by the marchers. These are almost exclusively oriented towards a Jesus celebration, with only one of the twenty banner and placard texts even indirectly referring to an element of moral protest (i.e. 'Jesus, the answer to soul pollution'). The placard texts had a Gospel theme, expressed by classic Scripture texts and evangelical slogans, with the large calico banners that formed the focal points of the march having a more upbeat slogan or text.[24]

Not all placards waved during the Jesus Marches played down the element of protest, however. Trevor Shaw refers to the confrontation in Palmerston North when the Jesus marchers accidentally crossed paths with the patrons of a performance of the stage show *Hair*. One of the placards in that march aptly read 'Give Hair a permanent wave goodbye.'[25] *Challenge Weekly*, in a report of the Palmerston North march, comments that the city was at that time 'breaking into new areas of notoriety with two wife-swapping clubs, black magic being practised openly in some schools, a prospect of a strip club opening, and unprecedented gang warfare in what has always been a very conservative centre.'[26] Despite the celebratory emphasis, moral concern therefore continued to be a prominent feature of the Jesus Marches in many centres.

The final and largest of the Jesus Marches took place in Wellington on Sunday 8 October 1972, when a crowd variously estimated from 15,000[27] to 'more than 25,000'[28] marched to Parliament House. This march had been well advertised in church newspapers, and, as with the other marches, many people came from other centres to participate. The tone of this march was affirmative rather than aggressive; it was effectively a public declaration of faith in Christ, rather than a demand for legislative action. Nevertheless, moral concern was still a key element. Captain Brian McStay of the Salvation Army, one of the speakers at the final rally, declared that 'a nation is changed only when the members of that nation change their values—change their attitudes.'[29] While the desire for an amelioration of the moral climate of the country was unaltered, the focus was now attitudinal, rather than legislative. The Covenant—which was presented by the marchers, and received by the Prime Minister, John Marshall, on behalf of the Government—was not a demand for legislative reform. Rather, it was a declaration of the need to pray for the

Government, to praise God for the positive things that were happening in the nation, and to proclaim the Gospel of Jesus Christ.[30]

How successful were the Jesus Marches? Despite the marchers' concern for national righteousness, little direct impact appears to have been made on the morality of the nation. (There is, for example, no evidence of a causal connection between the Jesus Marches and the drop in the level of indecent publications the following year.)[31] Rather, the marches functioned as a protest against what the participants perceived to be a catastrophic moral decline in society, and embodied a grass roots movement in the churches, particularly amongst the youth and the laity. Nevertheless, the marches did not find favour with all sections of the Christian community. Several march committees failed to gain the necessary support from the local churches. The Dunedin Jesus March, for example, had to be cancelled due to lack of support. An Anglican member of the *ad hoc* organising committee for the Dunedin march commented that 'the committee did not attract all the representatives it needed to ensure the march would be a success. The Pentecostal churches gave strong support to it, and there were representatives from the Otago University Evangelical Union, the Open Air Campaigners, and some others.'[32] However, some of this lack of support may also be because the march was to have been held in the depths of a Dunedin winter!

Other churches were opposed on principle to the emphasis of the marches. For example, the editor of the *New Zealand Methodist*, in an editorial written before the first Jesus March took place in Auckland, was disparaging towards the participants in the marches. He described them as 'limping for Jesus', and stated that

> It is not a "Jesus" march at all, but a morality march—with morality very narrowly defined.... The marchers' emphasis is on "righteousness," which is spelt out mainly in terms of individual (especially sexual) morality.... To exalt principles of individual morality and law and order while censoring out (as is intended) reference to evils like apartheid, the Indochina conflict, economic exploitation at home and abroad, and then to call it a "Jesus march," is to misrepresent the Gospel.[33]

Much of this editorial was repeated in the 'From the Churches' column in the *New Zealand Herald*, which noted, however, that the *New Zealand Methodist* editorial was 'written before Friday night's march.'[34] The editor's assessment, although possibly a valid criticism of the original intentions for the Jesus March as expressed in the publicity material for the March for Righteousness, was, in the event, somewhat premature. The march in Auckland, as in other centres, took on a celebratory character, and this change in emphasis highlighted the somewhat prejudicial nature of the editorial. Consequently, while there appeared to be little response to the march itself, the editorial attracted heavy criticism in letters to the editor of the *New Zealand Methodist*.[35] By contrast, other observers, such as Professor Lloyd Geering, were generally more temperate and balanced in their assessment.[36]

In one sense, the Jesus Marches were not novel. They were modelled on the Jesus Marches in the United States from 1969 on—themselves an adaptation by the American Jesus People of the antiwar protest marches of the late 1960s.[37] They also followed the example of the British Festival of Light. The march in Auckland was not the first Jesus March in this country. A Gather for Jesus March, organised by the Victoria University Christian Union, had been held on 17 March 1972 in Wellington. This was the culmination of a special outreach week at the University, and was 'a protest against the evil of this world and a demonstration of faith in Jesus Christ.'[38] Neither was the Charter of Righteousness presented at that march the first such document to be submitted to the civic authorities.[39] The difference was essentially one of scale, and the significance of the Jesus Marches lay more in their indirect, rather than direct, effects. They brought together some 70,000 people around the country, and gave voice to a united expression of conservative concern over moral decay.[40] In so doing, they provided an example of the power of collective action, and became a catalyst for increasing conservative Christian mobilisation over the next fifteen years.

The Jesus Marches also had other effects on the life of the Christian community. Similar Jesus Festivals continued annually for some years, usually under the auspices of the Full Gospel Businessmen's Fellowship International,[41] to 'continue the momentum'[42] generated by the marches. These had the effect of reinforcing the sense of Christian unity, transcending denominational barriers,[43] which was one of the marches' most powerful legacies: 'The march also did something in that it brought together some elements of the Christian community which would normally be reticent about a public demonstration of love and loyalty to the Lord Jesus and a stand for righteousness. Unity was in evidence.'[44] This public demonstration in the streets was a new feature, at least for Protestants. While Catholics had a tradition of public marches of commitment and witness,[45] the style of public display implicit in the Jesus Marches was quite new in the Protestant community.

Since much of the impetus for the Jesus Marches came from Pentecostal and Charismatic Christians,[46] this sense of unity greatly facilitated the growth of these movements throughout the 1970s. Charismatic solidarity was reinforced by the Christian Advance Ministries Charismatic Conference held in Palmerston North in January 1973. Pentecostal involvement in the Jesus Marches also did much to break down barriers between the various Pentecostal groups, including the Indigenous Churches.[47] The ministry of Ern Baxter and others over the next two years reinforced this increasing Pentecostal openness, and led to the landmark conference at Snell's Beach in March 1975.

To summarise: the increasing liberalisation of moral (especially sexual) ethics in the 1960s led to a conservative reaction, which took two forms. Firstly, it led to the formation of organisations, such as the Society for the Protection of the Unborn Child and the Society for the Promotion of Community Standards, to address specific issues. Secondly, it tapped into a more generalised, but largely unfocused, feeling of conservative Christian unease, which found expression in the Jesus Marches. These marches were catalytic for the later development of the conservative Christian moralist movement in New Zealand. They represented an increasing recognition of the need for 'Christians... to be more visible, and [to] let their convictions be *known* more widely.'[48] They also led to the formation of specifically targeted moralist action groups such as the Concerned Parents Association and the Save Our Homes Campaign.[49] Furthermore, they had the effect of producing an informal ecumenism, which, in the longer term, had marked effects on the expansion and development of the Charismatic and Pentecostal movements in New Zealand. Many of the changes that took place in the Pentecostal movement—and in the Indigenous Churches—in the 1970s can be traced directly back to the influence of the Jesus Marches. In that respect, they were catalytic for the future development of the Pentecostal movement.

Notes

1. Trevor R. Shaw, comp., *The Jesus Marchers 1972* (Auckland: Challenge Publishers, 1972), 7. This book is a compilation of newspaper reports and articles on the Jesus Marches.
2. For a brief outline of the Festival of Light, see Roy Wallis and Richard Bland, 'Purity in Danger: A survey of participants in a moral crusade rally', *British Journal of Sociology* 30 (June 1979): 188–205. Fuller accounts are given in Flo Dobbie, *Land Aflame!* (London: Hodder and Stoughton, 1972), 28ff., and Capon, *... and there was light*, 5ff. Dobbie's narrative is a somewhat subjective account, written by the wife of a key participant in the Festival, and showing a tendency to triumphalism. Capon's account is more temperate, objective and balanced.
3. Shaw, *The Jesus Marchers*, 7. The reference is to Proverbs 14:34.
4. 'March for Righteousness plans major impact in Auckland', *Challenge Weekly*, 29 April 1972, 4.
5. '10,000 Strong for Jesus', *New Zealand Herald*, 5 May 1972, 3.
6. Ranchord, Interview. Emphasis as cited.
7. Jesus March: March for Righteousness, Auckland, 'Executive Committee Statement of Purpose', Auckland, 1972, Ephemera Collection, Alexander Turnbull Library, Wellington. (Mimeographed). I am indebted to Rev. Dr John Evans for a copy of this material. The text of the Festival of Light 'Statement of Intent' is given in Capon, *... and there was light*, 20.
8. Shaw, *The Jesus Marchers*, 27; Jesus March, 'Executive Committee Statement', Object (e).
9. 'Jesus People Reign in Queen Street', *New Zealand Herald*, 6 May 1972, 1.
10. Shaw, *The Jesus Marchers*, 29.
11. 'Jesus People Reign in Queen Street', *New Zealand Herald*, 6 May 1972, 1.
12. Although a Board of Reference was appointed, this appears to have been essentially only a figurehead, with the organisation of the marches resting in the hands of local committees.
13. Ranchord, Interview.

14. For examples of Muri Thompson's promotion of the Marches, see '"Jesus Marches" plan for N.Z.' *Otago Daily Times*, 6 April 1972, 5; and '"March for Jesus" plan', *Christchurch Press*, 13 April 1972, 11.
15. This Board of Reference included members of parliament, civic dignitaries, and ministers from various denominations, and was supplemented by local *ad hoc* committees in the various areas. Jesus March, 'Executive Committee Statement', 2. This Board of Reference was extended for the later marches. *National Jesus Festival News No.1*, 1 August 1972.
16. Blyth Harper, cited in Shaw, *The Jesus Marchers*, 27
17. Jesus March, 'Executive Committee Statement', 2.
18. 'Plan for Jesus March', *Christchurch Press*, 12 August 1972, 9.
19. Blyth Harper, cited in Neil, 'Institutional Churches', 126, note 3.
20. *Challenge Weekly*, 29 April 1972, 4.
21. 'Unprecedented Event: 10,000 march for Jesus in Queen Street', *Challenge Weekly*, 13 May 1972, 1.
22. Blyth Harper, '85,000 publicly witness by Marching for Jesus', *Challenge Weekly*, 21 October 1972, 2.
23. The text of this Address to the Mayor is given in Allan K. Davidson and Peter J. Lineham, ed., *Transplanted Christianity: Documents illustrating aspects of New Zealand Church History* (Auckland: College Communications, 1987), 329–30.
24. Peter J. Lineham, Research Papers, History Department, Massey University, Palmerston North. I am indebted to Dr Lineham for making these available to me.
25. Shaw, *The Jesus Marchers*, 11.
26. *Challenge Weekly*, 27 May 1972, 1.
27. 'Thousands Join in Jesus March', *Dominion*, 9 October 1972, 1. Another newspaper estimated the crowd at 20,000. 'Thousands of Jesus Marchers Ended Festival in Grounds of Parliament', *Evening Post*, 9 October 1972, 36.
28. Copeland, *Faith that works*, 42.
29. Cited in Shaw, *The Jesus Marchers*, 21.
30. ibid.
31. See above at chapter 21, page 144, Figure 14.
32. 'Jesus March Cancelled', *Otago Daily Times*, 18 July 1972, 1.
33. 'Editorial: Limping for Jesus', *New Zealand Methodist*, 4 May 1972, 2.
34. 'From the Churches', *New Zealand Herald*, 8 May 1972, 16.
35. 'Letters to the Editor', *New Zealand Methodist*, 18 May–15 June 1972.
36. Lloyd Geering, 'Religion Today', *Auckland Star*, 21 October 1972, cited in Shaw, *The Jesus Marchers*, 25.
37. The best account of the Jesus People is Ronald M. Enroth, Edward E. Ericson, Jnr., and C. Breckinridge Peters, *The Jesus People: Old-Time Religion in the Age of Aquarius* (Grand Rapids, Michigan: William B. Eerdmans Publishing Company, 1972). This surveys developments in the movement up to late 1971. Other accounts include Robert S. Ellwood, Jnr., *One Way: The Jesus Movement and its meaning* (Eaglewood Cliffs, New Jersey: Prentice-Hall, 1973); Kenneth Leech, *Youthquake: The growth of a counter-culture through two decades* (London: Sheldon Press, 1973), especially chapter 7; and Walter L. Knight, *Jesus People come alive* (Wheaton, Illinois: Tyndale House Publishers, 1971). For an account of the New Zealand Jesus People, see R.J. Thompson, 'The New Youth Fundamentalism', in *Perspectives on Religion: New Zealand Viewpoints, 1974*, ed. John C. Hinchcliff (Auckland: Universi-

ty of Auckland Bindery, 1975), 85–91; Jill McCracken, 'The God Squad', *New Zealand Listener*, 23 October 1972, 14–15; and Robert Keyzer, 'A Christian Revolutionary', *idem*, 13 November 1972, 10–11.
38. Shona Cobham, 'Gather for Jesus March in Capital', *Challenge Weekly*, 25 March 1972, 3.
39. Neil, 'Institutional Churches', 125, refers to the presentation of a Charter in December 1970.
40. Varying figures are cited for the number of marches that actually took place in 1972. *Challenge Weekly* cites 11 marches, and 85,000 participants. Harper, '85,000 publicly witness by Marching for Jesus', *Challenge Weekly*, 21 October 1972, 2. Trevor Shaw estimates the total participation at 70,000 people in 13 marches. Shaw, *The Jesus Marchers*, 7 and 16–17. Neil appears to cite Shaw, but lists only 12 marches, omitting the march in Tokoroa. Neil, 'Institutional Churches', 125.
41. As, for example, the Jesus 75 campaign. John Bluck, 'Jesus 75—a mixed blessing', *New Citizen*, 12 June 1975, 5.
42. Rasik Ranchord to Hank van der Steen, 2 February 1973, Majestic House Correspondence Files, Christchurch [hereafter cited as *MHCF*].
43. A Canadian visitor to New Zealand (and participant in one of the later marches) commented that 'everyone lost their denominational tags' in the marches. Paul Edmondson, *Challenge Weekly*, 5 August 1972, 6. Edmondson was visiting New Zealand under the auspices of the Christian and Missionary Alliance. He also added the comment that 'there was nothing about [the march] to suggest it was "made in America"'.
44. *Challenge Weekly*, 27 May 1972, 1. The reference is to the Palmerston North Jesus March.
45. An example is given in H.R. Jackson, *Churches and People in Australia and New Zealand 1860-1930* (Wellington: Allen and Unwin and Port Nicholson Press, 1987), 68.
46. Neil, 'Institutional Churches', 126, note 3.
47. Ian Clark, however, believes that the Jesus Marches 'were a *fruit* of coming together rather than a catalyst to bring us together. I think that's really the order of events.' Clark, Interview. Emphasis as cited. Clark stresses the role of Ern Baxter's ministry in New Zealand in 1974 in stimulating Pentecostal unity.
48. Ranchord, Interview. Emphasis as cited.
49. See below, chapters 24 and 25.

Chapter 23

The Moralist Movement and the Indigenous Churches

The 1972 Jesus marches represented a conservative Christian grass roots reaction to the increasing liberalization of moral standards in the 1960s. Although the marches were intended as once only events, they provided a catalyst—and sometimes also the model—for further moralist activism throughout the 1970s. This conservative Christian response to the permissive society formed part of a worldwide phenomenon, and laid the foundations for what became known as 'the New Christian Right.' Although this title refers specifically to the American context, it is also applicable to the development of similar moral activist movements elsewhere.[1] Their rise was significant since, as Liebman and Wuthnow have observed, it represented a change from '[political] abstinence ... to political action, at least for a substantial segment of evangelicals' and compelled the reexamination of sociopolitical theories.[2] The emergence of these moralist movements was the product of several shifts of focus in the early 1970s, when 'The sharp line between the kingdom of God and the kingdom of Caesar began to blur. Unwilling to turn their backs on what appeared to be a deepening moral crisis ... , evangelicals shifted their attention to the sphere of public life.'[3]

The first of these shifts of focus was an eschatological one. Many conservative Evangelicals held premillennial views, believing that the world order was doomed to become progressively more degenerate, with the climax of evil coming just before the second coming of Christ. For their part, the Indigenous Churches espoused a distinctive form of premillennial dispensationalism, based on the Bethel Temple teaching of W.H. Offiler. In the light of this pessimistic worldview, there was little point in trying to change the world, since it was, by its very nature, irredeemable. While various forms of premillennial belief remained prominent in the 1970s,[4] the rise of the new moral activist movements implied a move away from this viewpoint. The assumption of the moralist participants that it was possible to change the world for the better, or at least to halt the process of decay, was, in reality, at variance with their premillennial theology. In New Zealand, as elsewhere, this shift was largely an unconscious one. Nevertheless, this conceptual shift both reflected and stimulated the end of conservative Christian protest, exemplified by the Jesus Marches, and the beginnings of conservative Christian political pressure and the proliferation of lobbying groups.

The second shift of focus involved the conservative Christian response to secularisation.[5] Although no consensus has been reached on a definition of the process of secularisation, there is generally agreement that it has the effect of internalising religious authority. Religion thus becomes individualised and privatised, and effectively nullified as a source of authority in secular society. This abrogation of public religious authority leads to morality, both public and private, becoming a matter of individual determination and choice. Secularisation can therefore be seen as a catalyst for the liberalization of moral standards in the 1960s, and it was primarily the devaluation of religion implicit in this process that provoked the Christian moralist reaction. In the eyes of the moral activists, society had departed from Christian principles, and it was therefore necessary to return to traditional standards of morality. Since the activists' perception of morality was rooted in their Christian faith, this necessarily implied a return to traditional Christian belief. They therefore opposed secularisation as much as the liberalization of moral standards that resulted from it—indeed, for some sections of the movement, secular humanism was the enemy *par excellence*.[6]

The conservative Christian opponents of secularisation sought to reinstate Christianity as a legitimator of public morality. In the 1970s, this reinstatement was seen as a matter of the adoption by society of Christian principles. By the late 1980s, however, the strategy had changed to placing conservative Christians into positions of power. Nevertheless, the enemy (i.e. secular humanism) remained the same. Rob Wheeler's candidacy for the Mount Albert seat in the 1987 General Election was motivated by precisely this perception:

> A Satanic revival has touched New Zealand! Our nation has been converted to secular humanism, which is anti-Bible and anti-Christian! Satan has been at work at all levels, right up to the Government.... When we can send Christians into Parliament... we can effect a change in our nation that will touch the heart of every man and every woman. We need to be in every level of society.[7]

However, although this motivation was a religious one, the accompanying moralist activism represented a shift in attitude towards secular society. Richard Russell describes this reorientation as a 'growing crisis of the Evangelical world-view.' He comments that, in the context of British Evangelicalism, 'there has been a considerable shift from setting up a choice between "individual redemption" to "social amelioration" to seeing their relation as conjunctive.'[8] Furthermore, this represented a shift from a 'Christ OR culture' to a 'Christ AND culture' paradigm and parallels the movement towards a social gospel and the secularisation of the Christian faith in the early 1900s.[9] Russell may be correct in his insistence that the moralist movement represented a change in the Evangelical worldview. In New Zealand, the new concern with moralist issues rather than with an individualistic faith marked a modification of the style of Evangelicalism that had prevailed in this country since the 1959 Billy Graham Crusade. To some extent, it also represented a revival of the conservative concern that motivated the rise of the Temperance Movement in the 1880s.

The third, and most important, shift of focus produced by the Jesus marches was a consolidation of identity among conservative Christians. The marches had the threefold effect of focusing the attention of the participants on moral issues in the wider society, stimulating an awareness of the power of collective action, and producing an informal ecumenism. In so doing, they helped to promote a clearer sense of conservative Christian self-identity—especially within the Pentecostal and Charismatic movements—and stimulated the beginnings of concerted moral and political activism. Both of these consequences were reinforced by subsequent events, and greatly influenced the way in which the Pentecostal and Charismatic movements developed in New Zealand during the 1970s and 1980s. As will be seen, the formation of the Associated Pentecostal Churches of New Zealand in 1975 owed much to Pentecostal anxiety about moral issues. In responding to the sweeping changes in the society around them, however, the Pentecostal churches themselves began to change.

As the 1970s progressed, the Pentecostal movement became much more acceptable and respectable.[10] Colin Brown sees this as the result of deliberate efforts by some of the movement's leaders to achieve enhanced growth, and cites the erosion of hard-line Pentecostal ethical standards as a further element. However, the author would argue that these standards were redirected, rather than eroded. One of the major factors that contributed to this change was the movement's perceived need to influence society towards Biblical standards of righteousness. As will be seen, the need for a legitimate political voice was one of the prime motivating factors in the acquisition of Pentecostal respectability. These changes were reflected in an increasing Pentecostal self-awareness, which was manifest in moves towards organisational consolidation both between and within the various Pentecostal groups, and in involvement in various political lobbying groups. Their apprehension about a perceived catastrophic decline in the moral values of society, together with the growing organisational consolidation of the movement, form the twin motifs of Pentecostal development in the 1970s. The changes in the Indigenous Churches strongly reflect this double motif.

What moralist issues were important to the Indigenous Churches? The moralist movement of the 1970s was neither monolithic nor well-defined. Allanah Ryan describes it as 'a neo-conservative movement that is concerned with maintaining the authority of the family and traditional ideas about gender and sexual relations.'[11] While conservative Christians focused on a number of specific moral issues throughout the decade, not all of these excited the same degree of concern. Different groups had different emphases, which in most cases tended to be questions of individual morality rather than of social praxis, and centred on the preservation of the nuclear family. As Ryan puts it,

'The overall defining factor of the moral right is concern with the family. This institution is constantly being invoked as being in a precarious position and therefore in desperate need of preservation and protection from the destabilising influences of "permissive" society.'[12]

Pentecostal groups tended to emphasise moral issues of gender and sexuality, rather than social and economic issues.[13] Bob Horton, a member of the North Shore New Life Fellowship, and president of the Auckland chapter of the Full Gospel Businessmen's Fellowship International that had organised the Jesus 75 crusade, provides a good example. John Bluck cites Horton as having 'no doubt that homosexuality..., abortion and drugs [headed] the list of evils that threaten God's blessing on New Zealand.'[14] (Bluck, as editor of the *New Citizen*, makes an intriguing contrast to his article on the Jesus 75 campaign with the juxtaposition of a testimony from a campaign newsletter on the same page. This testimony reads:

> One committee member reported how he had been halted by a traffic officer after excessively speeding. Parking behind the car and obviously viewing the Jesus 75 (sticker), [the traffic officer] approached the sorrowful member reminding him of the limit. The driver admitted his guilt and after tapping his book, (the officer) proceeded to remind him again and then proceeded back to his bike. Praise the Lord for the freedom in Christ![15]

This somewhat cavalier attitude to the speed limit provides a strange contrast to the concern of the Jesus 75 campaigners about the moral standards of society.) Nevertheless, Horton's views were typical of those held within the Pentecostal movement. This focus on individual, rather than social, morality[16] reflected the Pentecostal emphasis on individual experience, as well as the fundamentalist approach to the Bible that formed the basis of the movement's teachings.

Oral and documentary sources made available to the author[17] show that the moralism of the Indigenous Churches appeared to have several specific foci. These included 'the introduction of sex education into our public schools',[18] 'teaching in schools that is contrary to Christian principles',[19] and 'concern on moral issues and the state of education in New Zealand.'[20] The issue of abortion appears briefly in the 1977 and 1983 files,[21] while correspondence in 1980 protested against the bringing of indecent films and stage shows into New Zealand.[22] Oral interviews with pastors of the New Life Churches contain references to the need to 'work towards preserving the nuclear family.'[23] This concern for the family was stimulated in part by the publication of Larry Christenson's book *The Christian Family*,[24] which, according to Rasik Ranchord, 'was very, very well received.... It came out at the right time [and struck] a chord in the hearts of the people. The people felt [that] we must work towards preserving the nuclear family.'[25]

The Save Our Homes Campaign, started in 1977 by Anne Morrow, wife of Pastor Peter Morrow, was a specific response to the perceived radicalism of the feminist movement.[26] Surprisingly, although homosexual law reform was causing public debate in 1975, there is no reference in the Majestic House

Correspondence Files throughout the 1970s to the issue. Nevertheless, the Indigenous Churches, along with other conservative groups, were later heavily involved in the campaign against the Homosexual Law Reform Bill in 1985.

These primary materials show that, while there were a number of areas of moralist concern, there were three major issues for the Indigenous Churches in the 1970s. The first of these was that of sex education in schools, which expanded into 'the state of education in New Zealand.' The preservation of the nuclear family and the mobilisation of a response to what was seen as destructive radical feminism were also important. Expressions of concern about abortion and pornography appeared to be more muted, and made in response to specific local situations. Homosexuality did not become a major issue for the Indigenous Churches until the mid-1980s, and references to other social issues in the 1970s, such as racism and sporting tours to South Africa, are noticeably absent.[27] The core of the Indigenous Churches' concern was the family, and in particular, the traditional Pentecostal patriarchal model of the nuclear family. This was described as 'a unit of love, security and training for children' in which 'the husband is the head of the home. The husband is to be the provider and protector.'[28] Consequently, the preservation of marriage—and by inference, of Biblical standards of human sexuality—was of paramount importance, as also was the perceived need to maintain the traditional gender roles of society.

It is therefore not surprising that the two specific moralist initiatives made by the Indigenous Churches in the 1970s were both in response to perceived threats to this family ideal. The introduction of the Accelerated Christian Education system in 1976 sought to safeguard the movement's children from the harmful effects of sex education in schools. The Save Our Homes Campaign the following year was a response to what was seen to be destructive radical feminism, and an attempt to preserve the traditional nuclear family. These two responses will be discussed in the next two chapters.

Notes

1. John Evans, for example, uses the title to describe the New Zealand phenomenon. John Evans, 'The New Christian Right in New Zealand', in *'Be Ye Separate': Fundamentalism and the New Zealand Experience*, Waikato Studies in Religion, Vol.3, ed. Bryan Gilling (Hamilton: University of Waikato and Colcom Press, 1992), 69–106.
2. Robert Liebman and Robert Wuthnow, 'Introduction', in *The New Christian Right: Mobilization and Legitimation*, ed. Robert C. Liebman and Robert Wuthnow (New York: Aldine Publishing Company, 1983), 4.
3. Robert Liebman, 'The Making of the New Christian Right', in ibid., 227.
4. The best known, although not altogether typical, exposition of this view is Hal Lindsey and C.C. Carlson, *The Late Great Planet Earth* (Grand Rapids, Michigan: Zondervan, 1976). This book achieved best-seller status among the Jesus People in the 1970s.

5. For discussions on the process of secularisation, see Lloyd Geering, 'What is Secularisation?' in 'Secularisation of Religion in New Zealand' (Wellington: University Extension, Victoria University, 1976). (Mimeographed.); *idem*, 'New Zealand enters the Secular Age', in *Religion in New Zealand*, ed. Christopher Nichol and James Veitch (Wellington: Tertiary Christian Studies Programme of the Combined Chaplaincies and the Religious Studies Department, Victoria University, 1980), 238-63; Peter Donovan, 'Distinctions without Difference: the Illusion of Diversity in New Zealand Beliefs', in ibid., 179-203; Michael Hill, *A Sociology of Religion* (London: Heinemann Educational Books, 1973), 228-51; *idem*, 'Religion', in *New Zealand: Sociological Perspectives*, 169-95; and *idem*, 'The Social Context of New Zealand Religion: "Straight" or "Narrow"?' in *Religion and New Zealand's Future*, ed. Kevin J. Sharpe (Palmerston North: Dunmore Press, 1982), 23-46.
6. Donald Heinz, 'The Struggle to Define America', in Liebman and Wuthnow, *The New Christian Right*, 133-34. In New Zealand, the Christchurch Integrity Centre was established in direct response to what were perceived as the inroads of Secular Humanism. Ryan, 'Remoralising Politics', in Jesson et al., *Revival of the Right*, 59.
7. Stephen Stratford, 'Christians Awake! Join the National Party, Save New Zealand', *Metro*, November 1986, 125.
8. Richard Russell, 'The growing crisis of the Evangelical world-view and its resolutions' (M.A. Thesis in Theology and Religious Studies, Bristol University, 1973), 98 Russell is specifically referring to the ten-year period from 1963 to 1973. I am indebted to Dr Chris Gousmett for this reference.
9. ibid., 100. Capitalisation as cited.
10. Brown, 'How Significant is the Charismatic Movement?' [1985], 104-5.
11. Allanah Ryan, '"For God, Country and Family": Populist Moralism and the New Zealand Moral Right', *New Zealand Sociology* 1 (1986): 104.
12. *idem*, '"For God, Country and Family": Populist Moralism and the New Zealand Moral Right' (M.A. Thesis in Education, Massey University, 1986), 6.
13. 'While Pentecostal respondents were more likely to emphasise the importance of moral issues, the Plymouth Brethren tended to be more concerned with other social and economic issues.' S.M. Wallace, 'An investigation of the political attitudes of members of Plymouth Brethren and Pentecostal churches in Christchurch' (M.A. Research Paper in Political Science, University of Canterbury, 1977), 38.
14. Bluck, 'Jesus 75—a mixed blessing', 5.
15. '[T]estimony from a campaign newsletter', *New Citizen*, 12 June 1975, 5.
16. David Arrowsmith observes that 'the core of the Conservative Christian's beliefs is the necessity for individual salvation. From this core spring his attitudes to religion, society and the economy. He believes in a religion whose precepts are universally valid, but which demand individual commitment; he believes in a code of ethics whose rules apply equally to all men, but which demand individual moral responsibility; he extols a social and economic system which forces the individual to make his own way.' David Arrowsmith, 'Christian Attitudes towards Public Questions in New Zealand in 1975' (M.A. Thesis in Political Studies, Auckland University, 1978), 116. A 1987 magazine article on Pastor Rob Wheeler demonstrates the accuracy of Arrowsmith's analysis. Brian Rudman, 'For God and National', *New Zealand Listener*, 28 March 1987, 28-29.
17. These primary materials include tape-recorded interviews with a number of pastors in the movement and newsletters, pamphlets and circulars put out by

various New Life churches. The most important source was the Majestic House Correspondence files, which contained the inwards and outwards correspondence of the Christchurch New Life Centre from 1971 onwards. I am grateful to Pastors Max Palmer and Alex Webster and to the staff of Majestic House for making this invaluable archival material available to me.
18. Peter Morrow to Dr Michael Harry, 10 April 1974, *MHCF*.
19. Rasik Ranchord to Dr Martin Viney, 2 September 1975, *MHCF*.
20. Rasik Ranchord to Graham Truscott, 9 September 1975, *MHCF*.
21. The 1977 correspondence related to the impending passage of the Contraception, Sterilisation and Abortion Bill. That of 1983 related to opposition to the proposed Abortion clinic at Coronation Hospital, and contains letters in support of Doug Kidd's Status of the Unborn Child Bill, then before Parliament.
22. Max Palmer to G. Twentyman, Commissioner of Police, 19 March 1980, *MHCF*. This correspondence related to the stage show 'Further Confessions of a Window Cleaner.'
23. Ranchord, Interview.
24. Larry Christenson, *The Christian Family* (London: Fountain Trust, 1971).
25. Ranchord, Interview.
26. Peter Morrow, open letter, 27 May 1977, *MHCF*, describes the Save Our Homes Campaign as a 'showdown with some of the feminists.'
27. There was, however, some reference to these issues in the *New Zealand Times*, published quarterly throughout 1976 by the newly formed Associated Pentecostal Churches of New Zealand.
28. Save Our Homes Campaign material, cited in M. Reid, 'Capitalism and the Family', *New Zealand Monthly Review* 198 (1978): 14, and thence in Ryan, 'Remoralising Politics', in Jesson *et al.*, *Revival of the Right*, 59.

Chapter 24

Moralist Initiatives I: Accelerated Christian Education

The catalyst for much of the moralist activism of the mid-1970s was the controversy over sex education in schools.[1] This issue was seen as constituting a tacit challenge to the authority of the nuclear family, and thus as a threat to the foundations of the social order. For conservative Christians, including members of the Indigenous Churches, issues such as abortion and homosexuality were problems of the wider society, and as such, did not directly impinge upon their immediate horizons. Sex education, however, was a threat of a different kind, an invasion of the Christian family by the permissive society. Children of conservative Christian parents could not avoid exposure to the new regime if it was introduced into the schools. Consequently, this issue threatened the worldview of the Christian family in a way that other issues did not, and therefore provoked a vigorous response. While various sections of the conservative Christian community responded in different ways, one specific initiative came from the Indigenous Churches. This was the introduction of the Accelerated Christian Education [ACE] system.

The sex education controversy began in 1973 following the deliberations of the Ross Committee, which explored the issues involved in developing programmes in human development and relationships in schools. The report of this committee—known as the Ross Report—was intended to provide a basis for discussion of teaching in 'the broad fields of human development and family and personal relationships, including sex education.'[2] In so doing, it placed the issue of sex education within the wider context of human relationships and moral responsibilities. However, the specific question of sex education was seized upon by opponents of the proposals, who felt that the moral dimensions were being ignored in the introduction of courses such as these into the schools.

Strong concern was generated on the issue, as can been seen by a letter from Peter Morrow in April 1974. This stated that a campaign had already begun in Christchurch 'to collect signatures for a petition to the Government.' It also refers to a 'meeting for Concerned Christian Ministers and Lay People' convened to discuss the issue, noting that there was a reasonable response to this. Two further meetings were to be arranged for late April 'to discuss and implement action against sex education in schools.'[3] These meetings led to the eventual formation in October 1974 of the Concerned Parents Association [hereafter cited as *CPA*],[4] to orchestrate conservative opposition to the issue. Morrow's letter provides evidence of a nascent moralist movement in Christchurch, supported by the Christchurch New Life Centre and other groups, at least six months before the appearance of the *CPA*. Evidently there was already a strong undercurrent of concern in some sections of the Christchurch community, and the *CPA* represented a consolidation, rather than an initiation, of this concern.

The *CPA* quickly became the most prominent of the groups opposing the introduction of sex education in schools.[5] Its stated purpose was to 'enable parents to become more informed and effective on educational issues.'[6] By so doing, it sought to mobilise conservative Christian concern in a concerted expression of opposition, and advocated the use of political lobbying methods, such as letters to Members of Parliament, to convey this concern. Rightly or wrongly, it saw the proposals of the Ross Report as opening the door for a take-over by the forces of permissiveness. According to the *CPA*, these forces comprised a number of liberal groups such as the family planning association, the radical feminist movement, homosexual groups, the association for abortion law reform, and promoters of indecent publications.[7]

The *CPA*'s perception of the take-over of society by a vocal minority was echoed by others. For example, the Hon. R.D. Muldoon—later to become Prime Minister of New Zealand—wrote in 1974 that

> The term "silent majority" is one of the saddest of the many catchwords of our time. If the talkers really are the minority, and on many issues they are, then the majority are losing by default, and that is the worst kind of loss of all. . . . If only there could be a crusade by the normal people which would match the crusading spirit of the subversive element.[8]

As will be seen, Muldoon assiduously courted the conservative churches during the 1975 election campaign. It could be claimed that he saw the activity of groups such as the *CPA* as part of this 'crusade by the normal people.' However, a more cynical view is that he recognised the political value of conservative Christian moral concern, and forged links with these groups for political advantage.

The debate over sex education in schools escalated when the Report of the Committee on Health and Social Education—more commonly known as the Johnson Report—was published in 1977.[9] This Report built upon, and extended, the earlier work of the Ross Committee and of the Royal Commission on Contraception, Sterilisation and Abortion.[10] However, moralist attitudes had hardened since the beginning of the controversy some four years previously. The *CPA* continued to oppose the whole idea of contraceptive information being available in schools, seeing this as an infringement of the sole rights of the parents to give their children moral education. Their position was not wholly defensible, since moral education did take place, whether intentionally or unintentionally, in the school. This was an automatic process, with the teacher-pupil relationship being the channel by which this moral education was imparted. For some of the opponents of sex education, this was the core of the issue. As they saw it, the question was not so much the content of the nonChristian curriculum but the character of the nonChristian teacher. They feared the adverse effects of exposing their children to the influence of a teacher who was, for example, a homosexual or a spiritualist. Although this was not a universal view of the opponents of sex education in schools, many of the objections made by the *CPA* appear to be based on this perception.

The moralist movement in the 1970s gained support from a variety of conservative Christian groups. Pentecostal churches formed a part, but only a part, of this constituency. In the case of members of the Indigenous Churches, opposition to sex education in schools was expressed by involvement with groups such as the *CPA*. The Indigenous Churches also participated corporately in the activities of the Associated Pentecostal Churches of New Zealand [*APCNZ*], including its submissions to the various Committees and Commissions on this and other questions.[11] There was, however, one distinctive initiative from the Indigenous Churches to the issue. This was the introduction of the Accelerated Christian Education (*ACE*) system into New Zealand in 1976.

Religious and moral education has had a chequered history in this country.[12] In nineteenth-century New Zealand, the dual roles of the Church as educator and inculcator of Christian morality were seen to be inseparable. This helped to lay the foundation for, and to mould the early shape of, education in this country. However, the authority of church schools was undermined by sectarian rivalry and their privileged position was eventually abolished by the 1877 Education Act, which made education free, secular and compulsory in New Zealand. Nevertheless, there were several exceptions to the secularity of the state school system. Bible in Schools teaching continued after 1897, exploiting a loophole in the legislation by means of the Nelson system, and Catholic schools remained outside the state education system as a parallel private school system. There were also a number of private church schools that continued to expand and multiply.

These church schools were something of an anomaly, and the majority of these were eventually integrated into the State system after the passage of the 1975 Conditional Integration Act. The result of this integration was that 'the remaining private [i.e. nonintegrated] schools ... form[ed] a very small group, representing perhaps only 2% of the school population.'[13] In part, the nonintegration of these schools was due to their fear that their special (i.e. religious) character would be lost in the integration process.[14] Many of the schools that did not integrate had their origins in a new Independent Christian School movement that developed in the 1960s and 1970s.[15] In part, this was a product of the influx of Dutch immigrant families in the 1950s, bringing with them the Dutch Calvinist tradition of parent-controlled Christian schools.[16] The first such independent Christian school was Middleton Grange School, which opened in Christchurch in 1964,[17] and soon became regarded as the flagship of the movement. The major period of growth for the movement appears to have been the early 1980s, when a number of other private schools were established.

The arrival of the Accelerated Christian Education [ACE] system marked the appearance of a new type of independent Christian school in New Zealand. Its foundations had been laid by the visit of Dr Howard, the founder of the *ACE* system, at the invitation of Rob Wheeler in February 1976. While in New Zealand, Dr Howard conducted a number of seminars on the 'potential establishment and administration of church-based Christian schools.' Some seventy to eighty people attended the first of these seminars in Auckland, many coming from as far away as Dargaville, Cambridge, Nelson and Invercargill.[18] Dr Howard returned to New Zealand for further seminars throughout 1976 and 1977, and interest in the *ACE* system continued to increase. Eventually the first two *ACE* schools were opened in February 1977, both run by local Indigenous churches. These were the Nelson Christian Academy and the Auckland Christian Fellowship School, which were linked to the Nelson New Life Centre and the Auckland Christian Fellowship, respectively.[19] These two schools were soon followed by others. By 1980 there were thirteen schools using the *ACE* materials, and five of these had already been registered by the Department of Education.[20]

Interest in the *ACE* system was not confined to the Indigenous Churches. Pastor John Tiplady recalls attending a meeting, addressed by Dr Howard, 'at the Auckland Baptist Tabernacle at the top of Queen Street.... A number of people from a number of churches right throughout the country ... heard him, and from that there sprung up a number of Christian schools.... All sorts of churches wanted to come in [and] find out about it.'[21] Nevertheless, interest did not necessarily translate into involvement. Despite the interest from 'all sorts of churches', it would appear that early support for Accelerated Christian Education was largely, although not exclusively, confined to Pentecostal churches, and especially to the Indigenous Churches. It also appears that this strong Pentecostal involvement was a new development for the *ACE* organisation, and was a source of embarrassment to Dr Howard, since his background was Fundamentalist and hence anti-Pentecostal.[22] The Fundamentalist emphasis and isolationist ethos of the *ACE* system would have had a certain attraction for the Pentecostal churches, but have been less palatable to nonPentecostal groups.

The *ACE* system of individualised instruction was strongly church based. It stipulated that *ACE*-system schools must be linked with a local church,[23] and vested full responsibility for the school in that local church and in its pastor. The school was held in the church buildings and the pastor was the *ex officio* principal of the school. Teaching was usually, although not always, carried out by a Christian teacher, assisted by members of the congregation and the Bible formed the basis of all subjects in the curriculum. Even secular subjects such as English and Mathematics had Biblical character objectives incorporated into the lessons. These appeared to place as great an emphasis on Bible memorisation and character development as on the process of education. In method, the system was a 'teach yourself' one, and designed to stimulate self-reliance and self-discipline. Pupils worked on their own through lesson books called 'Paces', marked their work and set their goals with minimal supervision from the teacher and assistance only in cases of difficulty.

The *ACE* programme was regarded by its advocates as being not only a system of education, but also a means of evangelism and of bringing revival to the church.[24] The goal was not education *per se*, but education to mould a revivalist orientation and an evangelical Christian lifestyle. Chris Gousmett has observed that the *ACE* methodology is strongly influenced by Burrows F. Skinner's psychological theories of behaviour modification.[25] Because of this, and the narrow fundamentalist focus of the *ACE* system, its opponents have branded it as brainwashing. Dr Howard, the founder of the system, admitted that the charge had some validity, but defended it by alleging that the 'secular humanist-oriented education system [also] uses the same idea to engrain evolutionary teaching.'[26]

Proponents of the *ACE* system made glowing claims for it. 'Government education experts in the United States have described the system as being ten years ahead of anything they now have, but unsuitable for the public education system because it has a one hundred per cent Christian-integrated syllabus.'[27] Conversely, the existing Christian school network was seen by the *ACE* promoters as Christian in name only. Thus the independent Christian schools at Middleton Grange and Silverstream were seen as not really Christian, since they used materials from the State school system.[28] However, other observers were equally critical of the *ACE* system, which has been described as 'a return to an idealized version of nineteenth century America, or [to] a view that society is so corrupt that the focus of most of life is to proselytize and await the return of Christ. Such groups... object to students studying much modern literature, including science fiction.'[29] This narrow focus reflected the strongly isolationist philosophy that underlay the *ACE* programme. This was the product of a dualistic sectarian worldview, which saw the world and the church as mutually exclusive, and the Christian family as a microcosm of the church. It was necessary to defend the family and to preserve Christian beliefs and group identity in an increasingly secular society. Private Christian schools formed a component part of this controlled environment, and the fundamentalist use of the Bible as the medium of instruction in the *ACE* system reinforced the sense of difference from the world.

This tendency towards isolationism found its logical conclusion in the formation of Christian communes. The Cooperites at Rangiora, and the Full Gospel Mission at Waipara are two examples of these. Neville Cooper, the founder of the Rangiora community, had at one time been an associate of Peter Morrow, but had severed his connections with the Indigenous Churches by the 1970s.[30] The Full Gospel Mission gained public notoriety in 1977, when newspaper headlines highlighted the membership of the Mission by *RNZAF* personnel and that the community kept a collection of firearms on the property.[31] Although Pentecostal in origin, neither of these groups had links with other Pentecostal churches. Rather they represented the extreme wing of separatist Pentecostalism.

Not all Pentecostalists were convinced of the need for separate Christian schools, however. Ken Wright, for example, observed that 'there was a ... fifty-fifty division [within the Palmerston North Christian Fellowship] over whether we should isolate our children into Christian schools, or whether we should be "salt" and "light" in the State schools.'[32] Rasik Ranchord, for his part, commented that

> People use the argument that Christian boys and girls should be attending secular schools so that they can be a testimony. I'm not convinced of that. I feel, especially for the primary school ages, that they should be protected and first built up in the faith, so that what is taught at home is followed through at school, and [thus] there is no dichotomy.[33]

Although Accelerated Christian Education was adopted by a number of Pentecostal churches, including some of the Indigenous Churches, its acceptance was not universal.

In the 1980s, this wing of the Independent Christian School movement continued to expand, with both primary and secondary schools being established. However, the *ACE* programme was by now being modified. Many schools changed or abandoned the *ACE* materials, which were found to be too American-oriented in content and too restricted in scope, and supplemented these with other materials, including some adopted from the State system. There was, however, little change in the methodology. The individualistic, Bible-centred method of education that characterised the *ACE* system continued to be the norm in this type of school. However, some of the churches that adopted the programme, such as the Rangiora New Life Centre, have now matured beyond this, seeing the need for a broader-based education system. There were also a number of practical difficulties. Some churches found *ACE* schools burdensome, both with financial support, and with the administrative demands on the local pastor. Some churches, for example the Dunedin Assembly of God, closed down their schools, while other *ACE* schools, such as the Hokitika Christian Academy, run by the Hokitika New Life Centre, struggled to survive.

The adoption of the *ACE* system by a number of Indigenous churches was a significant indicator of their sectarian worldview. *ACE* schools sought to create a controlled environment in which the Christian beliefs of the child were reinforced, rather than challenged, by what was taught. The emphasis was therefore on conformity and control, rather than on exploration and genuine education. Character development was seen to be as important as rote learning, and the fundamentalist orientation of the *ACE* programme was reflected in the use of the Bible as the medium of instruction. *ACE* education reinforced a flight from the world and strengthened the sectarian boundaries of the movement.

Nevertheless, support for the *ACE* system was not universal among the Indigenous Churches. Some churches examined the programme and, for various reasons—including educational standards—found it wanting. Others found the cost of setting up an *ACE* school to be prohibitive. Several churches that did set these up found that they tended to take over the resources of the church, and that the church eventually served the school, rather than *vice versa*. Others found that it introduced division within the congregation between those who supported—and could afford—*ACE* education, and those that could not. Nevertheless, a number of Indigenous churches led the way in the introduction of the programme to New Zealand. Their support provides evidence that the conservative, isolationist, sectarian worldview of the *ACE* programme was shared by many of the Indigenous Churches and that its introduction reinforced the movement's sectarian attitudes to education.[34]

It is unclear to what extent this type of Independent Christian School will remain a viable proposition in the late 1990s. Churches that had a strong sense of sectarian identity and a solid financial and organisational base appear to be in a good position to continue with *ACE* schools. On the other hand, the increasing financial stress caused by the general economic downturn may mean that many of the schools linked to smaller churches may be forced to close. The *ACE* school system, in its original form, may become remembered as a short-lived phenomenon, brought into this country in the 1970s as part of a conservative Christian reaction to sex education in schools. Nevertheless, they were significant in that they exemplified the sectarian attitudes of many of the Indigenous Churches to rapid social change.

Notes

1. Allanah Ryan gives a good summary of the development of this and other moralist issues in the 1970s. Ryan, 'Remoralising Politics', in Jesson *et al.*, *Revival of the Right*, 58–60.
2. New Zealand Department of Education, *Human Development and Relationships in the School Curriculum* (Wellington: Government Printer, 1973), 5.
3. Peter Morrow to Dr Michael Harry, 10 April 1974, *MHCF*.
4. Besides specific activist groups such as the *CPA*, conservative Christian media networks were also important in the orchestration of moralist concern. The role of *Radio Rhema* and *Challenge Weekly*, for example, in the formation of the conservative Christian moralist movement has not yet been sufficiently explored.
5. Paul Spoonley includes the *CPA* in his summary of 'New Zealand Groups that have Associations with or are Part of the Extreme Right, 1960–1983.' Paul Spoonley, *The Politics of Nostalgia: Racism and the Extreme Right in New Zealand* (Palmerston North: Dunmore Press, 1987), 302. Spoonley appears to be quite mistaken in his analysis, since he claims that the *CPA* is principally an antitax and antiliberal organization. He completely overlooks the concern with moral issues that formed this group's *raison d'être*.
6. Concerned Parents Association, *Home and School: Co-operation or Conflict? Human Development and Moral Values* (Christchurch: Concerned Parents Association, 1976), back cover.

7. 'Why are New Zealand parents concerned?' *CPA Newsletter*, April 1977, 2. This highly polemic article demonstrates the view of the *CPA* and its supporters that they were fighting against an orchestrated conspiracy of permissiveness, and gives a typical example of the *CPA*'s combative style.
8. R.D. Muldoon, *The Rise and Fall of a Young Turk* (Wellington: A.H. and A.W. Reed, 1974), 30–31.
9. New Zealand Department of Education, *Growing, Sharing, Learning: The Report of the Committee on Health and Social Education* (Wellington: Government Printer, 1977).
10. *Report of the Royal Commission of Inquiry: Contraception, Sterilisation and Abortion in New Zealand* (Wellington: Government Printer, 1977).
11. The *APCNZ* was one of twelve church groups that made submissions to the Statutes Revision Committee on the first version of the Family Proceedings Bill, 1978. W.R. Atkin, 'The Family in Society—A New Zealand Christian Perspective', in *Christians in Public Planning*, ed. Christopher Nichol and James Veitch (Wellington: Tertiary Christian Studies Programme of the Combined Chaplaincies and the Religious Studies Department, Victoria University, 1981), 31–32.
12. Ian Breward, *Godless Schools? A study in Protestant reactions to the Education Act of 1877* (Christchurch: Presbyterian Bookroom, 1967), is the best survey of the changing roles of church and state in New Zealand education. He also includes an appendix summarising the development of Protestant church schools. Another brief, but useful, historical survey of the early development of Christian Schools in New Zealand is an unpublished paper by Eric Dunlop, former Rector of Middleton Grange School, Christchurch. E.A. Dunlop, 'Christian Schools in New Zealand', Christchurch, 1978. (Mimeographed.)
13. Dunlop, 'Christian Schools', 2.
14. Colin McGeorge points out that 'Section 3 of the Integration Act guarantees an integrated school's special character.' Colin McGeorge, 'Religion in State Schools', in Colin McGeorge and Ivan Snook, *Church, State and New Zealand Education* (Wellington: Price Milburn, 1981), 29.
15. Dr Duncan Roper has set out the philosophy of education that underlay the approach of these independent Christian schools. Duncan Roper, 'Christian Education: What is it?' and *idem*, 'The school in society', in Association for the Promotion of Christian Schools, 'The school and the world: A one day seminar examining the task of making a Christian contribution to Education in New Zealand', Dunedin, n.d. (Mimeographed.) I am indebted to Dr Chris Gousmett for a copy of this material.
16. Liberton Christian School in Dunedin is a typical example of this type of school. See Harro W. Van Brummelen, *Telling the next generation: Educational development in North American Calvinist Christian Schools* (Lanham, Maryland: University Press of America, 1986) for the historical development of these schools in America. Despite the American context of Van Brummelen's book, his comments are also applicable to the Dutch Calvinist wing of the Christian School movement in New Zealand. I am grateful to Dr Bill Lee, chairman of the Dunedin Christian Schools Association, for pointing out this material.
17. The history of this school is set out in Eric Dunlop, *The Middleton Grange Story* (Christchurch: 25th Celebration Committee, Middleton Grange School, 1989).
18. 'Enthusiastic Response', *Challenge Weekly*, 7 February 1976, 1.

19. *CPA Newsletter*, June 1977, 4.
20. *CPA Newsletter*, August 1980, 8.
21. John Tiplady, Interview, Auckland, 2 March 1990.
22. Dr Chris Gousmett, Comment to author, Dunedin, 3 July 1991.
23. *Challenge Weekly*, 11 September 1976, 16.
24. Dr Howard claimed that 'Christian education is a key to spiritual awakening'; indeed, the 'depth and duration of revivals [in history were] directly linked to [the] depth and duration of current Christian education.' 'Education: A key to Revival', *Challenge Weekly*, 26 May 1978, 7.
25. Gousmett, Comment.
26. 'Enthusiastic Response to Christian Schools', *Challenge Weekly*, 7 February 1976, 1.
27. ibid.
28. Gousmett, Comment.
29. Van Brummelen, *Telling the next generation*, 281.
30. Lineham, 'Tongues must cease', 16.
31. Michael Hill, 'To define true heresy: deviance, conformity and religion', in Hill *et al.*, *Shades of Deviance*, 140–59.
32. Wright, Interview. The reference to salt and light is taken from Matt.5:13–16.
33. Rasik Ranchord to John Parr, late 1976, *MHCF*.
34. See above at chapter 14, pages 96–97.

Chapter 25

Moralist Initiatives II: The Save Our Homes Campaign

A second issue that evoked a specific response from members of the Indigenous Churches in the 1970s was that of feminism. This response—the Save Our Homes Campaign—reflected typical Pentecostal attitudes to women, conditioned by the movement's fundamentalist approach to the Bible and by its patriarchal model of gender roles. These attitudes were proof-texted by Biblical references such as Eph.5:22-23 'Wives, submit yourselves unto your own husbands, as unto the Lord. For the husband is the head of the wife.' and 1 Cor.14:34 'Let your women keep silence in the churches.' Given this fundamentalist patriarchal stance, and the media portrayal of feminists as radical and anti-Christian, it is not surprising that the Indigenous Churches should have reacted so strongly to the feminist movement.

The rise of this movement was, in part, a product of rapidly changing social conditions of the 1960s and 1970s. Although New Zealand lagged several years behind other parts of the world in this respect, feminist activism emerged with the formation of several Women's Liberation groups in 1970. These groups represented 'a new, and distinctive, form of feminism',[1] which is sometimes referred to as second-wave feminism, following on from the first-wave feminism of the suffrage movement in the late nineteenth century. Although this new feminist movement was initially small and radical, it expanded its constituency and became more middle of the road as the 1970s progressed. This deradicalisation process was reflected in the changing nature of the biennial United Women's Conventions from 1973 to 1979.[2]

The Save Our Homes Campaign in May 1977 was a specific response, initiated by members of the Indigenous Churches, to the growth of feminism.[3] This was motivated both by their conservative views on the roles of women and by their perception of the radical character of the feminist movement. It is interesting that both radical feminists and conservative Christians identified the issues in religious terms. The former often blamed the Catholic Church for the opposition that they met, as may be seen in a cartoon accompanying Sandra Coney's editorial in the feminist magazine *Broadsheet*. This depicts a group of female puppets, representing the Save Our Homes Campaign, being manipulated from behind the scenes by two men in episcopal regalia, i.e. the Catholic church.[4] Conversely, David Arrowsmith alludes to the 'undisguised anti-Christian stance of the Women's Liberation Movement', citing Coney's *Broadsheet* article 'Virgin Mary or Fallen Woman' to prove his case.[5] However, Coney's aggressive stance represents only one viewpoint within the feminist movement. Other articles in this issue of *Broadsheet*, which addressed the overall theme of Women and Religion, are much more moderate in tone. Thus, while attitudes of some Women's Liberationists could justifiably be termed anti-Christian—i.e. a rejection of traditional Christian perspectives and beliefs—this epithet is not applicable to all sections of the movement. Nevertheless, feminism as a whole tended to be viewed in terms of its radical elements, and this public perception was assiduously cultivated by some sections of the media in the 1970s.[6]

The attitudes of the Save Our Homes campaigners reflected the standard Pentecostal views of the role of women. Ivanica Vodanovich observes that within Pentecostalism, the woman's primary social role is

> located within the family as legal wife and mother. The belief system of the movement describes a pattern of divinely ordained order in which individuals are organised into families; they, in turn, are the building blocks of the nation. God's blueprint for the establishment of universal social order posits a world divided into nations. Families are the crucial intermediary between the individual and the nation—and because of their primary responsibility in the family women are key figures in the realization of His design. Yet the centrality of their role is contradicted by their subordinate status both within the system of beliefs and the social reality it sanctions.[7]

The motivation for the Save Our Homes Campaign came indirectly from preparations for the 1977 United Women's Convention in Christchurch. Anne Morrow, the organiser of the Campaign, commented that she and her colleagues had originally planned to take part in the United Women's Convention. However, they soon came to the conclusion that this was dominated by 'very few, very dogmatic, feminists, ... [who] were really using the United Women's Conference [sic] as a platform to press their beliefs.'[8] Mrs Morrow had obtained various documents, particularly the report of the 1974 Select Committee on Women's Rights, and as a result, 'saw what their aims were, and realised that they were behind this same Conference.' Consequently, she decided to 'expose what feminism was in terms of their own [documents] that they had drawn up. So I used their material and people were staggered when they realised what was going on.'[9] She felt that it was necessary 'to make an alternative stand, a positive stand for women.... You couldn't really go into [the Convention] and make a stand. We had to raise an alternative voice. That was how the "Save Our Homes" [Campaign] started. I felt... that we [should] actually set up ... the positives for what women should be into.'[10]

Anne Morrow and her colleagues[11] therefore planned the Save Our Homes Campaign as a Christian alternative to the United Women's Convention. The emphasis of the Campaign was intended to be positive, rather than negative, and 'to offset... a Christian belief [against the views of the feminists]. For example, as they sought to undermine the [role] of a mother, we... took a firm and a positive stand on the role of a mother. When it came to the family issues, we would raise a standard... in those kind of areas. I think we... addressed every issue they addressed.'[12] The Campaign took place in the same venues as, and imitated the format of, the United Women's Convention scheduled to take place three weeks later. It included an overseas speaker, and thirty-four seminars that generally mirrored those of the United Women's Convention workshops. There were also some distinctively Christian topics such as The importance of the home, Knowing God and Moral Issues.[13] This imitation by the Save Our Homes campaigners was viewed as an attempt to sabotage the United Women's Convention, and was greeted with outrage by feminists. Sandra Coney, for example, complained bitterly that

> The most blatant tactic being used to attempt to counteract feminist influence is the organisation of a convention three weeks before the UWC [United Women's Convention], the "Save Our Homes" convention, which carefully copies many of the features of the UWC. Knowledge of how the Convention Committee intended to organise the UWC was being fed to the organisers of the church conference by a woman who got herself onto the UWC Committee. And while one of the main organisers of the church conference, Mrs. Anne Morrow has stated that the "Save Our Homes" campaign has not been timed to "upstage" the United Women's Convention it is abundantly clear that, in fact, it has.[14]

Consequently, when the Save Our Homes Campaign opened in the Town Hall, an angry group of about fifty feminists occupied several rows at the rear of the audience, and created some disturbance before finally leaving.

The Save Our Homes Campaign attracted some two thousand registrants, with the final public meeting in the Christchurch Town Hall drawing an audience of nearly 2,500 people.[15] These meetings were addressed by a number of speakers, including Members of Parliament, civic dignitaries and speakers from within the Pentecostal movement.[16] A range of speakers such as this would indicate that the Campaign was both socially and politically conservative. It is not surprising that its statements could be caricatured as '"the usual reactionary comments expected from middle-aged, lower middle class, religiously-affiliated women" (which *is* how the campaign has been described!).'[17] The conservatism of the Campaign was demonstrated by the various speakers, who emphasised the need for strong family units, discipline in the home and the restoration of Christian principles in society.

However, the message of the Save Our Homes Campaign on the role of women was not entirely unequivocal. On the one hand, the conservative Christian emphasis on the individual, rather than on the collective, was characteristic of the whole Conference,[18] and the various speakers strongly affirmed the role of the individual woman. 'The Bible holds no stereotypes for women who want to do anything physically possible.... A woman can do all things in Christ.... God has a way of shattering stereotypes.'[19] True women's liberation was to be found only in Christ. It was defined as 'a state of mind in which [the Christian woman] comes to view herself as Christ sees her, created in the image of God—one whom he wants to make free and whole—able to grow and learning how to fully utilise the talents and gifts God has given her as an individual.'[20] The Save Our Homes Campaign was viewed as a means to this liberation. As Anne Morrow put it,

> Save Our Homes is *not* a reactionary back-to-the-home movement. It is a ringing affirmation of the roles of the female woman [sic] home-maker, child-raiser, wife, career woman, but above all a joyous and confident statement that a woman can be a totally fulfilled person in her own right when she finds herself "in Christ" and discovers [that] the Bible can be her daily handbook.[21]

Despite these affirmative statements, however, the submissive role of the wife was also strongly emphasised during the Campaign. This subordinate gender role was characteristic of the Pentecostal movement. Indeed, Ian Breward has commented that Pentecostal churches 'have a certain notoriety for the firmness with which they keep their women in a Patriarchal framework.'[22] A classic example of this framework was given by Minta Baker, the keynote speaker at the First National Conference of Ministers' Wives and Women in Leadership, organised by Anne Morrow in June 1983. Mrs Baker was quoted as saying that 'Jesus wants the husband to be the head, to lead and not to rule.... We [women] need to take responsibility for our attitudes and to repent if necessary. Our spirit needs to minister to our husband, so that we become one flesh, glued together.'[23] This submission principle—based on texts such as Ephesians 5:22-24 and 1 Peter 3:1-6—was held by some Pentecostalists to apply even in the case of wives who were physically abused by their husbands.

The submissive role of the wife was also an emphasis of Ray Mossholder's address on the opening night, reported by the *Christchurch Star* under the heading 'Message for wives: don't nag hubby.' This report said, in part, that 'women need to pray, not bray. That was the message of Ray Mossholder.... As soon as the wife tries to rule, the husband rebels, so she must learn that God can do it [i.e. change her husband's behaviour].'[24] However, Mossholder's address, if accurately reported, forms a strange contrast with two earlier newspaper interviews that quoted him as saying that 'I have no doubts or anxiety over women's liberation. It has been deeply valuable in that it has forced the Church to re-evaluate God's Word in relation to women and their role.' Mossholder appeared to maintain a middle of the road, rather than conservative, stance on feminism, and saw some dangers in the feminist movement. In his view, 'the struggle for equality has involved the degrading of men. Men who were often fighting to maintain their position felt very insecure.' Mossholder insisted that 'we don't want to stereotype men, or women, into a role',[25] but believed that 'the Scriptures provided a perfect model for male and female relationships.'[26]

For the Save Our Homes campaigners, the issue was not so much the equality and individuality of women as the way in which the feminist movement was seen to be pursuing this equality. Anne Morrow, for example, asked the rhetorical question

> Could I be a feminist? I would have to define what a feminist was to be able to say that, because if you use the general use of the word "feminist," [then] I could not say that, because it involves a very radical and anti-Biblical and "fighting for rights of women" [attitude], which I think is an imbalance. But I think I could be viewed as a feminist in view of wanting to see women extended, their potential realised, opportunities made for the giftings they have. If that is what you call a feminist, then I could well be one!²⁷

The opposition of the Save Our Homes campaigners was therefore to the radical, anti-Biblical, 'fighting for rights of women' attitude of the feminists, as much as to feminism *per se*. The crux of their concern was the family, and they took issue with what they perceived to be the tendency of the feminist movement to downgrade the traditional roles of wife and mother. A later article observes that

> There is much emphasis on the theory that a woman can only be truly fulfilled and an individual when she throws off the "shackles" of the home, relinquishes the God-given role of wife, homemaker and mother, burns her bra, and joins the work force shouting "liberation."
>
> Save Our Homes is not against women who find it necessary to go out of their homes to work, but does not believe that every woman must do this in order to be fulfilled.... Many women, content to be full-time homemakers and mothers have been pressured into feeling that they are the cinderellas of society, second class citizens, and often termed "cabbages."
>
> Save Our Homes wants to encourage women to realise their full potential in the home, and in the community.²⁸

What did the Save Our Homes Campaign achieve? While, as Sandra Coney charged, the immediate result of the Campaign was to 'divert attention and support away from the United Women's Convention',²⁹ Anne Morrow saw it as having national significance. In her words, 'the convention raised a banner for the family.... [It] restored the faith of a lot of women in what minority groups have made look mundane—wifehood, motherhood, and childraising.'³⁰ The activism of the initial Save Our Homes Campaign in Christchurch stimulated eight further Campaigns in other parts of New Zealand over the next two years. These followed a similar format to that of the original Campaign, including, in some cases, the practice of conducting parallel conventions to those of the feminist movement.³¹ Other legacies included the launching of the women's magazine *Above Rubies*, 'designed to encourage women in their calling as wives and mothers, in the true image in which God has created them.' Nancy Campbell, its founder, had presented a seminar on 'the role of a Mother' at the Christchurch Save Our Homes Campaign, and the magazine had developed out of the enthusiastic response to this.³² The Campaign's influence was also extended by the setting up of programmes geared to enabling churches to meet the social needs of their local areas. These programmes were designed to develop skills in areas such as financial and time budgeting, coping with stress, dealing with teenagers, anger management, and other areas of social need.³³

An important consequence of the Save Our Homes Campaign was the creation of links with women's organisations such as the Christchurch branch of the National Council of Women. This had the effect of bringing Pentecostal women's groups into the mainstream of New Zealand life. Of greater importance, however, was the way in which the Save Our Homes Campaign exemplified, and helped to reinforce, the growing political clout of the Indigenous Churches. This reflected the expansion of the movement, and in particular, of the Christchurch New Life Centre. The Campaign succeeded in enlisting not only the services of civic and political figures as conference speakers, but also support from several mainstream churches, representatives of which were members of the Campaign's steering committee.³⁴ The financial resources of the Campaign were considerable, and Sandra Coney ruefully comments that

> If [Christchurch Pentecostal church] power in numbers may be a carefully constructed fallacy, their money is not.³⁵ The Christchurch UWC started its organising with $100 in the kitty. I've heard figures ranging up to $10,000 quoted to me in connection with "Save Our Homes." You *need* that sort of money to pay for lavish newspaper advertisements, bring three speakers from the States and get Xeroxed hundreds of copies of newspaper articles to use as propaganda. Where does the money come from? Not from a simple group of home-loving mothers, as Mrs. Morrow, who just happens to be the wife of the "New Life Centre" pastor, would have us believe they were.³⁶

The Christchurch New Life Centre was one of the largest and fastest growing of the Indigenous Churches in the 1970s. Its expansion, although differing in scale, was characteristic of other Indigenous Churches and of the Pentecostal movement generally throughout the decade. Peter Lineham observed that 'in the 1970s these fellowships were among the most dynamic forces in the religious life in New Zealand.'³⁷ This dynamism was matched by increasing social influence, which was reinforced by that of charismatic Christians in the mainstream churches. The Save Our Homes Campaign was an example of this growing Pentecostal power. As a conservative response to change, however, it was more aggressive and proactive than the Indigenous Churches' other response, the introduction of the *ACE* system. This may reflect its origins in what was then the flagship of the movement, the Christchurch New Life Centre.

The numerical growth of the Indigenous Churches, as well as of other Pentecostal groups, in the 1970s was paralleled by a growing sense of self-identity and political clout. The gradual focal shift of conservative Christianity towards social and political activism channelled some of this dynamism towards the preservation of the nuclear family, which was perceived to be under threat. Consequently, members of the Indigenous Churches were often involved in the campaigns of moralist groups such as the Society for the Promotion of Community Standards and the Society for the Protection of the

Unborn Child. The introduction of the *ACE* system and the launching of the Save Our Homes Campaign represented specific initiatives in response to a perceived moral threat from the permissive society. Other, more broadly based responses were also beginning to emerge within the Pentecostal movement, and these had marked effects on the future shape of the New Life Churches.

Notes

1. Christine Dann, *Up from under: Women and Liberation in New Zealand 1970-1985* (Wellington: Allen and Unwin and Port Nicholson Press, 1985), 4. Dann's account, although somewhat sketchy, is the only systematic account of the feminist movement in New Zealand in the 1970s. Stella Casey [later Dame Stella Casey], Research Officer for the National Council of Women of New Zealand, comments that 'we are not aware of any history of the feminist movement dealing specifically with the 70s. . . . The whole movement is as yet very inadequately documented.' Stella Casey, Correspondence with the author, Wellington, 3 July 1991. A number of articles in *Women Together: A History of Women's Organisations in New Zealand— Nga Ropu Wahine o te Motu*, ed. Anne Else (Wellington: Historical Branch, Department of Internal Affairs, 1993) refer indirectly to the rise of the feminist movement in the 1970s.
2. United Women's Convention, *United Women's Convention 1975* (Wellington: United Women's Convention, 1976); Joy Browne et al., ed., *Changes, Chances, Choices: A Report on the United Women's Convention. 3-6 June 1977* (Christchurch: United Women's Convention, 1978); United Women's Convention, *United Women's Convention, Easter 1979* (Hamilton: University of Waikato, [1979]).
3. The Save Our Homes Campaign was held three weeks before the 1977 United Women's Convention, apparently to preempt the Convention itself. Letters in the Majestic House Correspondence Files describe the Campaign as 'a showdown with some of the feminists.' Peter Morrow, open letter, 27 May 1977, *MHCF*.
4. Sandra Coney, 'Editorial', *Broadsheet*, May 1977, 10.
5. Arrowsmith, 'Christian Attitudes', 87. The article to which he refers is Sandra Coney, 'Virgin Mary or Fallen Woman', *Broadsheet*, December 1974, 14–17.
6. Examples include the coverage of the 1977 United Women's Convention in Christchurch. In the opening session, a male Radio New Zealand reporter was thrown out of the Convention after being hit and abused by three lesbian activists. 'Male Reporter leaves after convention row', *Christchurch Star*, 4 June 1977, 1. This incident sparked intense media controversy. Subsequent headlines included 'Women toss out media; convention united no longer', *Christchurch Press*, 6 June 1977, 1; 'Lesbians "intended to disrupt" convention if men let in', *Christchurch Press*, 8 June 1977, 16; and 'Editorial: Butch spoils it for the majority', *Christchurch Star*, 7 June 1977, 8.
7. Ivanica Vodanovich, 'Woman's place in God's World', *New Zealand Women's Studies Journal* 2 (August 1985): 68–69. Vodanovich's article discusses Pentecostal and Charismatic views on the position of women and the pivotal role of the family. I am indebted to Dr Jane Simpson for pointing out this article.
8. Anne Morrow, Interview, Christchurch, 21 November 1989.
9. ibid.
10. ibid.

11. Although other women were also involved in the Save Our Homes Campaign, this was Anne Morrow's brainchild, and she exercised a dominant role within it. She was usually the person quoted by the media and this reflected her central role as organiser and convenor for the Campaign.
12. Anne Morrow, Interview.
13. Coney, 'Editorial', *Broadsheet*, May 1977, 10.
14. ibid.
15. '2,000 women meet to save homes', *Challenge Weekly*, 21 May 1977, 1.
16. ibid. These included the Hon. Bert Walker, the Minister of Social Welfare; Dr Gerald Wall, M.P. for Porirua and Mr (later Sir) Hamish Hay, the mayor of Christchurch. Other speakers included Superintendent John Jamieson, deputy head of the Police Force in Christchurch, the overseas speaker Ray Mossholder, and Anne Morrow herself.
17. Liz Andersen, 'Rocking the cradle—ruling the world?' *Challenge Weekly*, 29 May 1977, 6. Emphasis as cited.
18. As for example, Dr Anna Holmes' statement in the Abortion seminar that 'Abortion is seen as a logical solution to social problems when mankind is viewed collectively not individually.' Also the reporter's comment in the same article that 'time and again, in the seminar after seminar came the message: "if you can't love yourself you'll never be able to love anyone else".' Andersen, 'Rocking the cradle—ruling the world', *Challenge Weekly*, 29 May 1977, 5. Dr Holmes was also one of the speakers at the 'I'm pregnant—Help!' workshop at the United Women's Convention. Browne et al., *Changes, Chances, Choices*, 27.
19. Ray Mossholder, cited in Andersen, 'Rocking the cradle—ruling the world', *Challenge Weekly*, 29 May 1977, 7.
20. This statement was made during the 'Building a sense of self-worth' seminar. ibid., 5.
21. Anne Morrow, cited in ibid., 7.
22. Ian Breward, 'Selecting Documents for Australian Religious History', in *Australian and New Zealand Religious History 1788-1988: A Collection of Papers and Addresses delivered at the 11th Joint Conference of the Australian and New Zealand Association of Theological Schools and Society for Theological Studies held at Burgmann College, Australian National University, 5-8 September 1988*, ed. Robert Withycombe (Jamison Centre, A.C.T.: Australian and New Zealand Association of Theological Schools and Society for Theological Studies, 1988), 22.
23. First National Conference of Ministers' Wives and Women in Leadership, 'Precis of the Conference', Christchurch, 1983, *MHCF*.
24. 'Message for wives: don't nag hubby', *Christchurch Star*, 16 May 1977, 4.
25. 'Men and Women created equal', *Christchurch Press*, 12 May 1977, 12.
26. 'Life Style: What Bible really says about women', *Christchurch Star*, 13 May 1977, 7.
27. Anne Morrow, Interview.
28. 'Save Our Homes Supplement: Aiming to bring families together', *Challenge Weekly*, 30 March 1979, 9.
29. Coney, 'Editorial', *Broadsheet*, May 1977, 11.
30. 'Convention's benefits of "national significance,"' *Christchurch Press*, 17 May 1977, 12.
31. Both the United Women's Convention and the Save Our Homes Campaign were held in Hamilton; the United Women's Convention at Easter 1979, and the Save

Our Homes Campaign shortly after this. *United Women's Convention, Easter 1979*; 'Enthusiasm as hundreds gather to SAVE OUR HOMES', *Challenge Weekly*, 8 May 1979, 10-11.
32. *Challenge Weekly*, 12 October 1979, 10-11. From a first printing of 1,500 copies in September 1977, the circulation of the magazine had climbed to 60,000 by 1979. Nancy Campbell, 'Above Rubies: Bringing the trend in the nation back to God's way!' Broadbeach, Queensland, Australia, 1991. (Mimeographed.); *Challenge Weekly*, 12 October 1979, 10-11. The Australian director of *Above Rubies* advises that current circulation varies between 150,000 and 180,000 copies for each half-yearly issue. Val Stares, Correspondence with the author, Broadbeach, Queensland, Australia, 1 March 1993.
33. Anne Morrow, Interview.
34. Max Palmer to W.D.H. Smith, Buildings Registrar, Canterbury University, 1977, *MHCF*. However, this ecumenical support contrasts oddly with the lament of a participant that 'I could not help wishing that more delegates from the "mainline" churches were present to support and benefit by such an occasion.' Blaikie, 'Out of the Innermost: Save our homes!' *Challenge Weekly*, 29 May 1977, 4.
35. Coney's claim that this power in numbers is fallacious was based on a somewhat flimsy argument. The 'Pentecostal Church behind "Save Our Homes" is unfamiliar to those of us living in the North Island; if there's a Pentecostal church in Auckland it must be very quiet.' Coney, 'Editorial', *Broadsheet*, May 1977, 11. However, the various local Indigenous Churches identified themselves by an assortment of titles. In the North Island, these churches were often called 'Christian Fellowships'; in the South Island, 'New Life Centres.' Although Coney correctly assesses the strength of Pentecostal conservatism in Christchurch, it is thus not surprising that she has failed to see the connection between the North and South Island wings of the Indigenous Churches.
36. ibid. Emphasis as cited.
37. Lineham, 'Tongues must cease': 16.

Chapter 26

Growth, Accountability and the Discipleship Controversy

The 1970s were boom years for New Zealand Pentecostalism and almost all groups associated with the movement experienced sustained growth during the decade. Some indication of the extent of this growth may be obtained from census statistics, which show that total Pentecostal adherence was 6,264 in 1966; 9,432 in 1971; 15,474 in 1976; and 31,005 in 1981.[1] However, these figures do not tell the whole story, since many Pentecostals preferred to identify themselves as 'Christian,' rather than as 'Pentecostal.' The indeterminate institutional boundaries within the movement, together with the reluctance of groups such as the Indigenous Churches to adopt an official denominational name, render the census figures less than conclusive. Nevertheless, Ray Galvin has estimated that by 1982

> The total membership of Pentecostal churches [stood] at about 36,000 and their weekly adult attendance [at] above 40,000; hence, *the Pentecostal worshipping community is now approaching the size of the Presbyterian* and is certainly bigger than the Baptist or Methodist [churches].... It is clear that *over the last fifteen years the centre of gravity of New Zealand Christianity has shifted somewhat in the direction of the Pentecostalist/Fundamentalist tradition.*[2]

Although this ongoing growth, which was paralleled by the formation of new Pentecostal alliances after the mid-1970s, helped to shape the contours of the movement, these changes were not always initially positive. For example, the increasing self-identity of the Charismatic movement from 1973 on was accompanied by a certain degree of distancing from its Pentecostal counterpart. However, this was not so much a severing of fellowship as a following of separate, although parallel, paths. Personal links between participants in the two movements generally remained warm and friendly. Nevertheless, the sense of unity in the Spirit between Pentecostal and Charismatic groups became more difficult to maintain. In the case of the Indigenous Churches, this was matched by the failure to recreate links with Ray Jackson's Associated Mission Churches of Australia[3] at the Asian-Pacific Ministers' Conference, convened in Melbourne in June 1973.[4] To some extent, the Indigenous Churches' reluctance to renew links with their Australian brethren reflected their independent polity. The autonomy of the local church remained the cardinal principle upon which relationships between local assemblies in the movement were modelled. There were, however, some indications that this polity of independence was beginning to change, and in this regard, the teaching of Pastor David Ellis on The Coverings[5] proved to be influential in the mid-1970s.

Ellis believed that although charismatic ministry was of itself authoritative, since it was a manifestation of the Holy Spirit, it must also be legitimated by submission to a covering—i.e. an authority in the church. The ministry of members of the congregation, for example, was to be exercised under the covering of their local pastors and leaders. This principle also applied to the pastors themselves, who were to be under a covering, usually of a more senior pastor in the movement. This covering functioned by means of personal relationship rather than through organisational structures. The effect of Ellis' teaching was to formalise a network of pastoral relationships both within and beyond the boundaries of the local assemblies, and so to provide a structural framework for the Indigenous Churches. Since these links were personal, rather than organisational, they were not seen as compromising the movement's traditional emphasis on the independence and autonomy of the local church. Nevertheless, Ellis' teaching legitimated this network of interrelationships and laid the foundation for later developments in the New Life Churches.

In part the covering teachings were an attempt to deal with the problems caused by the growth of the Indigenous Churches. These problems were twofold. Firstly, there was some concern over the quality of conversions to the movement, since not all of these appeared to be lasting.[6] Secondly, there also was considerable uncertainty how to deal with the growing number of independent charismatics who were not subject to any system of spiritual accountability. These issues challenged the neopentecostal movement in many different parts of the world, and Ellis' ideas were typical of teachings that were emerging among charismatic groups elsewhere. However, not all such teachings were universally accepted. Two, in particular, created widespread controversy and division in the charismatic movement, and especially, although not exclusively, in the United States. These were the Discipleship teaching of Juan Carlos Ortiz, and the Shepherding movement of Bob Mumford and others, which incorporated and extended Ortiz's teachings into a system of discipleship.

Juan Carlos Ortiz of Argentina had a strong concern for the practical implications of the lordship of Christ and for authentic Christian discipleship. He was a powerful writer and speaker, with a characteristic Latin flair for the dramatic, and his book *Disciple*,[7] which sets out the essence of his teaching, was widely read in New Zealand and elsewhere. His aim as a pastor was to bring each member of his congregation to a genuine love for one another that then 'must work itself out in a radical, no-nonsensical [sic] understanding of Christian discipleship.... The equipping and training of individual men and women for service is what the Church is all about.'[8] Ortiz believed that the pastor of the church had to move 'beyond Sunday morning.'[9] By this, he meant that the pastor's task was not just to preach to a congregation on Sunday morning, but to make disciples of his people in real life situations throughout the week. This was achieved by the formation of a cell group in the church, whereby the pastor would be able to relate in depth to a small handpicked group of people. In this way, he was able to personally train them as disciples themselves, and as trainers and disciple makers of others. The members of this mother cell group would then form and lead other individual cells in the church, and disciple the participants of these groups in the same way in which they themselves had been discipled. However, this involved a radical commitment by the disciple, both to the Lord and to the person leading the cell group,[10] as well as to meeting the needs of others in the cell group. Not all members of the congregation could meet such a costly level of discipleship, and Ortiz's teaching was often divisive when applied outside its original Argentinean context.

In the early 1970s, concern over 'the increasing numbers of nomadic charismatics who were free from any system of accountability'[11] led to the emergence of the Discipleship Movement in the United States.[12] This extended Ortiz's ideas into a system of discipleship and sought to deal with the problem of inadequate charismatic accountability by teaching 'a covenant love that evidenced devotion to God by submission to some man.'[13] A number of men with national and international ministries—e.g. Don Basham, Ern Baxter, Bob Mumford, John Poole, Derek Prince and Charles Simpson—were involved in this movement.[14] Mumford, however, was the leading figure and his views were widely circulated in the charismatic magazine *New Wine* and in other publications such as his book *The Problem of Doing Your Own Thing*.[15] Mumford equated doing your own thing with lawlessness and emphasised the need to provide an antidote to rebellion. This was remedied by an understanding both of spiritual authority—especially that of the father in the home and the pastor in the church—and of the nature of obedience. The fruit of this understanding was the spirit of obedience or learning to obey.[16] In Mumford's theology, obedience to God-ordained authority was central to authentic Christian living. Only in this attitude of submission, both individual and corporate, could the lordship of Jesus be fully realised in the church and the community.

Mumford's views were not entirely original, being based to some extent on the earlier ideas of the Chinese Christian leader, Watchman Nee,[17] and modified by the discipleship theology of Juan Carlos Ortiz. It is possible that Mumford took Ortiz's ideas further than Ortiz himself was prepared to go, since one commentator includes Ortiz himself among those who opposed Mumford's teachings.[18] The combination of Ortiz's emphasis on radical, costly, discipleship commitment to a leader, and Mumford's concept of a network of shepherd-sheep submission relationships, formed the doctrinal basis of the shepherding-discipleship movement. This enabled it to create a national network of followers who formed a pyramid of sheep and shepherds—every shepherd was a sheep to someone else.... The sheep were under the spiritual authority of the shepherd; they were discipled by the shepherd in such a way that through submission to his authority in an ongoing relationship the person might be brought to Christian maturity.[19]

The focus of the discipleship movement was behavioural, since for Mumford and his followers in the movement,

> Discipleship is uppermost [and] the goal ... is to effect a change in behaviour. It is achieved through being trained by a man (not a woman) [sic] with high spiritual motivation and who has been commissioned for the task by the Lord—a shepherd or elder. Discipleship involves submission to the shepherd as he points the way—and points out flaws in behaviour. The shepherd constantly chips away at the raw material, attempting to create a disciple patterned after the biblical model.... Those being discipled must consult with their shepherds about many personal decisions. In some cases, shepherds forbid marriages, reject school and vocational plans, demand confession of secret sins.[20]

There were considerable dangers in the discipleship process. The process could be applied in draconian ways, and the authority of the shepherd over the disciple abused. The overenthusiastic application of discipleship principles sometimes resulted in division, although in this respect the legacy of the movement was less devastating in New Zealand than in other countries. In the Philippines, for example, the discipleship teaching was introduced to the churches of the Anchor Bay Evangelistic Association. This was a Pentecostal group of more than sixty churches that had been established in the Philippines through the pioneer work of Emmanuel and Wave Bristle, and strongly supported by several New Zealand Indigenous churches. The results were calamitous. The Anchor Bay churches were split down the middle, with congregations being strongly divided. Some members were willing to pay the price and commit themselves to be discipled by their shepherd—i.e. their pastor. Others were more cautious in their acceptance of the new doctrine, and were therefore labelled as 'lukewarm', 'half-hearted', or 'compromising' Christians. The strife generated by this controversy, combined with the inroads of the Communist New People's Army into the areas where these churches were located, resulted in the decimation of Anchor Bay in the Philippines. This caused the almost total devastation of more than twenty years of sacrificial pioneer work carried out by the Bristles and other missionaries.

Horror stories such as these[21] were common to both sides in the controversy that erupted in America and elsewhere in 1975 over the discipleship teachings and which threatened to split the entire Charismatic movement. Although these teachings were an attempt to provide an answer to the issue of nomadic Charismatics, they were seen as threatening the Pentecostal and Charismatic movements in several ways. In particular, the promotion of extralocal submission,[22] whereby disciples submitted to various national and international leaders in the discipleship movement, was perceived to be the first step in the formation of a new denomination. This practice had the effect of dividing the loyalty of denominational Charismatics to their churches, and of vitiating the independence and autonomy of local Pentecostal groups. A series of meetings between prominent Charismatic leaders was held in 1975 in an attempt to defuse the issue.[23] Although these were only partially successful, a reconciliation between the major sectors of the Charismatic movement in the United States and the leaders of the discipleship movement was eventually achieved in March 1976.[24]

The application of the discipleship teaching, rather than the teaching itself, appears to have fuelled much of this controversy. Mumford himself clearly recognised the inconsistency between the principles of the movement and the way in which they were sometimes put into practice:

> There is in me a sense of responsibility and deep pastoral concern to adjust and correct abuses or misuses of the precepts which I and many other men have been teaching. Admittedly, there have been instances of wrong application or implementation of the principles. It is my desire, as well, to apologize personally for any lack of wisdom or any manifestation of immaturity on my part. However, the errors or problems, so far, are limited to the area of practice and application, and are not in the basic Biblical concepts that the Lord is bringing to our understanding.[25]

Mumford's assertion that the problem lay in the application, rather than the content, of the discipleship teaching appears to have been accepted by most of his opponents. This indicates that his perception of the need for some means of disciplinary control was shared by many participants in the Charismatic movement. By the mid-1970s, the first flush of charismatic enthusiasm was beginning to wane, and the need for some form of structure to preserve the integrity of the movement was becoming more evident worldwide. The various but similar teachings of Mumford, Ortiz and others—including New Zealand's David Ellis—all represented different approaches to the same issues. The discipleship movement, despite its failings, was beneficial in that it focused Pentecostal attention on seeking a solution to these problems.

Surprisingly, the discipleship controversy had comparatively little adverse effect on New Zealand Pentecostal and Charismatic groups. Although several pastors in the Indigenous Churches had close links with the leading discipleship teachers, a number of whom visited New Zealand during the 1970s, the movement did not take root in this country. However, this did not necessarily imply a rejection of the discipleship concepts. Juan Carlos Ortiz, for example, toured New Zealand in November 1974, and while not all of his ideas were uncritically received, some discipleship teachings did find a certain degree of acceptance in the Indigenous Churches. Rasik Ranchord comments that 'the emphasis that people particularly took to heart was [Ortiz's] comment that we were raising up a generation of "hearers" of the Word, and therefore he put a lot of emphasis on making the people "doers" of the Word.'[26] This imbalance between hearing and doing produced what Ortiz termed the 'eternal childhood of the believer', by which he meant that 'People "heard" a lot, but had never come to a place of maturity.... [Ortiz] was looking for ways and means whereby people could [be] brought to a place of maturity... [and] how he could make them "doers" of the Word.... He often preached along the same theme for months on end until people began to do it.'[27]

However, although Ortiz's teachings 'seemed to strike a chord with people',[28] there remained a certain degree of caution. John Steele recalled that although 'we were tremendously excited about his zeal and fervour, and bluntness and directness, and the whole concept of the discipleship thing,... none of us embraced it at all... at the time.'[29] Consequently, although Ortiz's emphasis on discipleship was widely accepted, the movement as such did not take root in New Zealand. The reasons for this appear to be social and cultural, rather than doctrinal. Rasik Ranchord, for example, refers to the typical independence and egalitarianism of the average New Zealander, observing that

> I don't think a New Zealander is likely to give that degree of control to another person. Generally speaking, I think we tend to be quite independent, and "thinkers" in many ways. We don't accept "hierarchy" too well; we're much more of an egalitarian society, and I think that might have... militated against [the discipleship teaching here].... We like to be our own boss, and I don't think... people would have taken too kindly to [that degree of authority].[30]

These cultural characteristics meant that while the teachings of Ortiz and the other discipleship teachers were seen to have some applicability, they could not simply be transplanted into the New Zealand context. As Ranchord put it, 'Juan Ortiz... had some good principles in church structure. I cannot say that I accept all that he had to say, but I feel the Church in Argentina has got a hold of some principles which we in New Zealand could well incorporate in our assemblies.'[31] Ranchord goes on to emphasise that this incorporation could not be simply a transplant of Ortiz's teachings. As he saw it, there must be a vital relationship with the Lord first, otherwise the discipleship teachings could produce a very legalistic, dictatorial type of church order.

This cautious approach paid dividends. Although there was considerable dissension over the discipleship teachings, especially in the United States and in Australia, little controversy developed in New Zealand.[32] (The contention in Australia may be partly because Howard Carter, who had taken over the editorship of *Logos* magazine in Australia, became involved in the discipleship movement. The result of this was that *Logos* became a vehicle for the discipleship teachings, and Carter a strong proponent of the movement in Australia and elsewhere.) In this country, the strength and stability of the Charismatic and Pentecostal movements and the traditional independence of the average New Zealander provide possible explanations for the lack of adverse effects from the discipleship movement. Leaders in that movement continued to maintain good relations with the Indigenous Churches and other Pentecostal groups in New Zealand, meeting with only minimal opposition on their visits,[33] although their views were not received uncritically. The outcome was that the effects of the discipleship movement were largely beneficial in so far as New Zealand Pentecostal churches were concerned and the teaching itself applied in much more moderate ways.

In the case of the Indigenous Churches, David Ellis' covering teachings preempted many of the concerns of the discipleship movement, which therefore simply reinforced ideas that were already beginning to emerge. However, the application of these ideas appears to have been somewhat selective. At one level, the discipleship and covering teachings both reinforced, and provided further legitimation for, the strong leadership roles held by pastors in the Indigenous Churches. Less readily accepted, however, was the idea of submission at pastoral as well as at congregational level. Given the movement's emphasis on the autonomy of the local church and its propensity for strong pastoral leadership, this autonomy tended to be effectively that of the local pastor, rather than of the local church. Nevertheless, the covering and discipleship teachings had the effect of sparking the beginnings of a move towards greater pastoral accountability, and hence towards some form of corporate structure, within the Indigenous Churches. Although the questions of how this accountability should operate and of what form this structure should take were not adequately resolved until the end of the 1980s, a process of evolution was taking place. This was reinforced by significant moves towards Pentecostal ecumenism in the mid-1970s.

Notes

1. Cited in Brown, 'How Significant is the Charismatic Movement?' [1985], 101.
2. Ray Galvin, 'Learning from the Sects', in *Towards an Authentic New Zealand Theology*, ed. John M. Ker and Kevin J. Sharpe (Auckland: University of Auckland Chaplaincy Publishing Trust, 1984), 99. Emphasis as cited. Galvin extrapolates from the estimated weekly attendance of the Assemblies of God to produce a membership figure for all Pentecostal churches.
3. This was the name by which the Bethel Temple movement in Australia was known. See Chant, *Heart of Fire*, 175–79, for an account of these churches.
4. See above at chapter 6, page 37.
5. David Ellis was pastor of the Ashburton New Life Centre until he died from leukaemia in late 1977. His views are set out in David J. Ellis, *The Coverings* (Christchurch: Estate of David J. Ellis, 1977); this book is a posthumous compilation by his widow, Norma Ellis, of his teaching on the subject. I am indebted to Janet Marsh for pointing out this book.
6. This issue was later addressed by Ray Comfort in his book *'Evangelical Frustration': The neglected key to genuine repentance* (Christchurch: Living Waters Publications, 1982). Comfort lamented that 'there is an estimated 80 per cent "fallaway" [sic] from evangelical altarcalls.' ibid., 7. He argued that the failure to retain these converts was due to the lack of genuine, life-changing repentance. As he saw it, the conversion process had been made human centred. People were converted because of their acceptance of the benefits of the Gospel, rather than because of a genuine conviction of their need as guilty sinners before God.
7. Juan Carlos Ortiz, *Disciple* (Carol Stream, Illinois: Creation House, 1975).

8. W. Stanley Mooneyham, Foreword to ibid., 6.
9. ibid., chapter 17, 131-38.
10. The basis for this commitment was found in Paul's injunction to 'be ye followers of me, even as I also am of Christ' (1 Cor.11:1, *KJV*).
11. H.D. Hunter, 'Shepherding Movement', in Burgess *et al.*, *Dictionary*, 784. This article gives a brief account of the Shepherding Movement—or, as it was sometimes known, the Discipleship Movement.
12. Kilian McDonnell gives an excellent account—including key documents—of the way in which the Discipleship Controversy developed in 1975-76. 'Seven Documents on the Discipleship Question', in *Presence, Power, Praise: Documents of the Charismatic Renewal*, 3 vols., ed. Kilian McDonnell (Collegeville, Minnesota: Liturgical Press, 1980), 2:116-47.
13. Hunter, 'Shepherding Movement', in Burgess *et al.*, *Dictionary*, 784.
14. McDonnell, *Presence, Power, Praise*, 2:116.
15. Bob Mumford, *The Problem of Doing Your Own Thing* (Fort Lauderdale, Florida: By the Author, 1973).
16. ibid., 7. These categories are the chapter headings in Mumford's book.
17. Mumford acknowledged his indebtedness to Watchman Nee's book *Spiritual Authority* (New York: Christian Fellowship Publishers, 1972). 'Circular Letter of Bob Mumford, November 1975', cited in McDonnell, *Presence, Power, Praise*, 2:141. Pat Robertson described Mumford's teachings as 'the Watchman Nee-Juan Carlos Ortiz "submission" teachings as expanded and put into practice by [Mumford] and [his] fellow teachers.' 'Open Letter of Pat Robertson to Bob Mumford, 27 June 1975', cited in ibid., 2:124.
18. Edward E. Plowman, 'The Deepening Rift in the Charismatic Movement', *Christianity Today*, 10 October 1975, 52. Vinson Synan, however, omits Ortiz from his list of critics of the shepherding movement. Vinson Synan, 'Reconciling the Charismatics', *Christianity Today*, 9 April 1976, 46. In any case, Ortiz was never affiliated to the *Christian Growth Ministries*—i.e. the Fort Lauderdale headquarters of the discipleship movement.
19. McDonnell, *Presence, Power, Praise*, 2:116-17.
20. Plowman, 'The Deepening Rift', *Christianity Today*, 53-54.
21. For other examples, see Hunter, 'Shepherding Movement', in Burgess *et al.*, *Dictionary*, 784.
22. This was later described as 'a move to build a chain of command linking many sympathetic local groups around the country to [the Discipleship teachers].' Peter Brock, 'The Secret Summit Reconstructed', *Christianity Today*, 4 April 1980, 45.
23. For an account of one such meeting—known as the Secret Summit—see ibid.
24. For details of the settlement achieved at this conference, see McDonnell, *Presence, Power, Praise*, 2:143-47.
25. Mumford, 'Circular Letter', cited in ibid., 2:132.
26. Ranchord, Interview.
27. ibid.
28. ibid.
29. John Steele, Interview, Dunedin, 14 February 1989. Steele was formerly pastor of the North Shore Christian Centre.
30. Ranchord, Interview.
31. Rasik Ranchord to Graham and Pam Truscott, 25 February 1975, *MHCF*.

32. Ranchord refers to 'real controversy going on re [the] Fort Lauderdale [discipleship] situation.... There has come such a polarising, both in the USA and Australia. Fortunately, the same situation hasn't developed in New Zealand.' Rasik Ranchord to David Ellis, 24 October 1975, *MHCF*.
33. In a letter to Ern Baxter, written regarding Charles Simpson's visit to Palmerston North at Easter 1976, Rasik Ranchord alludes to 'a group in Wellington who tried to stir up opposition regarding the discipleship question. On the whole, it seems to be all settling down.' Rasik Ranchord to Ern Baxter, 29 June 1976, *MHCF*.

Chapter 27

Moves towards Pentecostal unity: Ern Baxter and Jack Hayford

Leaders of the discipleship movement were not the only overseas speakers to visit New Zealand Pentecostal churches in the early 1970s. A number of Pentecostal and Charismatic speakers ministered in New Zealand, and two in particular had a major impact on the future shape of Pentecostalism in this country. These were Ern Baxter, who stimulated a *rapprochement* within the movement, and Jack Hayford, whose ministry at the Snell's Beach Conference in 1975 laid the foundations for a new openness between the various Pentecostal churches. This openness led to the formation of a new Pentecostal umbrella group, the Associated Pentecostal Churches of New Zealand.

Ern Baxter had a long experience in the Pentecostal movement. He had ministered together with William Branham in the late 1940s, when the postwar healing revival was just beginning in the United States. He had also had some involvement with the Latter Rain movement in 1948.[1] Baxter was a gifted Bible teacher, with the reputation of being a prince of preachers, and visited New Zealand several times in the early 1970s. (It should be noted that at the time of his visits to New Zealand he was not yet involved with the discipleship movement, as he did not affiliate with this group until late 1974.) His visits played a major part in laying the foundation for later developments in the Pentecostal movement in New Zealand. Ian Clark recalls that

> One of the major factors in Pentecostals flowing together was Ern Baxter. No question about Ern Baxter in my mind. He talked about things which no-one else was willing to talk about,[2] and he opened the hearts and minds and understanding of people of their sinfulness in division in a way that hadn't been seen before. I was profoundly personally affected by Ern Baxter, and I still cherish to this day a vision of the united Pentecostal movement in this country.[3]

Pentecostalism, as a movement, has had a long history of division in New Zealand and elsewhere. Given the individualistic nature of the Pentecostal experience of the Spirit, it is perhaps not surprising that the movement has tended to be somewhat prone to divisiveness. The Assemblies of God was the first group to split off from the Pentecostal Church of New Zealand, seceding from that group within three years of its establishment following the Smith Wigglesworth campaigns in 1924.[4] The arrival of the Apostolic Church in the early 1930s further divided the movement. Ian Clark comments that

> Despite what would be said by Apostolics, they *did* tear the Assemblies of God to pieces, and many of the old leaders of the Assemblies of God ended up in the Apostolic Church as Apostles and Prophets and what not. Whole congregations had problems over it.... There was that... "heritage" of splits and divisions [that] took a long time to heal; there was a lot of mistrust. When I became... General Secretary [of the Assemblies of God] in 1971, I was warned *never* to trust the Apostolic Church.... It was still very real at that time.[5]

The secession of Ray Jackson and his followers—the forerunners of the New Life Churches—from the Pentecostal Church of New Zealand in 1946 was therefore not a unique event. The generation by fission of groups such as these, as well as the spread of other independent Pentecostal groups tended to reinforce the atomistic nature of the movement. Consequently, it is not surprising that Baxter's ministry should have been so to the point, and that it produced a consciousness of the need to heal these divisions.

There had previously been some attempts to bring unity to the Pentecostal movement in New Zealand.[6] Moves towards a unity conference, initiated by the Apostolic Church in 1964, led to the formation of the New Zealand Pentecostal Fellowship (hereafter cited as the *NZPF*) in 1966. However, this was a somewhat circumscribed unity, since not all Pentecostal groups were represented. The Apostolic Church, the Assemblies of God and the Elim Church were members of the *NZPF*, with the National Revival Crusade also being invited to join. However, the Indigenous Churches were excluded. While their absence was, in part, due to their traditional attitudes of independence and of antipathy towards other churches, it would also appear that the other Pentecostal churches had refused to allow them to join. Ian Clark commented that his understanding of the situation was that the *NZPF* 'was really formed to keep the... [Indigenous] Churches out; that's the bottom line.... In those days [i.e. the early 1960s] your greatest enemies were other Pentecostals. It was really quite tragic.'[7] The reason for this ostracism was that the Indigenous Churches were still identified as 'Jesus Only'—i.e. unitarian Pentecostal—by the other Pentecostal churches, and consequently were unwelcome.

This policy of exclusion appears to have been directed at the Indigenous Churches as a movement, rather than against its adherents personally. Rob Wheeler recalls a *NZPF* seminar organised during the 1965 visit of Oral Roberts to New Zealand.[8] Wheeler had written to James Worsfold, then secretary of the *NZPF*, to inquire whether 'the Indigenous Churches [were] allowed to come in on this [seminar]?' According to Wheeler, the response was '*No!* But you're very welcome as individuals and your people.'[9] Thus, although individuals in the Indigenous Churches were welcome, the movement itself was unacceptable to the other Pentecostal churches. By the late 1960s, however, the *NZPF* had voluntarily disbanded.[10] In part, this was the product of a perception that its structure was too inflexible to accommodate the rise of other neopentecostal and charismatic groups.[11] Its disbanding was also, according to Ian Clark, due to the recognition that the exclusion of groups such as the Indigenous Churches was unjust and wrong. The *NZPF* was therefore allowed to die a natural death.[12]

Ern Baxter visited New Zealand several times as a Convention speaker in the early 1970s and his ministry was the catalyst that sparked a renewed search for Pentecostal unity. John Tiplady comments:

> I think the vision of [Pentecostal unity] was laid by people like Ern Baxter, who'd been through the country in the early '70s and had very powerfully got across the message that the Body of Christ was one, and it needed to be outworked in a practical way. So that seed was sown there [by Ern Baxter] and... was perhaps the major initial thrust towards proposed unity that came later.[13]

The Conventions at which Baxter ministered provided him with access to many sections of the New Zealand Pentecostal movement, although not all of these were receptive to his exhortations to unity. In particular, Baxter 'was treated by some persons within [the] Assemblies of God with extreme scepticism.'[14] However, the views of this antiunity camp were not held by the majority of Assemblies of God pastors. Consequently, as a result of the seed sown by Ern Baxter, links between the various Pentecostal groups began to develop. Although this *rapprochement* was most marked in Auckland, where an informal Pentecostal Ministers' Fraternal was set up, it was also taking place in other parts of New Zealand. Rasik Ranchord recalls that by 1975, 'There was a growing desire among the Pentecostal churches...to build bridges throughout the Pentecostal community in New Zealand.... There were senior leaders who were quite open, and... some of them had ministered in churches other than their own stream. So there was some... rapport and confidence already built up.'[15] Nevertheless, the Auckland Fraternal provided the platform for the Pastors' Convention with Jack Hayford[16] held at Snell's Beach, north of Auckland in March 1975.

This Convention is universally recognised by the Pentecostal churches as being a major turning point in the history of the movement in New Zealand.[17] While this was not the first combined Pentecostal Convention, it was among the most widely representative of its kind. It brought together more than 160 pastors from all Pentecostal groups and from all parts of New Zealand. Pastors of the Indigenous Churches—and in particular, Shaun Kearney—were heavily involved in the Convention,[18] which was uniquely successful in initiating Pentecostal unity.

There were several reasons for this success. The first of these was the rapport and confidence that had developed out of the links established between the different Pentecostal groups as a result of Baxter's ministry. A second factor was the growing Pentecostal unity in the Auckland region, as demonstrated by the Auckland Pentecostal Ministers' Fraternal. The Convention expanded this into a nationwide sense of unity, and 'spread the seeds of what had been sown in Auckland and throughout the country and got it going.'[19] The third, and most decisive factor, however, was the role of Jack

Hayford as the keynote speaker of the Convention. Rasik Ranchord believes that

> [Hayford] was the right person to bring because of his ability to relate, particularly with the human aspect of things, and the way he shared his own heart, his struggles and his failures, . . . his type of ministry seemed to open people up. And it certainly engendered a much more honest and open attitude towards people of other Pentecostal churches. . . . He showed the human face in ministry, not just his success side. . . . His openness before the brethren was an example to us, that we needed to be a bit more open towards one another. And so, slowly out of that, came the conviction to form the Associated Pentecostal Churches of New Zealand [hereafter cited as *APCNZ*].[20]

A later press report released by the *APCNZ* describes Hayford as bringing 'a ministry that shared his successes and his problems and strengthened our resolve to work together, fellowship together, and speak with one voice on issues that were of vital importance to the nation. . . . His ministry was particularly relevant at this time in the history of the churches in New Zealand.'[21]

Hayford's willingness to be honest and open was therefore a major catalyst in bringing a healing of relationships among the various Pentecostal churches represented at the Convention. The result was that long-standing barriers were broken down, and a new sense of Pentecostal unity generated, the most visible product of which was the formation of the *APCNZ*. This was set up as an umbrella group to represent and to speak on behalf of its member Pentecostal churches. It comprised the Apostolic Church, the Assemblies of God, the Christian Revival Crusade, the Elim Pentecostal Church, and the Indigenous Churches of New Zealand. This new association, which had no organic connection with its somewhat exclusive predecessor, marked the beginning of a new era in Pentecostal relationships in New Zealand, which has continued until the present day. Ian Clark recalls the way in which Pentecostal unity was achieved at the Convention:

> There were those who were all for pell-mell uniting all the Pentecostals into one body. And there were others who shrank back from that, if not in horror, [then] in trepidation, and in the finish, a compromise was reached. There were plenary sessions to begin with . . . , but it became evident to the leadership of the various Pentecostal groupings that the plenary sessions wouldn't achieve [unity]. . . . The key to the breakthrough was at a meeting down in the old farmhouse on the Snell's Beach property, when the leaders of all the groups . . . sat together,[22] and . . . said "Yes, we want to flow together. Yes, we want to forget the past. Yes, we want to be brethren together. Yes, we do want to love one another. But we want to take it in stages, like a 'courtship' rather than [to] 'get married' straight away." We decided that I [as secretary of the *APCNZ*] would act as a "clearing house," that we would open our pulpits more to one another, and that we would make representations on social and moral issues, and I was appointed spokesman to do that. And we did it.[23]

This new unity had some important outcomes, and Clark's allusion to 'representations on social and moral issues' is significant. It describes a new Pentecostal activism on moralist issues that did much to shape the development of the Pentecostal movement in the late 1970s and throughout the 1980s. This activism reflected both the burgeoning growth of the movement and an increasing sense of identity and political power, especially as channelled through the *APCNZ*. The effects of this will be explored in the next chapter.

Notes

1. For a brief biographical note on Baxter, see S. Strang, 'Baxter, William John Ernest ("Ern")', in Burgess *et al.*, *Dictionary*, 52.
2. Although Clark did not explain what specific issues Baxter was addressing, it would appear from the context that he was referring to division and disunity within the Pentecostal movement.
3. Clark, Interview. As will be seen, Clark presented a proposal in 1979 that all New Zealand Pentecostal groups amalgamate to form a single united Pentecostal movement in New Zealand.
4. ibid. James Worsfold plays down the role of division in the establishment of the various Pentecostal groups. Nevertheless, a comparison of Worsfold's references to the founding members of the various Pentecostal groups will demonstrate the frequency with which allegiances could, and did, change in the movement. Worsfold, *History*, *passim*.
5. Clark, Interview. Emphasis as cited. Clark is careful to emphasise that this distrust of the Apostolic Church by the Assemblies of God is now a thing of the past.
6. For an account of previous attempts to form a united Pentecostal body in New Zealand, see Worsfold, *History*, 310–22.
7. Clark, Interview. Clark cautions, however, that his information concerning this period is second hand, since he was employed in the diplomatic service overseas from 1963 to 1970. He is also careful to point out that the barriers between the Indigenous Churches and the other Pentecostal churches were not unique. He cites the 'cleavage' and 'breakdown of relationship' that characterised the New Zealand Pentecostal movement in the late 1920s and 1930s. As he puts it: 'And it was only later that God began to say to us "Hey, we really need to heal these divisions" [*sic*], and it was in the '70s that this took place.' ibid.
8. See Worsfold, *History*, 315–16.
9. Wheeler, Interview. Emphasis as cited.
10. Worsfold, *History*, 320.
11. ibid.
12. Clark, Interview.
13. Tiplady, Interview.
14. Clark, Interview.
15. Ranchord, Interview.
16. Jack Hayford was pastor of the thriving Four Square Church of Van Nuys, California. His congregation included people such as Pat Boone and other Hollywood luminaries. See S. Strang, 'Hayford, Jack William Jr.', in Burgess *et al.*, *Dictionary*, 349.
17. Ranchord, Interview.

18. John Tiplady describes Shaun Kearney as being the prime mover both in the Auckland Pentecostal Ministers' Fraternal and in the Convention that resulted from it. Tiplady, Interview.
19. Tiplady, Interview.
20. Ranchord, Interview.
21. *APCNZ*, Press Release, 31 October 1975, *MHCF*.
22. The only major Pentecostal group not represented at this meeting was the Elim Churches of New Zealand, since Gilbert Dunk, their General Secretary, did not attend the Convention. However, Dunk did take part in the later delegation to the Prime Minister, and the Elim churches were affiliated to the *APCNZ*.
23. Clark, Interview.

Chapter 28

The significance of the 1975 Snell's Beach Convention

The *APCNZ* was important for the future development of New Zealand Pentecostalism, and gave organisational shape to the growing *rapprochement* between the Pentecostal churches. However, the moralist concerns associated with its formation were equally significant. One of the first actions of the *APCNZ* was to send two delegations, one to the Prime Minister, Wallace 'Bill' Rowling, and the other to the Leader of the Opposition, Robert Muldoon. The stated purpose of these delegations was to 'discuss moral and social issues causing concern to the Pentecostal churches.'[1] Most of the pastors interviewed during the author's research linked the formation of the *APCNZ* with the sending of the two delegations, as did all references in documentary materials sighted by the author. It is therefore evident that moralist concern provided, at least in part, the motivation for the setting up of the *APCNZ*. Rasik Ranchord, for example, recorded that 'In a previous discussion, the Prime Minister had told me it was a pity that the Christian church was divided on certain moral issues. This led (*inter alia*) to the formation of [*APCNZ*] ... so that on ... moral issues, we could tell the Government that we were backed by at least 15,000 people.'[2]

Pentecostal consciousness of the need to have an effective political voice on moral issues to counter a perceived threat from the permissive society therefore appears to have been an important factor. John Tiplady confirms that this

> was one of the major reasons for proposing a closer unity.... The [Pentecostal] churches were trying to do everything in an un-united [*sic*], uncoordinated, way, and the various "streams" really didn't have the strength of impact on Government that they could have if they united, so that was the reason for the delegations. It said "Hey, we're united, and a significant force within New Zealand society."[3]

The reference to a 'significant force within New Zealand society' may indicate that Pentecostal motivation owed as much to a perceived upward mobility as to a desire to influence social morality.

Response to the delegations was mixed. A report in the Wellington *Evening Post* commented briefly on the 'strong views on social [and] moral issues' expressed by the delegation to the Prime Minister.[4] The national radio network also conducted three interviews with members of the delegations. A somewhat self-congratulatory *APCNZ* press release later reported that the discussions with Mr Rowling and Mr Muldoon were

> frank, cordial and positive, and covered education in schools, and the outcomes of relaxed laws on homosexuality, censorship, law and order, and liquor.[5] We spoke at length of the power of Jesus Christ to change lives and made a plea for the protection of the public interest against vociferous minority groups. We also made reference to the movement into schools during liberal arts periods of astrology and witchcraft, and the consistent attacks in these classes on authority and the family foundation. Although the Prime Minister and Mr Muldoon were reserved at the outset, their reception became warm and the sittings were extended. The Prime Minister gave us more than an hour of his time and Mr Muldoon, three quarters of an hour. We concluded with prayer and assured both men that we upheld them before God continually.[6]

A more cautious assessment appeared in an article in *Challenge Weekly*. This was based on a report from the *APCNZ* representatives, and noted that

> While not everything that the Pentecostal churches shared may have been received, a great deal of it was, and it is clear that both the Prime Minister and the Leader of the Opposition are concerned that a high moral and spiritual standard should be obtained in our country.... While Mr Rowling gave no particular commitment after the meeting, Mr Muldoon did say that he would represent our views to the National Party caucus the following day.[7]

Both Mr Rowling and Mr Muldoon had urged Christian involvement in the political arena. *Challenge Weekly* previously reported the Prime Minister as making 'a strong public statement approving and urging the involvement of Christians in politics.'[8] Similarly, the Leader of the Opposition was quoted by Rasik Ranchord as saying that '"Parliamentarians receive deputations from all kinds of people except Christians."... [Muldoon] strongly suggested that [Christians] should go out in the public and speak to our local M.P.s, approach the Prime Minister, and also make submissions to the appropriate committees.'[9] There was evidently an awareness, particularly by the Leader of the Opposition, of the depth of feeling over moral issues, and, it would seem, an attempt to use that concern to political advantage. Both conservative and liberal Christian groups were courted by the politicians in the runup to the 1975 election. The Clergy for Rowling campaign was an example of liberal Christian involvement in politics,[10] while conservative Christians were assiduously cultivated by the National Party. Mr Muldoon took part in a Jesus 75 rally in Auckland in June,[11] and, together with other National Party M.P.s, addressed a 'pre-morning service' [*sic*] at the Christchurch New Life Centre in late September.[12]

The effects of the delegations were indirect, rather than direct. Ian Clark comments that although there was little achieved by way of concrete results, 'the very fact that we had expressed these things gave them pause. That's all we can say; that we could talk to "Bill" Rowling in his office..., I think, was the significant thing.'[13] There was therefore a sense in the Pentecostal movement of having arrived. Clark refers to the 'amazement of... other Christians' who had been 'trying to do this [i.e. send delegations to the Prime Minister] for years, and the Pentecostals come along and just do it!'[14] Clark's claim is not entirely accurate, since several interdenominational deputations had visited the Prime Minister in the mid-1960s about the Vietnam war.[15] Nevertheless, the Pentecostal groups believed that they had succeeded where other churches had failed. This is a good indicator of the sense of self-identity and political power that was developing in the movement in the mid-1970s. This somewhat triumphalist self-understanding was demonstrated in events such as the Save Our Homes Campaign, and helped to reinforce the emerging moralist movement in the late 1970s and early 1980s.

This engagement with the political process represented a major shift in the attitude of Pentecostal churches, and may reflect the way in which the concerns of mainstream churches were filtering through to the Pentecostal movement. This process appears to have applied as much to the new Pentecostal ecumenism as to the concomitant political involvement over issues in the wider society. Not all the member churches of the *APCNZ* shared this change of attitude to the same extent. Ian Clark comments that despite the involvement of Frank Houston and himself—Superintendent and General Secretary, respectively, of the Assemblies of God—in both delegations, the Assemblies of God remained hesitant about political involvement. As he puts it: 'in the *AOG* there is a real reserve, especially at the highest levels, towards being linked with any political party. We feel that would be quite fatal for us.'[16] In the case of the Indigenous Churches, John Tiplady notes that the delegations marked the beginning of political awareness and involvement, and commented that from the perspective of the Auckland churches, these 'really sparked off the thought that it wasn't "ungodly" to get involved in the political arena. Up to that point, I think there was an influence that we were to be "in the world but not of it" to the extent that we didn't have any input or... any concern for the political process. That [attitude] was changed.'[17]

This change in attitude did not imply that the Pentecostal churches' conservative views on the problems of society had altered. Their newfound involvement in politics did not lead necessarily to a liaison with the National Party, despite, for example, the reported mutual admiration between Muldoon and the Pentecostal organisers of the Jesus 75 Rally. (Muldoon was reported as saying that he 'enjoyed the [Jesus 75 Rally]. This is what the country needs more of.' Conversely, Bob Horton, the organiser of the Jesus 75 Rally, replied that he valued Mr Muldoon's support. Horton commented that 'we have a very open ear there' in Mr Muldoon and informed him that 'we're going to influence people to vote for men with good moral principles who know right from wrong.'[18]) Rasik Ranchord insists that there was no 'deliberate working to align with a party',[19] and Ian Clark observes that such political involvement as did exist was because

Conservative Christians have recognised in the National Party a higher dedication to those things which we believe are good for society, and the fact that we see the Labour Party as having a lot of liberals, radicals and hostile elements in it as far as the churches are concerned. There's nothing formal in this; it's just an association of aims and views. There's things in the National [Party] we don't like either![20]

Other conservative political parties, such as Social Credit, also received support from some Pentecostal churches. While the National Party was the chief beneficiary of this informal 'association of aims and views', Rasik Ranchord cautions that although

It did happen that it *seemed* as if some of the ones that were more conservative appeared to be... from the National Party.... I think it would be a wrong association to say that [the Indigenous Churches] were simply with the National Party, because some may have later taken that view.... [It was] not so much supporting the Party, as individuals in the Party.[21]

Nevertheless, this informal convergence of views had hardened into some overt Pentecostal support for the National Party by the mid-1980s. The involvement of Pentecostalists in the political process became more direct. Both the main political parties recognised the potential benefits of this growing constituency and sought to encourage contacts with Pentecostal churches. Several examples may be cited of this. The Majestic House Correspondence Files contain correspondence with both National and Labour Members of Parliament. These include letters from National M.P.s specifically thanking the Christchurch New Life Centre for its support on particular issues.[22] The Labour Party also sought Pentecostal support. The *Otago Daily Times* reported in 1985 that 'five years ago [i.e. in 1980], Mr Lange had urged Labour candidates, particularly rural ones, to make contact with Pentecostal churches. Diligent provincial members maintained a close awareness [of] and contact with these churches.'[23] However, members of Pentecostal churches tended to support the National Party rather than Labour. The most high-profile example of the new Pentecostal political involvement was Rob Wheeler's candidacy for the Mount Albert seat for National in the 1987 General Election.[24] Wheeler's political stance was a personal one, and did not necessarily reflect the views of others in the Indigenous Churches. Nevertheless, several other Pentecostal Christians also stood as National Party candidates. These included Donald Crosbie, who contested the Miramar seat in the 1984 election, and Andrew Stanley in Onehunga and Andrew Cowie in the St. Albans electorate three years later.

Another product of this newfound Pentecostal unity was a 'vision... for a very well-researched, but arresting, and even slightly shocking [sic] national tabloid newspaper aimed at the top decision-making bodies and the man in the street.'[25] This newspaper, produced by the *APCNZ* and entitled the *New Zealand Times*, appeared at approximately quarterly intervals throughout 1976. It was distributed by Pentecostal churches around the country, and had achieved a circulation of 44,000 copies by the third issue. The newspaper had a twofold aim: it was intended to be 'evangelistic, [and]...to raise an awareness that there were people who believed in certain moral standards.'[26] Consequently, its content was 'geared to reach the unchurched New Zealander with the message of the gospel and the Christian viewpoint on issues affecting our nation. It [was] not written for church people.'[27] The newspaper placed a strong emphasis on what it considered to be topical issues. The first issue in February 1976, for example, covered the 'School battle for child minds'—i.e. sex education in schools, the women's liberation movement and the drug problem.[28] This was followed by references to 'abortion, pornography, sports tours to South Africa, and New Zealand political life and economic conditions' in the second issue.[29] The third issue, two months later, attacked Alcoholism and Transcendental Meditation, and reported on the *APCNZ*'s submissions to the Royal Commission on Contraception, Sterilization and Abortion.

A change of focus was evident in the fourth issue, published in October 1976, with the approach being positive rather than combative. This issue dealt with 'family life' and 'God in politics', and featured Jimmy Carter, then running for the Presidency in America, as well as several testimonies and a summary of Pentecostal history in New Zealand. There was also some criticism directed at soap operas on television. The newspaper by this stage appeared to be running out of steam. The Distribution Report for the third issue complained that there was '*a problem of distribution*' and urged 'all churches to give attention to mass distribution of the *New Zealand Times* to those in their area.'[30] The apparent lack of interest of some Pentecostal groups may have reflected the feeling that the newspaper concept was somewhat grandiose,[31] and publication ceased with the October 1976 issue.

The *APCNZ* continued to issue statements and to make submissions to Government on behalf of its member churches, as well as to work towards Pentecostal unity. Conventions were held on an annual basis until the early 1980s, when the format changed to a biennial one. Nevertheless, Ian Clark believes that the *APCNZ* had begun to drift by 1977: 'With the departure of Frank [Houston] and me...in 1977, [*APCNZ*] lost a lot of its impetus. We'd had annual Conferences, and I think they were a *vital* thing.... The decision was made by the committee...to go to two-yearly meetings; that effectively took all the steam out of what God wanted to do. And, I think, we blew it.... [Since then] it's drifted.'[32] In part this drift has been due to lack of leadership by the *APCNZ*, which, as a loose association of churches, exists at the will of, and has no real jurisdiction over, its member groups. This has meant that, despite the theoretical goal of unity in the movement, there has been no real convergence of perspective among the Pentecostal churches. Clark laments that the *APCNZ* has

> never had a governing or a leadership role. It's been an ancillary to leadership. It's been alongside it; it's been a parachurch thing. But, it has to be more. It has to be given teeth somehow or other. I think the whole thing needs looking at again.... If people get the right identity of views, [unity] will happen. The whole key to unity in New Zealand is recognition of ministries.... When ministries are freely recognised within the various streams, unity will come.[33]

By 'recognition of ministries', Clark was referring to mutual acceptance of ministries by the various Pentecostal groups. This was difficult to achieve, and the sticking point appears to have been the insistence of the Apostolic Church on the role of apostles. These were defined as senior ministers who 'have a ministry of superintendent leadership within the Apostolic Church as a whole, the leadership being evidenced by the gifts and the spiritual attributes of the person concerned.'[34] This gave the Apostolic Church a more formalised and centralised polity than was palatable to most of the other Pentecostal groups. The Indigenous Churches, especially, found this polity difficult to accept because of their insistence on the autonomy of the local church. As will be seen, Clark was responsible for an extraordinary proposal in 1979 that aimed at resolving these differences and achieving this desired unity.

The formation of the *APCNZ* in 1975 raised several significant points in so far as the Indigenous Churches were concerned. Firstly, the issues of moral concern, and of organisational consolidation to articulate that concern, were interrelated and laid the foundation for much of their development in the late 1970s and beyond. Secondly, it is noteworthy that even at this stage in their development, the Indigenous Churches still had considerable difficulty in working cooperatively from their independent, nondenominational, stance. For example, all issues of the *New Zealand Times* state that 'the Associated Pentecostal Churches of New Zealand...compris[es] the Apostolic Church, Assemblies of God, Christian Revival Crusade, Elim Church, and other local Pentecostal churches.'[35] The Indigenous Churches were not specifically identified, coming under the rubric of 'other local Pentecostal churches.' Nevertheless, they were heavily involved with both the magazine and the other activities of the *APCNZ*. Peter Morrow was one of three Pentecostal leaders—the others being Frank Houston of the Assemblies of God, and James Worsfold of the Apostolic Church—who were interviewed in the first issue.[36] Evidently there was still some reluctance among the Indigenous Churches to adopt any collective title that would signify a move towards denominationalism. This was in spite of the close bonds of fellowship that were developing between the various groupings in the Pentecostal movement as a result of the Snell's Beach Convention. Nevertheless, perceptions in the Indigenous Churches, as within the wider Pentecostal movement, were beginning to change. These perceptions were exemplified in the correspondence over Ian Clark's proposals for Pentecostal unity.

Notes

1. 'Rowling and Muldoon meet Pentecostals', *Challenge Weekly*, 16 August 1975, 1–2.
2. Rasik Ranchord to Howard Carter, 8 August 1975, *MHCF*. Ranchord knew Prime Minister 'Bill' Rowling personally since they had studied Economics together at Canterbury University. Ranchord, Interview. It would appear that this enabled him to initiate the delegation to the Prime Minister.

3. Tiplady, Interview.
4. 'Strong views on social, moral issues', *Evening Post*, 5 August 1975, 13.
5. Surprisingly, the issue of abortion is not mentioned in the press release.
6. APCNZ, 'Press Release', 31 October 1975, *MHCF*.
7. 'Rowling and Muldoon meet Pentecostals', *Challenge Weekly*, 16 August 1975, 2.
8. 'P.M. urges Christian involvement', *Challenge Weekly*, 3 May 1975, 1.
9. Rasik Ranchord to Don Capill, 6 October 1975, *MHCF*.
10. See Arrowsmith, 'Christian Attitudes'; and Keith Rowe, 'Clergy for Rowling—the Almost Politicians', in *Dialogue on Religion: New Zealand Viewpoints 1977*, ed. Peter Davis and John Hinchcliff (Auckland: University of Auckland, 1977), 31-35.
11. Reported in Bluck, 'Jesus 75—a mixed blessing', 5.
12. Circular letter to Kath Shaw, 24 November 1975, *MHCF*.
13. Clark, Interview.
14. ibid.
15. For example, see Colin Brown, *Forty Years On: A History of the National Council of Churches in New Zealand 1941-1981* (Christchurch: National Council of Churches, 1981), 145. John Evans comments that although deputations such as these occurred frequently in the 1940s and 1950s, they were less common in the 1960s and 1970s. John Evans, Comment to author, Dunedin, 1991.
16. Clark, Interview. Clark also comments that the Assemblies of God was the least responsive of the Pentecostal groups to the formation of the *APCNZ*. Their rationale was that 'the *AOG* was booming, really; [so] why did they need the *APC*?' ibid.
17. Tiplady, Interview.
18. Bluck, 'Jesus 75—a mixed blessing', 5.
19. Ranchord, Interview.
20. Clark, Interview.
21. Ranchord, Interview. Emphasis as cited.
22. Telegram from the Hon. H.J. Walker, Minister for Social Welfare, 10 October 1977; Doug Kidd, M.P. to Christchurch New Life Centre, 30 November 1983; *MHCF*.
23. 'Moral Coalition seen as political threat', *Otago Daily Times*, 14 September 1985, 4.
24. For articles on Wheeler's candidacy, see Rudman, 'For God and National'; and Stratford, 'Christians, Awake!.'
25. *APCNZ*, Press Release, 31 October 1975, *MHCF*.
26. Ranchord, Interview.
27. Donald B. Crosbie, Publisher, *New Zealand Times*, to Pastors, 5 August 1976, *MHCF*.
28. Associated Pentecostal Churches of New Zealand, *New Zealand Times*, n.d. [February 1976].
29. Cited in Brown, 'How Significant is the Charismatic Movement?' [1985], 104.
30. *New Zealand Times* Distribution Report, 5 August 1976, *MHCF*. Emphasis as cited.
31. Ranchord, Interview.
32. Clark, Interview. Emphasis as cited. Clark dates the changeover of the secretaryship of the *APCNZ* from himself to Rasik Ranchord in 1977, and appears to place the decision to change to biennial Conventions in 1977 or 1978, thus making 1978 the last of the annual Conventions. However, Clark's dates may be not entirely accurate, since the Majestic House Correspondence Files contain letters signed by him—as secretary of the *APCNZ*—as late as 1979, and several

references in the Files indicate that these Conventions were still being held on an annual basis in the early 1980s.
33. ibid.
34. Murray Darroch, *Everything you ever wanted to know about Protestants but never knew who to ask* (Wellington: Catholic Supplies, 1984), 142.
35. This declaration appears on page 7 of the February, July and October 1976 issues of the *New Zealand Times*.
36. 'Want best for New Zealand', *New Zealand Times*, February 1976, 7.

Chapter 29

Towards Pentecostal Church Union?

In 1979, Ian Clark issued a discussion paper on Pentecostal Church Union that sparked extensive debate among Pentecostal pastors and leaders.[1] His paper was a provisional document intended to stimulate discussion and proposed the amalgamation of all New Zealand Pentecostal groups into a single church. In part, it was a response to Pentecostal growth, as Clark foresaw that the continuing expansion of the movement would lead to increasing division and pluralism. He warned that 'unless we get together now ... with the major five Pentecostal churches,[2] we're going to find we'll have six, seven, eight and nine [churches], and the task of unity ... will be ... much harder.'[3] His prediction proved accurate, since several new Pentecostal groups did start up in New Zealand in the 1980s. However, Clark now concedes that the idea of amalgamation 'was probably before its time.... Any overall Pentecostal union would never appear in the form which I suggested.'[4]

Clark's paper was a personal initiative rather than that of the *APCNZ* committee. Although he did not set out a blueprint for Pentecostal union, his proposal of a united Pentecostal church may have been, in part, stimulated by pragmatic considerations. One such was the perceived convenience of having Pentecostal marriage celebrants registered under a single submission from the *APCNZ*, as had earlier been suggested by the Registrar General of Marriage Celebrants.[5] The benefits of having a simpler, more efficient structure through a united church group, rather than the manifold problems involved with a loose association of unaffiliated churches, were not lost on Clark.

There were varying reactions to Clark's proposals, the most hostile of which came from his own church, the Assemblies of God. Clark himself commented that he had 'received a great deal of personal "flak" from [its] Executive Council over that.'[6] In the case of the Indigenous Churches, John Tiplady recalls that the reactions of churches in the Auckland region to the proposals were varied and that 'A lot of different motivations came out [in the responses] from different ministry. I think Ian [Clark] was very disheartened by the reactions that emerged; perhaps it was idealistic.... It died, really, because of people looking at the practicalities of the thing, and saying it would never work, rather than embracing the vision.'[7] The Indigenous Churches in other parts of the country appear to have been equally ambivalent about Clark's proposals. Rasik Ranchord comments that

> There wasn't much enthusiasm generally among the leadership [of the Indigenous Churches].... I don't think anybody was that keen about it.... There was very much divided opinion. People felt first of all [that Clark's proposal]... was premature.... Overall, people just felt that [it] was not necessary to have a "super" organisation like that. It was rather that we ought to continue building those bridges of fellowship; that the *APC* would be the forum to build that kind of fellowship, plus the cross-pollination of ministry rather than organisationally to become one. So there was quite a bit of... coolness towards the idea.[8]

Much discussion over the idea of Pentecostal church union took place at pastoral level, both within and between the various Pentecostal groups, although nothing of this debate appeared to have reached congregational level. The discussion was conducted solely between pastors and leaders of the various Pentecostal groups. The issue was considered at the Indigenous Churches' Annual Conference in Christchurch in September 1979, and the official responses of the various Pentecostal groups were debated at a gathering of *APCNZ* leaders two months later. Given the general coolness towards the idea throughout the Pentecostal movement, it is perhaps not surprising that no steps towards implementation of Clark's proposals appear to have been taken.

A variety of responses can be discerned from within the Indigenous Churches to Clark's paper. Correspondence relating to the issue in the Majestic House Correspondence Files provides an illuminating focus on these responses and on the character of the movement at the time. Two letters from Rob Wheeler to Max Palmer and Peter Morrow set out the views of the North Island Indigenous Churches, and Max Palmer's return letter to Rob Wheeler summarises the South Island perspective. A final letter from Rob Wheeler and Peter Morrow to Jim Williams,[9] Chairman of the *APCNZ* Steering Committee, written on behalf of the National Conference of Indigenous Churches, contains their official response to Clark's proposals. These letters reveal a considerable difference of opinion on the issue.

Rob Wheeler strongly supported some form of structural unity, both within the Indigenous Churches, as well as between the various Pentecostal groups.[10] He comments: 'many of our young pastors are very figity [*sic*: fidgety] about the unrelatedness of our fellowships, and have been pushing here in the North for a closer structural organising of our Indigenous Churches.'[11] In his follow-up letter, he stated that he had sent a copy of Ian Clark's paper to each of the North Island Indigenous pastors. He describes this as 'an attempt to "scratch the itch" that many of the North Island ministers are plaguing me with regarding our closer cooperation.' The issue appeared to be a contentious one, at least in the North Island, and Wheeler's action was therefore an attempt to keep the pastors fully informed on the issues involved. He hoped that each pastor would 'speak, not in the heat of the emotion of the moment, but rather after weighing things up in the privacy of their own study.' This, he hoped, would 'clear the air' and not let the issue 'brood underground.' He insisted that he was not forcing the issue of structural unity, but rather 'letting our men know of the two subjects that need to be discussed while at the Indigenous Churches Conference in Christchurch.'[12]

Wheeler listed some specific questions in Clark's paper that required a collective response from the Indigenous Churches:

> We would need to spend some time [at the Annual Conference] ... to look at this as it involves such things as:
>
> (a) Do we want to go beyond a National Presbytery[13] and move closer to the Assemblies of God pattern of a Chairman, Vice-Chairman and Secretary?
> (b) What is our conviction on credentials and recognition of our ministers?
> (c) What criteria is [sic] required should we go this far?[14]

There appeared to be a certain degree of urgency in coming to a consensus on the issue. As Wheeler saw it, the 'subject of Pentecostal Unity [is one on] which we have to give an answer as from the Indigenous Churches to the [APCNZ] leaders in Wellington in November [1979].'[15] He was convinced, however, that the issue was not only urgent but critical. He insisted that 'if we by-pass this at this Convention [in September] our fellowship will disintergrate [sic] and become totally isolated with each Assembly "rowing his own boat" and "doing his own thing"' [sic].[16] Nevertheless, he warned that the consensus must be complete. If even ten percent of the Indigenous Churches were not for total Pentecostal unity or for Indigenous cooperation, then it would be foolish to continue with Clark's proposals for union. This would defeat the whole purpose of the idea and simply be divisive.[17]

Max Palmer's letter five days later—apparently written on behalf of Peter Morrow—responded to Wheeler's comments, and set out the position as the South Island Indigenous Churches saw it. The outlook of these churches appeared generally to have been rather different from that of their counterparts in the North Island.[18] Palmer saw no point in having a 'structure for structure's sake', pointing out that 'fellowship' and 'structure' were not synonymous terms. He also raised the curious argument that 'in times of crisis or persecution, a nationally-structured church is vulnerable.'[19] The need for fellowship was recognised, however. Palmer acknowledged that the South Island churches 'do need and desire...fellowship on a deeper level and relationship, and do recognise Ian Clark as secretary of *APCNZ*.' Nevertheless, they also felt 'that [the] purpose of our freedom as individual autonomous fellowships could be lost.'[20] This latter statement encapsulated the core of Palmer's objections, namely that organisational structure represented a danger to the freedom and life of the autonomous local assemblies. Effectively, this was simply a reiteration of the classic Latter Rain emphasis on autonomy that formed the basis of the Indigenous Churches' polity.

Palmer's responses reflected a differentiation between charismatic and organisational forms of authority as well as the movement's traditional emphasis on the freedom and autonomy of the local church. His major objection to the idea of having a chairman, vice-chairman, and secretary—after the pattern of the Assemblies of God—was that the chairman could become *'too influential.'* As an example of this, he instanced Ralph Read, whose tenure as General Superintendent of the Assemblies of God had 'tightened up [the] system' of that church.[21] In so far as ministerial credentials were concerned, Palmer pointed to the belief of the Indigenous Churches that recognition of ministry could only be given on the basis of *proven ministry* and *character*. This meant that the life of the minister, together with his charismatic gifting, was the crucial determinant in the acceptability of his ministry. Palmer argued that this process of recognition could not be carried out at a national level, since the size of the movement had produced an anonymity that prevented an accurate personal assessment of the minister.[22] The recognition of ministry therefore could be effective only at a local level, where the minister was known and appreciated, rather than at a national level.

Palmer's most important objection, however, was that Wheeler's proposals could possibly create more division than unity, and that there was real danger of 'little schisms' developing all over the country, if a structure was established.[23] (Palmer appears to have failed to recognise that an emphasis on local recognition of ministry could be even more divisive than Wheeler's proposals.) Nevertheless, he argued that there was real love and fellowship already in the Pentecostal movement and that this must be guarded. Consequently, the South Island Indigenous Churches were not favourable to the idea of any Pentecostal organisational structure. The proposal to list all Pentecostal marriage celebrants under the category of the *APCNZ*, previously suggested by Ian Clark, was, as Palmer put it, 'as far as we could go at present.'[24]

The Indigenous Churches debated the issue at their Annual Conference in Christchurch in September 1979. Their official response was contained in a letter from Rob Wheeler and Peter Morrow to the *APCNZ*, which sets out the points of agreement that had emerged from the Indigenous Churches' Conference, i.e.

1. We agree on the general principle of unity among the five Pentecostal churches in N.Z.
2. This unity needs to be formed by the Spirit rather than by structural organization.
3. To develop this unity, there needs to be an inter-flow of various ministries from the five streams,[25] so that we get to know the various ministries and their expressions [sic].
4. This unity needs to begin at a local level, by inter-church relationship in any given city or town, as well as at the national level.
5. The annual Waikanae [*APCNZ*] National Conference ought to be continued as an essential element in fostering fellowship and unity, regardless of who the

speaker may be. This annual conference should be a top priority for all ministers from the five streams.
6. Due regard must be given to have ministry from senior brethren[26] among the various streams at the annual *APCNZ* National Conference as a complement to any overseas ministries.[27]

It will be noted from this letter that Rob Wheeler's views had not prevailed at the Conference, and that the movement's official response to Ian Clark's proposals parallels those set out in Max Palmer's letter.

However, several observations should be made concerning the conduct of the debate among the Indigenous Churches. Firstly, it would seem that discussion was initially conducted at a senior leadership level, and only later involved the rest of the pastors in the movement. Correspondence between Rob Wheeler and Peter Morrow—as the senior pastors in the North and South islands, respectively—preceded discussion at the National Conference. This appears to be typical of the leadership style of the movement, in that decisions were often made at senior pastoral level, with little communication with those outside this immediate circle. At no stage were the movement's congregations brought into the discussion. This demonstrated the penchant of the movement for discussing matters *in camera* and its perception of the role of the pastor as the institutional authority over the congregation.

Secondly, the different positions reflected the personalities of the proponents to some extent. Peter Morrow, as representative of the South Island churches was somewhat antistructure, stressing the personal aspects of fellowship and 'flowing together' as the foundation of the movement's polity. His emphasis on a spiritual unity based on charismatic ministry reflected his own prophetic calling and artistic temperament.[28] By contrast, Rob Wheeler was more organization oriented, emphasising the need to facilitate a more structured relationship both within and between the various Indigenous Churches, as well as with other Pentecostal bodies. His involvement with the movement from its earliest days had given him a strong sense of collective identity, which he wished to preserve and consolidate by means of an organised structure. Nevertheless, Wheeler's views reflected those of 'many of our young pastors', particularly in the North Island, who were critical of the unrelatedness of the movement, and who sought closer cooperation. By now an increasing diversity was becoming apparent among the Indigenous Churches.

To some extent, these differences of opinion represented two contrasting styles of Indigenous church. The South Island churches for whom Peter Morrow spoke appeared to have a stronger sense of identity than did their North Island counterparts, holding to a traditional Latter Rain charismatic emphasis on independence and autonomy. Conversely, the young pastors in the North Island—particularly in Auckland—to whom Rob Wheeler refers represented a newer wing of the movement. These pastors included some who had transferred into the movement from other churches such as the Baptist churches, bringing their ecclesial understanding with them. The difference of opinion on this issue therefore reflected the changing composition of the movement. It was now considerably larger than was the case in the 1960s, and consequently, much less homogeneous. The debate over Ian Clark's proposals raised issues that became much more prominent in the 1980s, and that laid the foundations for changes in the movement's polity throughout that decade. The resolution of these diverse perspectives and the evolution of a corporate polity were important tasks for the Indigenous Churches throughout the 1980s.

Notes

1. Although most of the pastors who were interviewed were familiar with this paper, the author was unable, despite a number of attempts, to locate or to obtain access to a copy. Nevertheless, the main thrust of the paper could be reconstructed from analysis of the reactions to it.
2. These were the five Pentecostal churches affiliated to the *APCNZ*, namely, the Apostolic Church, the Assemblies of God, the Christian Revival Crusade, the Elim Church and the Indigenous Churches.
3. Clark, Interview.
4. ibid.
5. Ian Clark, Secretary *APCNZ*, to pastors, 23 February 1979, *MHCF*.
6. Clark, Interview.
7. Tiplady, Interview.
8. Ranchord, Interview.
9. Jim Williams was senior pastor of the large Hamilton Assemblies of God.
10. Wheeler later described the structure of the Indigenous Churches in the late 1970s as 'very informal; too much so.' Wheeler, Interview.
11. Rob Wheeler to Max Palmer and Peter Morrow, 18 July 1979, *MHCF*.
12. ibid.
13. By this phrase, Wheeler meant a council of senior ministries, who would have oversight of the movement as a whole. He also used the term 'National Eldership' to denote the same form of polity.
14. Rob Wheeler to Max Palmer and Peter Morrow, 18 July 1979, *MHCF*.
15. Rob Wheeler to Peter Morrow and Max Palmer, 24 July 1979, *MHCF*.
16. Rob Wheeler to Max Palmer and Peter Morrow, 18 July 1979, *MHCF*.
17. Rob Wheeler to Peter Morrow and Max Palmer, 24 July 1979, *MHCF*.
18. Rasik Ranchord, however, cautions that the difference in the approaches of the churches in the North and South Islands to the issue was not a clear-cut one. Ranchord, Interview.
19. Max Palmer to Rob Wheeler, 23 July 1979, *MHCF*. There appears to have been no connection between the Indigenous Churches and Dr Douglas Metcalf's Full Gospel Mission, which had come under public scrutiny in 1977 when guns were found at the sect's Waipara headquarters. Nevertheless, the media furore surrounding the incident may have been in Palmer's mind when making this comment. See Hill, 'To define true heresy', in Hill *et al.*, *Shades of Deviance*, 147ff., for an analysis of the Waipara incident.
20. Max Palmer to Rob Wheeler, 23 July 1979, *MHCF*.

21. ibid. Emphasis as cited. Conversely, Frank Houston, Read's successor, had the opposite effect. His open hearted and effective leadership after 1966 laid the foundation for the later expansion of the Assemblies of God.
22. ibid. Emphasis as cited.
23. ibid.
24. ibid.
25. The use of this word to describe the five main Pentecostal groups reflects the emphasis of the Indigenous Churches on the 'flowing' [*i.e.* activity] of the Spirit. The nature and shape of the organisational channels through which the Spirit flowed were only of secondary, although growing, importance.
26. Senior brethren were seen as senior because of the leadership mantle of the Holy Spirit, rather than by length of service in the movement. In the case of the Indigenous Churches, these senior brethren were Rob Wheeler and Peter Morrow. John Walton has now been recognised—despite his comparatively late arrival in the movement—as leader in the movement, replacing Wheeler and Morrow, who have both retired.
27. Rob Wheeler and Peter Morrow to Jim Williams, n.d. [*circa* September–October 1979], *MHCF*.
28. Morrow had been an art teacher in Australia before entering the ministry. Wheeler, Interview.

Chapter 30

The Indigenous Churches in the 1970s: Growth and Dynamism

The 1970s were a golden era of rapid growth for many Pentecostal groups, including the Indigenous Churches. This growth was manifest in the proliferation and expansion of Pentecostal churches throughout the country and was paralleled by the spread of the Charismatic movement in the mainstream churches. It was accompanied by a sense of Pentecostal confidence that found expression in a new attitude of cooperation and in the beginnings of political activism on moralist issues. The excitement of these years is captured in a Newsletter produced in early 1976 by one of the Indigenous churches. This reported that 'during 10 nights of recent meetings in Auckland,[1] it is a conservative estimate that over 2000 people received the Baptism of the Holy Spirit. In one meeting alone, over 700 people recieved [sic] the Holy Ghost. PRAISE THE LORD.'[2] The Newsletter also commented that the Indigenous Churches were themselves experiencing vigorous growth:

> Reaching out for new people ... is the current theme among our churches. [The] Timaru Assembly has seen people come to Christ without fail every Sunday night since Christmas. Ashburton has seen 30 new people in the last 7 months. Motueka had 41 decisions last year, with new families being added again this year. They are planning another extension after their recent extension is completed.... Bro. Ivan Gutschlag has baptised over 20 people in Arrowtown since Christmas.[3]

The reference to the numbers being baptised is significant, since these churches practised Believers' Baptism, i.e. the baptism of believers by full immersion, rather than the christening of infants. These people represented converts to the movement, as did those added to the assemblies, and it is therefore evident that many of the Indigenous Churches were growing throughout this period. This expansion was most evident in Christchurch, where the New Life Centre was reported as having 'two pastors and a congregation of about 600' in 1975[4]; by 1979, the congregation numbered more than 1000.[5] However, Doug Allington comments that some of this increase was due to a migration of charismatic Christians, and cites the case of the Opawa Baptist Church. This church lost a significant number of its members to the Christchurch New Life Centre and the Spreydon Baptist Church in 1976 and 1977.⁶ This enlargement therefore appears to have been due as much to transfers of charismatic Christians from other churches, as to conversions *de novo* to the movement. Pentecostal growth in Christchurch was not unique to the New Life Centre, however. The Sydenham Assemblies of God also experienced something of a revival in the late 1960s and early 1970s, attracting many of the converts of the Jesus People. As a result of this increase, combined meetings of the Christchurch Pentecostal churches sometimes drew up to 3,000 participants. (This was the attendance at the final meeting of a Festival of Faith campaign with Frank Houston, sponsored by the Christchurch Pentecostal churches, and conducted for eight days from 19 to 27 September 1976. The campaign was so successful that the organisers felt obliged to extend it for a further week to 3 October.)⁷

This vigorous growth brought both change and dilemma to the Indigenous Churches. The small size of the movement in its early stages had some positive benefits. It meant that many of the members of the various local assemblies were personally acquainted with their counterparts in other areas, and frequently worked and worshipped together with them. For example, when the Dunedin assembly bought a church building in the late 1960s, several carloads of young people from the Timaru assembly came down to assist with painting it, and to share in ministry. This enabled the development of close bonds of fellowship, which were reinforced by the annual Conventions that brought the various Indigenous Churches together. At ministry level, the pastors in both the North and South Islands had working relationships based upon personal friendship. Rob Wheeler described the early movement as 'just...a bunch of ministers who are all buddies and...friends just sharing together. There was no sense of a "stream" of our own.'⁸ Although this informal relationship of friendship was characteristic of the earlier participants in the Indigenous Churches, it also attracted some of the later arrivals in the movement. One example of the latter was the Palmerston North Christian Centre, which 'felt the need to associate or identify with a particular group of churches...on the basis of friendship and relationship.'⁹ These close links became harder to maintain as the Indigenous Churches multiplied and became more anonymous. Consequently, the dilemma of how to preserve this pastoral network of personal relationships without surrendering the movement's characteristic emphasis on the independence of the local assembly was a major one.

A second dilemma was the need for some efficient form of collective administration. The importance placed by the Indigenous Churches on the autonomy of the sovereign local assembly made cooperation difficult to achieve, and this situation was intensified by the increasing size and complexity of the movement. In the 1960s, collective action within the Indigenous Churches was usually the product of individual initiative. Rob Wheeler commented that 'until...1965 when our first [New Zealand-wide] Conference was [held] in Nelson...we didn't really elect anybody;...whoever had the biggest initiative [and] most enthusiasm took [the lead].'[10] In the early 1960s, much of this initiative and enthusiasm came from Ron Coady, the organiser of the 1965 Nelson Conference. However, Rob Wheeler and, following the departure of Coady for the United States in late 1967, Peter Morrow were tacitly acknowledged as spokesmen for the movement. Rob Wheeler appeared in this capacity on the *NZBC* radio programme 'I Believe' that year. Since their role as spokesmen was to articulate the consensus from within, and on behalf of, the Indigenous Churches, this development provided something of a focal reference point for the movement. Together with the publication of the short-lived in house periodical *Church Bells*, their role helped to maintain some degree of cohesion in the late 1960s.

A corollary of the numerical growth of the movement was its increasing complexity. This required a greater degree of organisational administration, and led to the appointment of a National Secretary in the early 1970s to coordinate the movement's corporate activities. Rasik Ranchord was the first such appointee, and was later succeeded by Max Palmer, the incumbent. There was also a move towards an informal system of pooling missionary support from the various Indigenous Churches, so that all funds for missionaries were remitted from a single point rather than from individual assemblies. This facilitated more accurate monitoring of missionary needs and enabled shortfalls in support to be made up from undesignated funds.[11] One outcome of this united approach to missions was a publication entitled *Global Vision*, which appeared in early 1975, and which publicised the work of those missionaries supported by the various Indigenous Churches. Eventually this informal consolidation took organisational shape at the 1976 Pastors' Conference in Nelson. The Conference agreed that 'a committee be formed [out] of which a secretary[12] be appointed to look into the support of New Zealand missionaries overseas.'[13] For a short time at least, the administration of missionary support became more organised.

This Missions Committee appears to have been short-lived, since the author could locate no references to it beyond 1976. However, given the individualism of the Indigenous Churches, its speedy demise was perhaps not surprising.[14] Neal Patterson, the secretary of the Committee, appears to have had a thankless task, as may be seen from his circular letter to pastors in the movement complaining about a lack of communication. Consequently, his report was 'only as accurate as the information supplied to me in response to a letter sent to all Pastors requesting details of their missionaries and their missionary support on a monthly basis.'[15] Patterson went on to observe that

> As there are many gaps owing to information being withheld from some quarters, I come to the conclusion that perhaps some are a little hesitant, not being too sure as to where such a report as this is leading. Especially as it may hint to [sic] centralisation. Let me therefore mention the objectives put before you all at the Pastors' Conference.
>
> 1. That the committee, and subsequent report, be on an informative and advisory capacity only, and not legislative.

2. Thus in no way is the sovereignty of the local church jeopardised by centralisation.[16]

Clearly, there was a fear of centralisation and some of the Indigenous churches needed reassurance that the formation of the Missions Committee was not the first step along the way to becoming a denomination. It would appear that this fear was not successfully allayed and that the Missions Committee failed to gain the cooperation that it needed to operate and consequently went into recess.

A third dilemma, again a corollary of the rapid growth of the Indigenous Churches, was the increasing diversity of the movement, which had expanded by the end of the 1970s 'to the stage where it was no longer just a little family of ministers who all knew what was going on in each other's church. We were getting second-generation [churches]; we were getting almost "adopted" churches [in the movement].'[17] Many of the early Indigenous Churches had inherited the Latter Rain emphasis on the independence and autonomy of the local assembly. They consequently had strong misgivings over any moves towards centralisation, which was seen as opening the door to denominationalism. However, by the end of the 1970s, there was also a growing number of pastors, particularly in the North Island, who had come into the movement from other backgrounds, such as Baptist or Brethren. These young pastors did not share the movement's traditionally independent views to the same extent. Rather, they were, as Rob Wheeler remarked, uneasy about the 'unrelatedness of our fellowships', and exerted pressure on him for 'a closer structural organising of our Indigenous Churches.'[18] This increasing diversity of opinion provided the context for changes in the movement throughout the 1980s.

A fourth consequence of the rapid growth of the Indigenous Churches was a changing perception of the role of the pastor.[19] Several factors combined to produce this change. These churches were initially the product of charismatic revivalism, in which the revivalist—whether pastor or evangelist—was the anointed leader through whom the Spirit was mediated. This charismatic authority was counterbalanced by the manifestation of the Spirit in and through the congregational members, any of whom might be a vehicle for the Spirit. This opportunity to minister was not restricted to the operation of the gifts of the Spirit, such as prophecy or tongues. A feature of the movement in the 1960s was the practice known as Body Ministry. The practice was so called because all the members of the Body of Christ—i.e. the congregation—had the opportunity to minister, and shows marked similarities to that of the Brethren movement.[20] Any member of the congregation was free, as the Spirit moved them, to share a scripture or to preach a short, usually extempore, message around the communion table on Sunday morning. This practice was most effective in small groups, where each person was known and where trust could be maintained. However, it fell into general desuetude as the movement grew and the local assemblies became larger. The charismatic authority of the Spirit was increasingly channelled and moderated by the pastor and the right to speak became specialised and restricted to those who were recognised by the leadership as having a ministry. While spontaneous spiritual gifts continued to feature in the worship of the Indigenous Churches, the effect of this regulatory function was to replace the charismatic freedom of the Spirit with an official mode of leadership. This made the pastor, as the God-appointed leader of the congregation, the source of authority within the local assembly.

The numerical growth of the movement was also paralleled by an upward social mobility. This was reflected in the higher socioeconomic status of the congregation, members of which in the 1970s and 1980s often included professional and semiprofessional people, as well as university graduates. This had a spin off effect on the status of the pastoral ministry. The higher socioeconomic and educational levels of the congregation, from which trainee pastors were recruited, meant a gradual rise in the social status of the pastorate as these new pastors entered the ministry. This upward mobility was also reflected in the increasing number of Indigenous pastors with professional qualifications or university degrees in the secular field—including, in some cases, doctorates.[21] The perception that these pastors possessed a certain standing in the secular world prompted a number of other pastors in the movement to gain a qualification by other means. These qualifications were supplied by an American organisation, represented in New Zealand by Pastor Kevin Dyson, which granted degrees to pastors on the basis of their Bible studies and sermon materials. Although the standards have since risen, it was then possible to gain a doctorate after seven years of pastoral experience, as evidenced by the pastor's collected sermon materials, and the submission of a 3000-word essay. Various pastors, particularly in the Auckland area, took advantage of this offer, and the result was a growing number of pastors with paper qualifications. This practice attracted some severe criticism from other pastors in the movement, largely directed at the falsity of these qualifications. The trend has now shifted towards the obtaining of a more genuine theological qualification through *NZQA*-registered Bible Schools, and occasionally through University study.

The increasing polarisation of New Zealand society also had significant effects on perceptions of the pastoral role. The movement's concern for moralist issues reflected its inherent authoritarianism, which had some attractive power in an age of social uncertainty. This authority, however, was more than just 'the Bible says.' The growth of the movement enabled it to speak with institutional authority in its own right and this enhanced the role of the pastor as spokesman for that authority. The perception of the pastor as the authority figure in the movement was legitimated by the covering teaching of David Ellis, and, to a lesser extent, by the discipleship teachings of Ortiz and Mumford. The effect of this was to invest the pastor's role with a definite status and to produce a hierarchy within the movement in place of the charismatic freedom that had originally characterised it.[22]

By the end of the 1970s the Indigenous Churches could look back over two decades of sustained growth and change, and had become one of the most dynamic forces in New Zealand religious life. From their earliest beginnings as a small sectarian breakaway group, they had grown to become one of the largest Pentecostal churches in New Zealand, second only to the Assemblies of God. Together with other Pentecostal churches, they significantly affected the emerging Charismatic movement, and gave strong support to the nascent conservative moralist movement. The proliferation and expansion of the Indigenous Churches and other Pentecostal groups in the 1970s contributed to a sense of confidence and was paralleled by a new cooperation that found organisational form in the *APCNZ*. The movement therefore had much for which to be thankful.

On the other hand, the Indigenous Churches were themselves changing as a movement, in part as a result of this growth. These changes created problems for the movement. The expansion of the movement produced a growing anonymity as links of personal fellowship between the various Indigenous churches became harder to maintain. As well as this, the increasing complexity and diversity of the movement demonstrated the need for efficient corporate administration. Another factor was the changing perception of the pastor's role in the Indigenous Churches. The shift from a charismatic to a more official form of authority was reinforced by an upward social mobility and by the acquisition of institutional authority as the pastors acted as spokespersons for the movement. Although the Indigenous Churches' sectarian worldview remained largely intact, they were—largely unwillingly—beginning to develop a more denominational identity as the New Life Churches of New Zealand. In so doing, their traditional emphasis on the autonomy of the local church became increasingly dysfunctional. This process would accelerate in the 1980s, fuelled by disciplinary problems and by the need for a more cohesive collective format. But that is another story.

Notes

1. The reference is to the Jesus '76 campaign, organised by Bob Horton and the Auckland chapter of the *Full Gospel Business Men's Fellowship International*. Bluck, 'Jesus 75—a mixed blessing', 5.
2. Kindah Greening, 'From the Pastor's Desk', in Bethel Chapel, Invercargill, 'Newsletter', Invercargill, n.d. (Mimeographed.) Emphasis as cited. This newsletter appears to date from the end of February 1976, since it refers to the death of Catherine Kulman [*sic*: faith healer Kathryn Kuhlman] in the United States 'last week', i.e. 20 February 1976.
3. ibid.
4. Rasik Ranchord to Daniel Manjam, 30 September 1975, *MHCF*. The two pastors referred to were Peter Morrow and Ranchord himself.
5. Max Palmer to Chuck Lynch, 12 March 1979, *MHCF*.
6. Doug Allington, Comment to author, Christchurch, 4 October 1991. Allington was a student during 1991 at the International School of Ministry, conducted under the auspices of the Christchurch New Life Centre. Pastor Gordon Rosewall of the

Timaru New Life Centre confirms Allington's account. Gordon Rosewall, Telephone comment to author, Timaru, 9 March 1998.
7. Rasik Ranchord to Tony Wiltshire, 11 October 1976, *MHCF*.
8. Wheeler, Interview.
9. Wright, Interview.
10. Wheeler, Interview.
11. Rasik Ranchord to Dave Shaw, 3 April 1973, *MHCF*.
12. Ranchord commented at the time that the role of the Secretary would be an essential one in enabling the committee to work efficiently. As he put it, 'human nature being what it is, and especially in the Independent Churches, anything can start off in a promising way and lapse back into the old unreliability pattern! Remember the reports about *Church Bells*?' Rasik Ranchord to Neal Patterson, 26 July 1976, *MHCF*. Ranchord is referring to the demise of the movement's in house magazine *Church Bells* in the late 1960s, mainly through the lack of news and articles being contributed from the local Indigenous churches.
13. Neal Patterson, circular letter to pastors, 28 September 1976, *MHCF*.
14. For example, the Christchurch New Life Centre had, by December 1977, formulated their own Missionary Guidelines that 'now, to a great extent, determine our financial support practices.' Max Palmer to Rasik Ranchord, 14 December 1977, *MHCF*. It would seem that the Missions Committee was now defunct, and that the Christchurch assembly had reverted to 'our missionary support becoming more defined and concentrating on ones sent forth from here.' By this, Palmer meant the support of missionaries from within their own local congregation. ibid.
15. Patterson, circular letter to pastors, 28 September 1976, *MHCF*.
16. ibid.
17. Wheeler, Interview. By adopted churches, Wheeler meant those churches—such as the Palmerston North Christian Centre and Fairlie New Life Centre—which had affiliated with the Indigenous Churches from the Charismatic Renewal.
18. Rob Wheeler to Max Palmer and Peter Morrow, 18 July 1979, *MHCF*.
19. Bryan Wilson has analysed the ways in which the role of a Pentecostalist minister changes as the movement grows. Although Wilson's discussion is based on the Elim Foursquare Gospel Alliance of Great Britain, which differs from the Indigenous Churches in having a centralised organisation, much of his analysis is applicable to these latter churches. B.R. Wilson, 'The Pentecostalist Minister: Role Conflicts and Contradictions of Status', in Wilson, *Patterns of Sectarianism*, 138–57.
20. Peter L. Embley, 'The Early Development of the Plymouth Brethren', in *idem*, 218.
21. An example of the latter was Mike Fitzpatrick, youth pastor of the Dunedin Word of Life Tabernacle until mid-1992, who held a Ph.D. in Chemistry from the University of Otago. However, degrees or academic qualifications in theological subjects were noticeably absent in the movement. This reflected the general Pentecostal scepticism towards theological education, particularly in those institutions that were seen as modernist.
22. Wilson comments that, in the case of the Elim churches in Great Britain, that 'the bureaucratisation of the movement ... has replaced the early simple charismatic revivalism, [and] has resulted in the creation of a hierarchy.' Wilson, 'The Pentecostalist Minister', in Wilson, *Patterns of Sectarianism*, 141, note 2.

Chapter 31

Epilogue

The end of the 1970s was a high tide mark for the Pentecostal and Charismatic movements as a whole, including the Indigenous Churches.[1] Although there were pockets of vigorous growth throughout the 1980s, particularly in Auckland,[2] this was not shared by all Pentecostal groups. In the case of the Indigenous Churches, references to disillusionment and discouragement had begun to appear in the minutes of the regional leaders' meetings and in the Majestic House Correspondence Files by the mid-1980s.[3] This despondency was, to some extent, a product of the sense of letdown that followed the peaking of the movement. A more significant factor was the deaths of two young Indigenous pastors from leukaemia, Pastor David Ellis of Ashburton in late 1977 and Pastor Brian Strong of Auckland in August 1980. Given that the movement believed strongly in divine healing, and had prayed fervently for the healing of these two pastors, their deaths were devastating to its morale.[4] This depression was reinforced by the trauma that the Indigenous Churches experienced as a result of several instances of pastoral immorality—euphemistically called 'moral issues'—within their ranks in the mid-1980s. The necessity of formulating consistent disciplinary procedures to deal with these moral issues added a new urgency to the task of reaching a consensus over the movement's collective polity.

By 1982, regional groups of pastors had been formed, each with its own regional representative, to facilitate pastoral fellowship in the local regions. Pressure for a more clearly defined polity continued, however, and this network of regional representatives—which met quarterly to decide the affairs of the movement—had been elevated to a regional leadership by 1985. There was considerable debate over these moves towards an incipient hierarchy of pastors. Several of the regional groups expressed strong opposition to these changes, which were seen as vitiating the traditional autonomy and independence of the local Indigenous churches. The matter came to a head at the 1987 Annual Pastors' Conference, when Peter Morrow and Rob Wheeler were recognised as apostolic leaders with supervisory authority over the movement as a whole. However, a minority of the delegates felt that the new leadership structures had compromised the principles of independence and autonomy upon which the Indigenous Churches were founded. This conviction led to the resignation of approximately twenty pastors over the three months following the Conference, the majority of whom formed a new group of Pentecostal churches, the South Pacific Fellowship. This loose association of churches sought to return to the less structured charismatic format of the 1960s and 1970s.

The recognition of Wheeler and Morrow as apostolic leaders exemplified the evolution of the Indigenous Churches towards a more hierarchical style of leadership. Nevertheless, their apostolic role was only an advisory one, and did not necessarily represent an external jurisdiction over the local assemblies. Their authority was dependent on their relationship with the movement's pastors, and their intervention in the affairs of a local assembly was only undertaken at the invitation of its pastor. The movement continued to refine its organisational structures after 1987, and a number of examples of this can be cited. The first of these was the adoption of an official name—the New Life Churches of New Zealand—at the 1988 Annual Conference. Another was the issue of a draft paper entitled 'Church/Ministerial Guidelines' in 1990, which included job descriptions for the regional leaders and apostolic ministries as well as guidelines for the election of regional leaders. Other indications of the changes within the movement were the issue of an annually renewable accreditation card to pastors in 1989 and the distribution of a Handbook for Pastors in 1992. Official superannuation and sickness insurance schemes were also established. However, for a movement that had begun its expansion in the early 1960s as a healing revival, this latter development indicated how greatly the New Life Churches had changed over the years.

Clearly, the movement in the 1990s is markedly different from what it had been in the 1960s. In ethos, it is now upwardly mobile, both in its congregational composition as well as its ministerial personnel, and its pastors increasingly professional in outlook. This reflects both the burgeoning growth of the movement since its early days and the changes in its constituency after the 1960s. To some extent it also represented a growing maturity in the New Life Churches, and a process of transition—in sociological terms—from sect to denomination. Although the movement continues to see itself as strongly undenominational, a younger generation of pastors appears likely to maintain the process of change that has taken place over the last ten years. Despite the greater emphasis on organisation, the New Life Churches remain strongly charismatic in worship and ministry, with a continuing emphasis on the activity of the Holy Spirit. Nevertheless, they are now a different kind of movement from their earlier counterparts. This is evident in the sense of political clout that led to their involvement in the moralist movement, the development of an incipient hierarchical structure, and the increasing professionalism and status consciousness of their ministers. These are all factors indicating that the New Life Churches—

despite their best intentions—have changed considerably since the freewheeling days of the 1960s and 1970s.

Notes

1. Battley, 'Charismatic Renewal': 49.
2. Jack Leigh, 'Getting Religion', *New Zealand Women's Weekly*, 8 July 1985, 59-62. For the growth of the Auckland Assemblies of God, see Jonathon Harper, 'The Church that's taking over Auckland', *Metro*, November 1983, 122-25; and Tania Evans, 'God Almighty', *New Outlook* 14 (January/February 1985): 22-30. A similar report—on the Blenheim Elim Church—is Yvonne Dasler, ' . . . Then they came to Elim', *New Zealand Listener*, 24 April 1982, 18-21.
3. For examples of these, see Knowles, 'Some Aspects of the History of The New Life Churches', 279, footnote 86.
4. Alex Webster and Janet Marsh, former pastors in the Indigenous Churches, recalled that the movement as a whole was stunned by the deaths of these two pastors. Janet Marsh further commented that the Indigenous Churches tended to believe that they were invincible in matters of faith and consequently had not developed theological resources to explain failures such as this. Alex Webster and Janet Marsh, Comment to author, Dunedin, 14 May 1993.

Appendix I

The Pentecostals: See how they grow

The Religious Professions figures in successive five-yearly censuses from 1961 to 1996 clearly demonstrate the extraordinary growth of New Zealand Pentecostalism since the 1960s. These are summarised in Table 1.

Group	1961[1]	1966	1971	1976	1981	1986	1991	1996[2]
Apostolic	1,399	1,841	2,361	2,693	4,503	4,194	6,804	8,913
Assemblies of God	1,060	2,028	3,649[3]	5,581	12,528	14,352	17,226	17,520
Christian Fellowships		110	72	88	240	1,074		
Christian Revival Crusade[4]	63	284	75	75				
Church of Christ (NZ)	599	610	1,085	835	681			
Commonwealth Covenant	875	506	385	361	327	261	297	168
Elim Churches	197	169	121	259	1,263	2,157	2,352	3,018
Full Gospel[5]	350	1162	1333	702	327	348		
New Life (cited as Indigenous or Independent Pentecostal)			12	824	5,361[6]	2,796		
Pentecostal (only designation)	659	1,110	1,859	4,846	6,408	15,717	25,368	39,228
Other Bodies			19		462	999	756	273
TOTAL	5,202	7,820	10,971	16,264	32,100	41,898	52,803	69,120
Percentage five-yearly increase	N/A	50.33	40.29	48.25	97.37	30.52	26.03	30.90

Table 1: Total Pentecostal Adherents 1961–96, according to Religious Professions Responses in successive five-yearly New Zealand censuses.[7]

Several observations can be made from these statistics. Although the Pentecostal movement as a whole continues to grow, its momentum appears to have slowed in the 1980s and 1990s. In addition, the remarkable expansion of the movement must be seen against the massive increase in the 'Atheist-Agnostic' and 'No Religion' categories in the same period. It is difficult to escape the impression that although Pentecostalism has extended its constituency within the Christian Church, it has not yet had a numerically significant impact on unchurched New Zealanders as a whole. This is further emphasised by the fact that, although fast-growing, the number of all Pentecostal adherents totals less than 2% of the population.

However, it may be argued that these census statistics do not tell the whole story. Mark Twain's celebrated observation that there are three kinds of falsehood ('lies, damned lies, and statistics'[8]) might be applicable here. This is particularly true in the case of the Indigenous Churches, which, according to the census figures, had no adherents before 1971. However, there were nearly 60 churches in the nascent movement by 1965, and its first major Convention, held at Nelson at Easter 1965, attracted over 700 people and 27 ministers from all over New Zealand.[9]

None of this growth is reflected in the census figures; there are several reasons for this. Firstly, the name Indigenous Churches was not universally popular, and its use as a descriptive title was not widespread in the movement. Secondly, adherents of the movement preferred to use the designation 'Christian' or 'undenominational Christian'—or, less frequently, 'Pentecostal'—in identifying themselves. This reflected their understanding that denominationalism—defined as any system of centralised church government, whereby the affairs of a local assembly could be directed or controlled from headquarters—was 'Babylon.' As they saw it, God was calling His people in the last days to come out from this 'Babylonian' structure that held them in bondage. There was therefore a strong resistance to any denominational identity and it is only in recent years that this perception has been modified to any extent. The increase in the 'Indigenous Churches' category in the census may therefore be due, not only to the numerical growth of the movement, but also to an increasing sense of identity and self-awareness. This paralleled a shift away from its antidenominational roots and the increasing acceptance in the 1980s of a previously unpopular name.

Church Group	1983	1984	1986
Apostolic	38	40	44
Assemblies of God	109	120	130
Christian Revival Crusade	11	13	11
Elim Churches	19	24	31
Indigenous Churches	121	135	144
Other Groups	10	12	11
TOTAL PASTORS	308	344	371

Table 2: *APCNZ*-affiliated Pentecostal pastors, listed by church affiliation, 1983–84 and 1986.[10]

Thirdly, the unreliability of the census figures is borne out by the 47% decrease for the Indigenous Churches between the 1981 and 1986 census figures. This decrease is not corroborated by data from within the movement. An examination of the Associated Pentecostal Churches of New Zealand's pastoral listings for the period shows a continuing growth in the number of pastors affiliated to the movement, and by inference, the number of adherents. These figures are set out in Table 2. The initial resistance to denominationalism, and the difficulty of finding an acceptable collective title has therefore limited the validity of the census figures as a guide to the growth of the Indigenous Churches. It would appear that the movement is considerably larger than the census figures suggest. This is corroborated by the findings of DAWN Strategy New Zealand, an interdenominational research organisation set up in the late 1980s. These are summarised in Table 3.

Pentecostal Groups	1986	% of Total	1990	% of total
Assemblies of God	14,039	35.48	19,108	35.47
New Life Churches	12,525	31.65	12,660	23.50
Subtotal	**26,564**	**67.13**	**31,768**	**58.97**
Apostolic Church	6,500	16.42	6,326	11.74
Christian City Churches	NA	NA	1,120	2.08
Christian Fellowships	1,700	4.30	3,295	6.12
Christian Revival Crusade	1,000	2.53	1,878	3.49
Elim Churches	3,808	9.62	5,859	10.87
Harvest Churches	NA	NA	388	0.72
South Pacific Churches	NA	NA	3,238	6.01
TOTAL ATTENDANCE	**39,572**	**100.00**	**53,872**	**100.00**

Table 3: Pentecostal attendance, 1986 and 1990.[11]

The figure of nearly 54,000 for Pentecostal attendance in 1990 was greater than that of the Presbyterian and Anglican churches (i.e. 52,780 and 45,225, respectively). The Pentecostal churches had therefore become the largest Protestant grouping in the country on an attendance basis, second only to the Catholic Church, which exceeded 110,000 weekly worshippers. The attendance figures of these mainstream churches contrast markedly with their membership figures. A recent study has estimated that only 15% to 17% of mainstream church members attend their church regularly.[12] By contrast, Catholic, evangelical and Pentecostal sects had a much higher rate of attendance. The difference between membership and attendance figures indicate that members of Pentecostal churches, as typically sectarian groups, tend to be rather less nominal than some of their denominational counterparts. It remains to be seen whether this level of commitment can continue as the Pentecostal churches become less sectarian and more denominational and evolve towards maturity.

Notes

1. Responses for minor groups are not included in the statistical extracts for 1961 and 1966.

2. The detailed statistics for Religious Professions from the 1996 census had not yet been published at the time of writing.
3. This figure includes other responses, such as 'Samoan Assemblies of God', 'First Assemblies of God' and 'Pentecostal Assemblies of God.'
4. This figure includes 'Christian Revival' and 'National Revival' responses for 1961, 1966 and 1971.
5. This term includes a variety of titles, such as 'Full Gospel', 'Full Gospel Fellowship', 'Full Gospel Christian', etc.
6. This figure includes 66 responses as 'Independent Pentecostal' for 1981.
7. This data is derived from the tables in Colin Brown, 'How Significant is the Charismatic Movement?' [1985], 101, and Michael Hill, 'The Decline of Church-based Religiosity', 142. The figures in italics are supplementary, taken from *New Zealand Population Census 1961, Vol. 3, Religious Professions* (Wellington: Department of Statistics, 1964), 8–9; *New Zealand Census of Population and Dwellings 1971, Vol. 3: Religious Professions* (Wellington: Department of Statistics, 1974), 11–12; *1986 New Zealand Census of Population and Dwellings, Series C, Report 14: Religious Professions* (Wellington: Department of Statistics, 1988), 13–15; and *1996 Census of Population and Dwellings, National Summary* (Wellington: Statistics New Zealand, 1997), 37–38.
8. Mark Twain, *Autobiography*, vol. 1, 246, cited in *The Home Book of Quotations: Classical and Modern*, 10th ed., edited by Burton Stevenson (New York: Dodd, Mead and Co., 1967), 1112a.
9. 'Holy Easter Convocation', *Revival News*, May 1965, 3.
10. Associated Pentecostal Churches of New Zealand, 'Directory of Ministers' (Wellington: 1983). (mimeographed.); *idem*, 1984; *idem*, 1986.
11. Wolfgang D. Fernández, *Institutional Analysis: Initial Findings* (Waikanae: DAWN Strategy New Zealand, [1987]); DAWN Strategy New Zealand, *1990 Church Survey Report* (n.p.: DAWN Strategy New Zealand Committee, 1990), 12.
12. Alan C. Webster and Paul E. Perry, *The Religious Factor in New Zealand Society: A Report of the New Zealand Study of Values* (Palmerston North: Alpha Publications, 1989). These researchers found that 'when the percent "religious" is corrected for frequent sense of a spiritual presence or for weekly attendance, it comes to 15–17%. By these criteria, the evangelical sects, while being nominally one in ten in the population make up one in three of the "religious." The Catholics and the evangelical sects make up two out of three weekly worshippers. Anglicans make up less than one in five of the weekly attenders and the Presbyterians somewhat less. There is clear evidence of the mythical nature of the belief in the domination of religion in New Zealand by the mainline non-Catholic churches.' ibid., 22. These results tend to match those obtained in the earlier study of J.J. Mol, *Church-Attendance in Christchurch New Zealand: A Social Research Project* (Christchurch: Department of Psychology and Sociology, Canterbury University, 1962).

Appendix II

Biographies

Armitage, George. Pastor of the Tauranga Christian Fellowship since 1971.

Baker, Charlotte. American woman pastor who visited New Zealand in the early 1970s. Baker had some influence on the worship styles of the Indigenous Churches, particularly on those of the Christchurch New Life Centre.

Baxter, Ern. Canadian Bible Teacher, whose ministry in New Zealand in 1973–74 helped to stimulate the beginnings of a *rapprochement* between Pentecostal churches in this country.[1]

Bensley, Mike. One of Rob Wheeler's earliest co-workers in Full Gospel evangelism, currently co-pastoring with Pastor James Lai in an Asian New Life church in Auckland.

Bloomfield, Ray.[2] Ray Bloomfield's evangelistic ministry had a significant impact on the later development of the New Zealand Assemblies of God. This was due both to his powerful faith ministry and irrepressible personality and to the influence that he had on his protege, Frank Houston, who later became the Superintendent of the Assemblies of God. Bloomfield started a small Pentecostal mission in Auckland in the mid-1950s—the Ellerslie-Tamaki Faith Mission—later enlisting Houston as his assistant. Houston learned much from Bloomfield, and their joint ministry saw a level of supernatural power uncommon in New Zealand at the time and attracted people from all over Auckland.

Bloomfield later began healing meetings among rural Maori in the Waiomio valley near Kawakawa, 250 kilometres north of Auckland, in 1957. These meetings escalated into revival, and Bloomfield and Houston continued to travel between Waiomio and Ellerslie for some months, preaching and following up the converts. Bloomfield later relocated to Canada and Frank Houston took over the leadership of this revival until he became pastor of the Lower Hutt Assemblies of God in late 1959.[3]

Chandler, Trevor. Former Baptist lay missioner who became Frank Houston's co-worker in the Lower Hutt Assembly of God in the 1960s.

Clark, Ian George.[4] After serving overseas with the New Zealand Ministry of Foreign Affairs in the late 1960s, Clark became an Assemblies of God pastor in Lower Hutt and General Secretary of that movement between 1971 and 1981. He was also appointed the first Secretary of the Associated Pentecostal Churches of New Zealand—formed to facilitate united action from all the Pentecostal churches on moral issues—on its formation in 1975. Clark saw the role of the *APCNZ* as being more than this, however, and in 1979 he published a proposal to amalgamate all New Zealand Pentecostal churches into a loosely united body. His proposal provoked considerable discussion, but was eventually rejected, partly because of the perceived difficulty in merging the varied structural leadership styles of the Pentecostal churches. Clark's observation that failure to facilitate Pentecostal unity would open the door to further division turned out to be a prophetic statement. At the beginning of the 1980s there were five major Pentecostal groups (i.e. the Apostolic Church, the Assemblies of God, the Christian Revival Crusade, the Elim Church and the Indigenous Churches) in New Zealand. Other Pentecostal denominations started up in the 1980s, with the result that there were at least eleven different Pentecostal groupings in the country by 1997. Clark went on to pastor the Rotorua Assembly of God and in 1986 became Principal of the Assemblies of God Bible College in Auckland.

Coady, A. Ron.[5] Coady was Australian-born and a former Roman Catholic. After converting to Pentecostalism, he attended Ray Jackson's Bible School in Sydney in 1952 (from which most of the early leaders of the New Zealand Indigenous Churches came). Coady moved to New Zealand in 1957 and co-pastored the Tauranga Upper Room Fellowship with Rob Wheeler. Coady and Wheeler set up a successful Pentecostal evening Bible School in Tauranga, and this school produced pastors for the churches that resulted from the campaigns of Wheeler and other evangelists in the early 1960s. In early 1960 Coady moved to Timaru in the South Island to assist American evangelist A.S. Worley in his successful healing campaign there. This marked a new beginning for Coady, inspiring him to undertake his pioneer evangelistic campaigns throughout the South Island. Much of the growth of the Indigenous Churches in the South Island up to 1965 was a direct result of Coady's personal drive and energy and of his controversial, aggressive style of evangelism.[6] Coady moved to the United States in 1970. He adopted a semi-Catholic orientation and accepted ordination with the Syro-Chaldean Church of South India two years later. Coady then became bishop of a church with Syro-Chaldean associations, the Catholic Apostolic Church: Glastonbury Rite in Davis, California. He resigned his See in 1989, and has now returned to his first love, healing evangelism.

Collins, David. Pastor of the Fountain City Fellowship in Hamilton, Collins resigned from the Indigenous Churches following the movement's recognition of Rob Wheeler and Peter Morrow as apostles at the 1987 Pastor's Conference. Collins was a founding member of the South Pacific Fellowship, an umbrella group for those churches that had seceded from the Indigenous Churches over the issue of organisational structure.

Collins, Paul and Bunty. Paul Collins was an early co-worker with Ron Coady in his South Island campaigns. He and his wife Bunty moved to Thailand in 1962 to begin missionary work, setting up the New Life office in Bangkok to facilitate the distribution of Christian literature throughout Thailand. Although there are no direct organisational connections, the New Life Churches later adopted the name of this office as their corporate name. Since their return from Thailand in the late 1960s, they have been based in Australia.

Collins, Terry. Brother of Paul Collins, and founder of the Christchurch New Life Centre, later pastored by Peter Morrow. Collins moved on to Dunedin, founding the Dunedin Word of Life Tabernacle. He has been a missionary in the Philippines since 1971.

Conner, Kevin. Formerly an Australian Salvation Army officer, Conner became one of the students in Ray Jackson's 1952 Bible School. He has since played an important role as a teacher in the Indigenous Churches, often lecturing in the movement's Bible Schools (e.g. those of Rob Wheeler in Tauranga and David Jackson in Timaru). Conner's base of operations remained in Australia, although he later moved to the United States. His books continue to be widely influential in the New Life Churches and further afield.[7]

Copeland, Gordon. Roman Catholic layman, formerly associated with Ron Coady's Gospel Lighthouse Church in Nelson. Copland later became involved with the beginnings of the Catholic Charismatic movement in New Zealand.[8]

Davies, Ross. Formerly pastor of the Alive Christian Fellowship in Kamo, Whangarei. In 1986, Davies resigned from the Indigenous Churches in protest at their growing institutionalisation. Since his views were shared by a number of other pastors in the movement, Davies became the focal point of a secession that led to the formation of the South Pacific Fellowship in late 1987.

Dyson, Kevin. Pastor of the New Covenant Fellowship in Auckland, and promoter of a scheme by which pastors could obtain academic credit for their pastoral work. Dyson later resigned from the New Life Churches in the wake of the changes instituted at the 1987 Annual Pastors' Conference.

Ellis, David. Pastor of the Ashburton New Life Centre until his death in late 1977. Ellis' teachings on The Coverings preempted the concerns of the Discipleship movement and provided a basis for many of the later organisational changes in the Indigenous Churches.[9]

Hayford, Jack. Pastor of the thriving Four Square church of Van Nuys, California, and conference speaker at the landmark 1975 Snell's Beach Convention.[10]

Hodgkinson, Eric. Hodgkinson was, for some years, a member of the pastoral team at Palmerston North Christian Fellowship.

Holt, Keith. Ron Coady's co-pastor in Nelson in the late 1960s.

Horton, Bob. Member of the North Shore Christian Fellowship and president of the Auckland chapter of the Full Gospel Businessmen's Fellowship International in 1975. He organised and chaired the Jesus 75 Crusade, attended by Robert Muldoon during the 1975 General Election campaign.[11]

Houston, Frank.[12] Frank Houston was formerly a Salvation Army officer, and later became involved with Ray Bloomfield's Pentecostal church in Ellerslie, Auckland. Bloomfield and Houston conducted revival meetings among rural Maori at Waiomio in Northland, which was a forerunner of the healing revival that emerged after Tommy Hicks' visit to New Zealand in late 1957. In 1959, Houston became pastor of the Lower Hutt Assembly of God, a position that he was to hold for the next eighteen years. He became General Superintendent of the Assemblies of God in 1966, and his energetic leadership and open attitude towards other Pentecostal and mainstream churches were key factors in its expansion over the next eleven years. In 1977, Houston moved to Sydney, Australia, where he established a large Pentecostal church—the Christian Life Centre—which had planted nearly twenty churches in and around Sydney by 1989. The Christian Life Centre now has branches in more than sixty countries of the world.[13]

Jackson, David. Son of Ray Jackson and a student in his 1952 Bible School, David Jackson later worked with Peter Morrow in itinerant evangelistic work in Australia, New Zealand and the United States for several years. After his return to New Zealand in late 1961, Jackson became pastor of the Timaru New Life Centre until 1971. He later worked in Australia and the Philippines, returning to New Zealand briefly in the late 1980s, when he again became pastor of the Timaru New Life Centre. He now lives in Australia.

Jackson, Ray Snr.[14] Ray Jackson Senior was a former Bethel Temple missionary to Japan and Indonesia in the 1930s. He briefly visited New Zealand in 1942 as part of an evacuation convoy back to the United States, and returned three years later to work with the Pentecostal Church of New Zealand. However, his teachings provoked a secession from that church the following year, and laid the foundations for the movement that later evolved into the New Life Churches of New Zealand. Jackson was also responsible for introducing the teachings of the Latter Rain movement to New Zealand in 1948–49. Jackson opened a Bible School in Sydney in 1952, following his shift to Australia, and many of the early leaders of the Indigenous Churches came from this particular body of students. Jackson's connections with the Indigenous Churches of New Zealand became more tenuous after the mid-1950s. Nevertheless, his doctrinal emphasis and Latter Rain insistence on the autonomy of the local church remained characteristic of this movement. Jackson's churches in Australia (the Associated Mission Churches of Australia) were always a more sectarian group than were their counterparts in New Zealand, and failed to achieve any significant growth or influence.[15]

Jackson, Ruth. Wife of Ray Jackson and an accomplished pianist, Ruth Jackson played a major part in establishing the characteristic practice of singing in the Spirit in the forerunners of the New Life Churches.

Kearney, Shaun. One of Rob Wheeler's early Bible students in Tauranga and pastor of the North Shore Christian Fellowship for a number of years. Kearney played a major role in the formation of the Auckland Pentecostal Ministers' Fraternal and in the organisation of the historic Snell's Beach Convention in 1975. This Convention stimulated a new Pentecostal unity and resulted in the formation of the Associated Pentecostal Churches of New Zealand.

Kiteley, Violet. American woman pastor who visited New Zealand in the late 1960s and early 1970s and who had an influential prophetic ministry among the Indigenous Churches.

McAlpine, Campbell. Brethren visitor to New Zealand, who helped to lay the foundation for the emergence of the Charismatic movement among the Brethren and in other churches in the early 1960s.[16]

McCracken, David. Pastor of the Manukau New Life Christian Centre until 1988.[17]

McMillan, Jim and Dinal. Pastors of the Kawerau Christian Fellowship. Dinal McMillan is of Ngati Kahungungu descent.

McNabb, Bernie. Ron Coady's assistant pastor in Nelson in the mid–1960s.

Morrow, Anne (neé Botherway).[18] Wife of Peter Morrow, and recognised within the New Life Churches as a senior minister in her own right. She has taken a strong leadership role in women's issues. In particular, she organised and led the Save Our Homes Campaign (a conservative Christian convention intended to provide a balance to what was perceived as destructive radical feminism) in 1977. She also coordinated the Indigenous Churches' responses to the 1984 Forums on the United Nations Convention of the Elimination of All Forms of Discrimination Against Women and acted as spokesperson for these responses. She has led the movement towards greater recognition of women's ministry roles in the New Life Churches.

Morrow, Peter.[19] Peter Morrow was Australian-born and a former Anglican and high school art teacher. Following his conversion to Pentecostalism, he was a student in Ray Jackson's 1952 Bible School and later engaged in informal evangelistic work for some years in Australia, New Zealand and the United States. On his return to New Zealand in the late 1950s, Morrow assisted Rob Wheeler and A.S. Worley in their evangelistic campaigns, particularly in the initial follow-up of converts. He moved to Christchurch in late 1962 to take over the pastorate of the newly formed Christchurch Revival Centre (later renamed Christchurch New Life Centre). Morrow's open attitude towards other churches enabled him to have considerable influence on the nascent Charismatic movement in the later 1960s. This was by way of teaching meetings, such as those held at Adullam's Cave (a coffee bar run by his church) and by personal contact. By the late 1970s, Morrow's congregation had grown to more than 1,000 people, making it one of the largest Pentecostal churches in New Zealand.

Peter Morrow was also spokesperson for the South Island Indigenous Churches. This senior role, together with his international standing as a conference speaker, led to his recognition as an apostle by the movement in 1987. Morrow has suffered ill health in recent years, largely due to a savage attack (which nearly cost him his life) by a machete-wielding former psychiatric patient that same year.

Mossholder, Ray. American pastor and keynote speaker for the Christchurch Save Our Homes Campaign in 1977.

Mumford, Bob. American Charismatic pastor, author, and leading figure in the Discipleship movement in the 1970s.[20]

Offiler, W.H. Pastor of Bethel Temple in Seattle, Washington. Offiler's teachings, passed on by his disciple Ray Jackson, shaped the doctrinal foundations of the early Indigenous Churches.

Ortiz, Juan Carlos. Argentinean pastor, author and conference speaker. Ortiz's teachings, expanded and put into systematic form by Bob Mumford, were the catalyst for the emergence of the Discipleship movement in the mid-1970s.[21]

Palmer, Max. One of the pastors in the Christchurch New Life Centre. A former accountant, Palmer succeeded Rasik Ranchord as secretary of the Indigenous Churches and has exercised an efficient administrative oversight in the movement for a number of years. He has served on the boards of World Outreach and Asian Outreach, and is currently on the board of *CFTN* (the Canterbury community television channel, associated with Lifeway Bible School in Warkworth, Auckland). He is also National Secretary for the Associated Pentecostal Churches of New Zealand and national trainer for Prepare/Enrich NZ.

Patterson, Neal. Former pastor of the Napier Christian Fellowship and Missions Secretary for the Indigenous Churches for several years in the mid-1970s.

Pollock, Ada (neé Saunders). Ada Pollock was responsible for A.S. Worley's return to Timaru after an earlier campaign there in April 1960. Worley's second campaign resulted in more than 600 conversions to Christ and the beginnings in the South Island of the movement that later became the New Life Churches.[22]

Ranchord, Rasik. Ranchord was born in Fiji and came to Christchurch in the early 1960s to study commerce at Canterbury University, where he was converted from Hinduism to Christianity. As a result of his conversion, Ranchord was forbidden by his Hindu parents to use the family name and thus was known for a time as Rasik Lal. He joined the Christchurch Revival Fellowship in the mid-1960s, eventually becoming Peter Morrow's assistant pastor and later the inaugural secretary of the Indigenous Churches. Ranchord had links with Prime Minister Wallace 'Bill' Rowling, with whom he had studied economics at Canterbury. This may have been a factor in his involvement with the delegations to the Prime Minister and the Leader of the Opposition following the formation of the Associated Pentecostal Churches of New Zealand in 1975. Ranchord later relocated to Wellington, where he is currently pastor of the Wellington Abundant life Centre.

Ravenhill, David. Son of American pastor Leonard Ravenhill—author of the internationally known book *Why Revival Tarries*—Ravenhill was on the pastoral staff of the Christchurch New Life Centre in the late 1970s and early 1980s. He was Principal of the New Life Family Bible College until he returned to the United States in 1985.

Robb, Edna. Mrs Robb was a convert of A.H. Dallimore's Revival Fire Mission in Auckland in the 1930s. Following a visit to Tauranga at the end of 1939, she became the pastor of a Revival Fire Mission outreach held in the Otumoetai school. She continued to lead this house church until 1950, when it amalgamated with Ray Jackson's Bethel Temple group. This merger formed the nucleus of the church that evolved into the Tauranga Christian Fellowship, effectively the oldest of the New Life Churches of New Zealand.

Shaw, Dave. Pastor of the Dunedin Word of Life Fellowship until 1986.

Shearer, David. Pastor of the New Plymouth New Life Christian Fellowship. Shearer had begun to express his concern at the increasing institutionalisation of the Indigenous Churches by 1986. Together with Ross Davies, Shearer formed a nucleus for opposition to the more structured organisational format then emerging in the movement.

Stanley, Andrew. Direction of Youth with a Mission in the early 1980s and later a pastor on the staff of the North Shore Faith Centre in Glenfield, Auckland. Stanley was one of the more prominent activists in the Indigenous Churches in the 1980s and stood for Parliament in the 1987 General Election.[23]

Steele, John and Julie. Pastors of the North Shore Faith Centre in the 1980s.

Stephen, Bill. Pastor of the Motueka New Life Centre.

Thrift, Allan. An early co-worker with Ray Jackson after 1949. Thrift's ministry has been largely among Bay of Plenty Maori, especially in the Te Teko area. He later became pastor of the Henderson Christian Fellowship in Auckland.

Tiplady, John. Former physical education teacher and currently pastor of the North Shore New Life Centre.

Wagener, Owen. Pastor of the Living Word Church, a New Life church in Kohimarama, Auckland. Wagener was deeply committed to the moralist campaign against the Homosexual Law Reform Bill in 1985, and helped to organise the collection of signatures in the Auckland area for the Homosexual Law Reform Petition.

Walker, Dal and Dorothy. Dal and Dorothy Walker were well known for their long missionary service in Indonesia. Dal Walker was converted under the ministry of A.H. Dallimore in 1931, while Dorothy Walker's father, Harry Roberts, was Superintendent of the Pentecostal Church of New Zealand. The Walkers became involved in pastoral and evangelistic work in the Pentecostal Church of New Zealand, and were supporters of Ray Jackson's teaching on 'the Name' when this controversy broke out in 1946. The Walkers arrived in the newly independent republic of Indonesia in March 1949, where they worked on the island of Roti, in the Timor group. They later opened Bible Schools in Malang, East Java, and in Bali, and ministered effectively throughout Indonesia, becoming well known for their evangelistic passion and enthusiasm. After being forced to relocate in the Philippines due to the rising Communist influence of the late Sukarno era, they eventually returned to Indonesia and set up a Bible School in Tawangmangu, Central Java. This school has become highly regarded throughout Indonesia, and some 2,600 graduates have gone into the ministry in the thirty years since the school opened. After Dal Walker's death in a car crash in 1974 and Dorothy Walker's later return to New Zealand, the school was run by their daughter and son-in-law, Carol and Sam Soukotta. The school currently has a student roll of more than 250, and offers a four-year degree-level training course that is fully accredited by the Indonesian government.[24]

Wallis, Arthur. Brethren visitor to New Zealand, who helped to initiate the Charismatic movement among the Brethren and in other churches in 1963 and 1964.[25]

Walton, John.[26] Walton was originally a member of the Exclusive Brethren, but was expelled for heresy in 1969 after he had become involved with the Charismatic movement. He then attended a Baptist church that in the mid-1970s became an Indigenous Church. He rose rapidly through the ranks of the Indigenous Churches of New Zealand, and contributed in its progress towards a more structured movement. This resulted in the recognition of Rob Wheeler and Peter Morrow as apostolic leaders at its 1987 Annual Conference. Walton replaced Rob Wheeler as one of the two leaders of the movement in 1989. By the early 1990s Walton was the sole head of the New Life Churches (Peter Morrow also resigning due to failing health).[27]

Wást, Bruce. Wást has been pastor of the Dunedin Word of Life Fellowship since 1986.

Webster, Alex, and Marsh, Janet. This husband and wife team were formerly pastors of the Kaikoura New Life Centre and missionaries to Thailand. More recently, they were on the pastoral staff of the Christchurch New Life Centre, where they had particular responsibility for the International School of Ministry. They resigned their positions in 1991 to undertake theological study at the University of Otago, and currently both hold pastorates in the Methodist church.

Wheeler, Rob.[28] Rob Wheeler's career spans the entire history of the New Life Churches. He was a member of Ray Jackson's Bethel Chapel church in Auckland from 1946 and attended Jackson's 1952 Bible School in Sydney, Australia. Wheeler returned to New Zealand in June 1953, initially taking over the pastorate of the Auckland church, and becoming pastor of the Tauranga Upper Room Fellowship the following year. He resigned this in late 1957 to begin itinerant tent crusade evangelism, modelled on the pattern of Oral Roberts and others in the United States. The success of these campaigns led to the creation of a group of independent Pentecostal churches that eventually evolved into the New Life Churches. Wheeler also conducted numerous short-term evening Bible Schools to provide Christian workers for these new churches, and in 1964 became pastor of the newly founded Auckland Christian Fellowship in Epsom, Auckland. In the 1980s, Wheeler became increasingly involved in political issues and unsuccessfully stood for the Mount Albert seat in the 1987 General Election. Wheeler was recognised as an apostle in the Indigenous Churches at their 1987 Annual Pastors' Convention, but resigned this role two years later due to ill health.[29]

Worley, A.S.[30] Worley was an independent Pentecostal evangelist from Walhalla, South Carolina, who was invited to come to New Zealand to conduct healing campaigns. Worley arrived in late 1959 and conducted a number of campaigns over the next twelve months. He had considerable influence on the new generation of healing evangelists then emerging in this country. Worley's ministry in New Zealand was notable for the healings that took place, particularly the filling of people's teeth as a sign of the power of God. His most significant contribution, however, was his highly successful campaign in Timaru during June and July 1960. The Timaru revival ignited a wave of healing evangelism in the South Island and led to unprecedented Pentecostal growth in this country. The Indigenous Churches, for example, grew tenfold (from six to more than sixty churches) during the five-year period from 1960 to 1965. This expansion is directly attributable to the ministries of Worley and of the evangelists whom he inspired during his time in New Zealand.[31]

Worsfold, James. Apostolic pastor, and author of a pioneering book on New Zealand Pentecostalism, *A History of the Charismatic Movements in New Zealand*.

Wright, Ken. Former Charismatic Presbyterian elder who was associated with the Awapuni Baptist Church when it seceded from the Baptist Union about 1969. This group appears to have laid the foundations for the later development of the Charismatic Movement in Palmerston North. It also underwent a series of name changes, eventually subdividing into the Palmerston North Christian Centre and the Palmerston North New Life Centre, both of which are affiliated with the New Life Churches.

Notes

1. S. Strang, 'Baxter, William John Ernest ("Ern")', in Burgess *et al*, *Dictionary*, 52.
2. Published as Brett Knowles, 'Bloomfield, Ray (1924?-)', in *New International Dictionary of Pentecostal and Charismatic Movements*, ed. Stanley M. Burgess (Grand Rapids, Michigan: Zondervan, 2000, forthcoming). Used by permission.
3. Houston, *Being Frank*, 70-112.
4. Published as Brett Knowles, 'Clark, Ian George (1935-)', in Burgess, *New International Dictionary* (forthcoming). Used by permission.
5. Published as Brett Knowles, 'Coady, A. Ron (1928-)', in Burgess, *New International Dictionary* (forthcoming). Used by permission.
6. Coady, *I Shall Not Want*; *Revival News*, 1962-66.
7. Conner, *The Tabernacle of David*; idem, *Foundations of Christian Doctrine* (Blackburn, Victoria: Acacia Press, 1980).
8. Copeland, *Faith that works*.
9. Ellis, *The Coverings*.
10. S. Strang, 'Hayford, Jack Williams Jnr.', in Burgess *et al.*, *Dictionary*, 349.
11. Bluck, 'Jesus 75', 5; Leigh, 'Getting Religion', 59-62.
12. Published as Brett Knowles, 'Houston, Frank (1922-)', in Burgess, *New International Dictionary* (forthcoming). Used by permission.
13. Houston, *Being Frank*.
14. Published as Brett Knowles, 'Jackson, Ray Sr. (1903?-1990)', in Burgess, *New International Dictionary* (forthcoming). Used by permission.
15. Chant, *Heart of Fire*; Riss, *Latter Rain*.
16. Lineham, 'Tongues must cease': 23-27.
17. Leigh, 'Getting Religion', 59-62.
18. Published as part of Brett Knowles, 'Morrow, Peter (1930-) and Anne', in Burgess, *New International Dictionary* (forthcoming). Used by permission.
19. ibid.
20. S. Strang, 'Mumford, Bernard C., Jr. ("Bob")', in Burgess *et al.*, *Dictionary*, 631.
21. E.A. Wilson, 'Ortiz, Juan Carlos', in Burgess *et al.*, *Dictionary*, 654-55.
22. Henderson, *From Glory to Glory*, 2-4.
23. See Fran Pardon, 'The Moral Minority: Auckland's Right-Wing Christians are on the March', *Auckland Metro*, May 1982, 91.
24. Dorothy Walker, 'Indonesia have I loved', *passim*.
25. Lineham, 'Tongues must cease', 29-30; P.D. Hocken, 'Wallis, Arthur R.', in Burgess *et al.*, *Dictionary*, 878.
26. Published as Brett Knowles, 'Walton, John (1934-)', in Burgess, *New International Dictionary* (forthcoming). Used by permission.
27. Toomer, 'National church leader "walks with his people,"' 5.
28. Published as Brett Knowles, 'Wheeler, Rob (1932-)', in Burgess, *New International Dictionary* (forthcoming). Used by permission.
29. Rudman, 'For God and National', 28-29; Stratford, 'Christians Awake! Join the National Party, Save New Zealand', 124-37; 'Treasures of Grace: God holds the Copyright', *Bible Deliverance*, February 1961, 14-16.
30. Published as Brett Knowles, 'Worley, A.S. (1921-)', in Burgess, *New International Dictionary* (forthcoming). Used by permission.
31. Grice, *Apostle to the Nations*.

Appendix III

Maps: Growth of the Movement

It is difficult to ascertain a starting date for many of the churches in the movement. There are several reasons for this. While preliminary evangelistic campaigns often resulted in the immediate establishment of a local assembly, other churches were founded only after several such attempts. New Life churches also resulted from the transfer into the movement of previously established churches.

Furthermore, it should not be assumed that these New Life churches remained static. The Nelson assembly, known as the Gospel Lighthouse, was established following Ron Coady's campaigns in 1962, but was later reformed under the pastorate of Alister Lowe to become the Nelson New Life Centre. Likewise, the Kaikoura Mission was set up following a successful evangelistic campaign in early 1964, but went into recess the following year. It was reestablished as the Kaikoura New Life Centre several years later by members of the Christchurch New Life Centre. A comparison of the references below with current Pastoral Lists of the movement will demonstrate that not all such assemblies have survived into the 1990s.

The following maps have been drawn up using data collated from early periodicals of the movement and from commemorative materials produced by several New Life churches. The references contained therein were often indefinite and the maps should not be taken as a definitive statement of the spread of the movement. For example, Rob Wheeler's *Bible Deliverance* magazine frequently fails to distinguish between churches of other Pentecostal groups for whom he had conducted campaigns and those autonomous local assemblies that later became the New Life Churches. Nevertheless, the references on the map indicate what appears to have been a permanent New Life presence at the time in the localities cited. In some cases the date of origin can be stated with some certainty. In other cases, the reference to a local church indicates only that it was in existence at this date and presumably had been established some time earlier. The source data for these references are tabulated as follows:

Church	Source of Reference
Ahipara	'Missionary News', *Gospel Truth*, July 1964, 8.
Ashburton	'We take the Word of Life to Ashburton and Christchurch', *Revival News*, September 1962, 3.
Auckland	R.B.W., 'Auckland Crusade at Western Springs', *Bible Deliverance*, November–December 1964, 6-7.
Blenheim	'News Items', *Revival News*, July 1963, 11.
Chatham Islands	Mary Henderson, *From Glory to Glory: A History of the Timaru New Life Centre 1960-1980*, 27; 'We saw God work on Chatham Islands: By Ray, Ron, Elton', *Gospel Truth*, September 1964, 4-5.
Christchurch	Christchurch New Life Centre, 'Visitor Pack', 1989.
Cromwell	'Church News', *Church Bells*, June 1966, 12-13.
Dunedin	Word of Life Fellowship, 'Newsletter', June 1991.
Edgecumbe	Te Teko Fellowship, '25th Anniversary Celebrations 1961-1986', 7 and 41.
Eltham	'Thrilling scenes witnessed in Eltham Crusade with Brother Coady', *Revival News*, December 1965, 6-7.
Fairlie	Mary Henderson, *From Glory to Glory: A History of the Timaru New Life Centre 1960-1980*, 27; 'Church Reports', *Church Bells*, July 1968, 22.
Feilding	'Miracle Tent Mission in Feilding', *Revival News*, July 1964, 6-7.
Gisborne	Te Teko Fellowship, '25th Anniversary Celebrations: 1961-1986', 6.
Gore	Mary Henderson, *From Glory to Glory: A History of the Timaru New Life Centre 1960-1980*, 14; 'First Anniversary', *Revival News*, September 1962, 8-9.

Appendix III: Maps: Growth of the Movement   243

Greymouth	'Greymouth Fire', *Gospel Truth*, February 1965, 6.
Hamilton	'Newflashes', *Bible Deliverance*, August 1964, 4; 'Forever with the Lord', *idem*, 10.
Hastings	Tauranga Christian Fellowship, 'Jubilee Reunion 1939–1989', 9.
Invercargill	Mary Henderson, *From Glory to Glory: A History of the Timaru New Life Centre 1960–1980*, 14.
Kaikoura	'Kaikoura Holiday and Healing Festival', *Revival News*, January–February 1964, 8.
Kaitaia	'Missionary News', *Gospel Truth*, July 1964, 8.
Kawerau	Te Teko Fellowship, '25th Anniversary Celebrations: 1961–1986', 6.
Leeston	'Church News', *Church Bells*, September 1966, 21.
Levin	'Newflashes', *Bible Deliverance*, April 1965, 7.
Lower Hutt	'Gospel Bombardment: Attack on New Zealand', *Revival News*, August 1965, 11.
Masterton	'Gospel Bombardment: Attack on New Zealand', *Revival News*, August 1965, 11.
Motueka	Motueka New Life Centre, 'New Life Centre: A History', 2.
Mount Maunganui	'Newflashes', *Bible Deliverance*, October 1959, 19.
Murupara	Te Teko Fellowship, '25th Anniversary Celebrations: 1961–1986', 7.
Nelson	I. Copeland, '"And the word of God grew and multiplied" in Nelson', *Revival News*, June 1962, 3.
Opotiki	Tauranga Christian Fellowship, 'Jubilee Reunion 1939–1989', 10.
Palmerston North	'Gospel Bombardment: Attack on New Zealand', *Revival News*, August 1965, 11.
Putaruru	'In the Tent at Putaruru . . .', *Bible Deliverance*, February–March 1963, 10.

Rangiora	'Churches throughout N.Z. [sic] and Australia', *Gospel Truth*, September 1964, 8.
Rangitukia	'Regions Beyond—the Missionary Page: The East Coast Maori Work', *Bible Deliverance*, April 1959, 8–9.
Rotorua	Tauranga Christian Fellowship, 'Jubilee Reunion 1939–1989', 9.
Ruatoki	Te Teko Fellowship, '25th Anniversary Celebrations: 1961–1986', 41.
Ruatoria	'New Zealand: The Maori Work', *Bible Deliverance*, November 1960, 12.
Stewart Island	'Stewart Island Welcomes Gospel', *Gospel Truth*, August 1964, 5.
Stratford	Tauranga Christian Fellowship, 'Jubilee Reunion 1939–1989', 9.
Takapuna/North Shore	'Log Book... Regrets? or Rejoicings?', *Bible Deliverance*, Christmas Issue 1965, 15.
Taneatua	Te Teko Fellowship, '25th Anniversary Celebrations: 1961–1986', 41.
Tauranga	Tauranga Christian Fellowship, 'Jubilee Reunion 1939–1989', 2.
Te Araroa	'Regions Beyond—the Missionary Page: The East Coast Maori Work', *Bible Deliverance*, April 1959, 8–9.
Te Awamutu	'Gospel Bombardment: Attack on New Zealand', *Revival News*, August 1965, 11.
Te Teko	Te Teko Fellowship, '25th Anniversary Celebrations: 1961–1986', 5.
Timaru	Mary Henderson, *From Glory to Glory: A History of the Timaru New Life Centre 1960–1980*, 8.
Tokomaru Bay	'"Regions Beyond": The Missionary Page', *Bible Deliverance*, January–February 1960, 8.
Tokoroa	Tauranga Christian Fellowship, 'Jubilee Reunion 1939–1989', 9.
Tolaga Bay	'Church News', *Church Bells*, September 1966, 20.

Tuatapere/Orepuki	Mary Henderson, *From Glory to Glory: A History of the Timaru New Life Centre 1960–1980*, 14.
Turangi/Taupo	'Newflashes', *Church Bells*, September 1968, 21.
Waharoa	'Indigenous Full Gospel N.Z. [sic] Churches', *Church Bells*, July 1968, 5.
Waihau Bay	'Regions Beyond—The Missionary Page: News from the East Coast', *Bible Deliverance*, May 1959, 12–13.
Waihi	Tauranga Christian Fellowship, 'Jubilee Reunion 1939–1989', 9.
Waimana	A.S. Thrift, 'At Home ... "Moves in Maoriland,"' *Bible Deliverance*, August 1963, 14.
Waimate	'Eben-Ezer: The stone of help', *Revival News*, October 1962, 2.
Wainuiomata	'Church Reports', *Church Bells*, July 1968, 15.
Waioeka	A.S. Thrift, 'At Home ... "Moves in Maoriland,"' *Bible Deliverance*, August 1963, 14.
Waiohau	'Church Reports', *Church Bells*, September 1968, 7.
Wellington	'Churches throughout N.Z. [sic] and Australia', *Gospel Truth*, September 1964, 8.
Westport	'Church News', *Church Bells*, June 1966, 14.
Whakatane	Tera Woelders, 'A Dutch couple find Christ', *Bible Deliverance*, August 1959, 18.
Whangarei	'Churches throughout N.Z. [sic] and Australia', *Gospel Truth*, September 1964, 8.

246 New Life

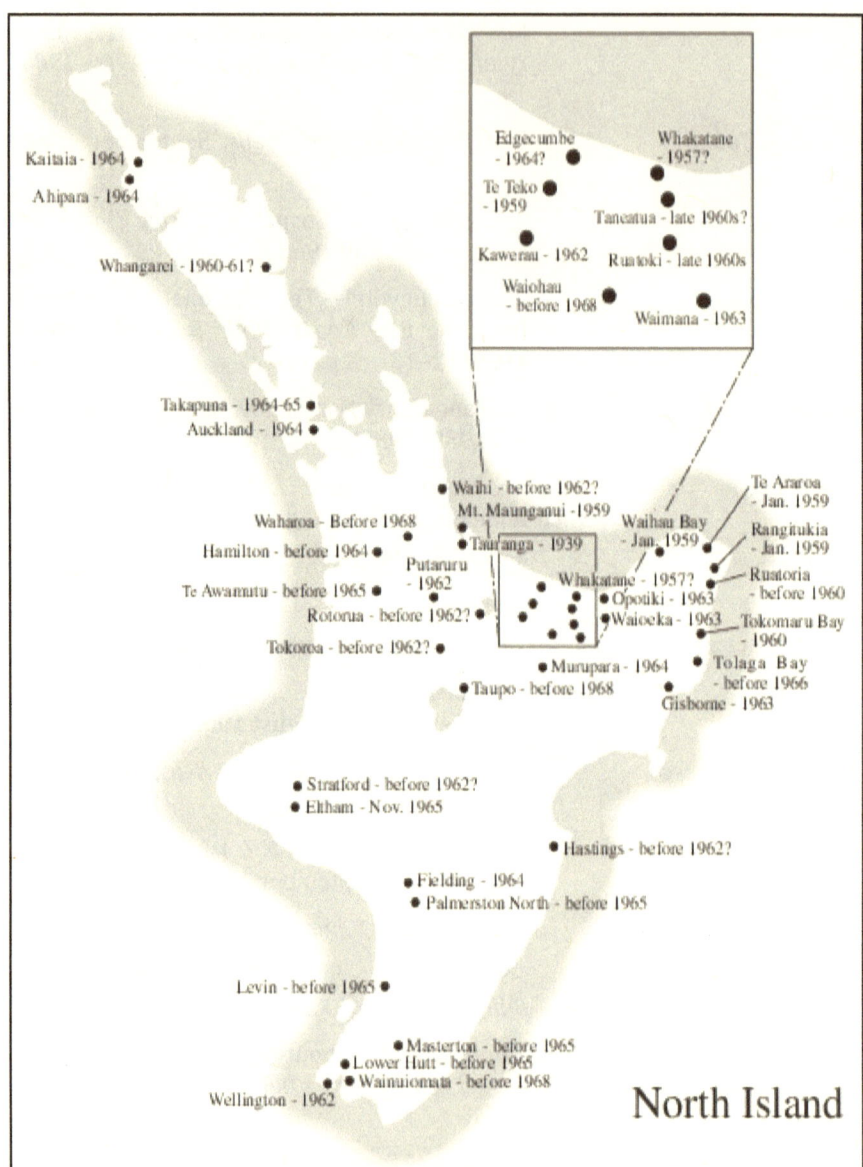

Figure 15: Growth of the Movement in the North Island

Appendix III: Maps: Growth of the Movement   247

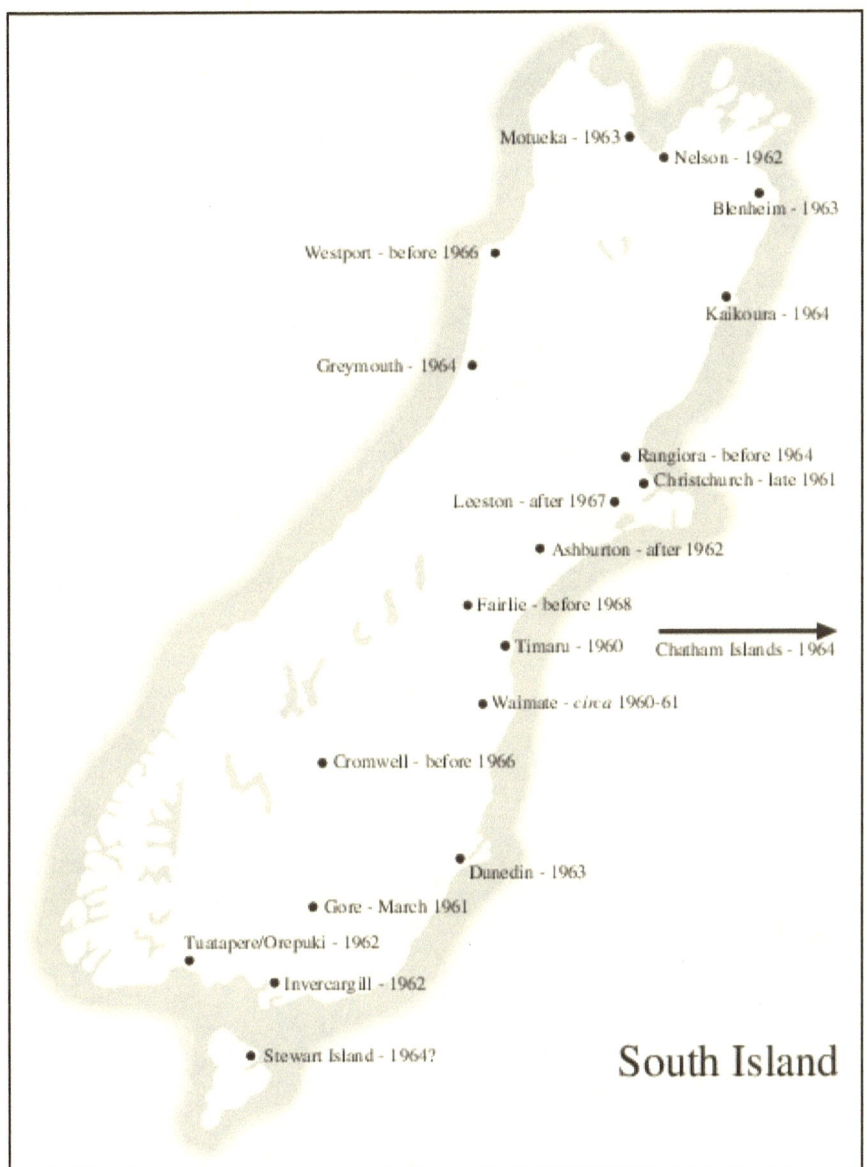

Figure 16: Growth of the Movement in the South Island

Bibliography

1. Oral Sources

1.1. Interviews

Bensley, Mike. Pastor, New Life Churches. Waikanae. Interview, 24 September 1987.

Clark, Ian. Retired Pastor and Bible School Principal, Assemblies of God. Auckland. Interview, 28 February 1990. Tape recording in author's possession.

Coady, Ron. Former Pastor, Indigenous Churches; now retired Bishop, Catholic Apostolic Church, Glastonbury Rite. Davis, California. Taped interview in response to Questionnaire, 24 March 1988. Tape recording in author's possession.

Collins, Terry. Former Pastor, Indigenous Churches; long-term missionary to Philippines. Dunedin. Interview, 21 December 1989. Tape recording in author's possession.

Davies, Ross. Former Pastor, Indigenous Churches; founder of South Pacific Fellowship. Whangarei. Interview, 1 March 1990. Tape recording in author's possession.

Jackson, David. Former Pastor, Indigenous Churches. Timaru. Interview, 19 November 1987. Tape recording in author's possession.

Mandie, Hanny. Former General Secretary of Indonesian *Gereja Pantekosta* [Pentecostal Church] movement. Waikanae. Interview, 22 September 1987.

McMillan, Jim and Dinal. Pastors, New Life Churches. Waikanae. Interview, 18 September 1990. Tape recording in author's possession.

McNabb, Bernie. Former Assistant Pastor in Nelson with Ron Coady. Richmond, Nelson. Interview, 18 January 1990. Tape recording in author's possession.

Morrow, Anne. Pastor, New Life Churches; wife of Peter Morrow. Christchurch. Interview, 21 November 1989. Tape recording in author's possession.

250 New Life

Morrow, Peter. Retired Pastor and Senior Leader, New Life Churches; husband of Ann Morrow. Christchurch. Interview, 13 May 1988. Tape recording in author's possession.

_____. Dunedin. Interview, 30 July 1990. Tape recording in author's possession.

Ranchord, Rasik. Pastor, New Life Churches. Christchurch. Interview, 21 November 1989. Tape recordings in author's possession.

Simpson, Jane. Lecturer in Religious Studies, University of Canterbury. Dunedin. Interview, 18 September 1987.

Steele, John and Julie. Pastors, New Life Churches. Dunedin. Interview, 14 February 1989. Tape recording in author's possession.

Thrift, Allan. Retired Pastor, Indigenous Churches. Auckland. Taped interview in response to Questionnaire, March 1989. Tape recording in author's possession.

Tiplady, John. Pastor, New Life Churches. Auckland. Interview, 2 March 1990. Tape recording in author's possession.

Walker, Dorothy. Retired long-term missionary to Indonesia; wife of Dal Walker. Wellington. Interview, 27 June 1996. Tape recording in author's possession.

Walton, John. Pastor and Senior Leader, New Life Churches. Pleasant Valley, Palmerston, Otago. Interview, 4 February 1989. Tape recording in author's possession.

Wheeler, Rob. Retired Pastor and Senior Leader, New Life Churches. Waikanae. Interview, 22 September 1987. Tape recording in author's possession.

Wright, Ken. Former Pastor, Indigenous Churches. Palmerston North. Taped interview in response to Questionnaire, April 1990. Tape recording in author's possession.

Wright, Lilian. Congregational member, Timaru Christian Fellowship Mission. Timaru. Interview, 18 November 1987.

1.2. Other Oral Sources

Allington, Doug. Pastor, New Life Churches. Christchurch. Comment to author, 4 October 1991.

Collins, David. Former Pastor, Indigenous Churches; Pastor, South Pacific Fellowship. Waikanae. Business meeting, 24 September 1987.

Donovan, Peter. Associate Professor of Religious Studies, Massey University. Dunedin. Open lecture, 19 June 1990.

Evans, John. Australian Uniting Church minister. Dunedin. Comment to author, 1991.

Gousmett, Chris. Theologian. Dunedin. Comment to author, 3 July 1991.

Hall, Bob. Senior Lecturer in Sociology, University of Canterbury. Christchurch. Comment re research hypothesis, November 1989.

Hotter, Bill. Congregational member, Christchurch New Life Centre. Christchurch. Comment to author, December 1989.

Jull, David. Ph.D. Student, University of Otago, Dunedin. Comment to author, 1998.
Kearney, Shaun. Former Pastor, Indigenous Churches. Melbourne. Comment at Asian-Pacific Ministers' Conference, June 1973.
Knowles, Zona. Congregational member, Timaru New Life Centre. Timaru. Comment to author, 26 November 1989.
Lineham, Peter. Senior Lecturer in History, Massey University. Palmerston North. Discussion re research, 6 March 1990.
Olssen, Erik. Professor of History, University of Otago. Dunedin. Comment re sociological analysis of congregational listings, 13 July 1989.
Rosewall, Gordon. Pastor, New Life Churches. Timaru. Telephone comment to author, 9 March 1998.
Steele, John. Pastor, New Life Churches. Waikanae. Business meeting, 24 September 1987.
Walker, Dal. Former long-term missionary to Indonesia; husband of Dorothy Walker. Tawangmangu, Indonesia. Comment to author, 1971.
Walton, John. Pastor and Senior Leader, New Life Churches. Pleasant Valley, Palmerston, Otago. Testimony given at public meeting, 3 February 1989.
Wást, Bruce. Pastor, New Life Churches. Dunedin. Comment to author, 1 October 1989.
Way, Audrey. Retired Secretary, Knox Theological Hall. Dunedin. Comment to author, 1990.
Webster, Alex and Marsh, Janet. Former Pastors, New Life Churches. Dunedin. Comment to author, 14 May 1993.
Wheeler, Rob. Retired Pastor and Senior Leader, New Life Churches. Waikanae. Business meeting, 24 September 1987.
_____. Auckland. Comment to author re Dissertation, 1989.
Winnington, Marion. Congregational member, Timaru New Life Centre. Comment made at the 25th Jubilee celebrations of the Timaru New Life Centre, October 1985.
Worsfold, James. Former Apostolic Pastor and Historian. Wellington. Comment to author, September 1990.

2. Archival Sources

Christchurch. Majestic House Correspondence files.
Dunedin. Brett Knowles Research Papers.
Dunedin. Knowles, Adrienne. *ICNZ Conference Notes*, 24 September 1987.
Dunedin. *New Zealand Evangel*. Microfilm 1927 to 1972.
Dunedin. Word of Life Tabernacle Correspondence files.
Palmerston North. History Department, Massey University. Peter J. Lineham Research papers.
Richmond, Nelson. Bernie McNabb. Scrapbooks of Newspaper clippings relating to early years of Nelson New Life Centre.
Rijswijk, Netherlands. Historical Branch, *Ministerie van Verkeer en Waterstraat, Directoraat-General Scheepvaart en Maritieme Zaken*

[Ministry of Transport (Land and Buildings), Director-General Shipping and Maritime Affairs]. *Tjinegara* Report Sheet.
Wellington. Alexander Turnbull Library. Ephemera Collection. Jesus March: March for Righteousness, Auckland. 'Executive Council Statement of Purpose', 1972. (Mimeographed.)
Wellington. James E. Worsfold Research Papers.
Wellington. Maritime Museum, Queen's Wharf. Wellington Harbour Board Records.
Wellington. Wellington City Elim Church. Board of Elders of the Pentecostal Church of N.Z. (Inc.), Minute Book 1934–51.
Wellington. Wellington City Elim Church. Executive Council, Representing the Board of Elders of the Pentecostal Church of N.Z. (Inc.), Minute Book 1934–51.
Wellington. Wellington City Elim Church. Wellington Pentecostal Evangelical Mission, Minute Book 8 July 1942–3 December 1951.

3. Periodicals

3.1. Journals

Colloquium 1:1–21:2 (Spring 1964–May 1989).
Historical Studies 9 (1959–60); 11–21 (1963–85).
Journal of Religious History 1:1–15:2 (December 1960–December 1988).
New Zealand Journal of History 1:1–23:2 (April 1967–October 1989).

3.2. Magazines

Bible Deliverance, April 1959–March 1966.
Broadsheet, December 1974; March–October 1977.
Christian Century, 4 November 1987.
Church Bells, June 1966–September 1968.
Gospel Truth, June 1964–April 1965.
'*Harvestime*' [sic], May 1961.
Lesbian-Feminist Circle, Summer–Autumn/Winter 1977.
Logos, August 1966.
New Life NZ, September 1987.
New Zealand Evangel, May 1958.
Pentecostal Messenger, December 1943.
Restoration, January–June 1967.
Revival News, March 1962–December 1966.
Salient, February–April 1972.
Time, 21 June 1971; 1990–91.

3.3. Newsletters

Auckland Christian Fellowship, Auckland. 'Newsletter.' November 1975–October 1976.

Bethel Chapel, Invercargill. 'Newsletter.' n.d. [February–March 1976].
Christian Fellowship Mission, Timaru. 'Signposts of Faith.' n.d. [December 1960].
Concerned Parents' Association. *Newsletter*, October 1975–December 1980.
National Jesus Festival News No.1, 1 August 1972.
New Life Centre, Nelson. 'New Life News.' July–November 1973.
New Life Churches of NZ, n.d. [October 1988].
Timaru Missionary Revival Centre, 'Newsletter: What's in a Name?', no date. (Mimeographed.)
United Full Gospel Fellowships, 'Newsletter', Wellington, February 1961. (Mimeographed.)
Word of Life Fellowship, Dunedin. 'Newsletter.' 2 June 1991. (Mimeographed.)

3.4. Newspapers

Associated Pentecostal Churches of New Zealand. *New Zealand Times*, February, July and October 1976.
Challenge Weekly, 1961–83.
Christchurch Press, 13 April 1972; 12 August 1972; March–June 1977; 1 November 1977; 28 December 1979; August–September 1980; 12 November 1980; 18–23 September 1987.
Christchurch Star, March–June 1977; 17–23 September 1987.
Christian Heritage Party, n.d. [1989].
Dominion, October 1972; 1–15 August 1975.
Dunedin Star Weekender, 25 September 1983; 9 October 1983.
New Citizen, 12 June 1975.
New Life, April–October 1993.
New Zealand Herald, 1–15 May 1972.
New Zealand Methodist, 4 May–15 June 1972.
New Zealand Truth, April–May 1961.
Otago Daily Times, May 1878; October 1878–March 1879; 18 June–14 July 1958; 24 March 1961; 17 April 1962; 6 April 1972; 18 July 1972; 14, 25 and 28 September 1985; 17 March 1992; 12 December 1998.
Timaru Herald, July 1959–December 1960; 12 October 1981; 7 May 1990.
[Wellington] Evening Post, February–March 1942; March and October 1972; 1–15 August 1975; October 1977.

4. Published Sources

4.1. Reference Works

Barrett, David, ed. *World Christian Encyclopaedia: A Comparative Study of Churches and Religions in the Modern World, AD1900-2000*. Nairobi: Oxford University Press, 1982. s.v. 'New Zealand.'

Burgess, Stanley M., ed. *New International Dictionary of Pentecostal and Charismatic Movements.* Grand Rapids, Michigan: Zondervan, 2000, forthcoming.

_____; McGee, Gary B.; and Alexander, Patrick H., ed. *Dictionary of Pentecostal and Charismatic Movements.* Grand Rapids, Michigan: Zondervan, 1988.

Devereux, Peter. ed. *The New Zealand Style Book.* rev. ed. Wellington: GP Publications Ltd., 1993.

Harvey, Van A. *A Handbook of Theological Terms.* New York: Collier Books, 1964.

Lineham, Peter J., and Grigg, Anthony R. *Religious History of New Zealand: A Bibliography.* 3rd ed. Palmerston North: Department of History, Massey University, 1989.

Orsman, H.W., ed. *The Dictionary of New Zealand English: A Dictionary of New Zealandisms on Historical Principles.* Auckland: Oxford University Press, 1997.

The Home Book of Quotations: Classical and Modern. 10th ed. Edited by Burton Stevenson. New York: Dodd, Mead and Co., 1967.

Turabian, Kate L. *A Manual for Writers of Term Papers, Theses and Dissertations.* 4th ed. Chicago and London: Univeristy of Chicago Press, 1973.

4.2. Books

Ahlstrom, Sydney E. *A Religious History of the American People.* New Haven: Yale University Press, 1973.

Anderson, Robert Mapes. *Vision of the Disinherited: The Making of American Pentecostalism.* New York: Oxford University Press, 1979.

Andrew, Maurice; Matheson, Peter; and Rae, Simon, ed. *Religious Studies in Dialogue: Essays in Honour of Albert C. Moore.* Dunedin: Faculty of Theology, University of Otago, 1991.

Balmer, Randall. *Mine Eyes have seen the Glory: A Journey into the Evangelical Subculture in America.* New York: Oxford University Press, 1989.

Bartleman, Frank. *What really happened at Azusa Street?* Edited by John Walker. Northridge, California: Voice Christian Publications, 1962.

Bennett, Dennis J. *Nine O'clock in the Morning.* Watchung, New Jersey: Charisma Books, 1972.

Bennett, Enid, and Donovan, Peter. *Beliefs and Practices in New Zealand: A Directory.* Palmerston North: Religious Studies Department, Massey University, 1980.

Best, Elsdon. *Maori Religion and Mythology: Being an Account of the Cosmogony, Anthropogony, Religious Beliefs and Rites, Magic and Folk Lore of the Maori Folk of New Zealand.* Dominion Museum Bulletin No.10, Section 1. Wellington: Government Printer, 1924.

Bezemer, K.W.L. *Geschiedenis van de Nederlandse Koopvaardij in de Tweede Wereldoorlog: Deel Twee [History of the Dutch Merchant Marine in the Second World War: Volume 2].* Amsterdam: Elsevier, 1986.

Blumhofer, Edith L. *The Assemblies of God: A Chapter in the Story of American Pentecostalism*. 2 vols. Springfield, Missouri: Gospel Publishing House, 1989.

Bradwell, Cyril R. *Fight the good fight: The story of the Salvation Army in New Zealand 1883–1983*. Wellington: A.H. and A.W. Reed, 1982.

Breward, Ian. *Godless Schools? A study in Protestant reactions to the Education Act of 1877*. Christchurch: Presbyterian Bookroom, 1967.

Brooks, Jocelyn; Tims, Kitty; Dawson, Lyn; Hirst, Yvonne; McIntosh, May; Penhale, Esther-Mary; Routledge, Louise; Trim, Marjorie; and Church, Toni. *Ill Conceived: Law and Abortion Practice in New Zealand*. Dunedin: Caveman Press, 1981.

Brown, Colin. *Forty Years On: A History of the National Council of Churches in New Zealand 1941–1981*. Christchurch: National Council of Churches, 1981.

Browne, Joy; Hargreaves, Anne; Kuiper, Alison; Livingstone, Joan; McKenzie, Margaret; Novitz, Rosemary; Roberts, Betty; and Sewell, Elizabeth, ed. *Changes, Chances, Choices: A report on the United Women's Convention, 3–6 June 1977*. Christchurch: United Women's Convention, 1978.

Bryant, George. *The Church on Trial*. Whangarei: Whau Publications, 1986.

Capon, John. *. . . and there was light: The story of the Nationwide Festival of Light*. London: Lutterworth Press, 1972.

Carr, E.H. *What is History? The George Macaulay Trevelyan Lectures delivered in the University of Cambridge, January–March, 1961*. Harmondsworth: Penguin Books, 1986.

Chant, Barry. *Heart of Fire*. Adelaide: Luke Publications, 1973.

Christenson, Larry. *The Christian Family*. London: Fountain Trust, 1971.

Clark, Ian G. *Pentecost at the Ends of the Earth: The History of the Assemblies of God in New Zealand (1927–2003)*. Blenheim: Christian Road Ministries, 2007.

Coady, Bro. [A.R.]. *I Shall Not Want*. Nelson: Faith Enterprises, n.d.

Comfort, Ray. *'Evangelical Frustration': The neglected key to genuine repentance*. Christchurch: Living Waters Publications, 1982.

Concerned Parents' Association. *Home and School: Cooperation or Conflict? Human Development and Moral Values*. Christchurch: Concerned Parents' Association, 1976.

Conner, Kevin J. *Foundations of Christian Doctrine*. Blackburn, Victoria: Acacia Press, 1980.

_____. *The Name of God*. Portland, Oregon: Bible Temple—Conner Publications, 1975.

_____. *The Tabernacle of David*. Portland, Oregon: Conner Publications, 1976.

Copeland, Gordon F. *Faith that works*. Lower Hutt: Barnabas Christian Trust, 1988.

Corry, Geoffrey. *Jesus Bubble or Jesus Revolution: The growth of Jesus Communes in Britain and Ireland*. London: British Council of Churches Youth Department, 1973.

Currie, Robert; Gilbert, Alan; and Horsley, Lee. *Churches and Churchgoers: Patterns of Church Growth in the British Isles since 1700.* Oxford: Clarendon Press, 1977.

Dann, Christine. *Up from under: Women and Liberation in New Zealand 1970-1985.* Wellington: Allen and Unwin and Port Nicholson Press, 1985.

Darroch, Murray. *Everything you ever wanted to know about Protestants but never knew who to ask.* Wellington: Catholic Supplies, 1984.

Davidson, Allan K. *Christianity in Aotearoa: A History of Church and Society in New Zealand.* Wellington: Education for Ministry, 1991.

_____, and Lineham, Peter J., ed. *Transplanted Christianity: Documents illustrating aspects of New Zealand Church History.* Auckland: College Communications, 1987.

Dearn, Ed. *Pornography Degrades.* Sydney: Renda Publications, n.d.

De Bres, Pieter H. *Religion in Atene: Religious Associations and the Urban Maori.* Wellington: Polynesian Society, 1971.

Dobbie, Flo. *Land Aflame!* London: Hodder and Stoughton, 1972.

Drummond, Andrew Landale. *Edward Irving and his circle; including some consideration of the 'Tongues' Movement in the light of modern psychology.* London: James Clarke and Company, [1934].

Dunlop, Eric. *The Middleton Grange Story.* Christchurch: 25th Celebration Committee, Middleton Grange School, 1989.

Edgar, S.L. *A Handful of Grain.* The Centenary History of the Baptist Union of New Zealand, Vol.4, 1945-1982. Wellington: New Zealand Baptist Historical Society, 1982.

Edwards, David L., and Robinson, John A.T. *The Honest to God Debate.* London: SCM Press, 1963.

Ellis, David J. *The Coverings.* Christchurch: Estate of David J. Ellis, 1977.

Ellwood, Robert S., Jnr. *One Way: The Jesus Movement and its meaning.* Eaglewood Cliffs, New Jersey: Prentice-Hall, 1973.

Else, Anne, ed. *Women Together: A History of Women's Organisations in New Zealand—Nga Ropu Wahine o te Motu.* Wellington: Historical Branch, Department of Internal Affairs, 1993.

Elsmore, Bronwyn. *Like Them That Dream: The Maori and the Old Testament.* Tauranga: Tauranga Moana Press, 1985.

_____. *Mana from Heaven: A Century of Maori Prophets in New Zealand.* Tauranga: Moana Press, 1989.

Enroth, Ronald M.; Ericson, Edward E., Jnr.; and Peters, C. Breckinridge. *The Jesus People: Old-Time Religion in the Age of Aquarius.* Grand Rapids, Michigan: William B. Eerdmans Publishing Company, 1972.

Facer, W.A.P., ed. *Legal Abortion in New Zealand: A Review of Opinions and Politics 1970-1977.* Auckland: New Zealand Rationalist Association, 1977.

Fletcher, Lionel B. *Mighty Moments.* London: Religious Tract Society, 1931.

Gee, Donald. *The Pentecostal Movement, Including the Story of the War Years (1940-1947).* Rev. ed. London: Elim Publishing Company, 1949.

Geiringer, Erich. *SPUC 'em all! Abortion Politics 1978.* Waiura, Martinborough: Alister Taylor, 1978.

Gerlach, Luther P., and Hine, Virginia H. *People, Power, Change: Movements of Social Transformation*. Indianapolis: Bobbs-Merrill Company, 1970.

Goff, James R., Jnr. *Fields White Unto Harvest: Charles F. Parham and the Missionary Origins of Pentecostalism*. Fayetteville: University of Arkansas Press, 1988.

Grice, Robert E. *Apostle to the Nations: An Authorized Biography of A.S. Worley, a Man of Faith and Miracles*. Walhalla, South Carolina: Faith Training Center, n.d. [1990].

Gritsch, Eric W. *Born Againism: Perspectives on a Movement*. Philadelphia: Fortress Press, 1983.

Habermas, Jürgen. *Legitimation Crisis*. Translated by Thomas McCarthy. Boston: Beacon Press, 1975.

Hall, Victor and Murray Wylie. *Journey to Ephesus: In Search of a Lampstand. A Biography of Restoration*. 2nd edition. Forest Glen, Vic.: Seedlife Publications, 2004.

Hames, E.W. *Coming of Age: The United Church 1913–1972*. Auckland: Institute Press, 1974.

Harper, Michael. *As at the Beginning*. London: Hodder and Stoughton, 1965.

Harrell, David Edwin, Jnr. *All Things are Possible: The Healing and Charismatic Revivals in Modern America*. Bloomington, Indiana: Indiana University Press, 1975.

———. *Oral Roberts: An American Life*. Bloomington, Indiana: Indiana University Press, 1985.

Henderson, Mary. *From Glory to Glory: A History of the Timaru New Life Centre 1960–1980*. Timaru: Dove Print, 1980.

High, Stanley. *Billy Graham: The personal story of the man, his message and his mission*. Kingswood, Surrey: World's Work (1913), 1958.

Hill, Michael. *A Sociology of Religion*. London: Heinemann Educational Books, 1973.

Hodgson, Peter C., and King, Robert H., ed. *Christian Theology: An Introduction to its Traditions and Tasks*. London: SPCK, 1982.

Hollenweger, Walter. *Pentecost between Black and White: 5 Case Studies in Pentecost and Politics*. Belfast: Christian Journals, 1974.

———. *The Pentecostals*. Translated by R.A. Wilson. London: SCM Press, 1972.

Hoover, Stewart M. *Mass Media Religion: The Social Sources of the Electronic Church*. Newbury Park, California: SAGE Publications, 1988.

Houston, Hazel. *Being Frank: The Frank Houston Story*. London: Marshall Pickering, 1989.

Hudson, Winthrop S. *Religion in America*. New York: Charles Scribner's Sons, 1965.

Hunter, James Davison. *American Evangelicalism: Conservative Religion and the Quandary of Modernity*. New Brunswick, New Jersey: Rutgers University Press, 1983.

Hutchinson, Warner, and Wilson, Cliff. *Let the People Rejoice*. Wellington: Crusader Bookroom Society, 1959.

Jackson, H.R. *Churches and People in Australia and New Zealand 1860–1930*. Wellington: Allen and Unwin/Port Nicholson Press, 1987.

Jesson, Bruce; Ryan, Allanah; and Spoonley, Paul, ed. *Revival of the Right: New Zealand Politics in the 1980s*. Auckland: Heinemann Reid, 1988.

Keegan, John. *The Second World War.* London: Hutchinson, 1989.

Kelley, Dean M. *Why Conservative Churches are Growing: A Study in Sociology of Religion.* New York: Harper and Row, 1972.

Kephart, William M. *Extraordinary Groups: the Sociology of Unconventional Life-Styles.* New York: St. Martin's Press, 1976.

Kinnear, Angus I. *Against the Tide: The Story of Watchman Nee.* rev. ed. Eastbourne, Sussex: Victory Press, 1976.

Knight, Walter L. *Jesus People come alive.* Wheaton, Illinois: Tyndale House Publishers, 1971.

Knowles, Brett. *New Life: A History of the New Life Churches of New Zealand, 1942–1979.* Dunedin: Third Millennium Publishing, 1999.

Knowles, Brett. *The History of a New Zealand Pentecostal Movement: The New Life Churches of New Zealand from 1946 to 1979.* Lewiston, NY: Edwin Mellen Press, 2000.

Leech, Kenneth. *Youthquake: The growth of a counter-culture through two decades.* London: Sheldon Press, 1973.

Leibman, Robert C., and Wuthnow, Robert, ed. *The New Christian Right: Mobilization and Legitimation.* New York: Aldine Publishing Company, 1983.

Lindsey, Hal, and Carlson, C.C. *The Late Great Planet Earth.* Grand Rapids, Michigan: Zondervan, 1976.

Lineham, Peter J. *New Zealanders and the Methodist Evangel.* Rotorua: Wesley Historical Society (New Zealand), 1983.

_____. *There we found Brethren: A History of Assemblies of Brethren in New Zealand.* Palmerston North: G.P.H. Society, 1977.

Lotz, David W.; Shriver, Donald W. Jr.; and Wilson, John F., ed. *Altered Landscapes: Christianity in America 1935–1985.* Grand Rapids, Michigan: William B. Eerdmans Publishing Company, 1989.

McDonnell, Kilian. *Charismatic Renewal and the Churches.* New York: Seabury Press, 1976.

_____, ed. *Presence, Power, Praise: Documents of the Charismatic Renewal.* 3 vols. Collegeville, Minnesota: Liturgical Press, 1980.

McEldowney, Dennis, ed. *Presbyterians in Aotearoa 1840–1990.* Wellington: Presbyterian Church of New Zealand, 1990.

McGeorge, Colin, and Snook, Ivan. *Church, State and New Zealand Education.* Wellington: Price Milburn, 1981.

Merritt, N.F.H. *To God be the glory: the first 10½ years of the Charismatic Renewal in St. Pauls.* Auckland: St. Paul's Outreach Trust, 1981.

Miller, Edward. *Thy God Reigneth: The Story of the Revival in Argentina.* Burbank, California: World Missionary Assistance Plan, 1968.

Mol, J.J. *Church-Attendance in Christchurch New Zealand: A Social Research Project*. Christchurch: Department of Psychology and Sociology, Canterbury University, 1962.

_____. *The Fixed and the Fickle: Religion and Identity in New Zealand*. Dunedin: Pilgrims South Press, 1982.

_____. *Western Religion: a country by country sociological enquiry*. The Hague: Mouton, 1972. s.v. 'New Zealand.'

Morrell, W.P. *The Anglican Church in New Zealand: A History*. Dunedin: Anglican Church of the Province of New Zealand, 1973.

Muldoon, R.D. *The Rise and Fall of a Young Turk*. Wellington: A.H. and A.W. Reed, 1974.

Mumford, Bob. *The Problem of Doing Your Own Thing*. Fort Lauderdale, Florida: By the Author, 1973.

Murray, Laurie. *Where to, World 1977?* Palmerston North: By the Author, n.d. [1977].

Nee, Watchman. *Spiritual Authority*. New York: Christian Fellowship Publishers, 1972.

New Zealand Broadcasting Corporation. *I Believe: A series of talks broadcast over NZBC stations in 1967*. n.p. [Wellington]: New Zealand Broadcasting Corporation, n.d. [1968].

New Zealand Department of Education. *Growing, Sharing, Learning: The Report of the Committee on Health and Social Education*. Wellington: Government Printer, 1977.

_____. *Human Development and Relationships in the School Curriculum*. Wellington: Government Printer, 1973.

New Zealand Homosexual Law Reform Society. *50/50: Fifty Questions and Answers about Homosexuality and the Law*. Wellington: New Zealand Homosexual Law Reform Society, 1968.

Ng, Sik Hung. *The Social Psychology of Power*. European Monographs in Social Psychology, Vol.21. London: Academic Press, 1980.

Nichol, John Thomas. *The Pentecostals* (formerly *Pentecostalism*). rev. ed. Plainfield, New Jersey: Logos International, 1971.

Niebuhr, H. Richard. *The Social Sources of Denominationalism*. New York: Meridian Books, 1959.

Offiler, W.H. *God and His Bible, or The Harmonies of Divine Revelation*. Seattle, Washington: Bethel Temple, 1946.

_____. *God, and His Name*. Seattle, Washington: Temple Publishing House, [1932?].

_____. *The Majesty of the Symbol, or Bible Astronomy*. Seattle, Washington: By the Author, 1933.

O'Regan, Pauline. *A Changing Order*. Wellington: Allen and Unwin and Port Nicholson Press, 1986.

Ortiz, Juan Carlos. *Disciple*. Carol Stream, Illinois: Creation House, 1975.

Osborn, T.L. *Healing the Sick*. 12th ed. Tulsa, Oklahoma: T.L. Osborn Evangelistic Association, 1959.

_____. *Impact*. Tulsa, Oklahoma: T.L. Osborn Evangelistic Association, 1963.

Osborne, J. *The Winds of the Spirit: An Introductory Study of the Charismatic Movement*. Auckland: Methodist Board of Publications, 1972.

Perry, Stuart. *Indecent Publication Control in New Zealand*. Wellington: McCrae Publishers, 1975.

Phillips, Roderick. *Divorce in New Zealand: A Social History*. Auckland: Oxford University Press, 1981.

Pittman, J.A. *Relevance, Relationship and Renewal: The Church—Yesterday and Today*. Wellington: Alfred and Isabel and Marion Reed Trust, 1978.

Pollock, John. *Billy Graham: The Authorised Biography*. London: Hodder and Stoughton, 1966.

Pratt, Douglas, ed. *'Rescue the Perishing': Comparative Perspectives on Evangelicalism and Revivalism*. Waikato Studies in Religion, Vol.1. Auckland: College Communications, 1989.

Quebedeaux, Richard. *The New Charismatics*. New York: Doubleday and Company, 1976.

Read, Ralph R. *Water Baptism: The Formula and its meaning. A Study of the Trinitarian Formula of Matthew 28 v.19 and the Formula of 'Oneness' Teachers: A Guide and a Refutation*. Christchurch: New Zealand Pentecostal Fellowship, 1966.

Report of the Royal Commission of Inquiry: Contraception, Sterilisation and Abortion in New Zealand. Wellington: Government Printer, 1977.

Riss, Richard M. *Latter Rain: The Latter Rain movement of 1948 and the Mid-Twentieth Century Evangelical Awakening*. Etobicoke, Ontario: Honeycomb Visual Productions, 1987.

Roberts, H.V. *Beware of the New Revelation on Water Baptism*. Auckland: Church Army Press, 1946.

_____. *New Zealand's Greatest Revival*. Auckland: New Zealand Pelorus Press, 1951.

Robinson, John A.T. *Honest to God*. London: SCM Press, 1963.

Sandeen, Ernest R. *The Origins of Fundamentalism: Towards a Historical Interpretation*. Historical Series (American Church), Vol.10. Philadelphia: Fortress Press, 1968.

_____. *The Roots of Fundamentalism: British and American Millenarianism 1800-1930*. Chicago: University of Chicago Press, 1970.

Shakarian, Demos, and Sherrill, John and Elizabeth. *The Happiest People on Earth*. Old Tappan, New Jersey: Spire Books, 1975.

Shaw, Trevor R., comp. *The Jesus Marchers 1972*. Auckland: Challenge Publishers, 1972.

Sherrill, John L. *They speak with other tongues*. London: Hodder and Stoughton, 1967.

Shiels, W.J., ed. *The Church and Healing: Papers read at the twentieth summer meeting and the twenty-first winter meeting of the Ecclesiastical History Society*. Oxford: Basil Blackwell for the Ecclesiastical History Society, 1982.

Shortland, Edward. *Maori Religion and Mythology*. London: Longmans, Green and Company, 1882.

Simmons, E.R. *A Brief History of the Catholic Church in New Zealand*. Auckland: Catholic Publications Centre, 1978.

Sinclair, Keith. *A History of New Zealand*. rev. ed. Harmondsworth, Middlesex: Penguin Books, 1984.

_____. *A History of New Zealand*. 4th rev. ed. Harmondsworth, Middlesex: Penguin Books, 1991.

Spoonley, Paul. *The Politics of Nostalgia: Racism and the Extreme Right in New Zealand*. Palmerston North: Dunmore Press, 1987.

Stern, Fritz, ed. *The Varieties of History From Voltaire to the Present*. New York: Meridian Books, 1956.

Strachan, C. Gordon. *The Pentecostal Theology of Edward Irving*. London: Darton, Longman and Todd, 1973.

Streiker, Lowell D., and Strober, Gerald S. *Religion and the New Majority: Billy Graham, Middle America, and the Politics of the 70s*. New York: Associated Press, 1972.

Synan, Vinson. *The Holiness-Pentecostal Movement in the United States*. Grand Rapids, Michigan: William B. Eerdmans Publishing Company, 1971.

Tauroa, Hiwi and Pat. *Te Marae: A Guide to Customs and Protocol*. Auckland: Heinemann Reed, 1988.

Taylor, William. *Story of My Life: An Account of what I have thought and said and done in my ministry of more than fifty-three years in Christian Lands and among the Heathen. Written by Myself*. Edited by John Clark Ridpath. New York: Eaton and Mains, 1895.

Thiselton, Anthony C. *The Two Horizons: New Testament Hermeneutics and Philosophical Description with Special Reference to Heidegger, Bultmann, Gadamer and Wittgenstein*. Grand Rapids, Michigan: William B. Eerdmans Publishing Company, 1980.

Thomas, David. *Battle of the Java Sea*. London: André Deutsch, 1968.

Tugwell, Simon; Every, George; Mills, John Orme; and Hocken, Peter. *New Heaven? New Earth?: An Encounter with Pentecostalism*. London: Darton, Longman and Todd, 1976.

Turley, Bruce, and Martin, Margaret Reid. *Religion in Education: Outlines and Reflections on the History of New Zealand Developments*. Wellington: Churches Education Commission, 1981.

United Women's Convention. *United Women's Convention 1975*. Wellington: United Women's Convention, 1976.

_____. *United Women's Convention, Easter 1979*. Hamilton: University of Waikato, [1979].

Van Brummelen, Harro W. *Telling the next generation: Educational development in North American Calvinist Christian Schools*. Lanham, Maryland: University Press of America, 1986.

von Münching, L.L. *De Nederlandse Koopvaardijvloot in de Tweede Wereldoorlog [The Dutch Merchant Fleet in the Second World War]*. Bussum: De Boer Maritiem, 1978.

Webster, Alan C., and Perry, Paul E. *The Religious Factor in New Zealand Society: A Report of the New Zealand Study of Values*. Palmerston North: Alpha Publications, 1989.

Wells, David F., and Woodbridge, John D., ed. *The Evangelicals: What they believe, Who they are, Where they are changing*. New York: Abingdon Press, 1975.

Whitworth, John McKelvie. *God's Blueprints: A Sociological Study of Three Utopian Sects*. Boston: Routledge and Kegan Paul, 1975.

Wilkerson, David; Sherrill, John and Elizabeth. *The Cross and the Switchblade*. movie ed. Old Tappan, New Jersey: Fleming H. Revell Company, 1975.

Wilson, Bryan, ed. *Patterns of Sectarianism: Organization and Ideology in Social and Religious Movements*. London: Heinemann, 1967.

Woodard, Christopher. *A Doctor Heals by Faith*. London: Max Parrish, 1953.

_____. *A Doctor's Faith holds fast*. London: Max Parrish, 1955.

Worsfold, James E. *A History of the Charismatic Movements in New Zealand*. Bradford: Julian Literature Trust, 1974.

Yarrell, Peter. *'Come, let us go . . .': the beginnings of Koinonia in the mountains of New Zealand*. Christchurch: Outreach Press, 1981.

Yska, Redmer. *All Shook Up: The Flash Bodgie and the Rise of the New Zealand Teenager in the Fifties*. Auckland: Penguin, 1993.

4.3. Chapters in Books

Aberle, David F. 'A Note on Relative Deprivation Theory as applied to Millenarian and other Cult Movements.' In *Millennial Dreams in Action: Essays in Comparative Study*, 209-14. Edited by Sylvia Thrupp. The Hague: Mouton, 1962.

Atkin, W.R. 'The Family in Society—A New Zealand Christian Perspective.' In *Christians in Public Planning*, 31-47. Edited by Christopher Nichol and James Veitch. Wellington: Tertiary Christian Studies Programme of the Combined Chaplaincies and the Religious Studies Department, Victoria University, 1981.

Barber, L.H. 'The Religious Dimension of New Zealand's History.' In *Religion in New Zealand Society*, 15-29. 2nd ed. Edited by Brian Colless and Peter Donovan. Palmerston North: Dunmore Press, 1985.

Battley, Donald. 'What is genuine and what is ephemeral in the Charismatic Wind?' In *Towards an Authentic New Zealand Theology*, 39-42. Edited by John M. Ker and Kevin J. Sharpe. Auckland: University of Auckland Chaplaincy Publishing Trust, 1984.

Bowman, Richard. 'Beyond the Pink Triangle: the New Zealand public's attitudes towards homosexuality.' In *Shades of Deviance: A New Zealand Collection*, 99-113. Edited by Michael Hill, Sharon Mast, Richard Bowman, and Charlotte Carr-Gregg. Palmerston North: Dunmore Press, 1983.

Breward, Ian. 'Have the Mainline Protestant Churches moved out of their colonial status?' In *Religion in New Zealand Society*, 67-80. 2nd ed. Edited by Brian Colless and Peter Donovan. Palmerston North: Dunmore Press, 1985.

_____. 'Selecting Documents for Australian Religious History.' In *Australian and New Zealand Religious History 1788-1988: A Collection of Papers and Addresses delivered at the 11th Joint Conference of the Australian and New Zealand Association of Theological Schools and Society for Theological Studies held at Burgmann College, Australian National University, 5-8 September 1988*, 19-25. Edited by Robert Withycombe. Jamison Centre, A.C.T.: Australian and New Zealand Association of Theological Schools and Society for Theological Studies, 1988.

Brown, C.G. 'Christianity in Australia and New Zealand.' In *Encyclopaedia of Religion*, Vol.13, 424-28. Edited by M. Eliade. New York: MacMillan Publishing Company, 1987.

Brown, Colin. 'Church, Culture and Identity: The New Zealand Experience.' In *Culture and Identity in New Zealand*, 237-59. Edited by David Novitz and Bill Willmott. Wellington: GP Books, 1989.

_____. 'Ecumenism in New Zealand: Success or Failure?' In *Religion in New Zealand Society*, 81-98. 2nd ed. Edited by Brian Colless and Peter Donovan. Palmerston North: Dunmore Press, 1985.

_____. 'How Significant is the Charismatic Movement?' In *Dialogue on Religion: New Zealand Viewpoints 1977*, 27-31. Edited by Peter Davis and John Hinchcliff. Auckland: University of Auckland, 1977.

_____. 'How Significant is the Charismatic Movement?' In *Religion in New Zealand Society*, 99-118. 2nd ed. Edited by Brian Colless and Peter Donovan. Palmerston North: Dunmore Press, 1985.

_____. 'Pentecostalism, Neo-Pentecostalism and Naturalistic Explanation.' In *The Religious Dimension*, 55-57. Edited by John C. Hinchcliff. Auckland: Rep Prep Ltd., 1976.

_____. 'Religion in New Zealand: Past, Present and Future.' In *Religion and New Zealand's Future*, 15-22. Edited by Kevin J. Sharpe. Palmerston North: Dunmore Press, 1982.

Chapman, Robert. 'From Labour to National.' In *The Oxford History of New Zealand*, 333-68. Edited by W.H. Oliver. Wellington: Oxford University Press, 1981.

Donovan, Peter. 'Distinctions without Difference: the Illusion of Diversity in New Zealand Beliefs.' In *Religion in New Zealand*, 179-203. Edited by Christopher Nichol and James Veitch. Wellington: Tertiary Christian Studies Programme of the Combined Chaplaincies and the Religious Studies Department, Victoria University, 1980.

Dunstall, Graeme. 'The Social Pattern.' In *The Oxford History of New Zealand*, 397-429. Edited by W.H. Oliver. Wellington: Oxford University Press, 1981.

Evans, John. 'The New Christian Right in New Zealand.' In *'Be Ye Separate': Fundamentalism and the New Zealand Experience*. Waikato Studies in Religion, Vol.3, 69-106. Edited by Bryan Gilling. Hamilton: University of Waikato and Colcom Press, 1992.

Galvin, Ray. 'Learning from the Sects.' In *Towards an Authentic New Zealand Theology*, 99–103. Edited by John M. Ker and Kevin J. Sharpe. Auckland: University of Auckland Chaplaincy Publishing Trust, 1984.

Geering, Lloyd. 'New Zealand enters the Secular Age.' In *Religion in New Zealand*, 238–63. Edited by Christopher Nichol and James Veitch. Wellington: Tertiary Christian Studies Programme of the Combined Chaplaincies and the Religious Studies Department, Victoria University, 1980.

Hawke, G.R. 'The growth of the economy.' In *The Oxford History of New Zealand*, 369–96. Edited by W.H. Oliver. Wellington: Oxford University Press, 1981.

Hill, Michael. 'Religion.' In *New Zealand: Sociological Perspectives*, 169–95. Edited by Paul Spoonley, David Pearson and Ian Shirley. Palmerston North: Dunmore Press, 1982.

———. 'Religion and Society: Cement or Ferment?' In *Religion in New Zealand*, 204–37. Edited by Christopher Nichol and James Veitch. Wellington: Tertiary Christian Studies Programme of the Combined Chaplaincies and the Religious Studies Department, Victoria University, 1980.

———. 'The Decline of Church-Based Religiosity and the Rise of Sectarianism.' In *Religion in New Zealand Society*, 119–42. 2nd ed. Edited by Brian Colless and Peter Donovan. Palmerston North: Dunmore Press, 1985.

———. 'The Social Context of New Zealand Religion: "Straight" or "Narrow"?' In *Religion and New Zealand's Future*, 23–46. Edited by Kevin J. Sharpe. Palmerston North: Dunmore Press, 1982.

———. 'To define true heresy: deviance, conformity and religion.' In *Shades of Deviance: A New Zealand Collection*, 140–59. Edited by Michael Hill, Sharon Mast, Richard Bowman and Charlotte Carr-Gregg. Palmerston North: Dunmore Press, 1983.

———, and Bowman, Richard. 'Churches in a changing world.' In *Religion and Change [International Religious Studies Conference]*, 235–72. Wellington: Victoria University, 1983.

Hoar, Peter. 'Young People and the Charismatic Renewal in a Catholic Parish.' In *Religion and New Zealand's Future*, 47–56. Edited by Kevin J. Sharpe. Palmerston North: Dunmore Press, 1982.

Kirkman, Allison. 'Propriety Promoted: Patricia Bartlett and the Society for the Promotion of Community Standards.' In *Shades of Deviance: A New Zealand Collection*, 26–40. Edited by Michael Hill, Sharon Mast, Richard Bowman and Charlotte Carr-Gregg. Palmerston North: Dunmore Press, 1983.

Knowles, Brett. 'Vision of the Disinherited? The growth of the Pentecostal Movement in the 1960s, with particular reference to the New Life Churches of New Zealand.' In *'Be Ye Separate': Fundamentalism and the New Zealand Experience*. Waikato Studies in Religion, Vol.3, 107–41. Edited by Bryan Gilling. Hamilton: University of Waikato and Colcom Press, 1992.

Lease, Gary. 'Youth, Religion and Politics in Contemporary America.' In *Religion's Response to Change*, 3–25. Edited by John M. Ker and Kevin J. Sharpe. Auckland: Auckland University Chaplaincy Publishing Trust, 1985.

Lineham, Peter J. 'Finding a space for Evangelicalism: Evangelical youth movements in New Zealand.' In *Voluntary Religion: Papers read at the 1985 summer meeting and the 1986 winter meeting of the Ecclesiastical History Society*, Studies in Church History, Vol.23, 477-94. Edited by W.J. Sheils and Diana Wood. Worcester: Basil Blackwell for the Ecclesiastical History Society, 1986.

———. 'Religion.' In *New Zealand Book of Events*, 342-52. Edited by Bryce Fraser. Auckland: Reed Methuen, 1986.

Mol, J.J. 'Religion and Churches.' In *Tasman Relations: New Zealand and Australia 1788-1988*, 263-77. Edited by Keith Sinclair. Auckland: Auckland University Press, 1987.

———, and Reidy, M.T.V. 'Religion in New Zealand.' In *New Zealand Society*, 264-82. Edited by S.D. Webb and J. Collette. Sydney: Wiley, 1973.

Oliver, W.H. 'The Awakening Imagination.' In *The Oxford History of New Zealand*, 430-61. Edited by W.H. Oliver. Wellington: Oxford University Press, 1981.

Openshaw, Roger. 'Upholding Basic Values: A Case Study of a Conservative Pressure Group.' In *Political Issues in New Zealand Education*. Edited by John Codd, Richard Harker, and Roy Nash. Palmerston North: Dunmore Press, 1987.

Roach, Kevin. 'The Growth of Roman Catholicism in New Zealand.' In *Religion in New Zealand*, 131-36. Edited by Christopher Nichol and James Veitch. Wellington: Tertiary Christian Studies Programme of the Combined Chaplaincies and The Religious Studies Department, Victoria University, 1980.

Rowe, Keith. 'Clergy for Rowling—the Almost Politicians.' In *Dialogue on Religion: New Zealand Viewpoints 1977*, 31-35. Edited by Peter Davis and John Hinchcliff. Auckland: University of Auckland, 1977.

Salmon, John B. 'Moral and Religious Education in New Zealand: Some history and some possibilities.' In *Under the Southern Cross*. Ocean Monograph no.4, 43-50. Edited by John Hinchcliff and Norman Simms. Auckland: Outrigger Publishers, 1980.

Sharpe, Kevin J. 'Religion for Modern Western Society.' In *Religion and New Zealand's Future*, 117-22. Edited by Kevin J. Sharpe. Palmerston North: Dunmore Press, 1982.

Stuart, W.J. 'Secularization and Sectarianism: The Struggle for a Religious Future for New Zealand.' In *Religion and New Zealand's Future*, 84-91. Edited by Kevin J. Sharpe. Palmerston North: Dunmore Press, 1982.

Tait, David. 'The Geering Controversy in Political Perspective.' In *Perspectives on Religion: New Zealand Viewpoints 1974*, 20-23. Edited by John C. Hinchcliff. Auckland: University of Auckland Bindery, 1975.

Thompson, R.J. 'The New Youth Fundamentalism.' In *Perspectives on Religion: New Zealand Viewpoints, 1974*, 85-91. Edited by John C. Hinchcliff. Auckland: University of Auckland Bindery, 1975.

———. 'Sects in New Zealand.' In *Towards an Authentic New Zealand Theology*, 89-97. Edited by John M. Ker and Kevin J. Sharpe. Auckland: University of Auckland Chaplaincy Publishing Trust, 1984.

———. 'The Baptism of the Spirit.' In *Under the Southern Cross*. Ocean Monograph no.4, 7-13. Edited by John Hinchcliff and Norman Simms. Auckland: Outrigger Publishers, 1980.

———. 'Theological trends of the World Council of Churches May 1979.' In *Under the Southern Cross*. Ocean Monograph no.4, 51-57. Edited by John Hinchcliff and Norman Simms. Auckland: Outrigger Publishers, 1980.

Tiwari, Kapil. 'Religious Movements of Indian Origin in New Zealand.' In *Religion in New Zealand Society*, 15-29. 2nd ed. Edited by Brian Colless and Peter Donovan. Palmerston North: Dunmore Press, 1985.

Vaughan, Martin, and Varelas, Angela. 'To be or not to be: the abortion controversy in New Zealand.' In *Shades of Deviance: A New Zealand Collection*, 114-25. Edited by Michael Hill, Sharon Mast, Richard Bowman and Charlotte Carr-Gregg. Palmerston North: Dunmore Press, 1983.

Veitch, James. 'Heresy and Freedom.' In *Religion in New Zealand*, 138-78. Edited by Christopher Nichol and James Veitch. Wellington: Tertiary Christian Studies Programme of the Combined Chaplaincies and the Religious Studies Department, Victoria University, 1980.

———. 'The Rise and Fall of Christianity in New Zealand.' In *Finding the Way: New Zealand Christians look forward*, 74-78. Edited by Margaret Reid Martin. Melbourne: Joint Board of Christian Education of Australia and New Zealand, 1983.

Weber, Max. 'The Nature of Charismatic Domination.' In *Max Weber: Selections in Translation*. Edited by W.G. Runciman. Translated by E. Matthews. Cambridge: Cambridge University Press, 1978.

4.4. Journal Articles

Battley, Donald. 'Charismatic Renewal: A View from Inside.' *Ecumenical Review* 38 (January 1986): 48-56.

Blaikie, Norman W.H. 'Religion, Social Status and Community Involvement: A Study in Christchurch.' *Australian and New Zealand Journal of Sociology* 5 (October 1969): 14-31.

———. 'What motivates Church Participation?: Review, Replication and Theoretical Reorientation in New Zealand.' *Sociological Review*, New Series 20 (February 1972): 39-58.

Breward, Ian. 'Religion and New Zealand society.' *New Zealand Journal of History* 13 (October 1979): 138-48.

Brosnan, Peter. 'Religion and Income in New Zealand: An Examination of Data from the 1981 Census.' *Australian and New Zealand Journal of Sociology* 24 (July 1988): 248-63.

Colquhon, James. 'The Revolt of Youth.' *New Zealand Monthly Review* IX (December 1968): 9-11.

Davidson, Allan K. 'A Protesting Presbyterian: the Reverend P.B. Fraser and New Zealand Presbyterianism 1892-1940.' *Journal of Religious History* 14 (December 1986): 193-217.
Davies, H. Merlin. 'Church and Nation.' *Landfall* 20:1 (March 1966): 20-24.
Downey, P.J. 'Being Religious in New Zealand.' *Landfall* 20:1 (March 1966): 31-37.
Evans, Tania. 'God Almighty.' *New Outlook* 14 (January/February 1985): 22-30.
Geering, Lloyd. 'The Church in the New World.' *Landfall* 20:1 (March 1966): 24-30.
Hadden, Jeffrey K. 'Religious Broadcasting and the Mobilization of the New Christian Right.' *Journal for the Scientific Study of Religion* 26 (March 1987): 1-24.
Harper, David. 'The Charismatic Renewal.' *Latimer* 76 (June 1982): 26-30.
_____. 'The Charismatic Experience II: Evolving Experience of God.' *Latimer* 77 (September 1982): 27-31.
Harré, John. 'To Be or Not to Be?' *Landfall* 20:1 (March 1966): 37-41.
Hill, Michael. 'Religious Adherence and Religious Practice in Contemporary New Zealand: Census and Survey Evidence.' *Archives de Sciences Sociales des Religions* 59 (1985): 91-114.
Hill, Michael, and Zwaga, Wiebe. 'Civil and civic: Engineering a national religious consensus.' *New Zealand Sociology* 2 (May 1987): 25-35.
Howe, Renate. 'Social Composition of the Wesleyan Church in Victoria during the Nineteenth Century.' *Journal of Religious History* 4 (June 1967): 206-17.
Lineham, Peter J. 'Tongues must cease: The Brethren and the Charismatic movement in New Zealand.' *Christian Brethren Review Journal* 34 (November 1983): 7-52.
Marriott, Wallace. 'Charismatic Renewal in the Anglican Church.' *Latimer* 55 (August 1976): 14-17.
Matheson, James G. 'New Zealand since the War.' *Landfall* 15:1 (March 1961): 58-67.
McEldowney, Dennis. 'Ultima Thule to Little Bethel.' *Landfall* 20:1 (March 1966): 50-59.
McGeorge, Colin. 'Some Old Wine and some New Bottles: moral and religious education in New Zealand.' *Journal of Moral Education* 4 (1975): 215-23.
Mol, J.J. 'Religion in New Zealand.' *Extrait des Archives de Sociologie des Religions* 24 (1967): 121-33.
_____. 'The Scope of Sociological Research in Religion in Australia and New Zealand.' *Colloquium* 4:3 (October 1971): 5-12.
Munro, Jocelyn. 'Religion, Age, Sex and Moral Issues: Some Relationships.' *Political Science* 34 (December 1982): 314-20.
Nichol, Frank. 'Theology in New Zealand.' *Landfall* 20:1 (March 1966): 42-49.
Oliver, W.H. 'Christianity among the New Zealanders.' *Landfall* 20:1 (March 1966): 4-20.
_____. 'The Church and the Churches 1: The Fruits of Fragmentation.' *Comment* 1 (Spring 1959): 15-19.

Parker, David. 'Evangelical Worship—Sacramental, Charismatic or Biblical?' *Colloquium* 19:2 (May 1987): 57–64.

Parsons, I.R.McK. 'Religion—a dead issue in Australian Universities?' *Colloquium* 4:2 (May 1971): 118–22.

Reidy, M.T. Vincent, and Richardson, James T. 'Roman Catholic Neo-Pentecostalism: The New Zealand Experience.' *Australia and New Zealand Journal of Sociology* 14 (1978): 222–30.

Reynolds, P.L. 'Religion and Voting in Auckland.' *Political Science* 24 (April 1972): 38–48.

Ryan, Allanah. '"For God, Country and Family": Populist Moralism and the New Zealand Moral Right.' *New Zealand Sociology* 1 (1986): 104–12.

Seligman, Adam. 'Collective Boundaries and Social Reconstruction in Seventeenth-Century New England.' *Journal of Religious History* 16 (1991): 260–79.

Simpson, Tony. 'New Life Style: The Jesus Revolution.' *Arts and Community* 7 (August 1971): 20.

Smith, Timothy L. 'The Disinheritance of the Saints.' *Religious Studies Review* VIII (1982): 22–28.

Thomas, Philip. 'Charismatics—Which Way?' *Latimer* 55 (August 1976): 1–6.

Veitch, James. 'Mapping Theological Contours.' *Forum* 37 (October 1984): 3–9.

Vodanovich, Ivanica. 'Woman's place in God's World.' *New Zealand Women's Studies Journal* 2 (August 1985): 68–79.

Wacker, Grant. 'Taking another look at the "Vision of the Disinherited,"' *Religious Studies Review* VIII (1982): 15–22.

Wallis, Roy, and Bland, Richard. 'Purity in Danger: A survey of participants in a moral crusade rally.' *British Journal of Sociology* 30 (June 1979): 188–205.

Wilson, Malcolm. 'News of the World: New Zealand.' *Christian Century* 82 (29 December 1965): 1611–12.

Young, Craig. 'The New Zealand Religious Right and Armageddon Theology.' *New Zealand Monthly Review* 27 (March 1987): 9–10.

4.5. Magazine and Newspaper Articles

Ansley, Bruce. 'The Growing Might of the Moral Right.' *New Zealand Listener*, 26 October 1985, 16–18.

Augsberger, David. 'The Private Lives of Public Leaders.' *Christianity Today*, 20 November 1987, 23–24.

Bluck, John. 'Jesus 75—a mixed blessing.' *New Citizen*, 12 June 1975, 5.

Brock, Peter. 'The Secret Summit Reconstructed.' *Christianity Today*, 4 April 1980, 45.

Chapple, Geoff. 'When the Spirit moves.' *New Zealand Listener*, 24 July 1976, 24–25.

Crawford, Janet. 'What do women want? Women are questioning male attitudes.' *Accent*, July 1988, 8–12.

Cryderman, Lyn. 'Bad News Bearers.' *Christianity Today*, 21 April 1989, 12.

Dasler, Yvonne. 'Then they came to Elim....' *New Zealand Listener*, 24 April 1982, 18–21.
Dawson, Selwyn. 'God's Bullies.' *Auckland Metro*, September 1985, 170–76.
Frame, Randy. 'A Bar-room Ministry Runs Amuck.' *Christianity Today*, 19 November 1990, 62 and 64.
Gordon, Richard. 'Fear and Loathing and the Moral Majority.' *Metro*, December 1985, 121–41.
Hands, Donald R. 'Towards liberation from shamed sexuality.' *Ministry*, Autumn 1992, 24–27.
Harper, Jonathon. 'The Church that's taking over Auckland.' *Metro*, November 1983, 122–35.
Hayward, Jeff. 'Back to Fundamentals.' *More*, December 1987, 208–19.
Kantzer, Kenneth S. 'The Road to Restoration: How should the church treat its fallen leaders?' *Christianity Today*, 20 November 1987, 19–22.
Keyzer, Robert. 'A Christian Revolutionary.' *New Zealand Listener*, 13 November 1972, 10–11.
Leigh, Jack. 'Getting Religion.' *New Zealand Woman's Weekly*, 8 July 1985, 59–62.
Loates, Lynne. 'State of Siege.' *More*, February 1990, 64–70.
Loryman, Gaynor. 'Growth of the Pentecostal Movement: A new relationship with Christ.' *Christchurch Star*, 27 October 1973, 7.
McCracken, Jill. 'The God Squad.' *New Zealand Listener*, 23 October 1972, 14–15.
Morey, Ann-Janine. 'Blaming Women for the Sexually Abusive Male Pastor.' *Christian Century*, 5 October 1988, 866–69.
Pardon, Fran. 'The Moral Minority: Auckland's Right-Wing Christians are on the March.' *Auckland Metro*, May 1982, 90–100.
Plowman, Edward E. 'The Deepening Rift in the Charismatic Movement.' *Christianity Today*, 10 October 1975, 52–54.
Poynton, Alex. 'Repent! Spiritual warfare on Wellington's street corners.' *New Zealand Listener*, 23 November 1984, 22–24.
Ray, Pauline. 'Religion is alive and selling downtown.' *New Zealand Listener*, 31 March 1979, 12–14.
_____. 'The Techniques of Loving Coercion.' *New Zealand Listener*, 7 April 1979, 16–18.
Reid, Tony. 'Patricia Bartlett versus Moral Rot.' *New Zealand Listener*, 15 November 1980, 24–25.
Rudman, Brian. 'For God and National.' *New Zealand Listener*, 28 March 1987, 28–29.
Stratford, Stephen. 'Christians, Awake! Join the National Party, Save New Zealand.' *Metro*, November 1986, 124–37.
Synan, Vinson. 'Reconciling the Charismatics.' *Christianity Today*, 9 April 1976, 46.
Toomer, Mark. 'National church leader "walks with his people."' *Challenge Weekly*, 8 May 1996, 5.

Wacker, Grant. 'America's Pentecostals: who they are.' *Christianity Today*, 16 October 1987, 16-21.

Wagner, C. Peter. 'America's Pentecostals: See how they grow.' *Christianity Today*, 16 October 1987, 28-29.

Willimon, William H. '"Heard About the Pastor Who...?" Gossip as an Ethical Activity.' *Christian Century*, 31 October 1990, 994-96.

Wright, Vernon. 'The Christian Connection.' *New Zealand Listener*, 25 July 1981, 20-22.

4.6. Other Published Sources

1986 New Zealand Census of Population and Dwellings, Series C, Report 14: Religious Professions. Wellington: Department of Statistics, 1988.

1996 Census of Population and Dwellings, National Summary. Wellington: Statistics New Zealand, 1997.

Ackley, A.H. 'He lives, He lives, Christ Jesus lives today!' No.631, *Redemption Hymnal*. Rev. ed. Eastbourne, Sussex: Elim Publishing House, 1955.

Baptist Union and Missionary Society of New Zealand. *Year Book.* 1958/59-1971/72.

Buttle, Francis. *The Elley-Irving Socio-Economic Indices: Practical Problems in their Use.* Research Report No.26. Palmerston North: Market Research Centre, Massey University, [May 1980].

Christian Heritage Party of New Zealand, 'Message from the President', [1989].

Church of the Province of New Zealand. *Proceedings of the General Synod.* 1957/58-1971/72.

Convention on the Elimination of All Forms of Discrimination Against Women: 'What's it all about.' A Review Paper. Wellington: Human Rights Commission, 1984.

DAWN Strategy New Zealand. *1990 Church Survey Report.* n.p.: DAWN Strategy New Zealand Committee, 1990.

Fernández, Wolfgang D. *Institutional Analysis: Initial Findings.* Waikanae: DAWN Strategy New Zealand, [1987].

Indigenous Full Gospel Churches of New Zealand. *The Miracle of New Life.* [1965].

Methodist Church in New Zealand. *Minutes of the Annual Conference.* 1958-71.

New Zealand Census of Population and Dwellings 1971, Vol. 3: Religious Professions. Wellington: Department of Statistics, 1974.

New Zealand Gazette. Wellington: Government Printer. 14 April 1965.

New Zealand Official Yearbook, 1984. 89th annual ed. Wellington: Department of Statistics, 1984.

New Zealand Official Yearbook, 1987-1988. 92nd annual ed. Wellington: Department of Statistics, 1987.

New Zealand Official Yearbook, 1988-1989. 93rd annual ed. Wellington: Department of Statistics, 1988.

New Zealand Parliamentary Debates, Vol.324 (23 September 1960); Vol.461 (8 March 1985); Vol.466 (24 September 1985 and 8 October 1985); Vol.472 (9 July 1986).
New Zealand Population Census 1961, Vol. 3, Religious Professions. Wellington: Department of Statistics, 1964.
Proceedings of the General Assembly of the Presbyterian Church of New Zealand. 1958-72.
Robson v. Hicks Smith and Sons Ltd. [1965] *N.Z.L.R.* 1113.

5. Unpublished Materials

5.1. Correspondence

Bensley, Mary. Auckland. Correspondence with the author, February 1998.
Casey, Stella. Wellington. Correspondence with the author, 3 July 1991.
Coady, A.R. Davis, California. Correspondence with the author, 1988-91, 1997-98.
Collins, David. Hamilton. Correspondence with the author, 1 May 1990.
Drinkwater, Ian. E-mail correspondence with author, 30 September 2014.
Hodgkinson, Eric. E-mail Correspondence with the author, 10 February 1998.
Richardson, Professor Herbert. Editor-in-Chief, Edwin Mellen Press. E-mail Correspondence with the author, 14 August 2014.
Stares, Val. Broadbeach, Queensland, Australia. Correspondence with the author, 1 March 1993.
Touwen-Bouwsma, Dr C. *Rijksinstituut voor Oolorgsdocumentatie* [Netherlands State Institute for War Documentation], Amsterdam, Netherlands. Correspondence with the author, 2 February 1990.
Wheeler, Rob. Correspondence with the author, 2 March 1998.
Worsfold, James E. Correspondence with the author, 14 January 1989.

5.2. Other Unpublished Materials

Associated Pentecostal Churches of New Zealand. 'Directory of Ministers.' Wellington, 1983, 1984, 1986 and 1989. (Mimeographed.)
Association for the Promotion of Christian Schools. 'The school and the world: A one day seminar examining the task of making a Christian contribution to Education in New Zealand.' Dunedin, n.d. (Mimeographed.)
Bethel New Life Centre. '25th Jubilee Celebrations.' Invercargill, September 1987. (Mimeographed.)
Bodger, Eleanor. 'Why women leave the Pentecostal church.' Research Proposal for Diploma in Social Work, University of Canterbury, 1991.
Campbell, Nancy. 'Above Rubies: Bringing the trend in the nation back to God's way!' Broadbeach, Queensland, Australia, 1991. (Mimeographed.)
Caton, E. 'A report on the Maori population of Dunedin, their religious affiliations, and participation in church life, and their reactions to the placing of a minister from the Presbyterian Maori Synod. Based on a survey

conducted from November 1967 to January 1968.' Presbyterian Maori Synod, Knox Theological Hall, Dunedin, 1968.

Christian Fellowship Mission, Timaru. Minutes of Business Meetings, 9 December 1961 and following. (Handwritten.)

Collins, David; Douglas, Brent; Dyson, Kevin; Wagener, Owen; and Davies, Ross. 'Indigenous Pentecostal Churches. Concept paper submitted to the members of INDIGENOUS CHURCHES OF NEW ZEALAND by the pastors of the Central North Island region.' Hamilton, n.d. (Mimeographed.)

Collins, David S.T. 'Women in Ministry.' Auckland, 1990. (Mimeographed.)

Court, J.H. 'Pornography and Sex Crimes: New evidence on an old controversy.' Paper presented during lecture tour of New Zealand, September 1979. (Mimeographed.)

Dunlop, E.A. 'Christian Schools in New Zealand.' Christchurch, 1978. (Mimeographed.)

Facer, W.A.P. 'Attitudes to Abortion in New Zealand.' Auckland: Abortion Law Reform Association of New Zealand, 1973. (Mimeographed.)

'First Occasional Symposium on Aspects of the Oneness Pentecostal Movement.' Cambridge, Massachusetts: Harvard Divinity School, 1984. (Mimeographed.)

Geering, Lloyd. 'What is Secularization?' In 'Secularization of Religion in New Zealand.' Wellington: University Extension, Victoria University, 1976. (Mimeographed.)

Hodgkinson, Eric. 'The Independent Pentecostal Movement.' Research Essay in New Zealand Religious History, Massey University, 1989. (Handwritten.)

Indigenous Churches of New Zealand. 'Directory.' Wellington, 1983, 1984, 1986, 1987, 1988 and 1989. (Mimeographed.)

'Introducing South Pacific Fellowship.' n.d. [December 1987]. (Mimeographed.)

Knowles, Brett. 'Vision of the Disinherited? An examination of the expansion of the Neo-Pentecostal and Charismatic Movements in the 1960s and 1970s and a suggested hypothesis for the social causes of their growth.' Paper presented at Postgraduate Seminar, Department of History, University of Otago, 4 October 1989.

Lineham, Peter J. 'Explaining the Attitude of Evangelical and Pentecostal Churches to Women?' Paper presented at 'Women, Men and God' Conference, Waikanae, 5 October 1991.

Missionary Revival Centre. 'Missionary Revival Centre.' Timaru, n.d. [1965?]. (Mimeographed.)

Morrow, Anne. 'Women in Ministry.' Christchurch, 1990. (Mimeographed.)

Motueka New Life Centre. 'New Life Centre: A History.' Motueka, n.d. [circa 1987]. (Mimeographed.)

New Life Churches of New Zealand. 'Directory of Pastors and Churches.' Christchurch, 1990 and 1991. (Mimeographed.)

Schoneveld, E.J. [Bert]. 'An exploration in Protest.' Research Essay, Knox Theological Hall, 1982. (Typescript.)

Strickland, D.R. 'Church growth Analysis: the fastest growing and declining Presbyterian churches in New Zealand.' Titirangi, 1985. (Typescript.)

'Tauranga Christian Fellowship: Jubilee Reunion 1939-1989.' Tauranga, 1989. (Mimeographed.)

'Te Teko Fellowship—25th Anniversary Celebrations, 1961-1986.' [Te Teko, 1986] (Mimeographed.)

Walker, Dorothy. 'Indonesia have I loved: Dal N. Walker 25 Years of Missionary Service 1949-1974.' Solo-Jateng, Java, Indonesia: Dorothy Walker, [1974].

Windsor Full Gospel Church. Circular letter. Windsor, Brisbane, Australia, 2 June 1963. (Cyclostyled.)

5.3. Theses and Dissertations

Arrowsmith, David. 'Christian Attitudes towards Public Questions in New Zealand in 1975.' M.A. Thesis in Political Studies, Auckland University, 1978.

Evans, John A. 'Church-State Relations in New Zealand 1940-1990, with particular reference to the Presbyterian and Methodist Churches.' Ph.D. Thesis in Church History, University of Otago, 1992.

Garing, M.N. 'Against the Tide: Social, Moral and Political Questions in the Presbyterian Church of New Zealand 1840-1970.' Ph.D. Thesis in Religious Studies, Victoria University of Wellington, 1989.

Gilling, Bryan D. 'Retelling the Old, Old Story: A Study of Six Mass Evangelistic Missions in Twentieth Century New Zealand.' D.Phil. Thesis in History, University of Waikato, 1990.

Ireton, Douglas. 'A time to heal: The appeal of Smith Wigglesworth in New Zealand 1922-24.' B.A. (Honours) Dissertation in History, Massey University, 1984.

_____. '"O Lord, How Long?": A Revival Movement in New Zealand 1920-1933.' M.A. (Honours) Thesis in History, Massey University, 1986.

Ker, Nola. 'Religion and Society in Interaction in New Zealand.' M.A. Thesis in Sociology, Victoria University of Wellington, 1984.

Knowles, Brett. '"For the Sake of the Name": A History of the "New Life Churches" from 1942 to 1965.' B.Theol. (Honours) Dissertation in Christian Thought and History, University of Otago, 1988.

_____. 'Some Aspects of the History of the New Life Churches of New Zealand 1960-1990.' Ph.D. Thesis in Church History, University of Otago, 1994.

Macleod, Duncan. 'J.D. Salmond's contribution to Religious Education in N.Z.' Dissertation in Church History, University of Otago, 1991.

Marquand, I.G. 'The New Zealand Presbyterian New Life Movement: A Case Study in Church Growth.' M.Th. Thesis in Church History, University of Otago, 1977.

Myers, Michael David. 'Organizational Change in the Auckland Catholic Charismatic Movement.' M.A. Thesis in Anthropology, Auckland University, 1978.

Neil, Allan G. 'Institutional Churches and the Charismatic Renewal: A Study of the Charismatic Renewal in the Anglican Church and the Roman Catholic

Church in New Zealand.' Diploma S.Th. Thesis in Church History, Joint Board of Theological Studies, 1974.

Paterson, Fraser. 'An historical analysis of issues within the Presbyterian Church of New Zealand, 1945–1985.' M.Th. Thesis in Church History, University of Otago, 1985.

Rayner, Anne. 'Social Characteristics of Pentecostalism: a sociological study of the Christchurch Apostolic Church.' M.A. Thesis in Sociology, University of Canterbury, 1980.

Rogers, Owen. 'The New Zealand Presbyterian New Life Movement.' B.D. Dissertation in Church History, University of Otago, 1990.

Russell, Richard. 'The growing crisis of the Evangelical world-view and its resolutions.' M.A. Thesis in Theology and Religious Studies, Bristol University, 1973.

Ryan, Allanah. '"For God, Country and Family": Populist Moralism and the New Zealand Moral Right.' M.A. Thesis in Education, Massey University, 1986.

Simpson, Jane M.R. 'Joseph W. Kemp and the impact of American Fundamentalism in New Zealand.' B.A. (Honours) Dissertation in History, University of Waikato, 1986.

Sloper, Geoffrey. 'Religion and Fertility: A Case Study among Pentecostal Christians in New Zealand.' B.A. (Honours) Dissertation in Geography, Otago University, 1978.

Waldegrave, C.T. 'Social and Personality Correlates of Pentecostalism: A Review of the Literature and a Comparison of Pentecostal Christian Students with Non-Pentecostal Christian Students.' B.Phil. Dissertation in Educational Psychology, University of Waikato, 1972.

Wallace, S.M. 'An investigation of the political attitudes of members of Plymouth Brethren and Pentecostal churches in Christchurch.' M.A. Research Paper in Political Science, University of Canterbury, 1977.

Index I

People

Adirek 106
Allington, Doug 215, 220, 221
Armitage, George 231
Arrowsmith, David 160, 174
Ashby, Bishop 128
Baker, Charlotte 231
Baker, Minta 176
Balfour, Rev. David 117, 137
Banks, John 4, 7, 9–11, 21, 23
Bartleman, Frank 29, 32, 103
Bartlett, Patricia 144, 146
Basham, Don 185
Battley, Donald 138
Baxter, Ern 151, 154, 185, 191, 193–95, 197, 231
Bennett, Father Dennis 113, 117, 120
Bensley, Mary 37, 74
Bensley, Mike 33, 34, 37, 42, 44, 49, 74, 231
Bilby, Chas. 9, 12, 80, 83, 115
Bloomfield, Ray 42, 46, 115, 116, 231, 234
Blumhofer, Edith 25, 31, 32, 116
Boone, Pat 197
Branham, William 21, 25, 41, 193
Brannen, Bill 109
Breward, Prof. Ian 176
Bristle, Emmanuel and Wave 186
Brown, Pastor Vin 52, 77–79
Brown, Prof. Colin 94, 114, 117, 120, 126, 146, 157
Campbell, Nancy 177

Carlisle, Frank 114
Carr, Rev. Clyde, M.P. 61
Carter, Howard 188
Carter, Jimmy 203
Casey, Dame Stella 179
Chandler, Trevor 115, 116, 118, 119, 122, 232
Christenson, Larry 158
Clark, Ian 36, 38, 46, 115, 154, 193–97, 200, 201, 203–5, 207–12, 232
Coady, Muriel 33
Coady, Ron......... xxi, 11, 15, 17, 33–35, 42, 53, 54, 57, 58, 61–64, 65–70, 71, 72, 74, 75, 78, 80, 81, 85–87, 89, 90, 100–103, 107–9, 116, 118, 217, 232–35, 241
Collins, Bunty 106, 107, 233
Collins, David 232, 233
Collins, Paul............ 65–67, 69, 70, 106, 107, 233
Collins, Terry 125, 233
Comfort, Ray 189
Coney, Sandra 173–75, 177, 178, 181
Conner, Joyce 33
Conner, Kevin......... 33, 34, 38, 74, 101, 109, 233
Cooper, Neville 167
Copeland, Gordon 102, 127, 233
Cowie, Andrew 202
Crosbie, Donald 202
Dallimore, A.H. 24, 123, 237, 238

275

Darby, J.N. 15
Davidson, Rev. Dr Alan .... xxi, 54
Davies, Ross 91, 233, 237
Dennehy, Father Cecil 127, 128, 130
Dornan, Andreé 125
Dowie, John Alexander 25, 43
Drinkwater, Ian 117, 119, 120
Du Plessis, Rev. David 120
Dunk, Gilbert 198
Dyson, Kevin 219, 233
Edmonds, Rev. David 136
Edmondson, Al 4–6, 7, 9, 10, 21
Edmondson, Paul 154
Eisenhower, President Dwight D. 39
Ellis, David 184, 187, 189, 219, 223, 233
Ellis, Norma 189
Evans, Dr John 152, 159, 205
Ferguson, Duncan 115
Findlay, Welburn 109
Firebrands, The 87
Fitzpatrick, Dr Mike 221
Fountain, Wyn 122
Galvin, Ray 182, 189
Garrett, Frank 122
Geering, Prof. Lloyd 150
Gousmett, Dr Chris 160, 167, 170
Gracie, Pastor Alf 24
Graham, Billy 36, 39–41, 43, 45, 93, 94, 157
Greenslade, Milton 115
Greenway, Dr Alf 115
Gutschlag, Ivan 215
Hall, Victor 32
Harper, Blyth 148
Harper, Rev. Michael 117, 120, 134
Hart, G.L. 100
Hawtin, Ern 22
Hay, Sir Hamish 180
Hayford, Jack 193, 195–97, 233
Henderson, Mary 62, 78, 106
Henderson, Ruth xxii
Hicks, Tommy .... xxiii, 42, 43, 49, 57, 234
Hickson, J.M. 43, 47
Highstead, Pastor Reg 69
Hill, Prof. Michael 94, 98

Hodgkinson, Eric 114, 120, 122–24, 234
Holmes, Dr Anna 180
Holt, Keith 75, 234
Horton, Bob 158, 201, 220, 234
Hotter, Bill 93
Houston, Frank 38, 42, 46, 80, 115, 116, 118, 119, 201, 203, 204, 213, 216, 231, 232, 234
Houston, Hazel 35, 38, 46
Howard, Dr Donald R. 166, 167, 171
Hunt, Ian............ 42, 44, 49, 51, 52, 54, 68–70, 115, 120
Hunt, Mavis 44
Hurst, Earl xxii
Jacks, Graham 44
Jackson, David......... 1, 3–6, 33–35, 72, 73, 80, 87, 105, 106, 109, 115, 118, 233, 234
Jackson, Ray Richard 109
Jackson, Ray, Snr....... 1, 2, 4, 7–12, 17, 21, 23–26, 32, 33, 34, 36, 37, 54, 72, 74, 75, 83, 96, 97, 102, 107, 119, 122, 183, 194, 232–39
Jackson, Ron 109
Jackson, Ruth 21, 23, 24, 235
Jamieson, Superintendent John 180
Jeffreys, Stephen and George 25
Jenkins, Murray 87, 88
Johnson, Everett 69, 70, 71, 77, 78, 81, 82, 110
Johnson, Omar 34, 37
Jones, Dr Len J. 33, 37, 57, 105
Jull, David 70
Jull, Sandi xix
Kearney, Shaun 37, 38, 109, 195, 198, 235
Kiteley, Violet 235
Knowles, Adrienne .... xxii, 283
Knowles, Zona 58
Kuhlman, Kathryn 220
Kynaston, Alan xxii
Lai, James 231
Lal, Rasik
  See Ranchord, Rasik
Lawrence, D.H. 141, 146
Lee, Dr Bill 170
Lineham, Prof. Peter .... xvii, xxi, 26,

114, 119, 153, 178
Loryman, Gaynor 126, 127
Lowe, Alister 83, 85, 109, 115, 241
Lustenhower, Tina xxii
Mandie, Hanny 5
Marsh, Rev. Janet ....xxi, 189, 225, 238
Marshall, Rt. Hon. John 149
Marshall, Tom 115, 122
Matheson, Rev. Dr Peter .... xxi, 81
McAlpine, Campbell 114–16, 122, 235
McCracken, David 235
McGeorge, Colin 170
McGill, Father Bruce 177
McGill, Father John 177
McGregor, Bruce and Fay 50
McMillan, Jim and Dinal 235
McNabb, Bernie 235
McStay, Captain Brian 149
Metcalf, Dr Douglas 212
Morrow, Anne 158, 174–78, 180, 235
Morrow, Peter 15, 17, 33, 35, 38, 52, 59, 70, 74, 87, 99, 109, 115, 116, 121, 122, 124, 125–29, 134–37, 158, 163, 164, 167, 204, 208–11, 213, 217, 220, 223, 224, 233–36, 238
Mossholder, Ray 176, 180, 236
Muldoon, Rt. Hon. Robert 164, 199–201, 234
Muller, Father Ray 113, 120, 123
Mumford, Bob 184–87, 190, 219, 236
Munro, Pastor Ian 82
Murray, Laurie 58, 63
Necklen, Ray 68, 77, 82, 109
Nee, Watchman 185, 190
Neil, Allan 113–15, 117, 120, 123, 129, 130, 133–35, 138, 154
Offiler, Pastor W.H.................... 1, 8, 11, 14–16, 18, 23, 26, 155, 236
Ortiz, Juan Carlos 184, 185, 187, 188, 190, 219, 236
Osborn, T.L. 13, 46, 49
Palmer, Max.............. xxii, 161, 208–12, 217, 221, 236
Parham, Charles Fox 21, 31, 102

Paterson, Pastor W.W. 2
Patterson, Neal 217, 236
Pennington, Pastor E.E. 9, 16
Péron, President Juan 42
Pillay, Prof. Gerald xxi
Pollock, Ada (neé Saunders) 58, 236
Pollock, Jimmy 58
Poole, John 185
Prince, Derek 185
Ranaghan, Kevin 130
Ranchord, Rasik...... xxi, 122, 127–29, 134–36, 147, 148, 158, 168, 187, 188, 191, 195, 196, 199–202, 204, 205, 208, 212, 217, 221, 236, 237
Ratana, T.W. 43, 47
Ravenhill, David 237
Ravenhill, Leonard 237
Read, Pastor Ralph............ 17, 82, 115, 210, 213
Riss, Richard M. 22, 26, 31
Robb, Mrs. (Pastor) Edna 24, 52, 237
Roberts, Oral............ 39, 41, 42, 46, 80, 194, 239
Roberts, Pastor Harry (H.V.) 8, 9, 11, 12, 16, 18, 238
Robertson, Pat 190
Roper, Dr Duncan 170
Rosewall, Gordon 220
Rowling, Rt. Hon. Wallace ('Bill') 199–201, 204, 237
Salisbury, Bill 109
Salisbury, Hudson 122, 124
Saunders sisters 58
Schoch, David 34
Schoneveld, E.J. (Bert) 62
Shaw, Dave 237
Shaw, Trevor 149, 154
Shearer, David 237
Sherrill, John 117
Short, Des 115
Simpson, Charles 185, 191
Simpson, Dr Jane 179
Skinner, Burrows F. 167
Smith, Milton 122
Soukotta, Sam and Carol 238
Spoonley, Paul 169
Stanley, Andrew 202, 237

Steele, John 188, 190, 237
Steele, Julie 237
Stenhouse, Dr John xxi
Stephen, Bill 237
Strong, Brian 223
Synan, Vinson 190, 283
Thompson, Muri 148, 153
Thrift, Pastor Allan 23, 24, 51, 55, 71, 74, 91, 237
Tiplady, John 166, 195, 198, 199, 201, 207, 237
Touwen-Bousma, Dr C. xxii
Tregenza, Pastor Roy 71
Troeltsch, Ernst 94
Truscott, Graham and Pam 105, 110
Twain, Mark 228
Vodanovich, Ivanica 174, 179
Wagener, Owen 237
Walker, Dal 9, 11, 13, 105, 110, 238
Walker, Dorothy 11, 105, 110, 238
Walker, Hon. Bert 180
Wall, Dr Gerald, M.P. 180
Wallis, Arthur 114–16, 122, 238
Walton, John 124, 213, 238
Wást, Bruce 31, 238
Weber, Max 94
Webster, Rev. Alex .... xxii, 161, 225, 238
Wetering de Rooy, R.B. .... xxii, 5
Wheeler, Beryl 33, 44, 88
Wheeler, Rob .... xxiii, xxiv, 10, 12, 15–17, 19, 21, 27, 33–38, 42–44, 49–54, 57, 63, 65–74, 76, 77–80, 82, 83, 88–91, 93, 98, 99, 100, 103, 108, 109, 115, 116, 121, 122, 124, 134–36, 148, 156, 160, 166, 194, 202, 205, 208–13, 216–218, 221, 223, 224, 231–33, 235, 238, 239, 241
White, Gilbert 42, 44, 115, 116, 118
White, Norman 42, 44, 54, 68–70, 91, 115, 116, 118
Wigglesworth, Smith 8, 11, 25, 43, 47, 58, 194
Wilkerson, David 117, 125, 130
Williams, Jim 208
Wilson, Prof. Bryan 95, 98, 99, 221
Winnington, Marion 61
Wonders, Mrs. Margaret 33
Woodard, Dr Christopher 47
Woodfield, Rev. Owen 137
Worley, A.S. 57–63, 65, 67, 78, 79, 82, 99, 103, 123, 232, 235, 236, 239
Worsfold, Cecily .... xxii, 6
Worsfold, James 16, 19, 31, 110, 124, 194, 197, 204, 239
Wright, Ken 114–16, 118, 119–21, 135, 168, 239
Wright, Lilian 60, 72
Wylie, Murray 32
Yong, Amos 283
Zimba, Kuda xix

Index II

Places

Ahipara 242, 246
Akatawara, Wellington 107, 108
Amsterdam .... xxii, 5
Argentina 42, 49, 184, 188
    Buenos Aires 42
Arrowtown 215
Ashburton 85–88, 215, 223, 233, 242, 247
Asia 283
Auckland .... xvii, 4, 6, 7–10, 12, 21, 23–25, 35, 36, 51, 55, 61, 62, 72, 74, 88, 90, 102, 107, 119, 123, 127–29, 142, 147, 148, 150, 151, 158, 166, 181, 195, 198, 200, 201, 207, 211, 215, 219, 220, 223, 225, 231–37, 239, 242, 246
Australia 2–4, 25, 33, 34, 36–38, 51, 69, 74, 80, 82, 96, 107, 109, 117, 183, 188, 189, 191, 213, 233–35, 239, 283
    Bendigo 33
    Brisbane 4, 82
    Melbourne ..... xxi, 33, 37, 97, 107, 183
    Sydney....... 3, 33, 35, 37, 232, 234, 239, 283
        West Ryde 33
Bay of Plenty 49–51, 237
Blenheim 4, 7, 8, 10, 11, 25, 68, 86, 225, 242, 247
Cambridge 166
Canada 21, 32, 37, 116, 231
    North Battleford, Saskatchewan ... 21–23, 26, 28
Chatham Islands 86, 242, 247
Christchurch .... xxii, 15, 25, 42, 68, 77, 79–82, 85–88, 93, 97, 107, 109, 115–17, 119, 125–30, 134–36, 138, 143, 148, 149, 160, 161, 163, 164, 166, 174, 175, 177–81, 200, 202, 208–10, 215, 216, 220, 221, 231, 233, 235–38, 241, 242, 247
Cook Islands 76
Cromwell 242, 247
Dargaville.................................... 166
Devonport, Auckland 24, 81
Dunedin ....xix, xxii, xxv, 31, 58, 66, 68, 69, 85, 86, 150, 168, 170, 216, 221, 233, 237, 238, 242, 247
Dutch New Guinea [Irian Jaya] 105
East Coast 49–52, 79
Edgecumbe 242, 246
Ellerslie, Auckland 231, 234
Eltham 242, 246
England 141
Epsom, Auckland 239
Fairlie 122–24, 221, 242, 247
Feilding 115, 118, 242, 246
Fiji 236
Foxton 69
Geraldine 66
Gisborne 50, 242, 246
Glenfield, Auckland 237
Gore 67–69, 71, 72, 85, 86, 108, 109, 242, 247

279

Governor's Bay, Christchurch 137
Great Britain 10, 40, 147, 221
Greymouth 243, 247
Gunn's Bush, Waimate 108, 109
Hamilton 81, 115, 180, 212, 232, 243, 246
Hastings 68, 243, 246
Henderson, Auckland 237
Hicks Bay 49, 50
Howick, Auckland 82
India 65, 87, 105, 115, 232
Indonesia .... xxii, 1, 2, 97, 105, 234, 238, 283
    Bali 2, 238
    Malang, East Java 238
    Roti 238
    Surabaya 1–3, 13
    Tawangmangu, Central Java 238, 283
Invercargill 66, 68, 69, 85, 86, 109, 166, 243, 247
Japan 2, 3, 105, 234
Jerusalem 283
Johnsonville, Wellington 107, 108
Kaikoura 86–88, 238, 241, 243, 247
Kaitaia 243, 246
Kamo, Whangarei 233
Kawakawa, Northland 42, 231
Kawerau 50, 51, 54, 235, 243, 246
Kohimarama, Auckland 237
Leeston 126, 243, 247
Levin 243, 246
London .... xxii, 5
Lower Hutt 25, 42, 115, 116, 231, 232, 234, 243, 246
Manawatu 117
Masterton 81, 243, 246
Miramar, Wellington 202
Mosgiel 85
Motueka 86, 215, 237, 243, 247
Mount Albert, Auckland 156, 202, 239
Mount Maunganui 49, 50, 243, 246
Mount Victoria, Wellington 4
Murupara 108, 243, 246
Nelson 15, 74, 75, 85–87, 102, 108, 109, 130, 165, 166, 216, 217, 228, 233–35, 241, 243, 247
New Plymouth 82, 237

North Shore, Auckland 38, 158, 190, 234, 235, 237, 244
Northland 42, 115, 234
Oamaru 68
Onehunga, Auckland 202
Opotiki 243, 246
Orepuki 81, 245
Otakiri 51
Otumoetai, Tauranga 24, 237
Pacific Islands 105
Palmerston North 54, 68, 82, 113, 115–24, 125, 129, 130, 135, 149, 151, 154, 168, 191, 216, 221, 230, 234, 239, 243, 246
Philippines 186, 233, 234, 238
Pukekohe 68, 77, 81
Putaruru 243, 246
Rangiora 167, 168, 244, 247
Rangitukia 49, 50, 54, 244, 246
Richmond, Nelson 130
Rotorua 232, 244, 246
Ruatoki 244, 246
Ruatoria 82, 244, 246
Silverstream, Wellington 167
Singapore 2, 97
Snell's Beach, Auckland 151, 193, 195, 196, 199, 204, 233, 235
South Africa 25, 114, 159, 203
Southeast Asia 105
Southland 64, 66, 81
St. Albans, Christchurch 202
Stewart Island 85, 86, 244, 247
Stratford 244, 246
Takaka 86
Takapuna 24, 244, 246
Taneatua 244, 246
Taupo 245, 246
Tauranga 15, 24, 25, 35, 42, 49–53, 57, 58, 65, 68, 73–76, 81, 102, 107, 115, 123, 231–33, 235, 237, 239, 244, 246
Te Araroa 49, 50, 54, 244, 246
Te Awamutu 81, 244, 246
Te Mahoe 51
Te Teko 49–51, 54, 71, 74, 237, 244, 246
Thailand 106, 107, 233, 238
    Bangkok 106, 233
    Chiangmai 106
Thames 81

Timaru .... xxii, xxiv, 25, 36, 57–64, 65–69, 71–73, 76, 80, 81, 83, 85–87, 95–97, 99, 100, 105–9, 115, 123, 136, 215, 221, 232–34, 236, 239, 244, 247
Tokomaru Bay 49, 50, 244, 246
Tokoroa 154, 244, 246
Tolaga Bay 244, 246
Tuatapere 81, 83, 85, 86, 90, 109, 245, 247
Turangi 245
United States of America 4, 10, 21–23, 33, 39–43, 45, 46, 97, 116, 127, 141, 151, 154, 167, 170, 178, 184, 185, 187, 188, 191, 193, 203, 217, 220, 232–35, 237, 239
   Ann Arbor, Michigan 138
   Davis, California 65, 232
   Fort Lauderdale, Florida 190, 191
   Greenville, South Carolina 57
   Los Angeles, California 21
   Sacramento, California 71, 77
   Seattle, Washington 1, 4, 8, 23, 236
   South Bend, Indiana 127
   Topeka, Kansas 21, 22
   Tulsa, Oklahoma 80

Van Nuys, California 197, 233
Walhalla, South Carolina 239
Vietnam, South 142, 201
Waharoa 245, 246
Waihau Bay 49, 50, 54, 245, 246
Waihi 245, 246
Waikaka Valley, Gore 67, 70
Waikanae 210
Waimana 245, 246
Waimate 66, 85, 109, 245, 247
Wainuiomata 127, 245, 246
Waioeka 245, 246
Waiohau 108, 245, 246
Waiomio, Northland 42, 231, 234
Waipara 167, 212
Wanaka 69
Wanganui 81
Warkworth, Auckland 236
Wellington .... xxii, 3–5, 7–11, 13, 35, 37, 42, 52, 77, 79, 81, 83, 89, 105, 109, 114, 115, 149, 151, 191, 200, 209, 237, 245, 246
Westport 63, 245, 247
Whakatane 50, 55, 108, 115, 245, 246
Whangarei 25, 35, 109, 233, 245, 246

About the author

Brett Knowles has served the Pentecostal movement for more than fifty years as an elder, ordained pastor, missionary, Bible teacher and Bible School principal, speaker and National Ministry Training Coordinator. He holds three theological degrees—including a Ph.D. in Church History—from the University of Otago, where he taught Church History in the Department of Theology and Religious Studies. He has also served on the staff of Sekolah Teologi Tinggi, Tawangmangu, Central Java, Indonesia and, latterly, as Director of Academic Resources and Senior Lecturer in Church History at Sydney College of Divinity in Australia, from which post he retired in 2008. He continues to contribute to teaching, the supervision and examination of postgraduate students and research.

Dr. Knowles' research interests include Pentecostal and Charismatic Movements, New Zealand Christianity and Culture, Crosscultural Aspects of Christianity in the Asian Region—especially prior to 1500 CE—and the Early Church. His primary area of expertise is New Zealand Pentecostalism. He has published *The History of a New Zealand Pentecostal Movement: The New Life Churches of New Zealand from 1946 to 1979* (Lewiston, N.Y.: Edwin Mellen Press, 2000), *Transforming Pentecostalism: The Changing Face of New Zealand Pentecostalism, 1920-2010* (Lexington, KY: Emeth Press, 2014) and numerous articles in this field. He has also edited and coedited a number of academic publications for the University of Otago. He is currently involved in the E21 Global Scholars Consultation, a select group of international Pentecostal and Charismatic scholars—led by Chairman Dr. Vinson Synan and Co-Chairman Dr. Amos Yong—in preparation for the 2015 Empowered21 Global Congress in Jerusalem.

Brett has been married to Adrienne for forty years; they have two children and two grandchildren.

www.ingramcontent.com/pod-product-compliance
Lightning Source LLC
Chambersburg PA
CBHW021755230426
43669CB00006B/81